Rabinal Achi

Also by Dennis Tedlock

Finding the Center: The Art of the Zuni Storyteller

Teachings from the American Earth: Indian Religion and Philosophy
(with Barbara Tedlock)

The Spoken Word and the Work of Interpretation

Popol Vuh: The Mayan Book of the Dawn of Life

Days from a Dream Almanac

Breath on the Mirror: Mythic Voices and Visions of the Living Maya

The Dialogic Emergence of Culture (with Bruce Mannheim)

Rabinal Achi

A MAYAN DRAMA
OF WAR AND SACRIFICE

Translated and interpreted by
DENNIS TEDLOCK

OXFORD
UNIVERSITY PRESS
2003

OXFORD
UNIVERSITY PRESS

Oxford   New York
Auckland Bangkok Buenos Aires Cape Town Chennai
Dar es Salaam Delhi Hong Kong Istanbul Karachi Kolkata
Kuala Lumpur Madrid Melbourne Mexico City Mumbai Nairobi
São Paulo Shanghai Singapore Taipei Tokyo Toronto

Published by Oxford University Press, Inc.
198 Madison Avenue, New York, New York, 10016
http://www.oup-usa.org

Oxford is a registered trademark of Oxford University Press

Library of Congress Cataloging-in-Publication Data
Rabinal-Achí. English
   Rabinal Achi : a Mayan drama of war and sacrifice / translated and interpreted by
Dennis Tedlock.
      p. cm.
Includes bibliographical references.
ISBN 0-19-513974-7
1. Rabinal-Achâ. 2. Quichâ drama—History and criticism. I. Tedlock, Dennis, 1939-
II. Title.

PM4231.Z95 E5 2002
897'.4152—dc21   2002030777

The illustrations in this book were prepared with the assistance of the McNulty Endowment of
the University at Buffalo of the State University of New York.

All photographs are by the author unless otherwise noted. Figures 23 and 49 are reproduced
courtesy of Michael D. Coe; figure 38 by permission of the University of Texas Press; figure 56
is Rollout Photograph K554 © Justin Kerr.

Book design by planettheo.com

Printing number: 9 8 7 6 5 4 3 2 1

Printed in the United States of America
on acid-free paper

Contents

Maps

Illustrations

Acknowledgments

Carroll Edward Mace has been generous from the very beginning of my work on *Rabinal Achi,* sharing his memories of his own research in Rabinal, providing copies of photos and manuscripts in his collection, and responding to my progress reports with encouragement.

Special thanks also go to Luis Enrique Sam Colop, whose insights into the language of the play unlocked meanings I would have missed. Visits to Rabinal have always been enlightening and entertaining, thanks to the warmth and generosity of José León Coloch, the man responsible for the production and direction of the play, and his wife, María Xolop. Barbara Tedlock and I wish them and their family every success in future productions of the play.

An earlier version of the translation served as the basis for a full stage production of the play at the State University of New York at Buffalo. For their brilliance as co-directors I thank Leandro Soto and Sally Goers Fox; for his magisterial performance as the play's shaman-narrator I thank Stephen M. Henderson. Dean Kerry Grant provided support from the College of Arts and Letters.

For information, comments, or suggestions I am grateful to Ruud van Akkeren, Luis Arata, Elizabeth Boone, Alain Breton, Stephen D. Houston, Maury Hutcheson, Mary Ellen Miller, Scott Pound, Dorie Reents-Budet, Francisco Rodríguez Rouanet, Karl Taube, Tamara Underiner, and the late Linda Schele. For editorial assistance I thank Donna Serwinowski.

The work of researching and writing this book was supported, at various times, by a translation grant from the National Endowment for the Humanities; a Fellowship in Pre-Columbian Studies at Dumbarton Oaks in Washington, D.C.; and a National Endowment for the Humanities Resident Fellowship at the School of American Research in Santa Fe, New Mexico.

Notes on Pronunciation

When words from the Mayan languages of Guatemala appear in italics they follow the 1988 spelling rules laid down by the Academia de las Lenguas Mayas de Guatemala, except that vowels are limited to the five found in sources that predate these rules.

With the following exceptions, consonants may be pronounced as in English: *j* is like Spanish *j,* with the tongue father back than for English *h;* *l* is like Welsh *ll,* with the tongue farther forward than for English *l;* and *q* is like Hebrew qoph, with the tongue farther back than for English *k.* Two other Mayan sounds are found in English but are spelled differently: *tz* is like English *ts* in "sets," and *x* is like English *sh.* The glottal stop, which is equivalent to *tt* in the Scottish pronunciation of "bottle," is indicated by *';* when it follows another consonant it is pronounced simultaneously with that consonant. Vowels are approximately like those of Spanish or Italian. Stress is always on the final syllable of a word.

Traditional spellings have been used for the title of the play and for names of the Mayan nations of Guatemala, such as Quiché, Cakchiquel, Pokomam, and Kekchí. For the names of Mayan languages the spellings of the Academia have been followed, as in the cases of K'iche', Kaqchikel, Poqomam, and Q'eqchi'.

Introduction

Many plays are performed in contemporary Mayan communities, but there is only one that dramatizes a time when Europeans had yet to appear over the horizon of the Mayan world. This same play is one of the few whose dialogue is entirely in a Mayan language. The town where the play is produced is Rabinal, in the highlands of Guatemala, and one of the play's two titles is *Rabinal Achi,* "Man of Rabinal." Whenever the characters are not engaged in dialogue they dance to the music of trumpets, which gives the play its other title: *Xajoj Tun,* "Dance of the Trumpets."

The character named Man of Rabinal is a warrior in the service of Lord Five Thunder, who rules the Rabinal nation from a fortress on a mountaintop. Guarding the boundaries of his court and kingdom are two characters who take their names, Eagle and Jaguar, from the sources of their spiritual power. Present within his court are his unmarried daughter, called the Mother of Quetzal Feathers; his wife, identified only as Lady; and a slave. For all these characters there is just one antagonist: Cawek of the Forest People, a renegade warrior from the ruling house of the neighboring Quiché nation. Man of Rabinal captures him and brings him before the court of Lord Five Thunder. In the end Cawek loses his head, but not before his status as a member of the nobility is given full recognition by his captors.

Considered as a dramatization of Mayan history, *Rabinal Achi* is mainly concerned with a series of events that reached a climax in the early fifteenth century. But when it is considered as a representation of Mayan culture, and the culture of Mayan royalty in particular, it reaches much deeper into the past. The ax and shield carried by each of the main characters are symbols of royal power that go back to the court dramas of what archaeologists call the Classic period, running from the fourth through the tenth centuries. The ancient axes took the form of an image of a deity with a stone ax blade mounted in his forehead, a celestial deity capable of hurling thunderbolts and meteors. When Cawek, Man of Rabinal, and Lord Five Thunder invoke "Sky" and "Earth," as they do almost every time they speak, they are using a shortened version of "Heart of Sky, Heart of Earth," an ancient epithet for the god of heaven-sent fire and the patron of kings.[1]

Events in the history of royal lineages provided subjects for dramas long before the Spanish arrived, but the dialogues were sung or chanted by choruses while the actors danced silently. The early missionaries intervened in Mayan theater on a massive scale, substituting Christian hymns for Mayan songs or suppressing traditional productions altogether. Meanwhile they introduced alternative dramas from the vernacular theater tradition of medieval Europe.[2] Despite these efforts, one of the most popular plays to emerge during the early colonial period had an all-Mayan cast of characters speaking all-Mayan dialogue, featured Mayan music played on long wooden trumpets, and dramatized the capture and sacrifice of a prisoner of war. *Rabinal Achi* is a direct descendant of this play.

As in the case of the plays that were introduced from Europe, many of which are still performed today, the dialogue in *Rabinal Achi* is scripted. The text currently in use is the latest in a series of versions that stretches back into the sixteenth century by way of manuscripts that have long since been discarded or lost. The composers of early versions lived in a time when many Mayan authors were adopting the roman alphabet as a medium for writing works in their own languages. The particular idea of using writing to create a script was a new one, coming with the introduction of European plays. Mayans had never used their own writing system to dictate, word for word, what performers would be expected to say.

The dramatists who scripted and produced ancestral versions of *Rabinal Achi* worked under the constant threat of censorship. Their solution to the problem of keeping the memory of Mayan court drama alive was to separate the words from the music and remove all but the outlines of the original religious content from public view. To this day the dialogue is spoken by actors rather than sung by a chorus, and the dance music is purely instrumental. Matters of religion are mostly the responsibility of the play's *K'amol B'e* or "Road Guide," a native priest-shaman who does most of his work behind the walls of houses and on mountaintops.

The most famous of the works produced by highland Mayan authors of the sixteenth century is the Popol Vuh, a sacred book whose story runs from the origin of the world to the second generation after the European invasion. A number of the historical events recounted in this and other writings of the same period are also mentioned in the dialogues of *Rabinal Achi*. The difference is that the composers of the script for the play created a montage, drawing upon episodes that occur as many as six generations apart in historical accounts and assigning them all to the generation of Man of Rabinal and Cawek of the Forest People.[3] But they did focus on one particular period: the tumultuous reign of Quicab, the most famous of Quiché kings. During the late fourteenth and early fifteenth centuries, he ruled over a confederation whose oldest members, in addition to the Quiché nation itself, were the closely related Rabinal, Cakchiquel, and Tzutuhil nations. Like other Quiché kings he was a member of the house of Cawek, the same lineage that gives its name to Cawek in the play.

Early in his reign Quicab launched a series of military expeditions that greatly expanded his domain, but while he was away on his grandest campaign a revolt broke out among his Quiché subjects at home. One of the instigators was his fifth son, who may well have served as the historical model for Cawek in the play. Against Quicab's objections, the rebels expanded the territory occupied by the Quiché nation at the expense of its Rabinal and Cakchiquel neighbors. The area affected by this invasion, as described by Quiché and Cakchiquel authors, coincides closely with the area invaded by Cawek and his army of rebels, as described in the dialogue of *Rabinal Achi*.

The play portrays Lord Five Thunder and Man of Rabinal as loyal supporters of an old order that has been disrupted by the unauthorized actions of Cawek. Rabinal territory has been invaded by members of the Quiché nation, but it was not the lords at the Quiché capital who "set them loose" but rather Cawek, acting on his own. As for ethnic rivalry between the two nations, the only substantive difference expressed in the play is the fact that Rabinal is the home of carved calabashes that serve as drinking vessels. Speaking from the Quiché side, Cawek can do no better than insist that where he comes from, the drinks are stronger and the Eagle and Jaguar dancers are fiercer. There were and still are linguistic differences between the two nations, but the script has all the characters speaking the same dialect of the same language. Some of the words and phrases they use are characteristic of Rabinal and neighboring towns, but Cawek actually uses these more often than the other characters.

By the time of the Spanish invasion, the breakup of the confederation that had once been ruled by Quicab was already a century or more in the past. The kingdom embracing the Quiché nation fell in 1524, but that did not give the invaders any territorial rights with respect to former Quiché allies. The lords of the Cakchiquel nation resisted until 1530, while the Rabinal lords held out until 1537. For early colonial audiences, a play that revived the memory of the confederation might have raised questions as to whether a united resistance to the Spanish invasion could have produced a different result. *Rabinal Achi* does not offer a direct answer to this question, but it does suggest that help from the direction of the Quiché capital would not have been what was needed anyway. Man of Rabinal reminds Cawek that there was a time when the two of them fought on the same side, but that Cawek caused heavy Rabinal losses by underestimating the strength of the enemy. This incident might well have brought to mind the more recent Quiché failure to deal effectively with the Spanish threat, which led, thirteen years later, to the submission of Rabinal.

The task of dramatizing events that took place before the Spanish invasion did not prevent the composers of the Rabinal script from paying attention to the new plays from Europe. As in the case of other Mayan writers of the early colonial period, they neither ignored what was European nor gave it uncritical acceptance. One particular imported play that seems to have caught their interest is *Carlomagno y los doce pares de Francia* or "Charlemagne and the Twelve Knights of France," ultimately based on the twelfth-century *Chanson de Roland.*[4] That play opens with a speech by Fierabrás, the chief antagonist, whose challenge to Carlomagno is answered by Oliveros, a knight. In the same way, *Rabinal Achi* opens with a speech by Cawek of the Forest People, who challenges Lord Five Thunder but is answered by Man of Rabinal. There are other parallels, but there are also various ways in which the plot lines of *Carlomagno* are reversed in *Rabinal Achi*. For example, when Fierabrás is defeated he humbles himself before Carlomagno and begs to begin a new life in his service, whereas Cawek is defiant before Lord Five Thunder and proudly accepts death.

While it is true that Cawek comes to a point where he sees very clearly what his end will be, this is not because he thinks he has reached the final moment in a destiny that has always been his. Instead he declares that "my day has been turned upside down / my birth has been turned upside down," meaning that the destiny he was given by the god who ruled the day of his birth was reversed when he was captured. This is an important point, because one of the recurrent themes running through the literature on the indigenous peoples of Mesoamerica is that their attitude toward life was and still is fatalistic.[5] They certainly have a long-standing desire to understand rhythms in the unfolding of time, but that does not require them to see the future as unalterable.

The representation of Cawek's death at the hands of his captors requires a major revision of received notions about the role of human sacrifice in ancient Mesoamerica. The prevailing view, which is not all that different from the lurid fantasies that appear in action comics and movies, is that the peoples of this region were driven by their belief in gods with an enormous appetite for blood, and especially for torn-out human hearts. But in the play, as in ancient Mayan sculpture and painting, the focus is not on heart extraction but on decapitation, a practice that is hardly exotic from a European point of view.[6] More importantly, as the play reveals and as ancient Mayan inscriptions confirm, the so-called victims were the deadly enemies of those who sacrificed them. And most important of all, the play makes it clear that prisoners were put on trial before they were sacrificed. In other words, a sacrifice was also an execution. Cawek confesses to multiple offenses against his captors, offenses that took a toll in Rabinal land and lives and threatened the life of Lord Five Thunder himself.

Looking at *Rabinal Achi* from this perspective, we can better understand why similar plays enjoyed widespread popularity during colonial times. For Mayans, such productions recalled a time when the legitimate use of lethal force, which underlies the authority of all states, had yet to be usurped by foreign invaders. As for the foreigners themselves, they sought to extinguish the very memory of such a time, repeatedly issuing bans against these plays from 1593 until 1770. In stating their reasons they evaded the political and judicial issues by denigrating Mayan religion and warning that representations of human sacrifices would lead to real ones. After four centuries a shift in perspective is overdue, to put it mildly. Today we find ourselves in a doubly awkward position, ignoring the judicial dimension of ancient Mayan ceremonies while at the same time forgetting the religious roots (and continuing religious overtones) of civil executions in our own society.

Out of all the dramas that centered on the capture, trial, and execution of a prisoner of war, the one performed in Rabinal is the only surviving example. In several other towns there are plays that retain such features as axes, shields, a log drum with keys that produce different tones (sometimes accompanied by trumpets), and an all-Mayan cast of characters. But these plays lack scripts, and their story lines have drifted far away from political and historical issues. Only *Rabinal Achi,* among all the plays performed in Mayan towns today, proclaims that history did not begin with the arrival of Europeans.

With the end of the Guatemalan civil war of the early 1980s came the flowering of a Mayan cultural revival. Questions of linguistic and ethnic identity were debated between those who sought Mayan unity and those who promoted the uniqueness of their own particular districts or towns. In the case of Rabinal and two neighboring towns, there was a controversy as to whether the local language should be considered a dialect of K'iche',[7] the most widely spoken of all Mayan languages, or whether it should be given the status of a separate language, called *Achi* after the play. In terms of linguistics as practiced in the academy, the case for a separate language is weak. People from Rabinal and people who speak even the most distant of K'iche' dialects have little difficulty in conversing with one another.[8] But in terms of the historical events that damaged the relationship between the two nations, as represented in the play, the choice of K'iche' as a name for the language they share is an unfortunate historical accident. It was in Quiché territory that Spanish missionary linguists first studied this language, and they followed the practice of members of the Quiché nation in calling it K'iche' or Quiché. Linguists, anthropologists, and historians have been calling it by that name ever since.

There are two extant versions of the *Rabinal Achi* script.[9] The story of the older one begins in 1850, when Bartolo Sis of Rabinal made a copy of a previous version that has long since been lost. Five years later Rabinal received a new parish priest in the person of Charles Étienne Brasseur de Bourbourg, who was an avid collector of manuscripts bearing on American antiquities. Among his many famous acquisitions was the only surviving copy of the K'iche' text of the Popol Vuh. In Rabinal he did not succeed in gaining direct access to the Sis manuscript or its predecessor, but he did persuade Sis to read the text aloud to him while he made his own copy. In 1857 he left Guatemala for Paris, where he turned to the task of preparing his finds for publication. His *Popol Vuh* saw print in 1861, followed by *Rabinal Achi* in 1862.[10] In both books the texts were accompanied by translations into French.

Brasseur sent a copy of the *Rabinal Achi* volume to a man who had been his servant and guide during his stay in Rabinal, and at some point the play's directors began using the printed version of the text to rehearse their actors. In 1913 the owner of the book allowed the current director, Manuel Pérez, to make a handwritten copy of the text of the play. Pérez made various editorial changes, altering spellings to conform to local practice and rewording some of the lines to make them sound better. His version of the text has served as the script for subsequent directors, including the present one.

In 1994 Alain Breton published a facsimile of the Pérez manuscript, accompanied by a transcription and French translation. Breton claimed that Pérez had worked from some prior manuscript version of the text rather than from Brasseur's book, but in fact Pérez made no secret of his reliance on the printed version, reproducing details of its typographic design and copying one of its page numbers. The true value of his version of the text lies not in its supposed connection to some older manuscript but in its documentation of the editorial sensibilities of a person who had acquired his knowledge of the play not only by reading its lines but by hearing them and speaking them from memory as well.[11]

Six Spanish versions of *Rabinal Achi* have been published, variously based on the 1862 French translation by Brasseur de Bourbourg, an unpublished French translation by Georges Raynaud that dates from the 1920s, a 1929 Spanish translation of Raynaud by Luis Cardoza y Aragón, and the 1994 French translation by Alain Breton.[12] English versions, one of them complete and the other three partial, have been based, in turn, on Brasseur's French and/or the Spanish translation of Raynaud's French.[13] The only translators who have worked directly from the original language of the play rather than from French or Spanish are Brasseur, Raynaud, Breton, and myself.

The magnitude of the problems with previous translations may be judged by the handling of a sentence Cawek addresses to Eagle and Jaguar in his final speech: *Mata qatz jumerwachil kiniwitzmarisaj.* In Raynaud, as translated by Cardoza y Aragón, this comes out as "Que me maten en un instante," while Breton has "afin qu'en un instant vous me fassiez devenir plumage."[14] The problems with these renditions begin with their failure to fit the context of the ongoing dialogue. In his previous speech Cawek described Eagle and Jaguar as toothless, clawless, and otherwise less than awe-inspiring. It therefore seems unlikely that he would now expect them to be capable of killing him swiftly, as Raynaud and Cardoza y Aragón would have it, or causing him to sprout instant feathers, as Breton would have it.

If we reconsider Cawek's sentence word by word, the first problem we have to deal with is that *mata* makes the whole thing negative, a fact ignored in both of the quoted translations.[15] The second word, *qatz,* means "certainly," and the first two words together mean "certainly not." The third word, *jumerwachil,* is not just "in an instant," but more literally "in one instant of the eyes," which is to say "one blink." So whatever Eagle and Jaguar are planning to do to Cawek, he is warning them *not* to expect to get it over with quickly.

The final word in the sentence is built around the verb stem *-itzma-,* which has to do with hair, fur, or feathers and means that they either grow or stand on end. Putting the stem back together with its prefixes and affixes, it means "you are going to cause my hair, fur, or feathers to grow or stand on end."[16] Among these possible meanings, the standing on end of Cawek's hair seems a more plausible choice than the growth of his feathers. Reassembling all four words and putting their meanings in English order, I come up with this sentence: "You certainly won't stand my hair on end in the blink of an eye." When I asked the current director of the play to explain what Cawek means by this statement, his response was simply, "He's saying they won't win," thus confirming that the statement is a negative one. In actuality Eagle and Jaguar do win, but not before Cawek has led them and all the other characters in a long walk, one that ends with his decapitation at stage center.

In making my own translation of *Rabinal Achi,* I have taken both the Brasseur and Pérez versions of the text into consideration. My written sources for the meanings of words and idioms include more than a dozen dictionaries, ranging from manuscripts penned by early Spanish missionaries to the printed works of contemporary Mayan linguists. I began my work in 1985, at a time when the play was not being performed in Rabinal and its future was uncertain. In the summers of 1988 and 1989 I traveled to Rabinal to meet with José León Coloch, the man responsible for the production and direction of the play. He was able to clarify the meanings of difficult passages (including the one just discussed), and he consented to recite long excerpts from the dialogue while I made sound recordings. He delivered the words just as he would have done when coaching actors at a rehearsal, or when taking a role himself. But the fact remained that I had yet to witness a full-dress production of the play, and I was reluctant to publish my translation without doing so.

Finally, in January 1998, I returned to Rabinal on the strength of a rumor that the play would be produced for that year's fiesta. The rumor proved to be correct, and Coloch allowed Barbara Tedlock and myself to make video recordings and take photographs of two complete performances. He himself played the role of Cawek of the Forest People. After years of wondering whether I would ever get a chance to observe the play, I found myself lending a hand in its very production, transporting actors, paraphernalia, and large bowls of stew around town in a rented pickup truck.

What makes the present translation of *Rabinal Achi* different from all others is that it proceeds not only from words on paper but from images and sounds on tape as well. Replaying the action made it possible to produce a script with stage directions, detailing the relationship of the movements of the actors to the music and dialogue. Replaying the speeches made it possible to study the ways in which the director and actors transform the script, which follows a prose format, into poetry. They break the text into short lines with deliberate pauses and string these lines together in groups by means of intonation, creating sequences of pitch and volume that start off high, work their way down, and then rise again. It would not have been possible to reconstruct these features of oral performance from the text alone. Close *reading* reveals numerous parallel couplets, but close *listening* reveals that a couplet is often combined with an unparalleled line to form a triad.[17] This creates a tension between the small-scale rhythms of couplets and the larger-scale rhythms of intonation.

Partly in the hope of drawing the reader further into the world of the play, I have translated proper names of persons and places whenever it seemed feasible. In so doing I have indulged in a habit I picked up from various speakers and writers of Mayan languages, whose attitude toward names is that they should be examined for meaning rather than allowed to remain undisturbed in their properness.

Earlier versions of the translation were read aloud and critiqued by students in my graduate seminar on ethnopoetics at the State University of New York at Buffalo. In 1996 a concert reading of the scene at the court of Lord Five Thunder was staged by members of the Institute of Maya Studies and myself at the Miami Museum of Science. In April 1998 a version of the entire play (under the title *Man of Rabinal*) was co-directed by Leandro Soto and Sally Goers Fox

1. Man of Rabinal (left) and Cawek of the Forest People as they appeared in 1998.
Around his waist Rabinal wears the rope that will later bind Cawek.

at the Katherine Cornell Theatre on the University at Buffalo campus.[18] They
added two new roles: a woman anthropologist who arrives at the scene of the
performance with a notebook and camera but ends up being drawn into the role
of the Mother of Quetzal Feathers, and a shaman-narrator who speaks the lines
of all the other characters. This last role was played by Stephen M. Henderson,
who sometimes found himself improvising lines that fit the poetic patterns of my
script in the same way the actors of Rabinal sometimes improvise lines that fit
the original script. The action unfolded in the arching mouth of a cave with a
sunlit village in the distance, which put the audience in the position of looking
out from the dark interior of the cave.

ON THE SCENE IN RABINAL

When the play is produced in Rabinal the first two performances take place on the
Saturday evening and Sunday morning preceding St. Sebastian's day, which falls
on January 20. Further performances take place on January 25, day of the conversion of St. Paul, the patron saint of Rabinal. The Sunday performance, which is the
one described here, is staged in front of the cemetery chapel at the west end of town.

2. Masks of Man of Rabinal (left) and Cawek of the Forest People (right), held in the hands of
Esteban Xolop, predecessor of José León Coloch as director of the play. Note the gill-like
slits in the cheeks of the masks, most clearly visible in Rabinal's left cheek.
Photo by Carroll Edward Mace.

During the first half of the play, the main image that confronts the viewer is
that of two masked actors armed with axes and shields, squared off on a stone
terrace that serves as their stage. Instead of exchanging blows, they make speeches
to one another. There is no printed program to explain who they are, but each time
one of them finishes speaking he names the other. The actor who wears a helmet
in the form of a coyote's head is the one in the title role, answering to the name
Rab'inal Achi, "Man of Rabinal" (figure 1, left). He calls his counterpart, who
wears the head of a jaguar, *Kaweq K'eche Winaq*, "Cawek of the Forest People"
(figure 1, right). Their wooden masks are painted with human features, except that
the skin is gold. Rabinal's mask is bordered in blue, while Cawek's is bordered in
green. So far as the local language is concerned, blue and green are two shades of
the same color, but there is a notable difference in the expressions they wear.
Rabinal's brow is furrowed with anger, but Cawek, though he is doomed, has a
calm expression (figure 2).

The masks have painted eyes, but hidden in the shadows cast by the brows
are slits for the masker's eyes. There is no opening for the masker's mouth, but the

3. Eagle from the back (left) and Jaguar from the front (right), as they appeared in 1998.

voice, instead of sounding muffled, has a deep resonance. Behind the painted mouth is enough empty space for the real mouth to give precise form to the sounds of the local language, including the sounds of ancient words whose meaning is no longer clear and the names of places whose locations have been forgotten. The voice comes out through slits, shaped and positioned like a pair of gills in the cheeks of the mask.

Rabinal and Cawek pace up and down at the center of the stage while they talk back and forth, following short east-west paths. They move in opposite directions as often as not, staying out of range of one another's axes, and their gazes meet only by accident. Meanwhile, two veiled performers silently walk up and down longer paths that define the northern and southern boundaries of the stage (figure 3). Their identities become clear only when they happen to turn away from the viewer, revealing what they carry on their backs. In this they are like the pairs of dancers who carry burdens in Maya vase paintings of the eighth century. The one who walks the southern path turns out to be Eagle, bearing a woodcarving of a two-headed eagle on his back, while the one who walks the northern path is

4. Lord Five Thunder (left), Mother of Quetzal Feathers (center), and Slave (right)
as they appeared in 1998.

Jaguar, carrying a woodcarving of two rampant jaguars. Rising from the center of
each carving is a pole topped by a basket-like structure whose ribs fan out above
the head of the carrier like the branches of a tree.

   Three more characters sit quietly on a bench at the west side of the stage,
facing east (figure 4). They can see straight down the main street of town to the
white parish church at the opposite end of it. Behind their bench a stairway rises
westward to the front door of a white chapel with a cemetery behind it. Today this
town sits in the middle of a valley, but five hundred years ago the palaces and
temples that formed its center were in a fortress on top of *Kaqyuq'* or "Red
Mountain," overlooking the valley from the north (figure 5). The ruins of the
fortress can be seen from down in the present town, and when people burn
offerings up there the smoke can be seen by day and the flames by night.

   The masker seated on the south end of the bench is costumed much like
Rabinal and Cawek, complete with an ax and shield, but instead of a helmet he

5. View of the town of Rabinal from the southeast; at center left is the dome of the parish church. Between the town and the misty mountains on the far horizon is the darker mass of Red Mountain; the ruins of Lord Five Thunder's fortress cover its summit and extend beyond the saddle to the right.

wears a boat-shaped hat festooned with long plumes. Halfway through the play Rabinal will go before him, addressing him as *Ajaw Job' Toj,* "Lord Five Thunder." Seated at the opposite end of the bench is a character whose mask is like all the others in having a mustache but who is otherwise dressed as a woman, with a long brocaded robe hanging down loosely over a tight sarong. When Lord Five Thunder needs something done, he addresses him-her as "man slave, woman slave." He has Man of Rabinal in his service as well, but their relationship is that of a king and his most trusted knight.

Between the lord and the slave sits a girl in early adolescence, unmasked. Her blouse is of finely brocaded cloth, tucked into her sarong. In her hair and around her ankles she wears bunches of shiny green feathers. She never speaks and is never directly addressed, but when Lord Five Thunder mentions her he calls her *Uchuch Q'uq' / Uchuch Raxon,* "Mother of Quetzal Feathers / Mother of Glistening Green." This is his way of saying that she is his daughter, and that her marriage will one day bring him and his wife wealth in the form of quetzal feathers and jade. His wife, who is silent like the girl, would be sitting to her left but is absent from this year's production. Even so, Man of Rabinal greets this missing woman as "lady" when he comes before the bench of the royal court.

The steps behind the bench give a good view of the play. Seated there is a man wearing a red and white head scarf, white shirt, red sash, and white pants. He accompanies the performers wherever they go, serving as their Road Guide. To prepare the way for this year's production he walked to places that are named in the play, praying and burning offerings at shrines on top of hills and mountains.

Just outside the stage to the south are two trumpeters and a drummer, dressed in red and white like the Road Guide. When they play the actors dance, promenade, or strike poses instead of speaking. Today the trumpets are elongated brass bugles, but as late as the eighteenth century they were long wooden trumpets like the ones depicted in ancient Mayan paintings. The drum, made by means of an ancient craft, is a recent replacement for one that rotted. It is a horizontal hollowed log, slit open on top to make a pair of keys. Using a pair of rubber-tipped sticks, the drummer produces three different tones.

The sound of the trumpets and the slit drum, in and of itself, announces that the performers are bringing *Rabinal Achi* into the present world from another one— a prior world, yes, but also a parallel one, in the sense that it is always there. The plays that were introduced into Mayan towns by Spanish missionaries are accompanied by different instruments: winds with double reeds, hide-covered drums with double heads, or the marimba, an instrument whose two rows of keys are made of the same wood as a slit drum. The same ears that hear dissonance and discordant rhythms when they listen to the trumpets and slit drum hear harmony and synchrony in the music played on the newer instruments. It may even be that over the centuries since the Spanish invasion, the musicians who play the trumpets and slit drum have worked to sharpen the difference between their music and that of other plays.

When the actors dance they move around the perimeter of a square, and when they promenade they move in a circle. These pathways locate them all in one world, whereas the dancers in dramas of Spanish origin typically confront one another in two parallel files. When it comes to costumes, the only thing that distinguishes Cawek from the men who capture and execute him is his particular color combinations, which are no more different from theirs than theirs are from one another. In contrast, the actors in dramas that confront Moors with Christians or Indians with Spaniards wear costumes that clearly divide them between two separate worlds. Cawek and his captors phrase their arguments in terms of a shared system of military and political values, whereas Moors and Indians face opponents who advertise themselves as seeking the victory of universal truth and good over local falsehood and evil.

A week from now, on the day of the apostle Paul, the play will be performed down by the parish church. That is when it will draw its largest audience—its largest visible audience, that is. Today, in front of the cemetery chapel, the actors are speaking to and for their ancestors as much as anyone else, including all those

6. A restored view of the main plaza at Red Mountain. The long building on the right side of the plaza
is the palace with nine stairways. The twin buildings at the far end and the
similar building at right are temples.
Detail from a drawing by Tatiana Proskouriakoff.

who ever acted in the play. Each time the dialogue between Rabinal and Cawek shifts from one to the other, the trumpets sound and they turn away from one another, looking toward the surrounding mountaintops while Cawek lets out a long, thin wail. It feels as though they wanted to leave this valley town in opposite directions and return to the places where their spirits dwell, one of them crossing the western mountains that separate him from his home at a faraway place called Red Earth, and the other following the path that leads to the top of Red Mountain, which is visible from here.

Acting in this play is not so much a matter of impersonating historical individuals—as if their lives could be relived in realistic detail—as it is a matter of impersonating their ghosts. All the ghosts except Cawek have their home in a cave beneath the ruins on Red Mountain, where they remember what they did when their bones wore flesh and the walls of their buildings supported roofs. Ordinarily the cave entrance is invisible, but some people have had the good fortune to dream their way to it and through it, descending into a brightly lit town where the characters of the play appear as they were in life. The Road Guide makes his visit to the ruins in the daytime, accompanied by the play's producer. Together they burn offerings for the spirits of the original characters, praying for permission to make their memories visible and audible in the waking world. Lord Five Thunder receives his offerings at the foot of the middle of the nine stairways that ascend the front of the main palace (figure 6).

In some ways *Rabinal Achi* has a greater resemblance to the Noh plays of Japan than to European forms of drama. In Noh productions, as in Rabinal, the ghosts of the characters must grant permission to proceed. Depending on one's point of view, the performers speak as if they had summoned distant ghosts into the same space with their bodies and their audience, or as if their own spirits had traveled to distant places while their bodies remained behind to tell the tale. Either way, they speak as mediums. Like the actors in *Rabinal Achi,* they seem to be living in a world where time moves more slowly than in real life and every action is deliberate.

The protagonist of *Rabinal Achi* is Man of Rabinal, in the sense that he overcomes adversity, but the main character is his antagonist. Cawek delivers more lines that anyone else, and the action centers around him. The situation is something like that of a Noh play about an encounter between two famous warriors: Kumagai, the protagonist, is confronted by the ghost of Atsumori, his defeated rival.[19] In the dialogue between them it is Atsumori who does most of the talking, and the story that unfolds is mostly about him.

Cawek and Rabinal are alone in the opening scene, but the actors who speak their lines make no attempt to simulate a private and spontaneous conversation. Their speeches are worded in such a way as to make it clear that they are addressing one another, but they project their voices beyond one another and beyond the limits of the stage. This is a "presentational" drama, but with the difference that the audience is not "out front" but on all four sides.[20] No one is in an ideal position to catch all of the words all of the time, but everyone has moments when they come through clearly.

Even a listener who does not know the language of the dialogue can hear that the actors are speaking in parallel verse, which reverses the effect of rhymed verse. What stands out are the parts of parallel lines that do *not* sound alike, as when Rabinal asks Cawek, *Ma at on ral sutz' / ma at on ral mayul?* "Weren't you born of clouds / weren't you born of mist?" Or when Lord Five Thunder considers the prospect of giving Cawek *kab'lajuj uk'ia / kab'lajuj umatul,* "his twelve drinks / his twelve poisons."

The actors in *Rabinal Achi* memorize their lines at rehearsals by repeating them after the director, who reads them aloud from the script. In actual performances the more experienced actors make frequent departures from the script, adding, subtracting, or rearranging words or lines in ways that are consistent with the style and substance of what they have learned at rehearsals.[21]

There is no scenery to represent the place where the dialogue between Cawek and Rabinal is taking place—unless, that is, we count the royal bench as the fortress and palace of Lord Five Thunder, the lines walked by Eagle and Jaguar as the outer limits of his authority, and the square of stone pavement between those lines as the surface of his territory. Cawek and Rabinal carry on their opening dialogue in the middle of the square, without any attention to the bench, and their statements gradually make it clear that they are indeed inside the lord's domain but outside his fortress.

Cawek declares his desire to chop through "the root, the trunk" of the ruling lineage of the Rabinal nation, as if he could terminate Lord Five Thunder's whole blood line. While he and Man of Rabinal argue back and forth, men swinging incense burners come and go just outside the limits of the stage, praying to their lineal ancestors as they enter and leave the chapel and the graveyard behind it. Their own audience is a strictly spiritual one, so they speak in low voices that can scarcely be heard under those of the actors. What Cawek desires is that when Lord Five Thunder dies, his soul will be left with no living voices to hear.

The only honorable choice for Man of Rabinal is to take Cawek prisoner and present him to Lord Five Thunder. This is a tragic turn of events, since there was a time when these two warriors fought on the same side. That was when Cawek came to Red Mountain in response to a call for Quiché military aid in a war against mutual enemies, the Uxab and Pokomam nations. But since then he has become a renegade, abandoning land he owned at a place called Red Earth, raising a rebel army, threatening the lords of his own nation, and then invading the domain of Lord Five Thunder. From the point of view of Man of Rabinal, having to treat Cawek as an enemy is "a terrible joke," since they ought to behave as brothers to one another. When Lord Five Thunder hears the news that Cawek has been captured, he imagines an alternative outcome in which the same man who is about to appear before him as a prisoner of war instead plays the role of a prospective son-in-law.

Like the characters in Noh plays, Cawek, Man of Rabinal, and Lord Five Thunder narrate many more past events than they reenact. Cawek's misdeeds catch up with him, but they are represented only in his words and in those of his captors. It is only the consequences of his deeds that are acted out in the play. Again as in Noh there is no attempt at realism, and time moves as slowly as it does for the dialogue. Rabinal speaks of roping Cawek, but he does not twirl an actual lasso and throw it over the head of his opponent. Instead, while the two of them hold still, a stage hand comes out and carefully ties the loose end of the rope carried by Rabinal around Cawek's upper arms. At the end of the play, when Cawek kneels to have his head cut off, all the characters dance around him, and those who have axes bring them down toward the back of his neck with unhurried movements, never quite touching his flesh.

Before Man of Rabinal takes Cawek in front of the royal bench, he accuses him of a whole series of hostile actions against the Rabinal nation and its lord. In each case Cawek admits his guilt without hesitation. When Rabinal presses him to explain his behavior he brings up the fact that he was never given the reward of land he was promised when he came to Red Mountain as an ally. Rabinal replies that the land was withheld for good reason: When Cawek was sent out on a spy mission among the Uxab and Pokomam he failed to observe that they were strong and already on the move, which resulted in a Rabinal defeat. Cawek has no real answer to this charge. All he can do is express the sorrow he felt and still feels at never having planted crops "in the bright mountains / bright valleys" of Rabinal.

Toward the end of the opening dialogue, Cawek reveals something he did in secret. When he headed home without his reward, he walked from hilltop to hilltop along the southern boundary of fertile land that had been given to Man of Rabinal. He stopped on top of each hill and lamented his fate, which had the effect of laying a curse on the land. The curse is in effect to this day, and each performance of the play brings it to mind. But thanks to the fact that Cawek confessed what he did before he was put to death and continues to reveal it each time his ghost is given voice by an actor, the curse can be counteracted. This is the duty of the man who serves as Road Guide for the performers of the play. Over a five-day period, he says prayers and burns offerings at each of the stopping places named by Cawek.

With the play more than half over, Rabinal brings Cawek before Lord Five Thunder. Again there are accusations, and again Cawek admits to his offenses. Clear about his fate, he makes his last requests. It is his desire to perform a series of acts that are the prerogative of persons of lordly rank like himself—"if only," he says, "to mark the greatness / of my death / my disappearance." For each performance he must "borrow" something or someone that belongs to Lord Five Thunder. So long as he has these borrowings in his possession it is as if he had become an adopted member of the society of his captors, but he has to give all of them back before his beheading.

The first of Cawek's last requests is for a drink called Quick Hummingbird, which is served to him in a type of vessel Rabinal artisans have long been famous for: a carved and painted calabash. The drink is said to bring dreams, and though Cawek is not portrayed as having a dream or a vision, he does raise the ongoing conversation to a mythic level. He begins to speak as if he were a character in the Mayan epic that accounts for the origin of the calabash tree, as told in the Popol Vuh. There was a time when this tree was barren, but when the lords of the underworld placed the severed head of a divine hero in its branches, it bore fruit that looked like skulls. Cawek wonders aloud whether the very calabash he now holds in his hand might be the skull of his own father or grandfather, thus placing himself in the lineage of the hero. Then, knowing that the twin sons of this hero avenged their father's death, he speaks of a future time when his own sons or grandsons might come into the possession of a carved calabash from Rabinal and remember what happened to him. In this way he casts his captors in the roles of lords of the underworld and, at the same time, implies that his death will be avenged.

The story of the calabash tree also implicates Lord Five Thunder's daughter, since one of the underworld lords had an unmarried daughter. She went to look at the tree, and when the skull of the hero spit in the palm of her hand she became pregnant with the twins who would later avenge him. Whatever this may imply about the future of Cawek's skull, all he can do for now is to ask for a dance with Lord Five Thunder's daughter. They dance facing each other but without touching, and she never opens her hands.

Cawek's next request is to "play a game" with Eagle and Jaguar. He dances with them, and as he does so they stare at him, click their teeth and claws, and scream—according to what he says about them after the dance, that is. During the dance Eagle and Jaguar remain silent, and the only visible evidence of their ferocity is the eagle and jaguar carvings they continue to carry on their backs. If there was a time when this dance involved the miming of combat, the only remaining trace is in the words spoken by Cawek.

In the last of his last requests, Cawek asks Lord Five Thunder to grant him thirteen score days to go to the mountains and valleys of his home and say farewell, but he gets no answer. What he does then, so far as his actions are outwardly visible, is to go out on the terrace, followed by all the other actors, and dance the perimeter of the same square that has been danced before, marking each corner by turning in a small circle. Spiritually, the space and time of his captors have now become the same as those of his homeland. The square has an invisible mountain at each corner and measures 65 days on each side, a quarter of the 260 days that make a full run of the Mayan divinatory calendar. When he is done with his journey through space and time he returns to the same date on which he started. He faces the other characters and says, with a touch of condescension, "Just now you were saying, 'He left!' / But I didn't leave. / I merely said farewell from here."

After his final speech Cawek leads all the other characters to center stage, where he kneels facing west while they dance around him making motions with their axes. The moment when his head comes off is represented only by the moment when they stop their motions. He then rises and joins the others in a final dance. Now it is as if he and all the other characters were ghosts again, on their way back to the parallel world where they lead lives that are visible only to dreamers. Shoulder to shoulder, they dance westward until they reach the foot of the steps that lead to the door of the cemetery chapel. There the actors hidden inside the costumes all kneel, and the Road Guide leads them in a prayer to their ancestors.

PART ONE

Rabinal Achi

or

Dance of the Trumpets

CHARACTERS

Cawek of the Forest People, *a warrior in the service of the lord of Quiché Mountain, Quiché Valley. Masked, carrying an ax in his right hand and a small round shield in his left.*

Man of Rabinal, *also called Man of Glory, a warrior in the service of Lord Five Thunder. Masked, carrying an ax and shield, and with a rope coiled around his waist.*

Lord Five Thunder, *ruler of the Cawuks and Rabinals. Masked, with an ax and shield.*

Lady, *wife of Lord Five Thunder. May be veiled. This role sometimes goes unfilled.*

Mother of Quetzal Feathers, Mother of Glistening Green, *unmarried daughter of Lord Five Thunder and Lady, about twelve years old. May be veiled, with an ax in her right hand and a calabash in her left.*

Slave, *masked as a man but dressed as a woman. Carries an ax in the right hand and a calabash drinking vessel in the left.*

Eagle and Jaguar, *priests in the service of Lord Five Thunder. Veiled, carrying tall backpacks, one with the image of a pair of jaguars at its center and the other with a pair of eagles.*

Trumpeters, *two in number. Dressed in white with red head scarf and sash, each with a long trumpet.*

Drummer, *assisted by a drum carrier. Dressed like the trumpeters, plays a three-tone slit drum with a pair of rubber-tipped sticks.*

Road Guide, *dressed like the musicians, carrying a shoulder bag.*

The scene is a plaza or courtyard in a town surrounded by mountains.

Note on recitation: Each of the lines in a speech should be followed by a pause. When a line is indented it should be intoned in a somewhat lower voice than the preceding line, with a return to a higher voice when a new line begins at the left-hand margin.

7. The Mother of Quetzal Feathers, flanked by Eagle (right) and Jaguar (left) and followed by the rest of the cast, approaches the house of the Confraternity of St. Sebastian.

The performers walk toward the stage by whatever public street or road leads directly to it. In the case of the terrace in front of the cemetery chapel they enter from the east. On the west side of the stage is a bench that seats four, facing east; on the south side is a bench for three, facing north. ROAD GUIDE goes to a position offstage to the west (marked **X** *in the diagram on the next page) and observes the action from there. The musicians stand in front of the south bench facing north, with DRUMMER and his drum carrier (with the drum loaded on his back) between the two TRUMPETERS.*

The next to enter are (in order) EAGLE, CAWEK, RABINAL, LORD, QUETZAL, LADY, SLAVE, and JAGUAR; they form a north-south line along the west side of the stage, with CAWEK and RABINAL in front of the west bench. All face south except for CAWEK and RABINAL, who turn and face away from one another, one facing north and the other south.

The musicians play a fanfare, for which all the characters stand still, and follow with music, for which they all dance. They move around the stage as four separate parties, with EAGLE, who dances alone, in the lead. In second place come CAWEK and RABINAL, who dance as partners. Next come LORD, QUETZAL, LADY (if present), and SLAVE, all of whom dance together. In last place comes JAGUAR. In general they all follow a counterclockwise square path around the stage, but they begin by turning in small counterclockwise circles. EAGLE and JAGUAR turn their first cir-

*cles at the southwest and northwest corners of the square, while the two groups turn
theirs in front of the bench. After that they make circles whenever they reach a corner of the square:*

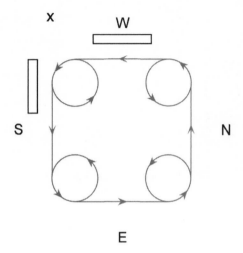

There are further fanfares when CAWEK *and* RABINAL *make their southeast
and northwest turns. At these times all the dancers stand still while* CAWEK *and*
RABINAL *face away from each other, raising their faces toward the surrounding
mountains and lifting their axes as high as their heads while* CAWEK *lets out a long,
high, fading cry: "Eeeeeiiiiiiiiii."*

After the second standstill, and when CAWEK *and* RABINAL *have danced the
complete square and come back to the west side again, there comes one last fanfare,
only this time all the dancers break into a walk. Now they follow a circular path
around the stage, and when they have all completed it the music ends. When* CAWEK
and RABINAL *reach the west bench they switch positions, so that* CAWEK *ends up
north of* RABINAL; *the others stand wherever they were when the music ended.*

CAWEK OF THE FOREST PEOPLE *speaks for the first time. He paces slowly back and
forth along a short east-west path, gesturing with his ax or rattling his shield to
emphasize a point or mark a transition. On a parallel path to the south* RABINAL
*paces independently. Whenever one of them reverses direction, he turns his back
toward the exterior of the stage. Their gazes meet only occasionally, and they stay
out of one another's reach.*

8. Cawek (at right), followed by Rabinal and Lord Five Thunder, dances around
the perimeter of the stage.

Come on out, lord who's been pierced
            lord who's been fitted with gems
however that may be
            let me take the lead
                        since I'm not finished
chopping through
            the root
                        the trunk
of that Lord of Walkers
            Lord of Workers
                        Cawuks and Rabinals
so say my words
            before Sky
                        before Earth
since I haven't many words
            to say to you, sir.
May Sky and Earth be with you, sir
            Man of Glory
                        Man of Rabinal.

Fanfare, with CAWEK *and* RABINAL *turning to face away from one another, then music, for which they move into place behind* EAGLE. *Everyone dances around the square as before, interrupted by two fanfares with standstills and ending with a fanfare for a walk around the stage. Again,* RABINAL *and* CAWEK *end up in front of the west bench.*

MAN OF RABINAL speaks for the first time. *He paces while gesturing with his ax or shield;* CAWEK *paces independently.*

> Listen!
> Brave man
>   Cawek of the Forest People:
> Is this what your words say
>   before Sky
>   before Earth?
> "Come on out, lord who's been pierced
>   lord who's been fitted with gems
> however that may be
>   let me take the lead
>   since I'm not finished
> chopping through
>   the root
>   the trunk
> of that Lord of Walkers
>   Lord of Workers
>   Cawuks and Rabinals."
> Is that what your words say
>   in the hearing of Sky
>   in the hearing of Earth?
> You delivered them
>   in range of my weapon
>   in range of my shield
> and my upraised ax blade
>   and my snail-shell bracelet
> my armband
>   my white paint
>   my gourd of tobacco
> and my strength
>   my manhood

9. A standstill, during which Cawek (left) and Rabinal (right) look in
different directions.

    so whether you see it coming
        or it happens without any warning
I shall catch you
        with my henequen rope
            my henequen cord
so say my words
        before Sky
            before Earth.
May Sky and Earth be with you
        brave man
            prisoner, captive.

Fanfare, with CAWEK *and* RABINAL *turning to look away from one another, then music and dance as before, interrupted by one standstill and followed by a walk.*

When the music stops the DRUMMER *sits on a low stool in front of the south bench while the drum carrier places the drum in front of him and retires. From now on the* TRUMPETERS, *who flank the* DRUMMER, *sit on the bench whenever they are not playing.* EAGLE *begins walking back and forth along a straight east-west path on the south side of the stage, turning toward the interior of the stage whenever he reverses direction;* JAGUAR *stays behind on the north side and begins walking an east-west path there:*

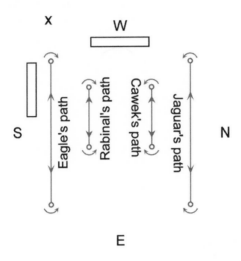

CAWEK and RABINAL *stop at their positions in front of the west bench while* LORD *sits on the south end of it, with* QUETZAL, SLAVE, *and* LADY *to his left.* ROAD GUIDE *sits down (at the position marked* **X** *in the diagram) and continues to observe. While* RABINAL *holds one end of his rope in his left hand, a stage hand ties the other end around the upper arms of* CAWEK, *leaving enough slack so that the two of them can stay well out of arm's reach.*

MAN OF RABINAL speaks for the second time. *He and* CAWEK *pace as before on the central paths shown in the diagram.*

> Listen!
> Brave man
> > prisoner, captive:
> Should thanks be given to Sky
> > to Earth?

10. Eagle (extreme left) and Jaguar (extreme right) walk paths that define the southern and northern
boundaries of the stage. On the bench (from left to right) are Lord Five Thunder, the Mother
of Quetzal Feathers, and Slave, there being no Lady in the 1998 production. In dialogue
in front of the bench are Rabinal (left) and Cawek (right). The Road Guide
is partially visible behind Rabinal.

Has Sky really given you up?
    Has Earth given you up?
So now you're under the power of my weapon
        under the power of my shield
and my upraised ax handle
        my upraised ax blade
my snail-shell bracelet
        my armband
            my white paint
                my gourd of tobacco.
Speak now:
Where is your mountain?
        Where is your valley?
Where did you blossom
        on the slope of a mountain
            on the floor of a valley?
Weren't you born of clouds?
        Weren't you born of mist?
Aren't you on the run
        in the face of violence
            in the face of war?

So say my words
>   before Sky
>   before Earth
since we haven't many words
>   to speak with you.
May Sky and Earth be with you
>   prisoner, captive.

Fanfare during which RABINAL *and* CAWEK *turn their backs to one another, as before, while* EAGLE *and* JAGUAR *stand still wherever they happen to be on their paths.*

CAWEK OF THE FOREST PEOPLE speaks for the second time.

Listen!
Alas, O Sky!
>   Alas, O Earth!
What are these words you speak, sir?
>   The words you speak
>   are hurtful right on their face, sir
before Sky
>   before Earth
>   in my teeth, in my face.
I am brave
>   I am a man
>   so say your words, sir.
"What place did you flee
>   in the face of violence
>   in the face of war?"
>   so say your words, sir.
Am I brave?
>   Am I a man?
Would a man of valor just run away
>   in the face of violence
>   in the face of war?
Yet this is what your words say, sir.
"Now reveal the face
>   of your mountain
>   your valley,"
>   so say your words, sir.

Am I brave?
    Am I a man?
Yet I should reveal the face
    of my mountain
        my valley?
Isn't it clear that I blossomed
    on the slope of a mountain
        on the floor of a valley?
I'm merely born of clouds
    I'm merely born of mist.
Why should I reveal

With the next two lines he lifts his ax toward the horizon and then lowers it toward the ground in front of him.

    my mountain
        my valley?
Better that Sky be left behind
    Earth be left behind!
So say my words
    before Sky
        before Earth
since we haven't many words
    to speak with you, sir
Man of Glory
    Man of Rabinal.
May Sky and Earth be with you, sir.

Fanfare.

MAN OF RABINAL speaks for the third time.

Listen!
Brave man
    prisoner, captive:
Is this what your words now say
    before Sky
        before Earth?
"Am I brave?
    Am I a man?

11. Rabinal (left) and Cawek (right) dialogue in the foreground; in the background (from left to right) are Road Guide, Lord Five Thunder, the Mother of Quetzal Feathers, and Slave, none of whom has a role in this scene. Rabinal carries a rope (looped around his waist), but in this production he did not use it until the end of Cawek's eighth speech.

And yet I should reveal
    my mountain
        my valley?
Isn't it clear that I blossomed
    on the slope of a mountain
        on the floor of a valley?
I'm merely born of clouds
    I'm merely born of mist,"
        isn't that what your words say?
Very well, if you refuse to reveal
    the face of your mountain
        the face of your valley
then Sky willing
    Earth willing
you'll just shout
    you'll just shriek

when I take you in
        before my lord
                before my liege
inside his great fortress
        inside his great walls
so say my words
        before Sky
                before Earth
and may Sky and Earth be with you
        prisoner, captive.

Fanfare.

CAWEK OF THE FOREST PEOPLE speaks for the third time.

Listen!
Alas, O Sky!
        Alas, O Earth!
Is this what your words say
        before Sky
                before Earth?
Could there be something out of place
        something wide of the mark
                about the words, the phrases
that we've been speaking to you, sir
        before Sky
                before Earth?
"Well, they will be wide of the mark
        they will be spoken in vain
until you reveal
        until you make clear
the face of your mountain
        the face of your valley.
If you refuse to make it clear
        then Sky willing
                Earth willing
you'll just shout
        you'll just shriek

when I present you
　　　to my lord, my liege."
So say your words, sir
　　　before Sky
　　　　　before Earth.
If you are willing, Sky
　　　if you are willing, Earth
then I shall indeed reveal
　　　the face of the mountain
　　　　　the face of the valley
　　　　　　　of this little house wren, this bird.
I am the brave
　　　I am the man
of the lord of foreign Cunén
　　　foreign Chajul:
the Lord Jaguar Man
　　　Jaguar Quiché
　　　　　the quick one.
I'm just a drop of water fallen from clouds and mist
　　　on my mountain
　　　　　on my valley.
Could there be something out of place
　　　something wide of the mark
　　　　　about the words, the phrases
that we've spoken to you, sir
　　　before Sky
　　　　　before Earth?
And may Sky and Earth be with you, sir
　　　Man of Glory
　　　　　Man of Rabinal.

Fanfare.

MAN OF RABINAL speaks for the fourth time.

Listen!
Brave man
　　　Cawek of the Forest People:

What a terrible joke you're someone I ought to help out.
　　　　What a terrible joke you're my elder brother.
　　　　　　　What a terrible joke you're my younger brother.
And I truly lost heart
　　　　when I saw you, sir
　　　　　　　when I spotted you, sir
outside the great fortress
　　　　outside the great walls
You, sir, are the one who makes the cries of coyotes
　　　　who makes the cries of foxes
　　　　　　　who makes the cries of agoutis and jaguars
　　　　　　　　　outside the great walled fortress.
You do it as an enticement, sir
　　　　for the children, the sons of light
they come out
　　　　in front of the great fortress
　　　　　　　in front of the great walls
the providers, creatures
　　　　of yellow honey
　　　　　　　fresh honey
the sustenance
　　　　of my lord, my liege
　　　　　　　Grandfather Lord Five Thunder.
And furthermore
what about those braves, those men
　　　　who became restless, agitated
　　　　　　　after you incited them, sir?
Didn't those twelve lords
　　　　those who rule each fortress
　　　　　　　each set of walls
cry out to us here
　　　　shout to us?
Didn't their words tell us this:
"Come quickly, sirs, boys
　　　　twelve brave boys
　　　　　　　twelve men
now come for your instructions, sirs
　　　　because the food in each bowl
　　　　　　　the drink in each jar

was dissolved
      tasted
            freshened
                  and absorbed.
Now only katydids
      only crickets
are left to chirp
      inside the fortress
            inside the walls
of the children of light
      the sons of light
since only nine
      now only ten
have returned
      to their fortress
            their walls.
So now we must finish the farm work
      of the children of light
            the sons of light
and this is when we must bring in their food
quickly gathering large beans
      gathering white-winged dove beans
            gathering red-feathered quail beans
                  gathering striped quail beans."
Aren't these the instructions that were given to us
      by those who are lords over us,
            those who have dominion?
Weren't there nine clenched fists
      nine forearms
those braves
      those men
who ended up buried
      shrouded
            by our lords
there at the place called
      Pitted
            and Planted?
How could your heart's desire
      not be fulfilled, sir

over those braves
    those men?
Now you will pay for your deeds, sir
    here at the navel of the sky
        navel of the earth
and now you've said goodbye
    to your mountain, sir
        your valley, sir
because this is where we chop clear through
    your root, sir
        your trunk, sir
here at the navel of the sky
    navel of the earth.
Perhaps no day
    no night will ever come to the sky
when you return
    to your mountain, sir
        your valley, sir.
Truly then, you are dead here
    you are lost, sir
here at the navel of the sky
    navel of the earth.
And so I'll bring word of you, sir
    before my lord
        before my liege
inside his great fortress
    inside his great walls
so say my words
    before Sky
        before Earth
since we haven't many words
    to speak.
May Sky and Earth be with you, sir
    Cawek of the Forest People.

Fanfare.

CAWEK OF THE FOREST PEOPLE speaks for the fourth time.

> Listen!
> Alas, O Sky!
>> Alas, O Earth!
> Brave man
>> Man of Glory
>>> Man of Rabinal:
> Is this what your words now say, sir
>> before Sky
>>> before Earth?
> "Why incite
>> the braves, the men?"
>>> so say your words, sir.
> Yes, it's correct that orders were given
>> by our lords
>>> our lieges
> but the first time it happened
>> it had nothing to do
>>> with my having to come
> to my mountain
>> my valley.
> A messenger had arrived there
>> from the navel of the earth
>>> navel of the sky
>>>> from a lordly fortress.
> Red Mountain
>> Shaker
>>> Dressed in Red
>>>> Tepecanic
> are the names of the rim, the face
>> of that fortress
>>> those walls.
> Didn't he bring ten score seeds of pataxte
>> five score seeds of cacao
> when he arrived
>> before my lord
>>> my liege?

Jaguar Lord
      Jaguar Man
           Jaguar Quiché
is the name of the rim, the face
      of my own fortress
           my own walls.
"The lord Jaguar Lord
      Jaguar Quiché
           should listen to this:
Since the Uxab
      the Pokomam
           desire the death
of the Lord of Walkers
      Lord of Workers
           Cawuks and Rabinals
we must do what is good and beautiful.
The Lord of Quiché Mountain
      Quiché Valley
should send into my sight
      his brave, his man
to come and cultivate
      the bright mountain
           bright valley
so that my fat
      my surplus
           might be forthcoming.
And when he comes to cultivate
      here at the navel of the sky
           navel of the earth
on the bright mountain
      in the bright valley
when he comes to plant
      when he comes to sow
then all the sprouts of our squash vines
      the sprouts of our bright seeds
           our bright abundance
               will travel their roads."

So said the announcement
> the cry of that messenger
>> before my lord.

And so my lord, my liege sent out
> his own announcement
>> his own cry:

"Listen! Listen!
> My brave, my man:

Give us your attention here
> because a messenger invited you.

He came from the navel of the sky
> navel of the earth

to arouse your strength
> your manhood

the power of your weapon
> the power of your shield

to traverse
> the length and breadth
>> of the mountains and valleys."

So said the announcement
> the cry
>> of my lord, my liege.

I'm going step by step right now
> I'm working the soil
>> I'm resetting the boundaries of the land

from the place where the day goes out
> to the place where the night enters

suffering through cold
> suffering through heat

starting from the place called
> Mountains in a Row
>> Pines in a Row

and so I have indeed aroused
> the power of my weapon
>> the power of my shield

and I have traversed
> the length and breadth
>> of the mountains and valleys

and there
I came to deliver
     my first announcement
         my cry
in front of the place called
     Thunderclap
         and then I came away from there
and then again
I came to deliver
     my second announcement
         my cry
there at the places called
     Big Tree
         Lord's Place
             Earthquake
                 and then I came away from there
and then again
I came to deliver
     my third announcement
         my cry
there at the place called
     Bountiful
         and then I came away from there
and next
I came to deliver
     my fourth announcement
         my cry
at the place called
     Between the Wasp Nests.
When I got there I heard, already in progress
     the sorrowful sound of the bloodletter's trumpets
         the bloodletter's drum
played for the twelve Golden Eagles
     Golden Jaguars.
It seemed as if the very sky were beating like a heart
     the very earth were beating like a heart.
The twelve Golden Eagles
     Golden Jaguars

were devastating when they screamed
          when they made an uproar there
along with the woman slaves
          man slaves.
So then
I spoke
          before Sky
                    before Earth
and this is what my words said
          before Sky
                    before Earth:
"Come on out, lord who's been pierced
          lord who's been fitted with gems
however that may be
          let me take the lead
                    since I'm not finished
chopping through
          the root
                    the trunk
of that Lord of Walkers
          Lord of Workers
                    Cawuks and Rabinals,"
                              so said my words.
Now, what's to be done
          about that oh-so-respectable lord?
I've yet to dismay him
          I've yet to teach him a lesson.
The words I spoke
          before Sky
                    before Earth
                              were mere talk
Man of Glory
          Man of Rabinal
and I've talked with you already, sir.
May Sky and Earth be with you as well, sir
          Man of Glory
                    Man of Rabinal.

Fanfare.

MAN OF RABINAL speaks for the fifth time.

> Listen!
> Brave man
>   Cawek of the Forest People:
> Is this what your words now say
>   before Sky
>   before Earth?
> The words you have spoken are true, sir
>   the words you have spoken aren't false, sir
> since a messenger truly went forth from here
>   since we truly sent him there
> to Quiché Mountain
>   Quiché Valley.
> But even so
>   it wasn't wrong
>   it wasn't evil
> that we sent him there
>   so that he could be heard
> by the Lord Jaguar
>   Lord Jaguar Quiché
> since the Uxab
>   the Pokomam
> desired the death
>   the disappearance
> of the Lord of Walkers
>   Lord of Workers
>   Cawuks and Rabinals
> here at the navel of the sky
>   navel of the earth.
> "We must do what is good and beautiful:
> The Lord of Quiché Mountain
>   Quiché Valley
> should send
>   his brave
>   his man
> to come and cultivate
>   the bright mountain
>   bright valley

to come and plant
        to come and sow
just as we plant
        just as we sow
then all the sprouts of our squash vines
        the sprouts of our bright seeds
            our bright abundance
                will travel their roads."
So said our original words
        before Sky
           before Earth.
But even so
we advised you in vain, sir
        we instructed you in vain, sir
here at the navel of the sky
        navel of the earth.
"Thanks be to Sky
        thanks be to Earth
you, sir, have come here
        before our fortress
           our walls.
And so now
        we must all raise our weapons
           we must make war.
We shall make war on the Uxab
        the Pokomam.
But before that
        I shall give you a task, sir
           a message to carry, sir.
You, sir, must run over there
        on the great road
to the place called
        Bird's Drinking Water
           Pieces of White Lime in a Row.
But don't give the Uxab
        the Pokomam
           their heart's desire, sir.

Don't let them get loose, sir
     from their mountain
          their valley.
Dismay them, sir
     deceive them, sir
here at the navel of the sky
     navel of the earth,"
          so said my original words, sir
but even so
you, sir, did not succeed
     in seeing
          observing
the Uxab
     the Pokomam
because they transformed themselves
     into gnats
          into flies
               into ants
                    into conqueror ants.
Now they go through scene after scene
     episode after episode
          telling how they took the length of that mountain
the one called
     Below the Cave
          Under Ripe Yellow Corn.
It was only when I had sent out
     my own lookout
          my own scout
before Sky
     before Earth
it was only then that I observed
     the Uxab
          the Pokomam.
And then
my heart skipped a beat
     my heart was wounded
at seeing you, sir
     at spotting you, sir

because you gave the Uxab
       the Pokomam
               their heart's desire, sir.
So then I delivered
       my announcement
               my cry to you, sir:
"Listen! Listen!
Brave man
       Cawek of the Forest People:
For what reason
       did you, sir, allow
               the Uxab
                       the Pokomam
to get loose
       from their mountain
               their valley?"
Alas, O Sky!
       Alas, O Earth!
After all
we had banished them
       from our own mountain
               our own valley
until you, sir, delivered
       your announcement
               your cry
to the Uxab
       the Pokomam.
Just what did they say in reply?
So say my words
       before Sky
               before Earth
since we haven't many words
       to speak with you, sir.
May Sky and Earth be with you, sir
       Cawek of the Forest People.

Fanfare.

CAWEK OF THE FOREST PEOPLE speaks for the fifth time.

> Listen!
> Brave man
>> Man of Glory
>>> Man of Rabinal:
> Is this what your words say, sir
>> before Sky
>>> before Earth?
> "For what reason
>> did you, sir, allow
>>> the Uxab
>>>> the Pokomam
> to get loose
>> from their mountain
>>> their valley?"
>>>> so say your words, sir.
> Well then
> I delivered
>> my announcement
>>> my cry
> to the Uxab
>> the Pokomam:
> "Listen! Listen!
> You Uxab
>> you Pokomam
> come on, pay attention
>> to your orders
>>> your instructions
> from the navel of the sky
>> navel of the earth,"
>>> I said over there
> and then
> the Uxab
>> the Pokomam
>>> said in reply:
> "Listen! Listen!
> Brave man
>> Cawek of the Forest People:

Even if we got away
>from our mountain
>>our valley
we do not yet have many descendants here
>among my children
>>among my sons.
There are some
>under black clouds
>>under white clouds
suffering through cold
>suffering through heat
shaded by quetzal feathers
>shaded by glistening green
under the golden pataxte
>under the golden cacao
under the golden money
>under the silver money
under the pickings
>the cuttings
among my children
>among my sons.
But these children of mine
>these sons of mine
don't find it difficult
>to grow their sustenance.
Here the only things that need care
>are pataxte seeds by the score
>>cacao seeds by the score
because they'll be pickers
>they'll be cutters
as long as there are days
>as long as there is light.
As for the children, the sons
>of that Man of Glory
>>Man of Rabinal
it's only by burning with pain
>by burning with anguish
that they'll ever manage
>to grow their sustenance

as long as there are days
    as long as there is light.
And they only see what's close to them
    when they look back
        when they look ahead.
They're twisted out of shape
    they're crippled.
Such are the predecessors
    and such will be the successors
of that Man of Glory
    Man of Rabinal
as long as there are days
    as long as there is light."
So said the announcement, the cry
    of the Uxab
        the Pokomam
            because of their troubled hearts.
And then I said to them there:
"Listen! Listen!
You Uxab
    you Pokomam:
Is this what your words now say
    before Sky
        before Earth?
'As for the children, the sons
    of the brave man
        Man of Rabinal
it should not be that the effects
    of their persistence
        their determination
extend to all four edges
    all four corners
to the width of the earth
    the length of the earth
at a day's journey
    or two days' journey
because of their strength
    their manhood.'

And these children and sons of yours, sir
    on the other hand
are simply dismayed
    astonished by their persistence.
They put things in order
    they finish what they start
when they come out
    in their mountain
        their valley.
So you desire that just one
    or else two
should reach
    their fortress
        their walls
because your children, your sons
    are simply dismayed
        simply astonished
by their persistence
    their determination.
'As for the children, the sons
    of that brave man
        Man of Glory
            Man of Rabinal
just one or two
    should come out
and just one or two
    should return
to their fortress
    their walls.'
Isn't that what your words say?'"
So I said over there
    to the Uxab
        the Pokomam.
May Sky and Earth be with you, sir
    Man of Glory
        Man of Rabinal.

Fanfare.

MAN OF RABINAL speaks for the sixth time.

> Listen! Listen!
> Brave man
> > Cawek of the Forest People:
> Now you, sir, have heard
> > the announcement
> > > the cry
> the Uxab
> > the Pokomam
> > > sent back here.
> Alas, O Sky!
> > Alas, O Earth!
> To tell the truth
> you brought down suffering
> > at the navel of the sky
> > > navel of the earth
> on the heads of our children
> > the heads of our sons
> and to tell the truth
> you did not plant crops
> > in the bright mountains
> > > bright valleys.
> This is remarkable
> > it's amazing
> since you, sir, have spent
> > so many days
> > > so many nights
> at the navel of the sky
> > navel of the earth.
> Also, you spent
> > the power of your weapon, sir
> > > the power of your shield, sir
> and you used up
> > all the strength of your arms, sir
> > > the strength of your shoulders, sir
> > > > it no longer came to you.
> And to tell the truth

12. Man of Rabinal at a night performance.

you, sir, did not plant crops
        at the navel of the sky
                navel of the earth.
Since you know, sir
        where the boundaries of the land are
why must you run, sir
        crossing the length and breadth
                of the mountains and valleys?
And to tell the truth
I who am a brave man
        a Man of Glory
                Man of Rabinal
have many descendants
        among my children
                among my sons

here at the navel of the sky
   navel of the earth.
So say my words
   before Sky
     before Earth
and may Sky and Earth be with you as well, sir
   brave man
     Cawek of the Forest People.

Fanfare.

CAWEK OF THE FOREST PEOPLE speaks for the sixth time.

Listen! Listen!
Alas, O Sky!
   Alas, O Earth!
To tell the truth
I did not plant crops
   here at the navel of the sky
     navel of the earth
in the bright mountains
   bright valleys.
Was it only for the sake of desire
   was it only for the sake of longing
that I spent so many days
   so many nights
at the navel of the sky
   navel of the earth?
Didn't my courage
   my manhood
     come here with me?
Alas, O Sky!
   Alas, O Earth!
"I'm going back, then
   to my own mountain
     my own valley."
So said my words
   before Sky
     before Earth.

I have traversed
>   the length and breadth
>   of the mountains and valleys
and there
I measured the distance in cords
>   to the place called
>   Water Jar Point
and my words said
>   before Sky
>   before Earth:
"Isn't it right
>   that I should gain recognition
as Lord of Water Jar Mountain
>   Lord of Water Jar Valley
by planting my sandals
>   on the heads of the children
>   the heads of the sons
of the Man of Glory
>   Man of Rabinal?"
>   so spoke my troubled heart.
And what's more
"Would that Sky could feel such pain
>   Earth could feel such pain!"
>   so said my words.
And then I came further
and then I measured the distance in cords
>   to Henequen Mountain
>   Henequen Valley.
I delivered
>   my announcement
>   my cry:
"Alas, O Sky!
>   Alas, O Earth!
Can it be true to say
I never planted crops
>   here at the navel of the sky
>   navel of the earth?"
And then I descended
>   to Healing Waters

and this time
        when I looked out over the land
the yellow-colored, white ears of ripe corn
        yellow sustenance, white sustenance
                bird-footed bean shoots
spread out ahead of me
        spread out behind me, over the land
and my words said
        before Sky
                before Earth.
"Isn't it right
        that I should protect
                a little bit of land
spread out ahead of me
        spread out behind me
with the power of my weapon
        the power of my shield?"
And so
I left the prints
        of my sandals on that land
spread out in front
        spread out behind.
So I left that place
and then I measured the distance in cords
        to the place called
                Croaking Frog Point at Belted House.
Again I left that place
and then I measured the distance in cords
        to the place called
                Worn-out Trumpet Point.
And so
I trumpeted there
        because of my troubled heart
for thirteen score days
        and thirteen score late nights
because I did not plant crops
        here at the navel of the sky
                navel of the earth
in the bright mountains
        bright valleys

and my words said
    before Sky
        before Earth:
"Alas, O Sky!
    Alas, O Earth!
Can it be true to say
    that I did not plant crops
here at the navel of the sky
    navel of the earth?
Was it only for desire
    was it only for longing
that I spent so many days
    so many nights?"
So said my words
    before Sky
        before Earth.
"And I've also spent the strength
    of my elbow
        my shoulder.
My courage
    my manhood
        no longer come to me,"
so said my words
    before Sky
        before Earth.
"I'm going back, then
    to my own mountain
        my own valley,"
            said my words.
"And so I have traversed
    the length and breadth
        of the mountains and valleys,"
            so said my words.
May Sky and Earth be with you as well, sir
    Man of Glory
        Man of Rabinal.

Fanfare.

MAN OF RABINAL speaks for the seventh time.

> Listen!
> Brave man
>> Cawek of the Forest People:
> What about the children of light
>> the sons of light?
> For what reason
>> did you incite revolt
>>> among the children of light
>>>> the sons of light?
> Even though it wasn't your right
>> you set them loose
>>> from their mountain
>>>> their valley.
> "Whether or not you set them loose
>> then, Sky willing
>>> Earth willing
> I shall shake the sky
>> I shall shake the earth,"
>>> so said my announcement
> because *I* was going step by step
>> *I* was working the soil
>>> *I* was resetting the boundaries of the land
> starting from the place called
>> Look-See Point
> when you, sir, incited
>> the children of light
>>> the sons of light
> to get behind the power of your weapon, sir
>> the power of your shield, sir
> But then
> your heart was unashamed, sir
>> at hearing my announcement
>>> my cry
> and then
> I traversed the length and breadth
>> of the mountains and valleys

and there
I measured the distance in cords
    to the place called
        Sculpture Tree
and from there
I sent out
    my announcement
        my cry to you, sir
and you, sir, had already set loose
    the children of light
        the sons of light
there at the places called
    Big Tree
        Lord's Place
            Earthquake.
They came within a very short distance
    of Quiché Mountain
        Quiché Valley.
And then
    they turned in this direction
taking by force
    the length and breadth
        of the mountains and valleys.
With their bellies grumbling
    since the worms in their bellies were grinding away
        they turned this way.
Even now
    they have yet to return
        inside their own fortress
            inside their own walls.
Now, instead
they have settled
    at the place called
        Spilt Water.
Also, of course, you, sir
    came to draw out
        my lord, my liege
there at the place called
    Bath.

Wasn't I, too, going step by step?
       I was working the soil
           I was occupied
I was resetting the boundaries of the land
       there at the place called
           House Point
               by the Rocks that Face Each Other.
So it was only
       my lookout
           my scout
I sent this way
       before Sky
           before Earth
just a large drop of water from a cloud
       a drop of water from a mist
left spattered
       before the great fortress
           great walls.
And from there
I sent over
       my announcement
           my cry
before Sky
       before Earth
           and my words said:
"Listen! Listen!
Brave man
       Cawek of the Forest People:
What about my lord
       my liege?
For what reason
       did you come to draw him outside
the great fortress
       great walls?
It simply wasn't right for you
       to bring him outside
the great fortress
       great walls,"
           so said my words

but even so
your heart did not cry, sir
    at hearing
my announcement
    my cry.
My words said this:
    "Whether or not you drew out
        my lord, my liege
then, Sky willing
    then, Earth willing
I shall shake the sky
    I shall shake the earth!
Sky be my road
    earth be my road,"
        so said my words
but then
your heart did not cry, sir
    at hearing
my announcement
    my cry.
I traversed
    the length of the mountains
        clear across the breadth of the great valley
and there
I used a cord to measure
    the perimeter of the great walls.
But this
    was all I saw:
just a drop of water from a cloud now
    just a drop of water from a mist now
spattered now
    before the great fortress
        great walls.
Now katydids
    only crickets
were left to trumpet
    left to trill
inside the great fortress
    great walls.

My heart skips a beat over this
    my heart deserts me.
Again I traversed
    the length and breadth
        of the mountains and valleys
and then
when I reached
    my lord, my liege
he had heavy fortifications behind him
    fortifications in front of him
        inside the plastered hive
so then
I arrayed
    the power of my weapon
        the power of my shield
and my upraised ax handle
    my upraised ax blade
along with my courage
    my manhood.
Only in this way
    could I look after
        my lord, my liege.
There was a terrible silence
    in back, in front
        and inside the plastered hive.
But then
I got him safely out of there
    under the power of my weapon
        the power of my shield.
To tell the truth
    if it were not for me
        and this is certain
you would have chopped clear through
    the root
        the trunk
of my lord
    my liege.
And this is the reason
    I have kept watch over him

with the power of my weapon
  the power of my shield.
And so it came about that I brought
  my lord, my liege
    inside his own fortress, own walls.
Didn't you, sir, finish off
  two or three branches of the nation
    down in the canyons, up on the heights
there at the places called
  Standing Jaguar
    Sparkling Dust
      Reed Rattles
        Drumbeat
          Mace Valley
            Sapota Tree?

So how could your heart's desire
  not be fulfilled, sir
over these braves
  these men?
Now you will come to pay for it, sir
  here at the navel of the sky
    navel of the earth.
And so I must take your story, sir
  inside the great fortress
    great walls
before my lord
  my liege
And so you have now taken leave, sir
  of your mountain, sir
    your valley, sir
because this is where we chop clear through
  your root, sir
    your trunk, sir
here at the navel of the sky
  navel of the earth.
Since this is the truth
  we haven't many words to speak with you, sir.
May Sky and Earth be with you, sir
  Cawek of the Forest People.

Fanfare.

13. Cawek of the Forest People.

CAWEK OF THE FOREST PEOPLE speaks for the seventh time.

> Listen!
> Brave man
>   Man of Rabinal:
> Is that what your words say, sir
>   before Sky
>   before Earth?
> These are true words
>   not false words

that you have spoken, sir
>   before Sky
>   >   before Earth
in my teeth
>   in my face.
And truly it is I
>   who am to blame.
Orders were given for a second time
>   by our lords
>   >   our lieges:
"They have invited us
>   they have called us,"
so said the words
>   of our lords, our lieges
from the rank of Lord Thunder
>   to the rank of Lord Knife
at Old Camp and Whisker Place
>   on each level
>   >   on each layer.
Gathered Cane Plants
>   Gathered Lakes
>   >   Gathered Canyons
>   >   >   Gathered Birds
are the names of the mouths
>   the faces
of those lords of ours
>   those lieges of ours.
"'You must come, sirs
>   twelve braves
>   >   twelve men.
Get here quickly, sirs
>   take your leave, sirs,'
so said their words
>   for you, sir.
'And so
as the food in each bowl
>   the drink in each jar

is dissolved
    tasted
        freshened
            and absorbed
inside the great fortress
    great walls
then only nine
    or ten
of the children of light
    the sons of light
will remain inside their fortress
    their walls,'
so said their words
    for you, sir.'"
And so
because I had not planted crops
    here at the navel of the sky
        navel of the earth
and because of
    my troubled heart
I incited the children of light
    the sons of light
to go on the road
    and make a turn.
When they were set loose
    the creatures of yellow honey
        fresh honey
were buzzing
    in the breadnut trees
        over their sustenance.
"I have cared for them."
So said my words
    before Sky
        before Earth.
"Isn't it right
    that I incited
these children of light
    these sons of light?

They're becoming aroused at my mountain
  my valley,"
    so said my words.
"I must take myself
  before my lord
    my liege
at Quiché Mountain
  Quiché Valley,"
    so said my words.
And there was
a little bit of land
  spread out in front
    spread out behind
yellow-colored, white ears of ripe corn
  yellow sustenance
    white sustenance.
But then
I gave it up
  there at the place called
    Red Earth
because
this heart of mine went away
  with the children of light
    the sons of light.
But even so
when you, sir, delivered
  your announcement
    your cry
my heart took notice
  my heart cried out
at hearing
  your announcement, sir
    your cry, sir.
And this was when
  you, sir, arrived there
    at Sculpture Tree
and then

you, sir, delivered
        your announcement, sir
                your cry, sir.
And after that
I set loose
        the children of light
                the sons of light
at the places called
        Big Tree
                Lord's Place
                        Earthquake.
It was only by a short distance
        that the children of light
                the sons of light
fell short of reaching
        my mountain
                my valley
Quiché Mountain
        Quiché Valley.
And then
the children of light
        the sons of light
                turned their gaze in this direction.
Since the worms in their bellies were grinding
        since the worms in their bellies were grumbling
they were seizing
        the length and breadth
                of the mountains and valleys.
And so
        because of that
they have yet to return
        inside their own fortress
                their own walls.
So now, instead
they have settled
        at the place called
                Spilt Water.
And truly it is I
        who am to blame

for drawing out
>your lord, sir
>>your liege, sir
there at the place called
>Bath
>>even though bathing was his only concern.
There I raised
>the power of my weapon
>>the power of my shield
and brought him down
>because of my troubled heart
>>because I had not planted crops
at the navel of the sky
>navel of the earth.
And so
I confined him
>inside the fortress, the plastered hive
I whitewashed him in back
>I whitewashed him in front
>>inside the plastered hive.
And truly it is I
>who am to blame
>>just as your words say, sir.
"You, sir, have finished off
>two or three branches of the nation
>>down in the canyons, up on the heights
there at the places called
>Standing Jaguar
>>Sparkling Dust
>>>Reed Rattles
>>>>Drumbeat
>>>>>Mace Valley
>>>>>>Sapota Tree."
And truly it is I
>who am to blame
>>because of my troubled heart
and this is where I will pay for it
>here at the navel of the sky
>>navel of the earth.

Isn't this what has been said
      in my teeth
            in my face
a mere squirrel
      a mere bird?
And isn't this what was done to him, sir
      to your lord?
Isn't this
      what your words say, sir?
"I will take your story, sir
      before my lord
            my liege
inside the great fortress
      inside the walls.
And now you, sir, have taken leave
      of your mountain, sir
            your valley, sir
because this is where
      we shall chop clear through
            your root, sir
                  your trunk, sir
here at the navel of the sky
      navel of the earth,"
            so say your words, sir.
But isn't it right
      that we should do what is good
            and beautiful?
We are elder and younger brother
      one to the other.
Let me make arrangements, sir
      let me make plans, sir
concerning my golden metal
      my silver metal
and the power of my weapon
      and the power of my shield
my upraised ax handle
      my upraised ax blade
likewise all my clothes

With the next line, still pacing, he lifts his right foot higher than usual.

along with my sandals

in order to work here, to serve

your children, sir

your sons, sir

here at the navel of the sky

navel of the earth.

It would be a mark of greatness

to let me go away, sir

to my mountain

my valley

so say our words

before Sky

before Earth.

May Sky and Earth be with you as well, sir

brave man

Man of Glory

Man of Rabinal.

Fanfare.

MAN OF RABINAL speaks for the eighth time.

Listen!

Brave man

Cawek of the Forest People:

Is this what your words now say, sir

before Sky

before Earth?

"Isn't it right

that you should let me make arrangements

let me make plans

concerning my golden metal

my silver metal

and the power of my weapon

and the power of my shield

likewise all my clothes

along with my sandals

in order to work here
        to be of service
at the navel of the sky
        navel of the earth?"
                so say your words, sir.
Would I go before my lord, my liege
        without taking those things?
"Well, perhaps this is the brave
        perhaps this is the very man
                with whom we've been concerned
outside the great fortress
        great walls
for thirteen score days
        and thirteen score nights—
he who is the dream
        from which we cannot awaken.
And so
I've let him make arrangements
        concerning his golden metal
                his silver metal
and his upraised ax handle
        his upraised ax blade
likewise all his clothes
        along with his sandals."
Wouldn't that be what I'd have to say
        before my lord
                before my liege?
"And so
I have let him go away
        to his mountain
                his valley."
Wouldn't that be what I'd have to say
        before my lord, my liege?
But I am perfect
        I am complete
                because of my lord, my liege.
There is the matter of my own golden metal
        my own silver metal.

There is also
>   the power of my weapon
>   the power of my shield
and my upraised ax handle
>   my upraised ax blade.
I am perfect
>   I am complete
because of my lord, my liege
>   inside the great fortress
>   inside the great walls.
Therefore I will bring your story, sir
>   inside the great walled fortress
>   before my lord, my liege.
And if my lord, my liege
>   says this:
"Let him go away, sir
>   to the mountain
>   and valley that are his own,"
if my lord says this
>   then I will let you go away, sir.
But if my lord, my liege
>   says this:
"Bring him in here, sir
>   in my teeth, in my face.
I have yet to look him in the teeth, in the face
>   to see how brave he may be
>   how manly."
If my lord, my liege
>   says this
>   then I'm taking you in, sir
so say my words
>   before Sky
>   before Earth.
May Sky and Earth be with you, sir
>   brave man
>   Cawek of the Forest People.

CAWEK OF THE FOREST PEOPLE speaks for the eighth time.

> Listen!
> It will be just as well, then
>> brave man
>>> Man of Rabinal
> if you, sir, take my story
>> before your lord, sir
>>> inside the great fortress, great walls.
> Take it, sir.
> May Sky and Earth be with you as well, sir
>> Man of Glory
>>> Man of Rabinal.

Fanfare. JAGUAR stops near the eastern end of his path and faces center. RABINAL takes CAWEK to that position. A stage hand ties RABINAL's end of the rope that binds CAWEK around the waist of JAGUAR. RABINAL then walks to a position in front of LORD. EAGLE continues pacing his full path.

MAN OF RABINAL speaks for the ninth time. *He paces up and down before the west bench as he speaks.*

> It's a clear day, lord.
>> It's a clear day, lady.
> Thanks be to Sky
>> thanks be to Earth
> you, sir, are exalted here
>> you, madam, are canopied
> beneath the shade of quetzal feathers, glistening green
>> inside the great fortress
>>> inside the great walls.
> Also
> I am here
>> I who am your brave, sir
>>> I who am your man, sir.
> I have arrived here
>> in your teeth, sir, in your face, sir
> inside the great fortress
>> inside the great walls.

And as for that brave, that man
    the particular one with whom we've been concerned
for thirteen score days
    thirteen score nights
        outside the great walled fortress—
he who is the dream
    from which we cannot awaken—
even so
Sky has given him up
    Earth has given him up
and he has fallen
    under the power of my weapon
        the power of my shield.
I have thrown a lasso
    I have thrown a lariat
with my henequen rope
    my henequen cord
and my upraised ax handle
    my upraised ax blade
my snail-shell bracelet
    my armband
        my gourd of tobacco.
Even so
I had to pry open the mouth
    of the brave, the man
since it wasn't quick and easy
    to get him to reveal the face
of his mountain
    his valley
in my teeth, in my face
    I who am brave, I who am a man.
This is the brave
    this is the man
who makes the cries of coyotes
    who makes the cries of foxes
        who makes the cries of agoutis
a fiction outside the great fortress
    the great walls

so as to decoy
    so as to entice
        the children of light, the sons of light.
This is the brave
    this is the man
who finished off
    nine or ten
        children of light, sons of light.
This is also the brave
    who came to draw you out, sir
        there at Bath.
This is the brave man
    who finished off
        two or three branches of the nation
down in the canyons, up on the heights
    at the place called
        Standing Jaguar
            Sparkling Dust
so how could his heart's desire
    not be fulfilled
over these braves
    these men?
Weren't we warned about this
    by our lords
        our lieges
by those who have lordship
    in each one of the fortresses
        each set of walls
from the rank of Lord Thunder
    to the rank of Lord Knife
at Old Camp and Whisker Place
    on each level
        on each layer?
Gathered Cane Plants
    Gathered Canyons
        Gathered Lakes
            Gathered Honey
            Gathered Birds

are the names
        of their mouths
                their faces.
And yet to come
        is his payment for this
here at the navel of the sky
        navel of the earth.
And this is where
we shall chop clear through
        his root
                his trunk
here at the navel of the sky
        navel of the earth
my lord, sir
        Lord Five Thunder.

LORD FIVE THUNDER speaks for the first time. *He gestures with his ax or shield while he speaks; RABINAL stands still whenever he speaks.*

My brave
        my man:
Thanks be to Sky
        thanks be to Earth
you, sir, have arrived here
        inside the great fortress
                inside the great walls
                        in my teeth, in my face
I who am your lord, sir
        I who am Lord Five Thunder.
Thanks be to Sky, indeed
        thanks be to Earth, indeed
if Sky has given up
        if Earth has given up
                this brave, this man
if he has fallen
        under the power of your weapon, sir
                the power of your shield, sir

and you, sir, have thrown a lasso
        you, sir, have thrown a lariat
                over this brave, this man.
Make haste, then
        bring him in here, sir
                in my teeth, in my face.
I have yet to look him in the teeth
        yet to look him in the face
to see how brave he may be
        how manly.
But even so
you, sir, will advise
        the brave, the man
that he must not howl
        he must not shriek
when he enters
        the gate of the great fortress
                gate of the great walls
because
there are loved ones here
        adored ones
inside the great fortress
        inside the great walls
because
they are here:
        his twelve elder brothers
                his twelve younger brothers
workers in metal
        workers in jade
yet to reach perfection
        in their mouths, their faces.
Perhaps this is the brave
        who will help them reach perfection
                completion
inside the great fortress
        inside the great walls.
Also here, of course
are his twelve Golden Eagles
        Golden Jaguars

also yet to reach perfection
    in their mouths, their faces.
Perhaps this is the brave
    who will help them reach perfection.
Also here, of course
are the bench adorned with metal
    raiment adorned with metal
but with rich raiment
    or without rich raiment
perhaps this is the brave
    perhaps this is the man
        who will come to be enthroned.
Also here, of course
are his twelve drinks
    his twelve poisons
        Quick Hummingbird by name
the mead that burns
    bites
        sweetens
            delights.
When I drink it
    it brings me dreams
here inside the great walled fortress
    the lord's drink.
Perhaps this is the brave
    who will come to taste it.
Also here, of course
is the double warp
    the tamped weft
        the weaving tightly done
the work of my mother
    my lady.
Perhaps this is the brave
    perhaps this is the man
who will be the first to show
    its border
        its face.
Also here, of course
    kept safe

14. Lord Five Thunder and the Mother of Quetzal Feathers.

is the Mother of Quetzal Feathers
        Mother of Glistening Green
goods that come from
        End of the String at Fish in the Ashes.
Perhaps this is the brave
        perhaps this is the man
who will be the first to show
        her mouth
                her face
who will come to dance her round and round
        here inside the great fortress
                inside the great walls.
Perhaps this is the brave
        who could become a father- or son-in-law
                a brother-in-law
inside the great fortress
        inside the great walls

if he were respectful
    if he were dignified
if he bowed
    if he lowered his face
        when he entered here
so say my words
    before Sky
        before Earth
and may Sky and Earth be with you, sir
    Man of Glory
        Man of Rabinal.

MAN OF RABINAL speaks for the tenth time.

Lord Five Thunder
if I may be allowed
    before Sky
        before Earth:
My words for you, sir
    now say:
Since this strength of mine
    this manhood of mine
was your gift, sir
    your present, sir, to me
        in my teeth, in my face
I must therefore leave
    my weapon here
        my shield here.

As he speaks these lines he turns the concave side of his shield up and lays his ax on top of it. Holding the shield from beneath with both hands, he gives it to LORD, *who takes it with both hands and places it on his lap.* RABINAL *goes on speaking and pacing, but with his hands folded together in front of him.*

Guard them, sir
    put them away, sir
inside their box
    upon their shelf

so that they may rest now
        just as I may rest
because
I will also leave *him*—
        he who was the dream
                from which we could not awaken—
here inside the great fortress
        inside the great walls
so say my words
        before Sky
            before Earth.
May Sky and Earth be with you, sir
        my lord, my liege
            Lord Five Thunder.

LORD FIVE THUNDER speaks for the second time.

My brave
        my man:
Do your words, sir, say this
        before Sky
            before Earth?
"Since this strength of mine
        this manhood of mine
this weapon of mine
        this shield of mine
are your gift, sir
        your present, sir
            in my teeth, in my face
I am leaving them
        for you to guard, sir
            to put away, sir
inside the great walled fortress
        inside their box
            upon their shelf."
Is this what your words say, sir?
For what reason
        would I guard them
            put them away

inside their box
       upon their shelf?
What then would be the name
       of your means of defense, sir
in the course of descending
       ascending
from the highlands
       from the lowlands?
Also, what would be the name
       of the means of defense
              of our children, our sons
who have ventured forth
       in their persistence
              their determination
on all four edges
       in all four corners?
There could always be one more time
       or two more times
when you, sir, would need to arouse
       this strength of yours, sir
              this manhood of yours, sir
this weapon of yours, sir
       this shield of yours, sir
              these gifts from me to you, sir
my brave, my man
       Man of Glory
              Man of Rabinal.
May Sky and Earth be with you as well, sir.

As he speaks these last lines he returns the shield, with the ax on top of it, to RABINAL, who takes it with both hands but then picks up the ax with his right, leaving the shield in his left.

MAN OF RABINAL speaks for the eleventh time.

Very well, then.
If I should need to arouse
       this strength of mine
              this manhood of mine

your gift, sir
        your present, sir
                in my teeth, in my face
well then
I could arouse them
        once more, twice more
so say my words
        before Sky
                before Earth.
And so
I take leave of you, sir
        inside the great fortress
                inside the great walls.
May Sky and Earth be with you, sir
        my lord, my liege
                Lord Five Thunder.

LORD FIVE THUNDER speaks for the third time.

Very well, then
        my brave, my man
                may it turn out well.
Don't get tripped, sir
        don't get wounded, sir
my brave, my man
        Man of Glory
                Man of Rabinal.
May Sky and Earth be with you, sir.

Fanfare. RABINAL *returns to* CAWEK, *who is still tied to* JAGUAR *by a rope.*

MAN OF RABINAL speaks for the twelfth time. *He paces up and down on an east-west path to the south of* CAWEK.

Listen!
Brave man
        Cawek of the Forest People
this much is certain:
        I brought your story

inside the great fortress
>inside the great walls
>>before my lord, my liege.
And then
my lord, my liege
>said this:
"You, sir, will advise
>the brave, the man
that he must not shriek
>he must not howl.
Instead he must bow
>he must lower his face
when he enters
>the gate of the great fortress
>>gate of the great walls
here at the navel of the sky
>navel of the earth
because
there are loved ones here
>adored ones
inside the great fortress
>inside the great walls
because
perfection
>completion are here
inside the great fortress
>the great walls.
There are his twelve elder brothers
>his twelve younger brothers
workers in metal
>workers in jade
who are yet to be perfected
>in their mouths, their faces.
Perhaps this is the brave
>perhaps this is the man
who will help them reach perfection
>completion.
Also here, of course

are his twelve Golden Eagles
      Golden Jaguars
also yet to reach perfection
      in their mouths, their faces.
Perhaps this is the brave
      perhaps this is the man
           who will help them reach perfection.
Also here
is the bench adorned with metal
      the seat adorned with metal
           the throne adorned with metal.
Perhaps this is the brave
      perhaps this is the man
           who will come to be enthroned.
Also here
      kept safe
is the Mother of Quetzal Feathers
      Mother of Glistening Green
           of jade
                of precious beads
goods that come from
      End of the String at Fish in the Ashes.
Whether her mouth has ever been shown
      or her face has never been shown
perhaps this is the brave
      perhaps this is the man
who will come to show her mouth
      her face.
Also here, of course
are his twelve drinks
      his twelve poisons
the mead that burns
      the mead that bites
           the lord's drink
inside the great fortress
      inside the great walls.
Perhaps this is the brave
      perhaps this is the man
           who will come to taste it.

Also here, of course
is the double warp
     the tamped weft
          the weaving tightly done
the work of my mother
     my lady.
Perhaps this is the brave
     perhaps this is the man
          who will be the first to show its face.
Also here
he could become a father- or son-in-law
     a brother-in-law
here inside the great fortress
     inside the great walls,"
          so said my lord, my liege.
And so
I have advised you, sir
     that you must not shriek, sir
          you must not howl, sir
when you enter there, sir
     at the gate of the great fortress
          gate of the great walls.
You must bow, sir
     you must kneel, sir
          when you enter there, sir
before my lord, my liege
     Grandfather Lord Five Thunder
so say my words
     before Sky
          before Earth
since we haven't many words
     to speak.
May Sky and Earth be with you, sir
     Cawek of the Forest People.

SLAVE rises from the west bench and goes to RABINAL and CAWEK, pacing immediately to the west of them and never taking his-her eyes off CAWEK.

Cawek of the Forest People speaks for the ninth time. *He paces as usual while he speaks, despite the rope that limits his movements;* Jaguar *walks back and forth just enough to allow this.*

> Listen!
> Brave man
> > Man of Rabinal:
> Is this what your words now say
> > before Sky
> > > before Earth?
> "I have brought your story, sir
> > before my lord
> > > before my liege
> inside the great fortress
> > inside the great walls
> > > and his words say this:
> 'And so
> you, sir, will give notice
> > to the brave man.
> Bring him in here, sir
> > in my teeth, in my face
> > > at the gate of the great fortress.
> I have yet to look him in the teeth
> > I have yet to look him in the face
> to see how brave he may be
> > how manly.
> Advise him, sir
> > that he must not shriek
> > > he must not howl
> when he enters here
> > in my teeth, in my face.
> He must bow
> > he must lower his face
> if this brave, if this man
> > is respectful
> > > and dignified
> because
> there are loved ones here
> > adored ones

> inside the great fortress
>> inside the great walls,'
>>> so said my lord, my liege."
> Is this what your words say, sir?
> Am I brave?
>> Am I a man as well?
> If I must simply bow
>> if I must lower my face
> well then, this is my way of humbling myself
>> well then, here is my weapon
>>> here is my shield
> this is my upraised ax handle
>> my upraised ax blade.
> They will be my means for humbling myself
>> my way of going down on my knees
> when I enter there
>> at the gate of the great fortress
>>> great walls.
> And would that I could just bring down
>> the greatness
>>> the day of birth
> of your lord, sir
>> your liege, sir.
> Would that I could just bind
>> his lower lip
>>> to his upper lip
> inside the great fortress
>> great walls.

As he speaks the next words he makes a move for RABINAL *and* SLAVE *comes between them.*

> Now then:
>> You try it first, sir
> Man of Glory
>> Man of Rabinal.

Pulling JAGUAR *behind him, he follows* SLAVE *and* RABINAL *around a tight counterclockwise circle. They stop with* SLAVE, *who has* RABINAL *at his/her right, facing front toward* CAWEK, *who has* JAGUAR *at his left.*

SLAVE speaks for the first time.

> Brave man
> > Cawek of the Forest People:
> Sir, do not kill
> > my brave, my man
> > > Glorious Man of Rabinal.

RABINAL takes the rope that binds CAWEK to JAGUAR and stands behind CAWEK. JAG-
UAR returns to pacing the north side of the stage, EAGLE having been pacing the
south side all this while. During a long fanfare CAWEK, followed by RABINAL and
SLAVE, begins walking a counterclockwise circular path around the stage. When
CAWEK arrives at the east side he turns west, followed by the others, and walks
straight to the west bench, standing in front of LORD as the music ends. RABINAL
unties CAWEK and retires to a position south of the bench, facing north. SLAVE stands
near the north end of the bench, facing south into the space that separates the bench
from CAWEK.

CAWEK OF THE FOREST PEOPLE speaks for the tenth time. *He paces back and forth*
on a north-south path in front of the west bench; SLAVE paces within a smaller space
and never takes his-her eyes off CAWEK.

> It's a clear day, man.
> Certainly I myself am here
> > and what has arrived already
> through the gate of the great fortress
> > through the gate of the great walls
> where you are honored, sir
> > where you are canopied, sir
> what has certainly reached here already
> > in your teeth, sir, in your face, sir
> > > is my *story*:
> I who am brave, I who am a man.
> As a result
> > your own brave, sir
> > > your own man, sir
> Man of Glory
> > Man of Rabinal

has delivered
        this announcement, this proclamation
                in my teeth, in my face:
"I took the news there
        before my lord, my liege
                inside the great fortress
and this word was sent back
        by my lord, my liege:
'Now bring him in here, sir
        this brave, this man
                in my teeth, in my face.
I have yet to look him in the teeth
        yet to look him in the face
to see how brave he may be
        how manly.
But first
you, sir, must serve notice
        on this brave, this man
that he must not shriek
        he must not howl.
He must bow down
        he must lower his face
when he enters
        the gate of the great fortress
                gate of the great walls.'"
Such was your announcement, sir
        your proclamation, sir
                as it was delivered
by your brave, sir
        in my teeth, in my face.
Am I brave?
        Am I a man?
Then if it comes down to bowing
        if it comes down to lowering my face
very well then
here is my way of being humble
        my way of kneeling
well this is how I humble myself
        this is how I get down in the mud:

With his next two lines he turns the concave side of his shield upward and strikes it twice with the broad side of his ax.

> Here is my weapon
> > here is my shield
> and now I must bring down your day, sir
> > your birth, sir.
> I must bind
> > your upper lip, sir
> > > to you lower lip, sir.
> Now then, come on and try it, sir
> > oh lord.

He makes a move toward LORD *with his ax raised;* SLAVE *grabs his arm and holds him back, then circles him clockwise.*

SLAVE speaks for the second time.

> Brave man
> > Cawek of the Forest People:
> Sir, do not kill
> > my lord, my liege
> > > Lord Five Thunder
> inside the great fortress
> > inside the great walls
> > > where he stays, where he sits.

Slave sits on the bench.

CAWEK OF THE FOREST PEOPLE speaks for the eleventh time. *Again he paces up and down in front of* LORD.

> And so
> you must turn me away, sir
> > from my seat, from my throne.
> As far as my mountain is concerned
> > my valley
> my day has been turned upside down
> > my birth has been turned upside down.

15. Cawek of the Forest People kneels before Lord Five Thunder. To the lord's left are the Mother of Quetzal Feathers and Slave.

Such is my seat
         such is my throne.
Why was I protected against cold?
         Why was I protected against heat?
So say my words
         before Sky
                  before Earth.
May Sky and Earth be with you, sir
         Grandfather Lord Five Thunder.

He kneels before LORD *and bows his head slightly.*

LORD FIVE THUNDER *speaks for the fourth time.*

Brave man
         Cawek of the Forest People:

Thanks be to Sky
	thanks be to Earth
		you have come at last, sir
inside the great fortress
	inside the great walls
where I am honored
	where I am canopied
		I who am Grandfather Lord Five Thunder.
Now then
	go ahead and *speak,* sir
		and go ahead and *talk,* sir
because it's a terrible joke
	to come and make
the cries of coyotes
	the cries of foxes
		the cries of agoutis
a fiction
	outside the great fortress
		outside the great walls
so as to entice
	so as to serenade
		and decoy
the children of light
	the sons of light
who were drawn outside
	in front of the great walled fortress
		into the breadnut trees.
They were the most persistent
	the most determined
among the creatures
	of yellow honey
		fresh honey
my sustenance
	I who am Grandfather Lord Five Thunder
		inside the great fortress, great walls.
Likewise it was you, sir
	who got nine or ten
		children of light, sons of light
			to go on the road.

They came within a very short distance
    of reaching Quiché Mountain
and if it hadn't been for my brave
    my man
        they would have turned their attention here.
Truly, over there
you, sir, were chopping through the root, the trunk
    of the children of light, the sons of light.
Likewise it was you, sir
    who came to draw me out, sir
        at Bath.
And furthermore
you set me up there, sir
    in range of your weapon, sir.
You confined me, sir
    inside my plastered hive.
You, sir, whitewashed my back
    my face
and there, truly
you did your best, sir
    to chop clear through
        my root, my trunk.
And so
    because of this

With his next lines he gestures to his right, toward RABINAL.

    my brave
        my man
    Man of Glory
        Man of Rabinal
has put me on top here
    sheltered me here
with the power of his weapon
    with the power of his shield.
If it were not for my braves
    my men
then truly

you, sir, would be chopping through
>my root
>>my trunk.
Because of this
I came to be present
>inside the great walled fortress.
Likewise, sir
you finished off
>two or three branches of the nation
>>down in the canyons, up on the heights
there at the places called
>Standing Jaguar, Sparkling Dust
>>Reed Rattles
>>>Drumbeat
>>>>Mace Valley
>>>>>Sapota Tree.
So how could your heart's desire
>not be fulfilled
over these braves
>these men?
What could it be
>that provoked you to come *here,* sir
>>moved you to come *here*, sir?
Didn't those braves
>those men
end up buried there
>shrouded
over there at Pitted
>and Planted?
Weren't there nine clenched fists
>nine forearms?
Those were the braves
>the men
who ended up buried
>shrouded.
We are the ones who buried them
>we who are their lords
>>we who are their lieges

inside each fortress
>   inside each set of walls.
And now you, sir, will pay for it
>   here at the navel of the sky
>>   navel of the earth.
So now
you have taken leave, sir
>   of your mountain, sir
>>   your valley, sir
and truly you are dead, sir
>   you are lost
here at the navel of the sky
>   here at the navel of the earth.
So may Sky and Earth be with you, sir
>   Cawek of the Forest People.

RABINAL walks around to the north end of the bench and sits down; CAWEK rises for his next speech.

CAWEK OF THE FOREST PEOPLE speaks for the twelfth time. *He paces a north-south path in front of the bench as he speaks.*

Lord Five Thunder
if I may be allowed
>   before Sky
>>   before Earth:
There is truth in the words
>   truth in the declarations
you have made, sir
>   before Sky
>>   before Earth.
Truly it is I
>   who am to blame.
Your words, sir, say:
"Did you make them go out, sir
>   make them come back, sir?
The children of light, the sons of light
>   who were lured outside

16. Cawek (at right) paces as he speaks before Lord Five Thunder, at the left end of the bench.
The right end is now occupied by Man of Rabinal.

were the most persistent
the most determined
among all the creatures
of yellow honey
fresh honey
my sustenance
I who am Grandfather Lord Five Thunder
inside the great fortress
inside the great walls,"
so say your words, sir.
And truly it is I
who am to blame
because of my troubled heart
because I did not plant crops
in the bright mountains
bright valleys

here at the navel of the sky
　　navel of the earth.
Your words, sir, also say:
"Did you, sir, draw me out?
　　You *did* draw me out, sir
　　　　there at Bath.
Wasn't bathing my only concern
　　there at Bath?"
　　　　so say your words, sir.
And again, truly it is I
　　who am to blame
　　　　because of my troubled heart.
Your words, sir, also say:
"Did you, sir, finish off
　　two or three branches of the nation
down in the canyons
　　up on the heights

He raises his ax and sweeps it across half the horizon.

there at Standing Jaguar
　　at Sparkling Dust
　　　　at Reed Rattles
　　　　　　at Drumbeat
　　　　　　　　at Mace Valley, Sapota Tree?"
So say your words, sir.
And truly it is I
　　who am to blame
　　　　because of my troubled heart
because I did not plant crops
　　in the bright mountains
　　　　bright valleys
here at the navel of the sky
　　navel of the earth.
Your words, sir, also say:
"Take leave at long last, sir
　　of your mountain, sir
　　　　your valley, sir,"
　　　　　　say your words, sir,

"because here you are dead, sir
      you are lost, sir.
Here is where we chop clear through
      your root, sir, *your* trunk, sir
here at the navel of the sky
      navel of the earth,"
          so say your words, sir.
And truly it is I
      who am amazed at these words
          these declarations
here before Sky
      before Earth
          because of my troubled heart.
And if it is true that here I am dead
      I am lost
then my words say this
      in your teeth, sir
          in your face, sir:
If you are truly perfect, sir
      if you have everything, sir
inside the great fortress
      great walls
then lend me something you have, sir:
      your food, sir
          your drink, sir
the lord's drink
      Quick Hummingbird by name
the twelve drinks
      twelve poisons
the mead that burns
      that bites
          sweetens
             delights.
When you drink it, sir
      it brings you dreams
          inside the great fortress
             inside the great walls.
It serves to glorify my mother
      my lady.

I have yet to taste it
>yet to mark the greatness of the manner of my death
>>my disappearance
here at the navel of the sky
>navel of the earth
>>so say my words.
May Sky and Earth be with you as well, sir
Lord Five Thunder.

LORD FIVE THUNDER speaks for the fifth time. *CAWEK continues to pace.*

Brave man
>Cawek of the Forest People:
Do your words now say this
>before Sky
>>before Earth?
"Make me a gift, sir
>of your food, sir
>>your drink, sir
lend me something you have, sir
>I have yet to taste it,"
>>say your words, sir,
"if only to mark the greatness
>of my death
>>my disappearance."
There is something
>I'll give you
>>I'll have it brought
>>>to you, sir.

He turns toward SLAVE with his next lines.

Man slave
>woman slave:
Bring them here
>my food
>>my drink.
Offer it to the brave man
>Cawek of the Forest People

only to mark the greatness
of his death
his disappearance
here at the navel of the sky
navel of the earth.

SLAVE rises and CAWEK stops, facing north.

SLAVE speaks for the third time.

Very well, my lord
my liege.
I give it to the brave
to the man.

With the next lines SLAVE moves to a position in front of CAWEK and hands him the calabash; CAWEK takes it with both hands, leaving his ax and shield to hang from his wrists.

Well then
brave man
Cawek of the Forest People:
You have yet to try it, sir:
the food
the drink
of my lord
my liege
Grandfather Lord Five Thunder
inside the great fortress
of my lord, my liege
where he stays, where he sits
brave man.

Fanfare while CAWEK walks a counterclockwise circle around the stage. After coming back around to the west bench he turns his back to it and takes a couple of steps eastward; the music stops. He then takes four long draughts from the calabash, holding it in his right hand and tilting his head back. He faces east for the first draught, turns counterclockwise to the west for the second, clockwise to the north for the third, and counterclockwise to the south for the fourth. Then he returns to his position in front of LORD.

17. Cawek drinks to the west.

Cawek of the Forest People speaks for the thirteenth time. *As he paces he holds the calabash in his right hand, gesturing with it instead of his ax.*

> Listen!
> Lord Five Thunder!
>> Is this your food, sir?
>>> Is this your drink, sir?
> Really, it shouldn't be called a meal
>> it shouldn't be counted as a meal in my teeth, in my face.
> But then you, sir, have yet to taste
>> what I have at my mountain
>>> my valley.
> It's amazingly delicious
>> delectable
>>> it's sweet, it's honey

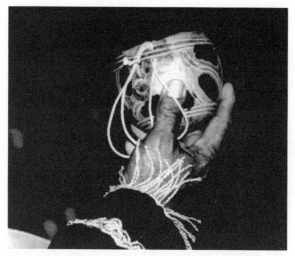

18. Cawek holds up the calabash.

it's amazing the way it tingles
            the way it bites
when I take a taste
            at my mountain
                        my valley
so say my words
            before Sky
                        before Earth.
Is this what you eat from, sir
            what you drink from, sir?

With his next lines he holds the calabash higher and shows it around as he paces.

Could this be
            the skull of my grandfather?
Could this be
            the skull of my father?
Is this what I'm looking at
            what I see before me?
Then won't this also become
            a work of some kind
                        an artifact

this bone of my crown
> bone of my head
carved in back
> and carved in front?
Then it'll be sent down there
> to my mountain
>> my valley
ending up as an even trade for
> five score seeds of pataxte
>> five score seeds of cacao
paid by my children
> my sons
at my mountain
> my valley.
My descendants will hear
> my grandsons will hear:

With his next lines he holds the calabash up again.

"This is the skull of our own grandfather
> our own father."
My descendants will hear
> my grandsons will hear
>> this remembrance of me
by my children
> my sons
as long as there are days
> as long as there is light.

With his next lines he stretches out his right arm at full length.

And as for
> this bone of my arm
when it becomes
> the handle of a metal rattle
they will marvel at the clatter
> they will marvel at the jangle
inside the great fortress
> inside the great walls.

He hands the calabash back to SLAVE.

And as for
     this bone of my leg
when it becomes
     the stick
          for a toponowos, a slit drum
they will marvel as long as there's a sky
     as long as there's an earth for them
here inside the great fortress
     inside the great walls
          so say my words.
Now lend me something you have, sir
     give it to me, sir:
something soft
     something delicate
the double warp
     the tamped weft
          the weaving tightly done
the work of my mother
     my lady.
This must be done for me right now
     inside the great fortress
          inside the great walls
on all four edges
     in all four corners
if only to mark the greatness
     of my death
          my disappearance
here at the navel of the sky
     navel of the earth.

LORD FIVE THUNDER speaks for the sixth time.

Brave man
     Cawek of the Forest People:
Whatever you may yet desire, you may ask
     I shall hand it over to you
only to mark the greatness
     of your death
          your disappearance

here at the navel of the sky
        navel of the earth.

With his next lines he turns toward SLAVE.

Man slave
        woman slave:
Bring it here:

As he continues SLAVE *rises, holding a folded cloth.*

the soft one
        the delicate one
the double warp
        the tamped weft
                the weaving tightly done
the work of my mother
        my lady
inside the great fortress
        inside the great walls.
Give it to the brave
        to the man
only to mark the greatness
        of his death
here at the navel of the sky
        navel of the earth.

SLAVE *speaks for the fourth time.* Stands in front of CAWEK, pacing back and forth
a few steps.

Very well, my lord
        my liege.
I give the brave
        I give the man
                his desire.

With the next lines SLAVE *unfolds the cloth and* CAWEK *stops pacing, facing north.*

Well then
brave man:
Here is the weaving
                tightly done
your desire
                your request.
                        I give it to you
but even so
don't abuse it
                don't wear it out.

Slave, facing Cawek, arranges the cloth so that it hangs like an apon from his sash.

Cawek of the Forest People speaks for the fourteenth time. *He paces while Slave remains standing at the north end of his path.*

Well sirs, you who are flutists
                well sirs, you who are drummers:
Could it be the mouth of my flute
                the mouth of my slit drum
                        that you are about to play, sirs?
Well sirs, if you did play
                my great instruments
                        my small instruments
and sirs, if you did play
                my Mexican flute
                        my Mexican slit drum
and sirs, if you did play
                my Quiché flute
                        my Quiché slit drum
then all the way from this place
                where I'm held prisoner
                        I'm held captive
clear over to my own mountain
                my own valley

With his next lines he ruffles his apron with his right hand.

the very sky would tremble
                the very earth would tremble.

19. Cawek, wearing the borrowed apron, dances with Slave.

But we would let our hair fall forward
    we would hang our heads
at the prospect of promenading
    dancing

With his next lines he extends his right arm, pointing at SLAVE with his ax.

    with this man slave
        woman slave
here at the navel of the sky
    navel of the earth

so say my words
before Sky
before Earth.
May Sky and Earth be with you, sirs
you who are flutists
you who are drummers.

Fanfare followed by music. CAWEK and SLAVE turn around one another in front of the west bench and then dance the counterclockwise square path around the stage, turning again at each corner. There are two fanfares during which they come to a standstill, one at the southwest corner and the other at the northeast. When they return to the west bench, a fanfare sends them walking around the stage in a circle. Then SLAVE sits on the bench and CAWEK stands before LORD, pacing.

CAWEK OF THE FOREST PEOPLE speaks for the fifteenth time.

Listen!
Lord Five Thunder
if I may be allowed
before Sky
before Earth:
So much for the things I have borrowed
the things I've been loaned.
The time has come for me to be divided
the time has come for me to be parceled out
in the mouth of the great fortress
great walls.
Guard these things, then
put them away, then
inside their box
upon their shelf
inside the great fortress
inside the great walls.
You, sir, have granted me
what I desired
what I requested
before Sky
before Earth.

I have danced them on and on
>> here inside the great walled fortress
on all four edges
>> in all four corners
and only to mark the greatness
>> of my death
>>>> my disappearance
here at the navel of the sky
>> navel of the earth.

He takes off the apron and hands it back to SLAVE.

And now my words say
>> before Sky
>>>> before Earth:
If you are truly perfect, sir
>> if you have everything, sir
inside the great fortress
>> inside the great walls
then make me a gift, sir
>> lend me something you have, sir:
the Mother of Quetzal Feathers
>> Mother of Glistening Green
>>>> of jade
>>>>>> of precious beads
who comes from
>> End of the String at Fish in the Ashes.
Whether her mouth has ever been shown
>> or her face has never been shown
I must show her mouth
>> I must show her face
I must dance her round and round
>> I must dance her on and on
inside the great fortress
>> great walls
on all four edges
>> in all four corners
if only to mark the greatness
>> of my death
>>>> my disappearance

here at the navel of the sky
        navel of the earth.
May Sky and Earth be with you as well, sir
        Lord Five Thunder.

LORD FIVE THUNDER speaks for the seventh time.

Brave man
        Cawek of the Forest People:
So is this
        what you desire, what you request?
Then I grant you
        your desire, your request
since this is where she is nourished
        where she is sheltered:

He turns and gestures toward QUETZAL.

the Mother of Quetzal Feathers
        Mother of Glistening Green
                of jade
                        of precious beads
goods that come from
        End of the String
                at Fish in the Ashes.
Whether her mouth has ever been shown
        or her face has never been shown
I give her to you
        brave man
only to mark the greatness
        of your death
                your disappearance
here at the navel of the sky
        navel of the earth.

He turns toward SLAVE.

Man slave
        woman slave:

20. Slave presents the Mother of Quetzal Feathers to Cawek.

Bring her forward
        the Mother of Quetzal Feathers
                Mother of Glistening Green.
Give the brave
        give the man
his desire
        his request
only to mark the greatness
        of his death
                his disappearance
here at the navel of the sky
        navel of the earth.

SLAVE rises and stands before QUETZAL.

SLAVE speaks for the fifth time.

> Very well
> my lord
> > my liege.
> I give her to the brave
> > to the man.
> Well then
> brave man
> > Cawek of the Forest People:
> I give you, sir
> > your desire, sir
> > > your request, sir
> but even so
> don't abuse her, sir
> > don't wear her out, sir
> this Mother of Quetzal Feathers
> > Mother of Glistening Green.

QUETZAL rises as SLAVE reaches toward her. Staying behind her with one hand on her right shoulder, SLAVE guides her to a position in front of CAWEK, who stands facing north.

> Just dance her on and on, sir
> > dance her round and round, sir
> inside the great fortress
> > inside the great walls.

Fanfare followed by music. After turning a circle in front of the west bench, CAWEK and QUETZAL dance the counterclockwise square, turning at each corner. They always face one another, with CAWEK dancing backward to move from one corner to the next, but they never touch. SLAVE dances also, staying right behind QUETZAL. There is one standstill, during which CAWEK does not turn his back to his dance partners. When they come back to the west bench a fanfare sends them walking a circle around the stage. CAWEK stops in front of LORD while QUETZAL and SLAVE sit down in their usual places.

CAWEK OF THE FOREST PEOPLE speaks for the sixteenth time.

> Lord Five Thunder
> if I may be allowed
>> before Sky
>>> before Earth:
> The one I have borrowed
>> the one I've been loaned
>>> has been given to me by both ends.
> I've held her out straight here
>> I've made flourishes here
> on all four edges
>> in all four corners
> inside the great fortress
>> great walls.
> Guard her, sir
>> shelter her, sir
> inside the great fortress
>> great walls
>>> so say my words.
> Give them to me now, sir
>> lend me something you have, sir:
> the twelve Golden Eagles
>> Golden Jaguars
> who will be my companions
>> on the last day
>>> the last night
> before the helmet
>> before the lance.
> Now lend me something you have, sir
>> I'm going to play a game here

While speaking the next two lines he bangs his shield with his ax at the places marked with accents.

> with the pówer of mý wéapon
>> the pówer of mý shiéld
> on all four edges
>> in all four corners
> inside the great fortress

great walls
only to mark the greatness
        of my death
                my disappearance
here at the navel of the sky
        navel of the earth.
May Sky and Earth be with you as well, sir
        Lord Five Thunder.

LORD FIVE THUNDER speaks for the eighth time.

Brave man
        Cawek of the Forest People:
Is this what your words say
        before Sky
                before Earth?
"Give them to me now, sir
        lend me something you have, sir
the twelve Golden Eagles
        Golden Jaguars,"
                so say your words, sir.
I give you something to keep as your own, sir:
        the twelve Golden Eagles
                Golden Jaguars
just what you want, sir
        just what you ask, sir
                in my teeth, in my face.

With his next line he turns to his right and gestures toward EAGLE.

You then, my Eagle

Now he turns to his left and gestures toward JAGUAR.

you then, my Jaguar:
        It must be done.
Come on out:

With his next line he gestures toward CAWEK.

This brave
>>this man
will play a game with you here
>>with the power of his weapon
>>>>the power of his shield
on all four edges
>>in all four corners.

Fanfare followed by music. JAGUAR leaves his stage right path and falls in behind CAWEK, who moves to a position behind EAGLE. They dance the counterclockwise square, separately turning a circle at each corner. When CAWEK comes back to his starting place the usual fanfare shifts them into walking a circle around the stage. JAGUAR stays on his northern path when he gets there, CAWEK stops in front of LORD, and EAGLE returns to his southern path.

CAWEK OF THE FOREST PEOPLE speaks for the seventeenth time.

Lord Five Thunder
if I may be allowed
>>before Sky
>>>>before Earth:
Now that you, sir, have given me
>>just what I desired
>>>>what I intended
the Golden Eagle
>>Golden Jaguar
I've played out my game here
>>with the power of my weapon
>>>>the power of my shield.
But is that an *eagle* standing there, sir?
>>Is that a *jaguar,* sir?
Don't let any such thing be said
>>in my teeth
>>>>in my face
because
there are some that can stare
>>and others that can't stare.
There are some with nary a tooth
>>some with nary a claw.

But then you, sir, have yet to see my own
            at my mountain
                        my valley.
They are devastating when they stare
            they are devastating when they gaze
                        they are devastating when they scream
when they click
            their teeth, their claws.

LORD FIVE THUNDER speaks for the ninth time.

Brave man
            Cawek of the Forest People:
We have yet to see the teeth
            of the eagle
                        the jaguar
                                    that live on your mountain
whatever may be the stare, the gaze
            of this eagle of yours
                        this jaguar of yours
that live on your mountain
            live in your valley.

CAWEK OF THE FOREST PEOPLE speaks for the eighteenth time.

Lord Five Thunder
if I may be allowed
            before Sky
                        before Earth
to speak my words now
            in your teeth, sir
                        in your face, sir:
Now give me
            thirteen score days
                        thirteen score nights.
I have yet to say farewell
            to the face of my mountain
                        the face of my valley
where I walked
            where I moved

on all four edges
    in all four corners
in the course of searching
    striving
to provide myself
    with meals
        with morsels.

A north-to-south file forms in front of the west bench; RABINAL goes to the head of it while CAWEK falls in behind him, followed by LORD, QUETZAL, SLAVE, and LADY. As a fanfare sounds, CAWEK turns his back to RABINAL and gives his cry. JAGUAR and EAGLE join the file by stopping at the western ends of their northern and southern paths. When the music begins they all dance the square path as they did at the beginning of the play. There are standstills when RABINAL and CAWEK do their southwest and northeast circles. Then comes a second dance around the square without standstills, and when CAWEK has almost reached the west bench a fanfare sounds. He walks to center stage, facing east; all the other dancers walk a circle as far as the eastern side of the stage, where they form a straight row and come to a stop. EAGLE and JAGUAR stand at angles, facing center; the others look toward CAWEK.

CAWEK OF THE FOREST PEOPLE speaks alone.

Little Eagle, little Jaguar:
Just now you were saying, "He left!"
    But I didn't leave.
I simply said farewell from here
    to the face of my mountain
        the face of my valley
where I walked
    where I moved
in the course of searching
    for my meals
        my morsels
on all four edges
    in all four corners.
Alas, O Sky!
Alas, O Earth!
Didn't my courage
    my manhood
        come with me?

21. Cawek (at left) delivers his soliloquy while pacing up and down in front of the other characters, who are (from left to right) Eagle, Man of Rabinal, Lord Five Thunder, the Mother of Quetzal Feathers, Slave, and Jaguar.

Well, I've tried
      my road in the sky
           my road on the earth
I've returned to the meadows
      I've returned to the barrens
but my courage
      my manhood
           didn't come with me.
Alas, O Sky!
      Alas, O Earth!
Can it be true
      that I'm dead here
          I'm lost
here at the navel of the sky
      navel of the earth?
You then!
      My golden metal
           my silver metal

and you, strength of my weapon
        strength of my shield
my upraised ax handle
        my upraised ax blade
and likewise you
        all my clothes
            along with my sandals.
You then!

While speaking the next five lines, he turns toward the west and extends his ax in that direction.

        Go to our mountain
           go to our valley
then tell our story
        before our lord
        our liege
talk this way
        to our lord, our liege:
"'The road is closed
        for my courage
        my manhood
searching
        striving
        for our meals, our morsels.'
Say this
        to our lord
        to our liege."
Isn't that what you'll say
        if my fate is simply
        to die
           to disappear
here at the navel of the sky
        navel of the earth?
Alas, then, Sky!
        Alas, then, Earth!
If I am truly dead
        if I am lost

at the navel of the sky
> navel of the earth
then I shall resemble
> that squirrel
>> that bird
that died on the branch of a tree
> in the flower of a tree
while searching
> for his meals
>> his morsels
here at the navel of the sky
> here at the navel of the earth.
You then, Eagle
> you then, Jaguar:
Come now!
> Do your duty
>> do your work.
Do it now with your teeth
> your claws.
But you certainly won't stand my hair on end
> in the blink of an eye
because
I am truly brave
> coming as I do
>> from my mountain
>>> my valley.
May Sky and Earth be with you too
> little Eagle, little Jaguar.

Fanfare. All walk a counterclockwise circle around the stage, with CAWEK falling in behind EAGLE and JAGUAR bringing up the rear. When CAWEK has almost finished his circle, approaching west center, he begins to spiral inward toward the very center of the stage with the others following. He reaches the center at the same moment his spiral brings him into position to face west. As the music begins he kneels with his head bowed; the others shift to dancing and form a tight counterclockwise circle around him. As they progress around the circle they move inward toward CAWEK with each left step and farther away with each right. With each left step the right arm moves toward CAWEK; those who bear axes make a chopping motion (but without touching him), aimed at the back of his neck if they happen to be in the right position at the moment.

22. Cawek kneels as the other characters close in to do their work.

As RABINAL completes a full circuit of CAWEK, which finds him facing west, CAWEK rises with a fanfare and steps into place behind him. Everyone breaks into a walk, spiraling counterclockwise and outward until CAWEK reaches the middle of the east side. Then they dance the square, breaking into the usual groups to turn circles at each corner. When EAGLE comes back around to the east side of the stage he continues to the northeast corner and stays there; the rest fall in behind him, forming a line across the east side with JAGUAR at the south end. They all turn to face east and continue to dance in place for a few measures, keeping the left foot forward and shifting their weight back and forth between left and right; on the left shift they swing the right arm forward. Next comes a fanfare with a standstill.

When the music resumes they do an about face, dancing westward while staying in line. On the way, CAWEK turns with RABINAL while LORD turns with QUETZAL, SLAVE, and LADY; EAGLE and JAGUAR turn independently. All arrive at the west side with a fanfare and standstill. ROAD GUIDE rises and moves to a position in front of the others, facing west, and when the fanfare stops the musicians also face west. Everyone prays to the ancestors at the same time but independently; only murmurs can be heard.

PART TWO

Mayan History Onstage
and
Behind the Scenes

23. Yellow Monkey Lord (right center), with one trophy head mounted on his hat and another hanging from his shirt, steps toward two fleeing enemies (left). Behind him, a prisoner he has already taken is held by an assistant. Note that he wears the same ear ornament as his assistant, whereas their enemies all wear a different ornament.
Painting from a vessel made near San Agustín Acasaguastlán, Guatemala.

Kings and Captives

PRISONERS OF WAR

Stories of lordly warriors who were captured, presented at court, and then sacrificed provided subjects for Mayan sculptors, painters, and writers throughout what archaeologists call the Classic period (300-900 A.D.). During the eighth century in particular, prisoners of war became a major focus of attention. They appear, among other places, in scenes painted on cylindrical vases that were used for mixing chocolate beverages. Among the workshops where these vases were produced, three happened to be near Rabinal. One of them was fifty kilometers to the north, at the ruins known as Chamá. Another was sixty kilometers to the east in the middle part of the valley of the Río Motagua, near the present-day town of San Agustín Acasaguastlán. And a third was seventy kilometers to the west, near the town of Nebaj.

Two painted vases from the Motagua workshop depict scenes from the career of a warrior named *K'an Maax Ajaw*, "Yellow Monkey Lord."[1] They were commissioned by the lord he served, who ruled a domain named *Ch'aaj*, "Toasted Maize." A third Motagua vase that was painted for the same lord is known to have been excavated at Nebaj, but the location of his domain remains uncertain.[2] In the first of the two scenes that concern us here (figure 23), Yellow Monkey Lord advances on two retreating enemy warriors, leaving a prisoner he has already taken in the hands of an assistant. The prisoner, stripped of his spear and quilted armor, is still struggling. The second scene (figure 24) takes place in the court of the ruler

24. Yellow Monkey Lord (at left) presents the prisoner from figure 23 to the lord of Toasted Maize (at right). The prisoner has two trophy heads attached to his belt. Painting from a vessel made near San Agustín Acasaguastlán, Guatemala. Drawing by Jamie Borowicz.

of Toasted Maize, who sits cross-legged on a dais and leans forward to speak to the same prisoner who was struggling in the first scene. The captive is not in an attitude of total subjection, but he does kneel (which he may have been forced to do), and he has his arms folded over his chest and his face slightly lowered. Standing directly behind him is Yellow Monkey Lord, who holds onto him by the loose end of his sash.

In the Rabinal play, events like the ones in the two paintings are divided into four episodes that alternate between the capture scene and the court scene. First, Cawek of the Forest People is captured and left bound by Man of Rabinal; second, Rabinal brings the news to Lord Five Thunder; third, Rabinal goes back to get his prisoner; and fourth, he presents the prisoner to Lord Five Thunder. In productions of the late 1950s, once the prisoner had been taken, he and his captor danced around one another holding opposite ends of a sash, which recalls the sash that connects the prisoner and his captor in the second painting.[3] In the play the prisoner's physical resistance lasts all the way into the beginning of the fourth episode, when he lunges toward Lord Five Thunder and has to be restrained.

Yellow Monkey Lord's prisoner is shown partially stripped in the battle scene, but he wears a quetzal-feather headdress and a necklace for his presentation at court (figure 24). No one wears such items in the battle scene (figure 23), so they may belong to his hosts. Just as Cawek receives various items on loan from Lord Five Thunder, so the prisoner in the painting may have been loaned his finery by the lord on the dais.[4] As for the two trophy heads that hang from the prisoner's waist, they may be the property of his captor. Yellow Monkey Lord is the only person in the battle scene who wears such trophies, one on top of his hat and the other hanging from his waist. Just as Cawek is loaned a drinking vessel, which he takes to be the

25. Red Monkey Man (right) presents three bound captives (lower left)
to his lord, Shield Jaguar (upper left). Eighth-century relief panel from
near Las Pasaditas, Guatemala, now in the Kimbell Museum,
Fort Worth. Based on a drawing by Linda Schele.

skull of his own father or grandfather, so Yellow Monkey Lord's prisoner may have
been loaned a pair of heads that once graced the necks of his kinsmen.

In a scene carved on a limestone panel from a site near Las Pasaditas, on the
Río Usumacinta in northwestern Guatemala, three war captives are presented by
a victorious warrior to his lord (figure 25). According to the inscriptions, the
victor's name is *Aj Chak Maax*, "Red Monkey Man," and the lord on the dais is
Shield Jaguar, the ruler of Yaxchilán (a larger site on the opposite side of the river).
The prisoners were captured three days previously, on a Mayan date corresponding to August 24, 783.[5] Their clothing and ornaments were provided by
their hosts. The ropes that bind them are looped around their upper arms, which
is the way Cawek is bound by Rabinal.

26. Warriors armed with long spears in an eighth-century battle scene. Some of them bear shields,
all rectangular; the most obvious examples are at the extreme left. From the mural in Room 2
of Structure 1 at Bonampak, Chiapas. Detail of a copy painted by Antonio Tejeda.

BEARERS OF SCEPTERS AND SHIELDS

Throughout the play, Man of Rabinal, Cawek of the Forest People, and Lord Five
Thunder all carry an ax in the right hand and a small, round shield in the left. Such
arms do exist in Classic art, but they are ceremonial rather than practical. Classic
warriors carry long spears, and those few who use shields in the course of a battle
bear rectangular ones (figure 26).[6] In later art the long spears are often replaced by
the shorter spears (or darts) used with spear-throwers, and the shields are often
round. But no one is shown going into battle armed with an ax and shield, which
is the way Rabinal (figure 27, left) and Cawek are equipped when they confront
one another. Rabinal speaks of his ax and shield as being the source of his *al* or
"power," and he warns Cawek, just before capturing him, that he has come
chupam, "under" or (more literally) "inside" that power. As for the power of
Cawek's own ax and shield, Rabinal accuses him of using it to incite revolt among
the vassals of the lords he should be serving. Cawek's ultimate purpose, as he
himself describes it, is to use his ax for "chopping through / the root / the trunk"
of the lineage of the rulers of Rabinal.

In the Classic period, as in the play, the ax and round shield do not serve
their bearers as weapons in the ordinary sense, but rather as instruments of lordly

27. Man of Rabinal (left) and an eighth-century lord from the Temple of the Inscriptions at
Palenque (right). Each wears a feathered headdress, mask, short cape, and kilt, and each
carries an upraised ax in the right hand and a small round shield in the left.
Drawings by Jamie Borowicz (left) and Merle Green Robertson (right).

power. Scenes from the state occasions on which they were displayed are sculpted
on monuments all over the lowlands, from Uxmal, far to the north of Rabinal, to
Quiriguá in the east and Palenque in the far northwest (figure 27, right).[7] They
show standing lords wielding the so-called mannequin scepter, which is both an
ax and a figurine, in the right hand. In the left hand or else tied to the left wrist is a
small shield, either round or with rounded corners.

Lord Five Thunder bears an upraised ax and a round shield, though he seats
himself early in the play and rises only at the end (figure 28, left). But like Man of
Rabinal and Cawek of the Forest People, who either stand or dance through most
of the play, he is engaged in a properly Mayan display of lordly power. In Classic
reliefs, seated lords bearing the ax and shield appear at the lowland sites of Tikal,
Palenque, Pixoy (near Uxmal), and Chichén Itzá (figure 28, right).[8]

28. Lord Five Thunder of Rabinal (left) and a lord of tenth-century Chichén Itzá (right). Each has a
feathered headdress, mask, short cape, ax scepter, and round shield. The serpent crossing the
ancient lord's ax symbolizes lightning. Drawing at left by Jamie Borowicz.

The ax scepters held by Classic lords are icons of the patron deity of royal
lineages.[9] One of his legs takes the form of a serpent, with its head and mouth where
his foot would be, and sometimes this is his only leg (as in the case of figure 27).
Mounted in his forehead is an ax blade (figure 27) or else a burning torch or cigar
that points forward (figure 29, left). He is a celestial deity, one whose power is
visible in sudden flashes of light and audible in thunder. His serpent foot can be
seen when a shaft of lightning strikes the earth, and the sparks from his torch or
cigar are meteors. The face on the shield held by bearers of his image is that of a
more earthly being, a jaguar deity of fire (figure 29, right). The twisted rope below
and between the eyes is a cord of the kind used to spin a fire drill.[10]

Links between Classic Maya scepters and the axes of the Rabinal play are
provided by sixteenth-century highland Mayan authors who sought to preserve
the memory of the pre-Columbian past, using the roman alphabet but writing in
their own languages. In their accounts the patron deity of lordship, like his lowland
Classic counterpart, had only one leg. He made fire by pivoting on this leg as if it
were the shaft of a fire drill, which would seem to indicate that he combined the
attributes of the Classic gods of the scepter and shield. Vassals burned offerings at
a temple dedicated to him before making tribute payments to their lords. One of

29. The god of the manikin scepter (left) and the shield held by bearers of the scepter (right). From Late Classic reliefs in the Temple of the Inscriptions and Temple of the Sun at Palenque, Chiapas. Drawings by the author (left) and Linda Schele (right).

his names was *Tojil* (in K'iche') or *Tojojil* (in Kaqchikel), meaning "Thunderer," and when his image was displayed by a lord it was called *uq'ab' Tojil*, "handle of Thunderer," which is to say it was a scepter.[11] His Rabinal name was that of a day on the divinatory calendar, *Jun Toj*, "One Thunder," and the Cakchiquel sometimes called him *B'eleje Toj*, "Nine Thunder."[12]

The founders of the ruling lineages of the Quiché, Rabinal, Cakchiquel, and Tzutuhil nations obtained their images of Thunderer on a pilgrimage to a great eastern city where the royal emblem of the local lords, according to a Cakchiquel source, was a bat. That would be Copán, the easternmost city ever built by the Maya, where the emblematic hieroglyph of the ruling lineage features the profiled head of a bat. Its glory days began during the sixth century and ran through the ninth. While there, the pilgrims received ax scepters, royal titles, and the right to establish their own realms.[13] When they left they went into the highlands west of Copán, seeking places to establish shrines for the gods of their scepters and seats of lordship for themselves. By the time they were ready to proclaim their own glory, the Classic period had ended and Copán had been abandoned.

At Yaxchilán (figure 30), Dos Pilas, and elsewhere, reliefs of lords bearing an ax and shield carry captions that describe them as dancing.[14] These Classic dancers are linked to the Rabinal play by a drama of kingship that was performed among the Quiché and Cakchiquel right up to the time of the Spanish invasion.[15] It was called *Poqob'*, "Posts," or *Chanal Poqob'*, "Festival of the Posts," which suggests the tall posts that rise from the burdens of the Eagle and Jaguar dancers at Rabinal. An alternative name was *Upoq'ob' Tojil*, "Revelation of Thunderer."[16]

ak'ta, "to dance"

30. The ruler of Yaxchilán (right) and a lesser lord (left) dance with manikin
scepters; the shield of the ruler is strapped to his wrist. Enlarged at the top is the
glyph that identifies them as dancing, from the column indicated by the arrow.
Lintel 3 from Yaxchilán, Chiapas. Based on a drawing by Ian Graham.

Quiché lords held this festival "as a sign of their sovereignty. It was a sign of their fiery splendor and a sign of their greatness."[17] Images of the patron deity of lordship, normally kept hidden in deerskin bundles, became the subject of "a great display, a spectacle" in which they were "called by name."[18]

During the late fourteenth or early fifteenth century, a particularly spectacular production of the Revelation of Thunderer was mounted by Quicab *(K'iqab')*, the most celebrated of Quiché kings. The occasion was provided by the success of his military campaign against enemies who had killed his father. He had recovered the skull and other bones of his father and had brought back thirteen prisoners of noble birth who were sacrificed at some point during the ceremony.[19] All the lords of the nations that owed fealty to the Quiché king, including Rabinal, converged on the capital, and each one brought an image of the patron deity of lordship and danced with it. By attending the ceremony, they signaled their loyalty to the new king.[20]

Quicab scheduled his celebration for the twenty-day division of the solar year called *Tz'ikin Q'ij* or "Bird Days," which fell in December during his reign.[21] The event was memorable because, among other things, *tzatz chi ch'ab'i q'aq', kaq tijax,* "it was thick with flaming weapons, red knives."[22] These words could be a way of evoking the power of the ax scepters or other weapons carried by the participants in the dance, but in normal usage "flaming weapons" were meteors, and a "red knife" was an iguana that flew across the night sky carrying fire. In Mesoamerica in general, exceptionally bright meteors with sparks trailing behind them were and still are likened to iguanas.[23] The time of year in question was right for the Andromedid meteor shower, a large one through much of Mayan history.[24]

Also seen at the ceremony were *kaqulja Uk'ux Kaj,* "thunderbolts from the Heart of Sky." It was the wrong season for a thunderstorm, but meteors that reach the surface of the earth produce a sound like that of thunder.[25] In Quiché thought, the similarity between lightning and meteors goes beyond the fact that they both produce sudden streaks of light and thunderous sounds. Manifestations of the Heart of Sky called *ch'ipi kaqulja* and *raxa kaqulja,* "newborn thunderbolt" and "sudden thunderbolt," reached the earth in the form of fulgurites, glassy stones that congeal where lightning hits the ground. Such objects were said to have been shot from "the blowgun of a thunderbolt."[26] So it was that both lightning and meteors were seen as celestial weapons, delivering their power by means of stones. In this they resembled the blowguns, spears, darts, arrows, and axes of the earthly realm. As for the ax scepters, they were not weapons but rather served as transmitters, delivering the luminous power of the gods into the hands of human lords. The axes used in the Rabinal play are carved from wood and painted to look like European hatchets, but a sense of their original resplendence remains in the dialogue. Neither Rabinal nor Cawek speaks of his ax in plain terms, instead calling it "my upraised ax blade, my upraised ax handle" and repeatedly invoking its power.

MARKS OF LORDSHIP

In his opening speech Cawek challenges Lord Five Thunder, calling him a *worom ajaw / k'aqom ajaw,* literally "pierced lord / lanced lord."[27] This couplet is his way of recognizing that the ruler of the Rabinal nation has undergone a ceremony in which he was confirmed in his status as a lord. During the era represented in the play his face would have been pierced in two places, with one opening running through the septum of his nose and the other through the flap of flesh supporting his lower lip.[28] Along with being pierced came the right to insert precious stones or ornaments encrusted with stones in the perforations. In order to bring out this

31. A fourth-century ruler of Tikal named Jaguar
Lord of the Sky, wearing a nose ornament
composed of two precious stones.
Detail of a jade plaque now in Leiden.
From a drawing by Linda Schele.

implication of Cawek's statement in the present translation, it has been rendered
as "lord who's been pierced / lord who's been fitted with gems."

Cawek's challenge is answered by Man of Rabinal, who calls attention to the
fact that he himself possesses marks of noble status. He gives first importance to
his ax and shield, but he goes on to list four more items: "my snail-shell bracelet /
my armband / my white paint / my gourd of tobacco." Several Quiché and
Cakchiquel authors of the sixteenth century mention emblems of lordship similar
to these four, assigning their acquisition to a pilgrimage that came later than the
one on which the founders of royal lineages obtained the ax scepters.[29] To obtain
these new emblems and renew their right to rule, descendants of the founders went
northward through the territory of the Kekchí Maya, passing through *Karchaj* or
"Fish in the Ashes," a town mentioned in the play, and at some point they came to
the shore of a sea that must have been the Caribbean. Their ultimate destination
was the court of a great lord with the Nahuatl name Nacxit, who gave each of them
various insignia of nobility.

Among the items given out by Nacxit were the bracelet, armband, paint, and
gourd of tobacco that Man of Rabinal says he has in his possession. He uses K'iche'
terms for all these objects, but the sources that describe the pilgrimage tend to favor
foreign terms. In referring to his armband he uses the K'iche' word *k'alq'ab*,
whereas the authors of the Popol Vuh use *makutax*, from Nahuatl *macuetlaxtli*.
He calls his tobacco container *salmet*, combining K'iche' terms for "painted gourd"
(sal) and "tobacco" *(met)*, whereas they use the Yucatec term *k'us b'us* for the same

32. An eleventh-century Mixtec lord named Eight Deer has his nose pierced (left). Later in his story he is repeatedly shown with a horizontal nosepiece inserted through his septum (as at right). From Codex Zouche-Nuttall pages 52 and 78.

item.[30] The combination of Nahuatl and Yucatec, together with the mention of a lord named Nacxit, points to Yucatán as the region where the pilgrims reached their destination. The most likely candidates for a specific place are Chichén Itzá, where a foreign lord whose names included Nacxit established himself during the tenth century,[31] and Mayapán, whose lords promoted their thirteenth-century rise to power as a restoration of the lost glory of Chichén Itzá.

While the pilgrims were at the court of Nacxit they underwent a ritual the Cakchiquel account calls *ri orb'al tzam,* "the nose-piercing."[32] Maya lords of the Classic period are sometimes represented as wearing ornaments that dangle or jut out from the tips of their noses (figure 31), which were presumably pierced, but in most images their noses are free of jewelry, even when they are costumed for ceremonies. Whether or not the wearing of nose ornaments was a privilege of lordship in earlier times, it did not become a prominent marker of high status among the Maya until the transition between the Classic and Postclassic periods, which is to say the ninth and tenth centuries.

Throughout the Postclassic period, which ended with the Spanish invasion, the wearing of a long nosepiece that ran horizontally through the septum served as an international mark of lordship in Mesoamerica. In Mixtec books that tell the story of an eleventh-century lord named Eight Deer, he is shown going on a pilgrimage to have his nose pierced (figure 32, left), after which he is always depicted as wearing a nosepiece (figure 32, right).[33] Similar nosepieces first became prominent among Mayan lords at Chichén Itzá (figure 33, top left), among them lords bearing the ax scepter from earlier times (figure 28, right). All four of the surviving pre-Columbian images of Quiché and Cakchiquel lords show them

33. Lords wearing nosepieces, from ninth-century Temple 6E1 at Chichén
Itzá (top left), fifteenth-century Temple 2 at Iximché (top right), and a
sixteenth-century depiction of the investiture of the Aztec emperor
Motecuhzoma (bottom left). The lord from Iximché also wears a
labret; on the masks for *Rabinal Achi* (bottom right) the nosepiece
and labret have become a mustache and goatee.
Drawings by Linda Schele (top) and from the manuscript of Fray Diego
Durán's *Historia de las Indias de Nueva España* (bottom left).

wearing horizontal nosepieces, and one image shows a labret as well (figure 33, top
right).[34] Labrets are generally favored over nosepieces in depictions of Aztec lords,
but early colonial manuscripts sometimes show them wearing nosepieces (figure
33, bottom left). In the case of the masks worn by the actors in *Rabinal Achi* the
nosepieces have been transformed into broad black mustaches, while the labrets
have become small black goatees (figure 33, bottom right).[35]

The "gourd of tobacco" mentioned by Man of Rabinal, which he does not
carry in today's productions, would have been a bottle-necked gourd containing
tobacco and lime, both powdered.[36] This mixture was chewed rather than snuffed.
In Postclassic iconography, a tobacco gourd carried on the back indicates that the
person depicted is engaged in a priestly role (figure 34). No one is shown wearing
a nosepiece and carrying a gourd at the same time, but there were times when lords

34. A Mixtec priest bears an offering and wears a gourd of
tobacco on his back. The gourd (shown in top view) is the
kind that has warts. Sticking out of its opening is a
spoon for dipping out the tobacco.
From Codex Zouche-Nuttall page 2.

took on priestly roles. Aztec emperors and lords occupying lesser positions went
on priestly fasts when they were inaugurated, wearing tobacco gourds on their
backs. According to the Popol Vuh, Quiché lords not only waged war but went on
retreats in temples, fasting and praying for their subjects.[37]

Cawek is warned that he has come *chupam ral,* "in range" or "under the
power" of Rabinal's ax, shield, bracelet, armband, paint, and gourd of tobacco.
But not one of these items—not even the ax, as we have already seen—is a weapon
in the sense that its purpose is to deliver physical force on the battlefield. That
purpose is served by what Rabinal calls "my henequen rope / my henequen cord,"
which he uses to bring Cawek under physical control. Otherwise he is engaged in
a show of political and religious force. Whether or not we imagine him as wearing
a nosepiece and carrying a gourd simultaneously, he is asserting his legitimacy as
a player of both lordly and priestly roles.

THE BURDEN OF BEING AN EAGLE OR JAGUAR

Among the other characters in *Rabinal Achi* are two who spend most of the play
pacing up and down on opposite sides of the stage. On the south side is Eagle, and

35. An eighth-century dancer painted on a vase excavated at Buenavista, Belize (left), and the Rabinal dancer in the Jaguar role (right). Both carry burdens larger than their own bodies. Mounted at the level of their trunks and facing backward are jaguar images. Drawings by Jamie Borowicz.

on the north is Jaguar (figure 35, right). Each of them follows a straight path, turning to face in the opposite direction when he reaches the end. All the actions of the other characters are contained between the two parallel lines defined by their paths. Instead of wearing masks or helmets that identify them as having eagle and jaguar roles, like the sacrificial priests of central Mexico, they carry eagle and jaguar images on their backs, mounted in backpacks that tower over their heads and spread wider than their bodies.

The substitution of an image carried on the back for a mask worn on the face has its basis in a pan-Mayan metaphor whereby the term for a burden (*patan* in K'iche' and *kuch* in Ch'ol) is extended to mean "office" or "duty." In carrying visible burdens of office, the Rabinal Eagle and Jaguar are like the so-called Holmul

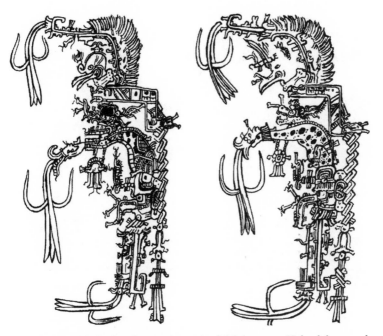

36. Side views of the backpacks worn by a pair of eighth-century Holmul dancers; the
one on the right is from the dancer in figure 35. The bird effigies sit on sky bands,
and each of the animal effigies carries a trophy head.
Drawings by Jamie Borowicz.

dancers painted on Classic Maya chocolate vases from pottery workshops in
northeastern Guatemala and western Belize, dating from the same period as the
paintings already discussed.[38] The dancer shown here (figure 35, left) was painted
for a lord named *K'ak' Tiliw Kan Chaak,* "Thunderbolt Fire that Burns in the Sky,"
who ruled at the town whose ruins are known as Naranjo but whose real name was
Maxam.[39] In most cases a pair of dancers is depicted, occupying opposite sides of
a vase. They are distinguished from one another only by what they carry on their
backs. Mounted in the burden of each dancer, at the level of his trunk, is an animal
facing backward, seated on the head of an earth monster and holding a shrunken
human head. Rising above the animal is an angled bracket representing the vault
of the sky, and perched on top of this is a bird with outspread wings.

Dancers in costumes like these could have given viewers a full picture of
their offices only by turning their backs, the very opposite of masking. In this
particular painting one dancer carries a peccary and the other a jaguar (figure
36). There is a difference in the birds as well, but otherwise the two costumes
are the same. The Eagle and Jaguar dancers of Rabinal also have matching
costumes (though the color schemes differ), and they carry their representations

37. The carved wooden plaques that serve as the core of the backpacks worn by the
Eagle and Jaguar dancers in Rabinal Achi. Drawings by Jamie Borowicz.

of animals at the same level above the ground as the peccary and jaguar carried
in the vase painting (as shown in figure 35). Whatever the animal figures depicted
on the vase were made of, the Rabinal animals are carved in relief on panels of
wood (figure 37). The carvings evoke the power of indigenous and foreign
nobility at the same time, making use of the European heraldry Mayans first saw
in the sixteenth century. One dancer carries the two-headed eagle of the Haps-
burgs, but the heads, instead of wearing crowns, are crested like the various
eagles and hawk-eagles of southern Mesoamerica.[40] The other dancer carries a
pair of rampant felines, but they are jaguars rather than lions. In place of the
Holmul sky bracket a pole rises from each carving, and at the top, instead of a
bird, is a basket-like device with long feathers radiating from its rim. In the case
of the backpacks carried in the Hummingbird Dance of Aguacatán, a town to the
west of Rabinal, there is a bird on top of the basket.[41]

In Aguacatán the carriers of burdens are armed with an ax and shield, but in
Rabinal they are like the Holmul dancers in dancing barehanded. When the time
comes for sacrifice, the Rabinal carriers join the other characters in dancing around
the prisoner. The dancers with axes make chopping motions toward his head or
neck at the end of each phrase in the music, but Eagle and Jaguar do this with their
hands alone, holding them flat and in the same position as an ax blade. We do not

38. Late Classic jaguar (left) and eagle (right) dancers, from central Mexico but rendered in the style of Mayan painting. From Portico A at Cacaxtla, Tlaxcala.

know what the dancers painted for the lord of Naranjo might have done with their hands at some other moment than the one depicted, but the animals mounted in their burdens hold trophy heads.

Leaving aside the question of backpacks, the pairing of performers in eagle and jaguar roles points to central Mexico. The earliest known depiction of such a pair is in the murals at Cacaxtla, in Tlaxcala, which are approximately contemporary with the murals at the Classic Maya site of Bonampak. Despite the fact that Cacaxtla lies far to the west of the Maya homeland, the style and much of the content of the paintings are distinctly Mayan.[42] Flanking a doorway that opens eastward are two figures costumed from head to toe as an eagle and jaguar (figure 38). As in the Rabinal performance, the eagle is on the south side and the jaguar on the north. Cradled in the arms of the eagle is a ceremonial bar like the ones Classic Maya kings are sometimes shown carrying in place of a scepter and shield. Like the brackets that hold up the birds that perch atop the backpacks of Holmul dancers, it symbolizes the sky.[43] The jaguar carries a bundle of spears whose points are dripping with blood.

Among the Aztecs of Postclassic central Mexico, knights costumed as eagles and jaguars staged sacrifices of prisoners of war that took the form of

39. A tethered prisoner of war and an Aztec Jaguar knight in combat. From the manuscript of
Fray Diego Durán's Historia de las Indias de Nueva España.

gladiatorial contests (figure 39). Each prisoner, with one foot tethered to a stone, faced an opponent drawn from a company of two eagles and two jaguars. Both combatants were armed with maces and shields, but the prisoner's mace was set with feathers instead of obsidian blades. The contest ended as soon as the prisoner's blood was drawn, after which he was flayed. On rare occasions he overcame his opponent, in which case one of the other knights took him on. One way or another, he met his end.[44] No such contest is enacted in the Rabinal play, but it is suggested by the dialogue. When the prisoner asks Lord Five Thunder to let him dance with Eagle and Jaguar, he says, "I'm going to play a game here / with the power of my weapon / the power of my shield," and he challenges his dance partners by saying, "Do it now / with your teeth, your claws." What happens then is that Eagle and Jaguar, who remain unarmed, dance around the stage with the prisoner.[45] They do not engage in combat, but afterwards the prisoner speaks as if some kind of contest had taken place, one in which he came out without a scratch. Addressing Lord Five Thunder, he says, "Is that an *eagle* standing there, sir? / Is that a *jaguar*, sir?" As far as he is concerned his opponents are toothless and clawless, unlike their counterparts among his own people. There is no mention of flaying.

In sum, the Eagle and Jaguar dancers of Rabinal are like Classic Maya Holmul dancers in being unarmed and in carrying their burdens of office on their backs, but they are like the knights of Postclassic Mexico in pairing eagle and jaguar identities and in playing a sacrificial role. In between are the eagle and jaguar of Cacaxtla, who are dressed like Mexican knights but are not armed for combat.

40. The Lord of Death holds a freshly severed head by the hair.
The inscription above the head identifies it as that of the lord
of Pia, a town tributary to the site of Pomona.
From a stucco relief at Toniná, Chiapas.
Based on a drawing by Linda Schele.

DECAPITATION AND QUESTIONS OF IDENTITY

The sacrifice that ends *Rabinal Achi* takes the form of a simulated decapitation. When the play was produced in Antigua in 1955, this caused great disappointment in the audience whose members had expected a heart sacrifice, and the directors of the 1970 Festival de Folklore in Cobán insisted that the actors direct their axes at the chest of the prisoner.[46] But a focus on decapitation—like the upraised axes and round shields borne by the actors with lordly roles, and like the burdens carried by the Eagle and Jaguar dancers—follows ancient Mayan traditions rather than answering to the expectations of those whose only model for the late pre-Columbian world is the central Mexican one. In the Classic inscriptions that record Mayan political history, one of the commonest verbs is *ch'ak*, "to chop," and the object acted upon is often someone's head.[47] In the play, Cawek of the Forest People uses the K'iche' cognate, *ch'ayik*, to describe what he would like to do to Lord Five Thunder.

41. This prisoner, with a rope around his upper arms, was the
lord of Palenque when he was captured. The caption on his
thigh gives his personal name, K'an Hok Chitam, and that
of his royal house. Monument 122, Toniná, Chiapas.
Based on a drawing by Linda Schele.

In Classic Maya art the actual moment of human sacrifice is seldom represented and heart extraction not at all, but there is abundant evidence for decapitation.[48] Perhaps the most vivid image is the one in a stucco relief at Toniná, which
shows a skeletal figure dancing while he grasps the hair of a freshly severed head
with its jaw slack and its tongue hanging out (figure 40). The figure is that of the
impersonator of an underworld god, a lord of death, while the head, according the
caption, belongs to a human lord from a placed called Pia, in an enemy kingdom
northeast of Toniná. This meeting of the divine and human realms makes it clear
that rituals of decapitation were conceived as reenactments of mythic events.
According to the Popol Vuh, the first of all decapitations was carried out by the
lords of death.[49]

Heads, and especially faces, have played a central role in Mayan notions of
identity and personhood throughout history. In art this is clearest in Classic works
that combine the likeness of an individual with a text giving his or her names.[50]
Skulls, though lacking in recognizable faces, retained their individuality so long as
the memory of the names of their owners was kept alive by their descendants. The
skulls of important ancestors were sometimes removed from tombs and venerated
separately from their bodies, a custom followed today among the Itzá Maya of
northern Guatemala.[51]

A second corporeal source of Mayan identity is the thigh. In reliefs at Toniná
(figure 41), Piedras Negras, and Yaxchilán, artists placed the labels that identify
prisoners of war on their thighs. The label at Toniná includes the prisoner's

42. The text labels the skull and leg bones as belonging to Lady
Twelve Macaw. They were exhumed by Lord Clear Sky
Scepter, her husband. Detail of Altar 5 at Tikal,
based on a drawing by Linda Schele.

personal name as well as that of his lineage. The placement of this information is
consistent with the meanings ascribed to the parts of the human body by contemporary diviners in the Quiché town Momostenango, who locate a person's patri-
lineage in the thigh on the right (male) side of the body.[52] In Classic Maya tombs
the parts of skeletons most frequently removed, other than the skulls, were the long
bones of the legs (especially femurs), suggesting that these, too, were potential
objects of veneration. An eighth-century ruler of Tikal risked entry into what had
become enemy territory in order to recover the skull and leg bones of his deceased
wife (figure 42).[53]

In the Rabinal play, much of the dialogue revolves around the question of
the prisoner's identity. When he himself first addresses this question, he speaks of
uwach nujuyub'al / nutaq'ajal, "the face of my mountain / my valley," which he is
reluctant to reveal to his captor. At the individual level, his "mountain" and
"valley" are the contours of his own physical body (including his head). At the
lineage level, they are the place where he and others like him were born. What his
captor wants him to reveal, at a minimum, is the identity (the "face") of this place,
which is to say the name (or names) by which it is distinguished from other places.
Eighth-century sculptors at Yaxchilán expressed the link between lineage and
place by showing the local rulers standing on the head of an earth monster who
wears the hieroglyphic emblem of their dynasty on its face (figure 43).[54]

Late in the play, when the prisoner is about to lose his head (and thus his face),
he considers the question of his personal identity in terms of time rather than place.
He says, *Pak'ab'am nuq'ij / pak'ab'am walaxik,* "My day has been turned upside
down / my birth has been turned upside down." By his "day" *(q'ij)* and "birth"

43. The head of an earth monster with the emblem glyph of the
ruling lineage of Yaxchilán covering its forehead. The profiled
feet at top center and right belong to lineage members who are
standing on the head. Detail from Stele 4 at Yaxchilán,
based on a drawing by David Stuart.

(alaxik) he means the date of his birth on the 260-day Mayan divinatory calendar.
To know when he was born would be to know *uwach uq'ij,* the "face of his day,"
which is to say the influence of that particular day on his character and destiny.
Highland Guatemalan holders of noble titles were often named for their dates of
birth, as in the case of *Ajaw Job' Toj* or "Lord Five Thunder" in the play, but Cawek
never reveals his own date. His statement that it has been "turned upside down"
suggests that this aspect of his being has been canceled by his capture or will be
canceled when he loses his head. A similar ideology may lie behind images of Classic
warriors that show them wearing effigies of trophy heads upside-down (figure 44).
An eighth-century scepter from a site in Campeche, a human femur with carved
decorations, was made to be held with the hip end down and the knee end up.[55]

    In most if not all languages of the Mayan family, the word for "face" (*wach*
in K'iche' and *ich* in Yucatec) is extended to mean "fruit," and it can also be used
in the sense of "species." Thus plants, like people and animals, reveal what kind
they are by their faces. This idea is given visual expression in an eighth-century
relief at Palenque that depicts a corn plant as a cosmic tree (figure 45, left). The
trunk of the tree has a head at the place where it emerges from the ground, which
is where its mouth is, but it is only by bearing fruit that a tree reveals its identity.
In this case the fruit takes the form of the heads and faces of the twin gods of maize,
whose long hair is corn silk. In another Palenque relief the same ground-level head
supports a prisoner instead of a cornstalk (figure 45, right). His hair is in the grasp
of a lord who is poised to harvest his head (and remove his identity) with an ax.

44. Four representations of severed heads hanging
upside-down from the waist of an eighth-century
lord. Detail of Lintel 9, Yaxchilán, Chiapas,
from a drawing by Ian Graham.

When a Classic Maya depiction of a king takes the form of a *te' tun* or "tree
stone," which is to say a carved stone stele, he is likely to be shown wearing a
costume that places him in the role of a tree. It is a cosmic tree, but it is also the tree
of his lineage. In Classic texts, to say that a young noble *och te'*, "enters the tree,"
is to say that he has been designated as the heir to a throne.[56] The tree itself has a
life that flows upward through its trunk and branches to its most recent fruit, an
idea that also finds expression in the Rabinal play. When Cawek speaks of his task
as a warrior, he makes it clear that he is not merely trying to hunt down Lord Five
Thunder as an individual. Rather, it is his desire to chop through "the root / the
trunk" of his enemy, as if to bring the life of his whole lineage to an end.

As part of his tree costume, the Classic king wears an apron that bears the
image of the face and mouth at the bottom of the tree's trunk (figure 46, right).[57]
Appropriately enough, the apron exactly covers his thighs, which then become the
trunk of his whole lineage, while his own face is the living fruit that makes this tree
different from all others. Lord Five Thunder owns an apron he describes as "the
double warp / the tamped weft / the weaving tightly done / the work of my mother
/ my lady." Today the acts of weaving and childbearing are intricately connected

45. At left a personified corn plant grows from the head of an earth monster, its forehead marked with
the cruciform glyph for k'an, "corn." The ears on the plant are the heads of twin maize gods and
the silk is their hair. At right, a lord with an upraised ax grasps the hair of a captive who is
seated on the head of the same earth monster. From relief panels in the Temple of the
Foliated Cross and House D of the Palace, at Palenque, Chiapas.
Drawing at right by Merle Greene Robertson.

in Mayan ideology, suggesting that the wearing of a cloth apron over the thighs,
whether in the world of the play or in Classic times, was a man's way of
acknowledging the roles of women in perpetuating his lineage.[58]

In the play the apron is worn by Cawek, who asks Lord Five Thunder to lend
it "if only to mark the greatness / of my death / my disappearance." Cawek, like the
lord, calls the apron the work of "my mother / my lady," as if it stood for the one he
might have worn at his own royal court, or as if the events leading to his decapitation
were an ironic ritual of adoption. Like the aprons of Classic lords, it covers his
thighs, and like them, he dances in it (figure 46, left). Afterwards, he rejects any
notion that this borrowed moment before his death could substitute for a real dance
in an apron, claiming that the music would have been better at his home court and
expressing indignation at having been given a slave as his dance partner.

The roles of thighs, trees, and fruit in the symbolism of lineages all come
together in an early colonial drawing that tells the story of the Xiu lineage of Yucatán

46. At left, Cawek of the Forest People, bearing his ax and shield, dances in an apron borrowed
from Lord Five Thunder. At right, an eighth-century ruler named Itzamnaaj K'awil, bearing
his ax and shield, dances in a tree costume whose apron (shaded) bears the face and mouth
of his tree's trunk. His mask is open, exposing his eyes, mouth, and chin.
From Dos Pilas Stele 1, Guatemala; based on a drawing by Linda Schele.

with a combination of Mayan and European imagery (figure 47).[59] The figure
reclining on the ground, wearing a peaked paper hat that marks him as a lord, is
Hun Uitzil Chac, the founder of the town of Uxmal. Growing from his right thigh
is the branching tree of his lineage; the marks on his left thigh may refer to his
mother's lineage. The tree bears abundant fruit, and each fruit (or face) is labeled
with the name of one of his descendants.

When Cawek is served his last drink in a vessel made from the dried and
hollowed fruit of a tree, he turns his thoughts to those who have lost their heads
before him. Contemplating the vessel (figure 48), he asks, "Could this be the skull
of my grandfather? Could this be the skull of my father?" He then imagines that
his own head will become "a work of some kind, an artifact," and that it will be
"carved in back and carved in front." These lines are favorites of the current
director and producer of the play, José León Coloch. The drinking vessel used in

47. The Xiu family tree, growing from the right thigh of the founder of Uxmal;
the woman is his wife. The branches show multiple generations of fruit,
beginning at a point well after the founder's time and reaching as far as
the early seventeenth century. From the *Crónica de Oxkutzcab*.

past performances has not always been the appropriate one,[60] but for him Cawek's
meaning is perfectly clear: "He's comparing his head to a calabash." In his own
productions, Coloch uses a carved calabash from Rabinal. Cawek also speaks of
the future of *ubaqil waqan*, "the bone of my leg," imagining that one of his femurs
will become the stick for a slit drum whose sound will live after him.

In musing over his drinking vessel and imagining the future existence of his
own head as a calabash, Cawek is alluding to an ancient myth that is illustrated in
Classic Maya paintings and narrated by the authors of the Popol Vuh. There may
be an allusion to a myth in his mention of his leg bone as well, but that story has
yet to come to light. The story told in the Popol Vuh concerns the transformation
of a fruitless (or faceless) tree into the first of all trees that bear calabashes, which
have the shape, thickness, and hardness of human craniums. This story is closely

48. Cawek of the Forest People contemplates the carved calabash vessel, made in Rabinal, from which he has been drinking.

bound to the identity of the Rabinal nation, whose tribute payments to the lords of the Quiché kingdom took the form of calabash bowls and drinking vessels. Rabinal artisans are famous to this day for their calabashes, which they decorate by cutting designs through a coat of lacquer of local manufacture.[61]

In the Popol Vuh, the story of the tree opens when two brothers are summoned to the underworld court of the Lords of Death.[62] They begin their journey by entering a cave near Fish in the Ashes. This is the site of the town known today as San Pedro Carchá, about forty-five kilometers north of Rabinal. At the time the Popol Vuh was written it was famous as a source of quetzal feathers and jade beads, and it has that reputation for the characters in the play as well.[63]

Once the two brothers arrive in the underworld, the Lords of Death amuse themselves by putting their guests to a series of tests whose results are rigged. The price the brothers pay for failing the tests is death. The severed head of the elder one is placed in a tree and his headless body, along with the complete body of his brother, is buried. Then the tree bears fruit for the first time, in the form of calabashes. Blood Moon, the daughter of one of the Lords of Death, hears rumors about this tree and goes to see it for herself.[64] The skull, which is still there among the calabashes, now acts on behalf of both of the slain brothers. It spits in Blood Moon's hand, making her pregnant with twins. Her condition angers her father, who sentences her to death. To escape this fate she leaves the underworld, emerging on the surface of the earth through the cave near Fish in the Ashes.

Now it happens that in the play, Lord Five Thunder also has an unmarried daughter. Not only that, but he describes her as "the Mother of Quetzal Feathers / Mother of Glistening Green / of jade / of precious beads / goods that come from / End of the String at Fish in the Ashes." Quetzal feathers and jade beads were metaphors used by parents for a daughter of marriageable age, expressing endearment but also alluding to her role as a possible source (or "mother") of wealth in the form of a high bride price.[65] By an extension of this same metaphor, the area around Fish in the Ashes becomes the place where all such daughters come from, ever since the emergence of Blood Moon.

Now we can see that when Cawek talks about the calabash in the play, he is maneuvering Lord Five Thunder, who wants his head, into the role of a Lord of Death. He is also maneuvering Lord Five Thunder's daughter, this woman who is described as if she came from Fish in the Ashes, into the role of Blood Moon. A short time later he will ask to dance with her, but by his own declaration he is already as good as dead. In this sense she is like Blood Moon, taking a dead man as a partner.

After Blood Moon escapes onto the surface of the earth she gives birth to twins named Hunahpu *(Junajpu)* and Xbalanque *(Xb'alanq'e)*. Eventually they seek revenge for the death of their two fathers, gaining access to the court of the Lords of Death by disguising themselves as entertainers.[66] For their most famous act, a series of sacrifices in which they bring the victims back to life, they begin by using a dog and then a volunteer from the audience. The second of these sacrifices is painted on a Classic Maya chocolate vessel from the area around Nakbé, near the northern border of Guatemala (figure 49).[67] The two actors have partially hidden their identities, but they are the lowland Maya counterparts of Hunahpu and Xbalanque, named *Hun Ahaw* and *Yax Balam*. They both wield stone axes with wooden handles, and one of them is in the act of bringing his ax down on the back of the neck of a bound prisoner while the other looks on. In the Rabinal play the dialogue makes it sound as though Eagle and Jaguar will decapitate the prisoner, but when the time comes all the actors dance around him, making chopping motions whether they wield axes or not.

49. In the court of an underworld lord, two masked actors wielding axes dramatize the decapitation of a bound prisoner. The artist has included clues to their true identity as Hunahpu (left) and Xbalanque (right). Only Hunahpu has spots on his body (here rendered as signs that also mark his divine status), while only Xbalanque has jaguar features, here reduced to a jaguar's paw mounted on the snout of his mask. Drawing from an eighth-century vase in the Princeton University art museum, reproduced by permission of Michael D. Coe.

In the myth, what happens after the sacrifice and revival of one of the spectators is that Hunahpu and Xbalanque take turns at sacrificing and reviving one another. The Lords of Death, carried away by this spectacle, volunteer themselves for sacrifice. The twins oblige but leave them dead, thus completing their quest for vengeance. Then they visit the place where the bodies of their two fathers lie buried and attempt to put the remains of the one who still has his head back together. In an attempt to bring him back to life in the flesh, they tell him to name each of his parts. He gets no further than naming "the mouth, the nose, the eyes of his face," which remain as features of skulls. They take their leave of him by promising that "you will be prayed to here" and "your name will not be lost."[68] In this way they establish the custom of venerating the dead by name and in the presence of their remains, especially their heads.

As for Cawek of the Forest People, he casts himself in the role of the twins' decapitated father. He raises the possibility of revenge by speaking of the day when his skull—or rather, a calabash from Rabinal—will come into the possession of his younger male relatives. Once that happens, he imagines them saying, "This is the skull of our own grandfather / our own father," and declares that they will remember him "as long as there are days / as long as there is light." The audiences of an earlier time would have understood these last lines as alluding to the first of all avengers.[69] When Hunahpu and Xbalanque departed from the grave of their fathers, one of them rose as the sun and the other followed as the full moon.

The myth from the Popol Vuh and the painted scenes from the Classic period give us an answer to the question as to whether there were dramatizations of sacrifices as well as real ones in pre-Columbian times. The plot of the episode in which Hunahpu and Xbalanque perform at the court of the lords of the underworld turns on this very distinction. They begin with represented sacrifices, complete with magical special effects that make them seem real, and then step out of their masquerade to perform real sacrifices on their official hosts. The episode ends when they make a speech to the horrified spectators, discarding their pretense at being itinerant actors and revealing their true identities as avenging sons.

In the world of human lineages, there was a radical alternative to the story of capture, sacrifice, and revenge. The Rabinal play reveals that this alternative could be given at least a small measure of expression even when a member of a rival lineage was brought before a ruler as a prisoner of war. When Lord Five Thunder first learns that Cawek has been captured, he considers what might be done with him when he arrives at the royal court. After raising the possibility of allowing Cawek to dance with the Mother of Quetzal Feathers he remarks, "Perhaps this is the brave man who will become a father- or son-in-law, a brother-in-law."[70] The focus of this remark is not on a possible relationship between Cawek and the Mother of Quetzal Feathers as individuals, but on a whole set of possible relationships between the male members of two separate lineages. As Coloch put the matter, Cawek could be "an in-law who gives or an in-law who takes. As a giver he would have to give his sister in marriage, and as a taker he would marry the sister of Rabinal. Or a giver could be someone who has a daughter ready for marriage, and a taker would be the one to marry her." But in the long run, Lord Five Thunder's statement turns out to be deeply ironic. When the moment arrives for him to grant Cawek's request for a dance with the Mother of Quetzal Feathers, he says, "I give her to you only to mark the greatness of your death, your disappearance." Out of two possible choices, the story enacted in the play is not the one in which men separated by a lineage boundary marry one another's sisters and daughters but rather the one in which they sacrifice one another's brothers and sons.

History as a Performing Art

MUSIC, DANCE, AND SONG

The main characters in *Rabinal Achi* resemble historical figures, the deeds they narrate resemble historical events, and most of the places they mention can be located in geographical space. The dramatization of events in the human past, like so many of the other features of the play, has roots among the ancient Maya. The oldest direct evidence has been found at Dos Pilas, in two seventh-century inscriptions on the risers of a stone stairway. The earlier of the two texts concerns an attack on Tikal that drove its ruler into exile, followed by a retaliatory attack on Dos Pilas. The text that was added later records the performance of a dance at Dos Pilas, one in which the two earlier occurrences were dramatized.[1]

Evidence bearing on the relationship between texts and oral performances during the Classic period is fragmentary, but it seems likely that dedication ceremonies for monuments included speeches, chants, or songs whose subject matter coincided, at least in part, with that of the inscriptions. The double-sized glyph block that commonly introduces monumental texts offers a clue to the nature of such performances. There has yet to be any agreement as to how to read the entire block, but its most prominent single sign, the one that serves as the foundation for its composition, is a schematic picture of a slit drum (figure 50). This sign could have been read as standing for the sound of first syllable in *tunk'ul,* a likely term for the slit drum in Classic inscriptions. In that case, it could then have been interpreted as spelling the word *tun,* referring to the 360-day year used in calculating the time intervals that form the opening subject matter of public inscriptions.

50. The initial glyph blocks from the tablets in the temples of the Cross (left), Sun (center),
and Foliated Cross (right) at Palenque. In each case the *tun* glyph is the one resting on
triple elements at the bottom. The cross-hatched areas represent slits on the top of the
drum and the dot represents a hole in its side. Based on drawings by Linda Schele.

But even when it was read this way it might also have been understood as a visual
allusion to the slit drum itself.[2] Drumming and the playing of other musical
instruments could have served as fanfares for speeches, as they do in *Rabinal Achi,*
or they could have accompanied the singing of a song whose words concerned the
same event as the inscription.

Hieroglyphic texts tend to be extremely terse, so their relationship to vocal
performances was probably more like that of a set of program notes than a libretto.[3]
By comparison, the alphabetic texts produced by sixteenth-century Mayan authors
are rich in detail and thematic development. Hieroglyphic writers had access to a
full range of phonetic signs, but the ability to spell out all the sounds of a language,
in and of itself, does not require an author to transcribe every word of an actual oral
performance or prescribe every word of a projected one. The explanation for the
expansiveness of later authors does not lie in their use of alphabetic writing but in
the conditions under which they wrote. They were responding, in part, to the
destruction of hieroglyphic texts, but they were also faced with missionary efforts
to take control of the performing arts. It was not only the visible words of endangered books they sought to conserve but also the audible words of endangered
performances for which those books provided prompts.

Many passages in the alphabetic works of the sixteenth century are written
as if they were intended as records of oral performances. The authors of the Popol
Vuh introduce their account of the origin of the calabash tree and the victory over
the lords of death by proposing a toast to their readers (or the audiences they
intended for readers). The Quiché authors of another document address their
reader's audience as *ix qamam, qak'ajol,* "you, our grandsons, our sons," and they
sometimes introduce a new topic by saying, *Wakamik k'ut xchita' chi alaq,* "And
today you will listen, sirs."[4] In the *Chilam Balam* or "Jaguar Spokesman" books
of Yucatán, a chapter that explains the meanings of metaphors used only by royalty

51. Eighth-century musicians, with two trumpeters (left) and a masked figure with a slit drum under
his arm (extreme right). Seated on the ground and reaching for the drum is a caiman-masked figure.
From Room 1, Structure 1, Bonampak, Mexico. Detail of a copy painted by Antonio Tejeda.

is written as a dialogue in which a pupil and his instructor address one another as
yume and *mehene*, "father" and "son."[5] Like Classic inscriptions, these works serve
to advance the claims of royal lineages, but nearly all inscriptions are written
exclusively in the third person.

Early alphabetic texts from all over Mesoamerica make it clear that the
memory of events in dynastic history was carried, at least in part, by songs. In all
cases the lyrics were in the first person, so that the singers sang in the voices of the
participants in the events. The Popol Vuh quotes words from a song of the
founders of the ruling Quiché, Rabinal, Cakchiquel, and Tzutuhil lineages, who
lament their departure from the city where they received their ax scepters. The
Chilam Balam books record the lyrics of a song of the survivors of the disastrous
end of an era at Chichén Itzá. In both cases the words take the form of a question-
and-answer dialogue.[6]

Most of the evidence for dynastic songs comes from sixteenth-century central
Mexico, where speakers of Nahuatl transcribed the words of numerous compositions that had been sung in royal courts. These songs were performed by choruses
singing in unison, in some cases accompanied by a horizontal slit drum like the one
used in the Rabinal play and in others by an upright hide-covered drum. Among
the roles assumed by the vocalists were those of victorious warriors like Man of

52. The musicians for the 1998 production of *Rabinal Achi*. The
man standing beside the far trumpeter is the drum carrier.

Rabinal and prisoners of war like Cawek. If there were two or more characters in
the same song, they were represented as taking their turns in a dialogue, one that
often consisted of questions and answers.[7]

The speeches of the Rabinal play are performed solo rather than in chorus,
and the musical instruments, rather than providing an accompaniment, are played
in alternation with the speeches. Otherwise, the speeches are very much like court
songs. Persons of lordly rank engage in dialogue about their own deeds and those
of other lordly persons, and in the latter half of the play they do so in the setting of
a royal court. But the most telling point is that a speaker usually quotes lines from
what his counterpart has just said before he ventures a response. The quotation is
interpreted as raising a question and the response is offered as an answer. The
result is that any one speech, even if it stood alone, would make sense as an account
of an exchange between two parties. Such speeches are similar to the monologues

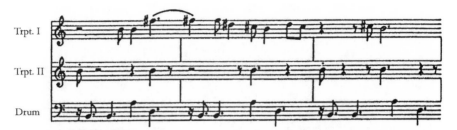

53. A characteristic passage from the music of *Rabinal Achi,* recorded in 1945 by Henrietta
Yurchenco and transcribed by David Friedlander.

of Western theater, in which a solo performer converses with an imaginary or
absent partner, but in Mesoamerica their closest correlation is with court songs
whose lyrics took the form of dialogues.

The clearest ancient Mayan counterparts of the instrumentalists who perform for *Rabinal Achi* are depicted in the eighth-century murals at Bonampak.[8]
The paintings are on the inside walls of a series of three rooms in a palace. Scenes
from a festival fill the first room, and the first sight that greets a person coming
through the doorway is that of dancers painted on the opposite wall. The band that
plays for the dancers is located on the inside wall that runs to the left of a person
entering the doorway (figure 51). The two most prominent musicians blow long
wooden trumpets. Facing the trumpeters is a masked man with a slit drum tucked
under his arm, and in his hand he holds what could be a drumstick.[9] Seated on the
ground in front of him, wearing a crocodile mask, is the drummer, who reaches
toward the drum. If he were to follow Mayan practice as described in early Spanish
accounts, he would place the drum on the ground in front of him in order to play
it. In contrast, the slit drums of central Mexico were set on mats or supported by
wooden trestles.[10]

In the Rabinal play, as in the Bonampak mural, dance music is provided by
two trumpeters and a drummer (figure 52). When the drum is transported it is
carried by a person other than the drummer, and when it is played it rests on the
ground. As recently as the eighteenth century wooden trumpets were still in use in
highland Guatemala, but the instruments played today in Rabinal are brass bugles
of more recent vintage, custom-made so as to have extra length similar to that of a
trombone.[11] The drum is still a slit drum, a recent replacement for one that rotted.
It was made by hollowing the trunk of a *sanik che'* or "ant tree," a lowland species
whose wood is valued for its resonance and is also used to make marimba keys.[12]
The slits are in the H-shape of ancient drums, creating two tongues. They are equal
in length, unlike marimba keys, but differ in thickness, producing two tones at an

54. Eighth-century chorus whose members gesture while they sing for the same dancers for whom the band plays in figure 51. From Room 1, Structure 1, Bonampak, Mexico. Detail of a copy painted by Antonio Tejeda.

interval of about a third when struck. A blow to the main body of the drum at either side of the tongues widens the total interval to a seventh. The drummer, like his counterparts at the time of the European invasion, uses a pair of sticks tipped with rubber,[13] but Cawek of the Forest People accuses his hosts of planning to use one of his leg bones once they have sacrificed him.

The music played by the Rabinal trumpeters and drummer has structural features that identify it as being of indigenous rather than European origin.[14] The melodic phrases, which are played by the higher of the two trumpets (see the top staff in figure 53), are consistent with a general Amerindian preference for contours whose overall trend is downward. As elsewhere in the music of the highland Maya, the voices of the instruments are far more autonomous than in Western polyphony. Because of differences in the structure and length of phrases from one instrument to another, any one of the three instruments is as likely to sound by itself as it is to sound in synchrony with either of the other two (compare the three staffs in figure 53).[15] This is but one expression of a more general Mayan aesthetic that finds expression in such arts as textile weaving and time reckoning. Multiple, overlapping temporal or spatial intervals are preferred to evenly spaced or evenly divisible intervals of the kind that make for frequent moments of temporal synchrony or spatial alignment.[16]

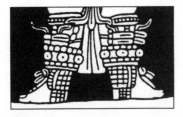

55. The dancing feet of lords from Yaxchilán Lintel 3 (upper left), Palenque Temple 18 tablet (lower left), and Rabinal Achi (right). The Rabinal dancers often place their feet at opposite angles before turning to one side (upper right). When one heel is lifted high the other is kept flat (lower right). The illustrations at left are based on drawings by Linda Schele (upper) and Merle Greene Robertson (lower).

There is at least one major difference between the providers of music in the Bonampak murals and those in the Rabinal play. As we have already seen, the performers to the left of the Bonampak doorway have musical instruments (figure 51), but that is only half the story. To the right is a separate group of performers who gesture instead of handling instruments and who move their feet as if shuffling slowly forward (figure 54). A caption inserted between two of them has recently been read as *k'ayom*, "singers."[17] All of this is consistent with early Spanish accounts of Mesoamerican musical performances, which make it clear that the playing of instruments was always accompanied by singing, that singing was choral, and that the members of a chorus danced while they sang. But when the Rabinal musicians play their instruments, the actors dance silently with one another, and when the musicians are silent the actors make speeches to one another while standing or pacing back and forth in front of one another. It seems apparent that at some point during the colonial history of the play, the words were separated from the music and dance.

Classic lords were not limited to the shuffle of the Bonampak chorus when they danced, but they did keep their feet close to the earth—on state occasions, at least. Judging from the available representations, their footwork was similar to that of the characters in the Rabinal play (figure 55). Instead of keeping on their toes,

56. Cawek of the Forest People dances with the Mother of Quetzal Feathers in the play (left), and a royal couple dances at their wedding in a Late Classic Maya vase painting (right). The vase is in the Kimbell Art Museum, Fort Worth, Texas. Photo at right by Justin Kerr.

the Rabinal dancers often have both feet flat on the ground before turning to one side, and when one foot is turned at an angle in preparation for a change in direction, the opposite foot may be turned at an equal but opposite angle. When one heel is lifted high the opposite one is flat on the ground or lifted only slightly, and there is never a moment at which both feet leave the ground.

Near the end of the play, Cawek of the Forest People dances with the Mother of Quetzal Feathers (figure 56, left). It is as if he were stepping out of his role as Lord Five Thunder's prisoner of war and instead becoming his son-in-law, if only for as long as the music lasts. A similar dance, performed by a bride and groom on the happier occasion of an actual wedding, is the subject of a Late Classic vase painting (figure 56, right). Cawek and Quetzal, like the couple in the painting, dance face to face, extending their lower arms without touching one another and keeping their feet close to the ground.

In the course of dancing, the actors in the Rabinal play move counterclockwise around the four sides of a square, marking their arrival at a corner by turning a small counterclockwise circle:

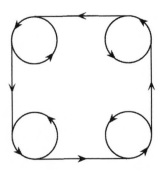

After two complete circuits they break into a fast walk, still moving counterclockwise, but this time they make a large circle whose diameter is equal to the width of the square. Images of dance formations in the pre-Columbian art of Mesoamerica are short on details, but they do make it clear that the counterclockwise completion of a closed path was the typical pattern of movement.[18] In contrast, the dance dramas introduced by Spanish missionaries typically divide the participants into two parallel files whose members dance into the intervening space and then return to their places.

The meaning of the square path traced out by the Rabinal dancers is suggested by a speech in which Cawek, addressing Lord Five Thunder, makes the last of a series of final requests. He starts off by saying, "Now give me / thirteen score days / thirteen score nights," referring to the 260 days of the divinatory calendar. What he wishes to do with these days is "to say farewell" to his homeland, "where I walked / where I moved / on all four edges / in all four corners." This combination of the passage of time with movement in space suggests a series of rituals whose timing follows the rhythm of the divinatory calendar. The time-reckoning of Rabinal no longer includes this calendar, but it is very much alive elsewhere. The priest-shamans of the Quiché town of Momostenango use it to schedule visits to four pairs of shrines, each of which lies in a different direction from the town center. The dates for one series of visits are separated by intervals of 65 days, thus dividing the 260 days into four equal parts.[19] The final ritual at a given shrine takes three days, suggesting the small circles the Rabinal dancers turn at each corner of their square.

A second series of four rituals follows a different rhythm, marking the passing of four successive years of 365 days each. The Mayan year intersects with the twenty day names of the divinatory calendar in such a way that only four names, spaced five days apart, can begin a new year. Each of the four days is governed by a lord, and each lord resides at one of the same shrines that figure in the rituals that divide the 260-day calendar into four parts. The closing of a given year takes five days, the same five that advance the beginning of the following year to a new day name. Again, this smaller interval calls to mind the circles that mark the corners of the square path followed by the Rabinal dancers.

Cawek does not wait for an answer to his request for time to visit the sides and corners of his homeland. Instead he dances the same square path that all the play's previous dances have followed, and all the other characters join him. In the physical world, then, his space continues to coincide with that of his captors. But prisoner though he may be in body, he is not so in spirit. When the dance is finished he remarks on the fact that he did not leave the place where he is being held, but then he adds, "I simply said farewell from here." To this he could have added, "I simply said farewell from today." According to the priest-shamans of Momostenango, the spirit familiars of all the shrines of the world are in communication with one another. A person saying prayers at one place can send messages to others, addressing them by name. In the same way, the lords of all the days are in communication, so that a person praying on one day can call upon other days by naming them.

There is no direct reference to the 365-day year in the play's dialogues, but there are subtle details that point to it. When Cawek returns a calabash drinking vessel and a piece of brocaded cloth he has borrowed from his hosts, he tells Lord Five Thunder to "put them away" or, more literally, "enclose them," using the verb stem *tz'api-*. This may be an allusion to the final five days of the year, which are called *tz'api q'ij*, "enclosing days." Appropriately enough, these days have an unlucky character. The year is also suggested by the fact that Cawek makes his request to say farewell to his homeland in his eighteenth speech. It happens that the first 360 days of the Mayan year are divided into eighteen named periods of twenty days each. The numbering of Cawek's speeches, which is noted in the script, stops with his eighteenth even though it is not his last.[20] The label for his final speech simply reads *utukel kach'awik*, "he speaks alone." Just as the last five days of the year stand alone, putting an end to a succession of twenty-day periods, so his last speech stands alone, closing down the series of speeches with which he prolonged his life.

TRACES OF SONGS IN SPEAKING PARTS

Though the dialogues of *Rabinal Achi* have never been sung during the known history of the play's performances, there are passages that suggest songs whose music, if it survives at all, can only be heard in the play's instrumental interludes. The change to speaking voices as the sole vehicle for the dialogues may well have been decided upon by the composers of the earliest script for the play, working under the eyes and ears of the invaders who taught them alphabetic writing. The early missionaries made particular efforts to stop the singing of indigenous songs on public occasions, demanding the substitution of hymns with lyrics translated into local languages. That would have left the speaking voice as the only possible medium for the public voicing of words that had once been sung.

There are abundant references to the playing of instruments in the dialogue of the Rabinal script, but there is nothing in the script that directly identifies any of the words as belonging to a song. To find lyrics that are clearly labeled as such, we must look to other alphabetic works by Mesoamerican writers. Among the common features of the songs recorded in these sources are exclamations of woe. Two favorite Nahuatl expressions of this kind are *Ayyo!* and *Ohuaya!* As loan words in Yucatec Maya they take the forms *Ayano!* and *Wayano!* in a song that laments disastrous events at Chichén Itzá. For K'iche' Maya only two short quotations from song texts are known, both of which begin with *Aqaroq!*[21] This is a K'iche' verb whose literal meaning is something like "Let it wait!" but whose effect is more like "Alas!" In the Rabinal play eleven different speeches or sections of speeches begin with this exclamation. Whether or not all eleven passages were based on songs, hearing *Aqaroq!* could have stirred memories of songs in the minds of playgoers of the past.

One of the play's best candidates for a song text is the opening passage of the first speech, delivered by Cawek of the Forest People. He is speaking before Man of Rabinal but making a threat whose ultimate target is Lord Five Thunder. Here are his words, divided at the places where José León Coloch pauses when he plays this role:

Katel uloq, worom ajaw	Come on out, lord who's been pierced
k'aqom ajaw	lord who's been fitted with gems
xa k'u xere	however that may be
qi chinab'e wa'	let me take the lead
keje mawi kanuk'iso	since I'm not finished
uch'ayik	chopping through
uwixal	the root
ukutamil	the trunk
Ajaw Chakachib'	of the Lord of Walkers
Ajaw Samanib'	the Lord of Workers
Kawuq Rab'inal.	Cawuks and Rabinals.

Cawek follows these lines with *kacha k'u ri nutzij,* "so say my words." This is partly his way of signaling that his speech is coming to an end, but he is also marking his words as a matter of record, a declaration of intent that is not limited to the present encounter. In his fourth speech, when he tells the story of how he came to use these words for the first time, he recites them again. This time he introduces them by saying *chiri k'ut / mi xnub'ixtaj,* "and then / I spoke," but early audiences might have heard this as a play on *mi xnub'ixaj,* "I sang."

Cawek's final speeches, in which he readies himself for death by sacrifice, have a number of points of similarity with a sixteenth-century song text from central Mexico. It comes from a collection of texts known as the *Cantares Mexicanos,* recorded by speakers of Nahuatl at the request of missionaries. In this particular song a condemned prisoner of war addresses Nezahualpilli, the ruler of Texcoco.[22] The lyrics, sung by a chorus, are preceded by a notation of the phrases to be played on the accompanying slit drum: *toto tiquiti tiquiti* at the beginning, and *tocotico tocoti* at the end. The first words are these:

Oya moquetz huehuetl, oo!	The drum is ready, oh!
Ma on netotilo teteuctin, aya!	Let the dance begin, noble warriors, ay!

There is an equivalent passage in *Rabinal Achi,* one in which Cawek addresses Lord Five Thunder, but it is far more developed, with twenty-one lines on the subject of music instead of one. Moreover, the passage has a defiant tone that is absent from the words of Nezahualpilli's prisoner:

Alaq b'a, ri ajsu'	Well sirs, you who are flutists
alaq b'a, ri ajq'ojom:	well sirs, you who are drummers:
Alata chike ri uchi' nusu'	Could it be the mouth of my flute
ri uchi' nuq'ojom	the mouth of my slit drum
ri mi xchitzaqta alaq?	that you are about to play, sirs?
Areta b'a, chitzaq alaq	Well sirs, if you did play
ri nunima tzaqab'alaj	my great instruments
nuch'uti tzaqab'alaj	my small instruments
areta puch chitzaq alaq	and sirs, if you did play
ri nuyaki su'	my Mexican flute
nuyaki q'ojom	my Mexican slit drum
areta puch chitzaq alaq	and sirs, if you did play
nu K'iche' su'	my Quiché flute

nu K'iche' q'ojom	my Quiché slit drum
k'ojb'al re	then all the way from this place
ri nukanab'	where I'm held prisoner
nuteleche'	I'm held captive
chi nujuyub'al	clear over to my own mountain
chi nutaq'ajal	my own valley
qi ta chib'irb'ot kaj	the very sky would tremble
qi ta chib'irb'ot ulew.	the very earth would tremble.

Cawek follows the subject of music with that of dance, putting them in the same order as the Mexican poem, but at this particular stage in the action he does not have the prospect of dancing with "noble warriors." He registers a complaint about his lack of a suitable partner as follows:

Chiqajta qawi'	But we would let our hair fall forward
chiqajta qajolom	we would hide our faces
chirech uyi'k	at the prospect of promenading
uxajik	dancing
kuk' achij mun	with this man slave
ixoq mun	woman slave
waral chuxmut kaj	here at the navel of the sky
chuxmut ulew.	navel of the earth.

In the Mexican poem, what the prisoner does next is to ask Nezahualpilli for the temporary use of valuables that belong to him:

Ma on netlanehuilo chalchihuitl	Lend out the precious jades
on quetzalli patlahuac.	the ample feathers of the quetzal.

There is a similar but far more detailed passage in *Rabinal Achi,* one in which Cawek again addresses Lord Five Thunder:

Chiyata chi b'a la chuwe	Then make me a gift, sir
chinkajta chi b'a chi ech la:	lend me something you have, sir:
ri u Chuch Q'uq'	the Mother of Quetzal Feathers
u Chuch Raxon	Mother of Glistening Green

ri yamanim	of jade
xteq'oqib'	of precious beads
ri petenaq	goods that come from
Tzam K'a'm Karchaj.	End of the String at Fish in the Ashes.
K'o saom uchi'	Whether her mouth has ever been shown
majab'i saom uwach	or her face has never been shown
chinsata k'u uchi'	I must show her mouth
chinsata k'u uwach	I must show her face
chinmesesejtaj	I must dance her round and round
chinjikikijtaj	I must dance her on and on
chupam unimal tz'aq	inside the great fortress
unimal k'oxtun	great walls
chi kaj pa	on all four edges
chi kaj xukutal.	in all four corners.

This passage shares its request for a loan of quetzal feathers and jade with the Mexican speech, but whatever such a request may have meant when addressed to Nezahualpilli, Lord Five Thunder understands it to mean that Cawek wants to dance with the Mother of Quetzal Feathers, a young woman whose marriage will one day bring gifts of feathers and jade.[23]

The prisoner of the Mexican poem follows his request for a loan of jade and feathers with a line alluding to his impending death:

Ayac ichan tlalticpac, ayyo!	No one has a home on earth, alas!

Cawek, in contrast, speaks of his death directly. "I must dance her on and on," he says of the Mother of Quetzal Feathers,

xata nima retalil	if only to mark the greatness
nukamik	of my death
nusachik.	my disappearance.

In making his various requests of Lord Five Thunder, Cawek always includes these three lines. Two of the items he asks for—a strong drink and a finely woven garment—are absent from the Mexican song.

Nezahualpilli's prisoner goes on to address those who will sacrifice him, making a more direct reference to his fate than before:

Zan nomac otitemic	Already you hold in your hand
motlahuazomal:	your flaying knife:
in ina tic ahuilitia icelteotl.	you give pleasure to the god.

Cawek employs metaphors to refer to the cutting instrument:

Ix b'a, ri kot	You then, Eagle
ix b'a, ri b'alam:	you then, Jaguar:
Kixpe ta b'ala!	Come now!
Chib'ana b'a ri ichak	Do your duty
chib'ana b'a ri ipatan	do your work.
chib'ana b'ala	Do it now
ri we'	with your teeth
ri wixk'aq.	your claws.

Nezahualpilli's prisoner next makes a statement of identity, one that includes his place of origin and the fact that the language he is presently speaking is, for him, a foreign one:

Zan ninonoalcatl	I am from Nonoalco
zan ca nicolintototl	a bird from the land of rubber trees
a nacomapan aya mexicatl.	but my mouth forms Mexican words.

Nonoalco roughly corresponds to the present-day Mexican state of Tabasco, which means that the prisoner's native language could be Nahuat, a dialect contrasting with the Nahuatl spoken by his captors, or else Mayan, either Ch'ol or Chontal. In Nonoalco he could have been bilingual throughout his life, in which case one of his two languages would be Nahuat. In any case the term he uses for the language that is foreign to him, here translated as "Mexican," is *mexicatl*, referring to Nahuatl. Cawek speaks less directly of his foreign status, but like the man from Nonoalco, he compares himself (if only in part) to a bird:

We qatz waral in kamel	If I am truly dead
in sachel	if I am lost

chuxmut kaj	at the navel of the sky
chuxmut ulew	navel of the earth
b'a re k'u xchiwachilib'ej	then I shall resemble
la' kuk	that squirrel
la' tz'ikin	that bird
la' xkam chuq'ab' che'	that died on the branch of a tree
chuxum che'	in the flower of a tree
chirech utzuquxik	while searching
la' re echa	for his meals
uk'uxun.	his morsels.

Cawek, like his counterpart from Nonoalco, finds himself speaking differently than he would at his place of origin, though he does not explicitly call attention to the fact. His own dialect of K'iche' would be the central one, spoken at the capital of the Quiché kingdom and different from the dialect of Rabinal. When he speaks of the "navel" of the sky and earth, he not only refers to the location where he is held captive, but he also uses a term for navel that is peculiar to the Achi dialect, spoken in Rabinal. In his own dialect the term would be *muxu'x,* but he uses Rabinal *xmut* instead. The term for the "four sides" (or "four edges") of the earth would be *kaj tz'uq* in his dialect, but he uses the Rabinal expression *kaj pa,* literally "four eaves" (or "four edges"). When he says that his descendants will think of him when they see a carved calabash from Rabinal, he describes the calabash as a *k'uxtub'al* or "remembrance," another term specific to Rabinal. And when he denigrates the Eagle and Jaguar priests of Rabinal, he describes them as having *jinta re'* and *jinta rixk'aq,* "nary a tooth" and "nary a claw," again following local usage.[24] A person from his own region might have been more likely to say something like *mawi jun re'* and *mawi jun rixk'aq,* "not a single tooth" and "not a single claw."

One could argue that the composers of the script were unaware of these dialect differences and unintentionally put Rabinal words in the mouth of Cawek, but in fact he uses the Rabinal term for "navel" much more often than any other character. It is as if the playwrights meant to portray him as fascinated by the strangeness of its sound and the irony of its meaning. Here he is, at a place that claims to be the navel of sky and earth, but as for his connection to his own place of birth, his captors keep turning the words of his play-opening declaration back on him, saying, "This is where we chop clear through / *your* root / *your* trunk, sir."

The difference in length between the Mexican song and the Rabinal speeches is probably accountable to a difference in verbosity between Mesomerican song and oratory rather than a contrast between the poetic preferences of Nahuatl and K'iche' speakers. The thing to be remembered about the song is that some of its lines would have been sung more than once, and that the *oo, aya,* and *ayyo* appearing in its text are probably the traces of refrains that would have been composed of exclamations and wordless vocal sounds of the kind that flow from music rather than language. A full performance of the song may well have taken as long as the corresponding speeches from the Rabinal play.

EVENTS RETOLD AND EVENTS REENACTED

During the early colonial period, audiences for dance dramas like *Rabinal Achi* would have been in a much better position to catch historical references and allusions than anyone is today. The play's own time is fixed in a world that precedes the coming of Europeans, and by now that world has receded far enough into the past to take on a mythic life of its own. Speeches that now seem lyrical or liturgical may once have come across as comments on political history. Narratives that now seem to belong together in the generation of the play's characters may once have evoked the multiple layers of a deeper past.

When the names, places, and events that figure in the lives of the play's characters are traced out by means of historical documents and archaeological evidence, they tell a story that runs much longer than any possible human life span. Here, as in some of the other Mayan dramas performed today in Guatemala and Chiapas, episodes from separate layers of history have been treated as the story of a single set of contemporaneous characters.[25] It has long been customary for students of Mayan culture and history to attribute such compositions to a Mayan preference for cyclical as opposed to linear time, but there are major problems with such an argument.

First, when we consider the historical context of the performances themselves, we are confronted with the fact that colonial authorities imposed narrow limits on the public representation of the pre-invasion world. In the case of Guatemala, the one public window that opened directly onto that world was provided by a drama called *Xajoj Tun* or "Dance of the Trumpets," whose actions included the sacrifice of a prisoner of war. It was widely performed during the colonial period, and it must have become densely laden with information about the past wherever it enjoyed some degree of continuity in the repertoire of a particular town. Even this one window worried Spanish authorities, who tried to close it again and again and in many different places (see the next chapter). Today there is only one local version of the Dance of the Trumpets that still tells an ancient story of war and sacrifice, and that is the version known as *Rabinal Achi.*

A second problem with consigning Mayan thinking about time to a compartment labeled "cyclical" is that dramas do not tell the whole story of Mayan representations of the past. In the case of the Rabinal play the very historical documents that allow us to perceive the layering of its events were authored by Mayans. These works, written in the roman alphabet but in the K'iche' and Kaqchikel languages, date from the sixteenth century, which also saw the first attempt to prohibit dances involving representations of sacrifice. In the case of the *Annals of the Cakchiquels,* the narrative is punctuated by dates from the 260-day divinatory calendar and by a succession of named 400-day periods. Otherwise the temporal framework of these documents is provided, at the most general level, by widely spaced occasions on which lineages received titles and emblems of lordship. Smaller intervals are marked by changes in the named locations that served as the seats of particular lordships, subdivided in turn by the successive reigns of named lords. Scattered unevenly across these reigns are notable events in the lives of particular lords, such as marriage alliances or military conflicts that reached over long distances—or, closer to home, construction projects, public celebrations of lordly power, and conspiracies aimed at seizing power. Most lords receive little more than a mention of their names, but a famous few are remembered as actors in multiple events.

Most of these same generalizations can be made about Classic Maya inscriptions. It is true that inscriptions on stelae include dates from the so-called long count, which measured time on a larger scale than the dates in alphabetic documents. But when it comes to recording a long succession of rulers, the texts carved on tablets at Palenque are similar to the Popol Vuh in their terseness, and the dynastic narratives painted on vases from Calakmul are limited to abbreviated dates very much like the ones in the *Annals of the Cakchiquels.*[26]

In Classic inscriptions, as in the alphabetic works of the highlands, the episodes in long narratives are not told in the exact order in which they occurred. Instead they are put together something like a cinematic montage, with forward or backward jump cuts to episodes that are discontinuous with the one at hand. On the tablet in the Temple of the Cross at Palenque, an account covering 175 years of dynastic history averages one flashback for every two forward moves. In the speeches of *Rabinal Achi,* the story of Cawek's past actions is told with a similar ratio between backward and forward moves.[27]

The actions of the characters in *Rabinal Achi,* considered apart from the stories they tell about themselves in their speeches, concern a single episode in their lives, centering around the capture and sacrifice of Cawek of the Forest

People. At this level the play is a representation of a series of customary actions in which the participants could be any captive, any captor, and any lord who received and sacrificed a captive in the Guatemalan highlands at any time during the last several centuries preceding the Spanish invasion. Even the names the characters give to one another are generic in quality, referring, with one exception, to categories of people rather than to individuals.

The one character whose name is not generic is *Ajaw Job' Toj,* "Lord Five Thunder." Among all the highland lords who were like him in being named for their days of birth on the divinatory calendar, no other Five Thunder is known.[28] Unfortunately, it is also the case that there is no further documentary evidence, outside the script of the play itself, for the existence of this particular Five Thunder. When he is considered strictly in terms of his role in the play, the strongest argument for the truth of his name lies in its poetic resonance. On days named *Toj* or "Thunder," the deity of the ax scepter received sacrifices and the lords who wielded the scepter received tribute payments. Rabinal lords called this deity by the name of a specific date, *Jun Toj* or "One Thunder." Present-day diviners give meaning to the day name *Toj* by playing on its sound to produce the verb *tojonik,* "to pay."[29] In the play, when the prisoner is about to be sacrificed, *Ajaw Job' Toj* tells him that the time has come for him to *tojorisaj,* "make payment."

Countering the poetic resonances of the name *Toj,* which almost makes it sound too good to be the true historical name of the lord in the play, is the number attached to it. If the composers of the script wished to avoid identifying him directly with the deity of the Rabinal scepter, they would have avoided calling him One Thunder. That would have left six, eight, nine, eleven, and thirteen as other important numbers on the highland ritual calendar, but not five, which seems more like an accident of a real birth than the result of an effort to invent an ideal date for a birth. The one possibility that keeps both history and poetry in the picture is that the composers chose the name of a historical lord, but did this not so much because he actually participated in the particular events that are narrated in the play, as because his name fit the poetry of the play.

None of the other characters has even the semblance of a personal name. Instead, they take their names from whole categories of people. When Lord Five Thunder calls his daughter *Uchuch Q'uq', Uchuch Raxon,* "Mother of Quetzal Feathers, Mother of Glistening Green," he is not revealing her personal name. Rather, he is using a parental figure of speech for an unmarried daughter who will become a source of wealth in the form of quetzal feathers and jade when a suitor comes to take her as a wife.[30] When he speaks of his knights as the *kab'lajuj Uq'anal Kot / Uq'anal B'alam,* "twelve Golden Eagles / Golden Jaguars," he is using their titles rather than their names. And when he addresses the androgynous character who waits on him, he simply calls him/her *achij mun, ixoq mun,* "man slave, woman slave."

Cawek comes no closer to speaking the name of the warrior who captures him than calling him *Q'alel Achi, Rab'inal Achi,* "Man of Glory, Man of Rabinal," which tells us he is dealing with a member of the Rabinal nation whose noble status, as indicated by the particular title he holds (Man of Glory), was not inherited but was rather conferred as a reward for military service.[31] For his part, Man of Rabinal calls his captive *Kaweq K'eche Winaq,* "Cawek of the Forest People," which reveals that the social relationship between the two of them is an asymmetrical one.[32] Cawek is the name of the first-ranking royal house of the Quiché nation, indicating that the captive is noble by birth. There is an asymmetry in their national identities as well. For much of their history, the lords of the Rabinal nation were members of a confederation that was headed by the lords of the *K'eche Winaq* or "Forest People," more commonly known as the *K'iche'* (Quiché) nation.

As for the meaning of "Forest People," that depends on who is using these words. When members of the Quiché nation used them to refer to themselves, they were calling up the memory of their rise to greatness from humble origins in a great forest. But when Man of Rabinal uses the same words while speaking angrily to the man who is his opponent and will soon be his prisoner, and when Lord Five Thunder later uses them while describing the prisoner's behavior as that of an animal, they shift the meaning. In everyday speech (as opposed to courtly poetry), "forest people" meant people who were foolish, rustic, and gross.[33]

Despite the fact that the actions performed during the play are generic, as are the names of all but one of its characters, the stories the characters tell about themselves and about one another recall specific historical individuals. The main difference is that in the play, a particular character may claim roles in events that historical accounts assign to separate individuals and even to separate eras. Cawek of the Forest People describes himself as a participant in events the authors of the Popol Vuh reckon as spanning six generations of the Cawek dynasty.[34] This telescoping of historical time and the removal of the names of the original participants in the events would seem to be two aspects of the same creative process by which the composers of the script constructed a drama.

In his opening speech Cawek describes Lord Five Thunder as the lord of a place called *Samanib'* or "Workers."[35] In so doing he evokes the remote era of the founders of the noble lineages of the Quiché, Rabinal, Cakchiquel, and Tzutuhil nations, who went together on a pilgrimage to a great city in the east and received ax scepters that gave them the right to rule.[36] When they returned they founded the towns that served as their first seats of power. For the Rabinal founder that town was Workers. Its ruins crown a high mountain ridge that marks the southeastern

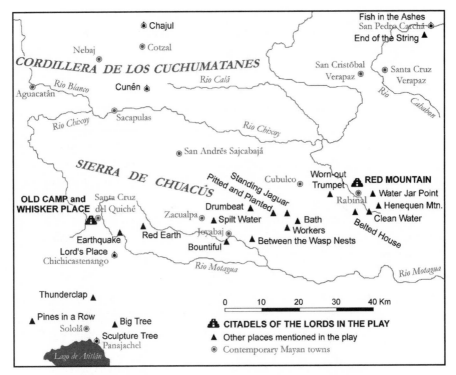

Map 1. The region defined by places named in the dialogue of *Rabinal Achi*.

border of Cubulco, which is the next town west of present-day Rabinal and shares the same dialect (see map 1). Lord Five Thunder is a descendant of the founder, but he belongs to a time when Workers was no longer the Rabinal capital and may have been falling into ruin.

When Cawek reveals the identity of the lord he serves, he again looks back to the era of the founders. Instead of naming anyone who would have been alive at the time of the various events in which he claims participation, he uses the names of the ultimate forefathers of the Quiché lords.[37] The names have been changed somewhat in the course of the copying and recopying of the script, but they are still recognizable. The lord Cawek names as *B'alam K'iche'* or "Jaguar Quiché" is *B'alam K'itz'e* or "Jaguar Quitzé" in older documents, which identify him as the founder of the royal house of the Caweks. The lord called *Ajaw B'alam Achi* or "Lord Jaguar Man" in the script is elsewhere called *B'alam Aq'ab* or "Jaguar Night," while the one called *la' Jukutaj*, "the Quick One" is *Majukutaj*, "Not Quick." These two founded the lineages that ranked second and third after the Caweks. The script has Cawek using all three names as if they belonged to a single individual.

Cawek of the Forest People and Man of Rabinal locate themselves in a later era when they speak of insignia of lordship other than the ax scepters obtained by the founders. When Cawek describes Lord Five Thunder as having been "pierced" and "fitted with gems," and when Rabinal calls upon the power of his bracelet, armband, white paint, and gourd of tobacco, they move the timeline forward to the pilgrimage to the lord named Nacxit, in Yucatán (as described in the previous chapter). It took place either one or four generations after the founders, depending on which historical source one follows.[38] Man of Rabinal evokes one of the events of the pilgrimage when he brings up an incident that took place when Cawek was supposed to be acting in the role of an ally rather than an enemy of the Rabinal lords.

When Cawek served the Rabinal lords as an ally, they were preparing for war with the allied nations called Uxab and Pokomam in the script. The Uxab, called *Yaki* or "Mexican" in some sources, were speakers of Pipil (an Aztecan language) who once lived among the Pokomam, whose own language (a Mayan one) is Poqomchi'. As late as the nineteenth century there were still speakers of Pipil in Salamá, a short distance east of Rabinal.[39] Among the present-day towns that speak Poqomchi' are San Cristóbal Verapaz and Santa Cruz Verapaz, to the north of Rabinal (see map 1).

The incident mentioned by Man of Rabinal took place when Cawek was sent into enemy territory as a combined emissary and spy. He failed to observe that the Uxab and Pokomam were strong in numbers, which became clear only when Man of Rabinal sent out a second spy of his own. A similar spy story is told by the authors of the *Annals of the Cakchiquels,* who describe it as taking place when the pilgrims were returning from their visit to Nacxit.[40] When they entered Pokomam territory they decided to gather intelligence before planning how to deal with the inhabitants. The first spies failed to carry out their mission, but a later one succeeded, correctly reporting that the Pokomam were very numerous.

In strict historical terms the play's spy story appears to be an anachronism, belonging to a much earlier time period than most of the other events in which the characters describe themselves as participants. But when we consider the story in theatrical terms it fits the play's general portrayal of Cawek as an ally turned enemy.

Another troublesome incident for which Man of Rabinal blames Cawek transpired at place called *Chatinib'al* or "Bath," whose location is uncertain.[41] It was an assassination attempt against Lord Five Thunder at a time when "bathing was his only concern." He was trapped inside a "plastered hive," which may have been a domed sweat bath of the kind that is still in use in the Guatemalan highlands. A similar incident occurred two generations after the pilgrims returned from Nacxit, when a Quiché king survived an attempt to assassinate him while he was

57. At a bathhouse, an assassin stabs a Mixtec lord named
Twelve Motion. At left is the fire for heating the bath.
From Codex Zouche-Nuttall page 81a.

bathing.[42] The name by which he is known, *K'otuja* or "Noble Bathhouse,"
probably derives from this event.

It may be that the play's authors borrowed the bath episode, changing the
identity of the protagonist. On the other hand, there is the possibility that baths
were customary sites for Mesoamerican assassination attempts in general, and that
the historical Lord Five Thunder was the object of one such attempt. In Oaxaca a
Mixtec lord named Twelve Motion was less fortunate than either Noble Bathhouse
or Lord Five Thunder. Several Mixtec codices picture him as meeting his end in
a sweat bath, stabbed in the chest with a knife his assassin had hidden inside an
object anyone would have expected to be brought inside a bathhouse: a bundle of
aromatic herbs (figure 57).[43]

Cawek locates himself in a time frame later than that of the historical spy and
bath incidents when he names the Quiché capital. He calls it *Q'umarmachi*, thus
combining the names *Q'umaraqa'j* or "Old Camp" and *Chi Ismachi'* or "Whisker
Place" in a single word.[44] During the reign of Noble Bathhouse the capital was a
citadel at Whisker Place, on a steep-sided headland that juts into a canyon. After
the attempt on his life most of the temples and palaces of the ruling lineages were
rebuilt at Old Camp, on a neighboring headland. The expanded capital was then
known by both names, right down to the time of the Spanish invasion.

The Rabinal capital is given four names by Cawek, names that reflect the
fact that it once belonged to the Uxab and Pokomam.[45] The first name, *Kaqyuq'*,
means "Red Mountain" in Poqomchi', the language of the original Pokomam
inhabitants. The second name, *Silik*, means "The One that Slides" in Poqomchi'

and "The One that Shakes" in K'iche', perhaps referring to past landslides. The third name, *Kaqokawunik,* is K'iche' for "Dressed in Red." The fourth name is a legacy of the Uxab, the speakers of Pipil who lived among the Pokomam. It is *Tepekanik,* derived from *Tepekumit,* which means "Jar Mountain." The ruins of this four-named citadel crown a mountaintop overlooking the present-day town center of Rabinal.

Red Mountain became a Rabinal citadel during the reign of the Quiché king Quicab *(K'iq'ab'),* who came three generations after Noble Bathhouse. All the Mayan writers who mention Quicab do so admiringly, in one case comparing his ferocity as a conqueror to that of Pedro de Alvarado. His reign was a long one, stretching over a period of forty or fifty years at the end of the fourteenth and the beginning of the fifteenth century.[46] While still a youth he launched a military campaign modeled on the story of the hero twins who went on a quest to the underworld, as told in the Popol Vuh. His purpose was to defeat the enemies who had captured and sacrificed his father and recover his father's bones. Aided in his quest by warriors from the Rabinal and Cakchiquel nations, he led his forces northeastward through the territory of the Uxab and Pokomam. Among their conquests was Red Mountain, which was afterwards occupied by the Rabinal nation.[47]

The play's version of the war against the Uxab and Pokomam differs from other accounts. Instead of beginning with Quicab's determination to avenge his father's death and leading to conquests that include Red Mountain, the story begins when Lord Five Thunder, who is already ensconced at Red Mountain, acts to prevent his own death at the hands of the Uxab and Pokomam. He wants to take the initiative by going to war against them, and with this in mind he asks the lords at the Quiché capital to send him warriors. As a reward for military service he offers land on which to settle and plant crops, presumably land to be taken from his enemies. Cawek accepts the offer, but in the end he returns home without receiving any reward. When he expresses his bitterness at having been denied land, Rabinal reminds him that his failure to report the true strength of the Uxab and Pokomam (as discussed earlier) resulted in Rabinal losses.

The story of Quicab's quest and that of Lord Five Thunder's request for help give opposite pictures of the relationship between the Quiché and Rabinal nations. In the one story a successful Quiché initiative results in new land for Rabinal, while in the other a Quiché warrior causes losses of land when he responds to a Rabinal initiative. One possible explanation for the inversion is that the composers of the play deliberately rewrote history, putting a Rabinal lord in the position of making the first move and avoiding the issue of the original ownership of the area commanded by Red Mountain. Another possibility is that Quicab's quest and Cawek's response to Lord Five Thunder's offer involve two successive historical events.

This would mean that after Red Mountain was occupied by the Rabinal nation, the Pokomam and Uxab planned to attack Lord Five Thunder and regain their lost territory. But this is a historical problem rather than a dramatic one. For purposes of the plot line of the play, the solution does not matter. Because of Cawek's resentment over the crops he never planted on the land he was never given, he eventually returns to Rabinal territory in the role of an enemy.

As for Quicab, he defeated those who had captured and sacrificed his father and took thirteen of their lords back to his capital as prisoners. They were sacrificed in the course of a spectacular production of the ceremony of the Revelation of Thunderer (as described in the previous chapter). The participants in the celebration included the current lord of Rabinal, quite possibly the historical Lord Five Thunder. Later in his career Quicab launched a series of expeditions that were conceived in terms of a four-directional cosmological scheme. Their purpose was to go "all around the borders of the earth, the Quiché earth, the Quiché mountains and valleys."[48] They reestablished the domain Quicab inherited and expanded it. The actions undertaken by a given expedition depended on whether the lord of a particular town in its path was ready to pay tribute or preferred to engage in a test of military strength.[49]

All the expeditions except the western one are mentioned or alluded to in the play.[50] Cawek seems to be referring to the northern expedition when he calls the ruler he serves "the lord of foreign Cunén / foreign Chajul,"[51] places which are directly north of Old Camp. In calling them foreign he is most likely referring to a language difference. Today the people in most districts of Chajul speak Ixil, a language that belongs to a separate branch of the Mayan family from that of Quichean languages, though there are some districts that speak K'iche'.[52] Cunén, though its people speak K'iche' today, may have been an Ixil-speaking town at the time of the northern expedition.

Cawek explains his return to Rabinal territory, which lies east of Old Camp, by claiming that he is conducting the business of the eastern expedition. He tells Man of Rabinal, "I'm working the soil / I'm resetting the boundaries of the land / from the place where the day goes out / to the place where the night enters." Man of Rabinal replies that he, too, was busy resetting boundaries until he heard the news of Cawek's attempt to assassinate Lord Five Thunder in his bath and came home to investigate. The expedition from which he departed, judging from the itinerary he describes for it, was the southern one. Among the places he visited was *Pan Ajachel* or "Sculpture Tree," a Cakchiquel town located directly south of Old Camp on the north shore of Lake Atitlán. According to other sources, the southern expedition was led by Quicab himself, who began by going to the lake.[53] He then turned southwestward to the Pacific coastal plain, but the play has Man of Rabinal returning home before the expedition progressed that far.

Man of Rabinal does not object to the eastern expedition as such but rather to the way Cawek has been conducting himself in the course of it. He asks, "For what reason / did you incite revolt / among the children of light / the sons of light?" Children and sons of light are the subjects of lords, referred to in this way because lords trace their genealogies all the way back to a time of darkness, whereas commoners came into existence when the present sun had already lighted the world. Rabinal continues, "Even though it wasn't your right / you set them loose / from their mountain / their valley," which is to say that Cawek turned the eastern expedition into a migration of commoners. According to the *Annals of the Cakchiquels*, Quicab had forbidden his subjects "to travel the roads,"[54] meaning that he did not wish them to migrate. But his southern expedition kept him away from the capital for a long time, and there was growing unrest among members of the Quiché nation who lived at the center of the kingdom. Dissident Quiché lords, together with commoners who included veteran warriors, began plotting a revolt.

Among those who plotted against Quicab were his two youngest sons, one of whom seems likely to have served as the principal historical model for Cawek of the Forest People. This son, known to his enemies by the nickname *Tata Yak* or "Father Fox," held the noble title *Chituy*, which gave him fifth place in the line of succession.[55] Man of Rabinal never makes a direct mention of either the nickname or the title, but he seems to display a knowledge of both when he says to Cawek, "You, sir, are the one who makes the cries of coyotes / who makes the cries of foxes / who makes the cries of agoutis and jaguars." By juxtaposing foxes with agoutis, he inflicts a triple insult on Cawek. First of all, agoutis are easily frightened rodents that shriek when they flee.[56] Second, a list of animals like this one would normally follow foxes with pumas, not agoutis. And third, the term for agoutis, *utuy*, is a pun on Father Fox's title, *Chituy*.

Quicab was never formally deposed, but by the time he returned to the capital he had been forced to surrender much of his access to wealth and power. Meanwhile the rebels were engaged in a new form of conquest, expanding the territory occupied by people of the Quiché nation at the expense of its closest allies.[57] According the *Annals of the Cakchiquels*, Quicab opposed a plan to attack *Chiawar* or "Lord's Place," the citadel where the Cakchiquel lords held court, and gave the lords advance warning when he realized he could not prevent it.[58] Quicab is not mentioned by name in *Rabinal Achi*, but according to the play's account of the invasion of Rabinal territory by Cawek of the Forest People, Man of Rabinal and Lord Five Thunder were forewarned by the lords at the Quiché capital.[59]

In the *Annals*, as in *Rabinal Achi*, a distinction is made between the authority of the legitimate rulers at the Quiché capital, which is never questioned, and the activities of rebels. In the *Annals* the term used to identify the nationality of the

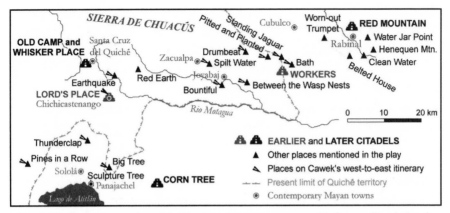

Map 2. The internal expansion of the Quiché nation at the expense of its former allies during the reign of Quicab. Cakchiquel lords, who had formerly ruled from Lord's Place, moved to Corn Tree, while Rabinal lords, whose original seat was at Workers, moved to Red Mountain.

rebels is *K'eche Winaq*, "Forest People." Another Cakchiquel source goes a step further and calls them *Kaweq K'eche Winaq*,[60] which is to say Forest People of the Cawek lineage—precisely the same people whose name is born by the single figure of Cawek in the play.

Cawek admits to Man of Rabinal's charge that he incited revolt among the subjects of the lords at the Quiché capital. When he set them loose, he says, they "were buzzing / in the breadnut trees / over their sustenance." The fruit of the breadnut tree, a broadleaf evergreen called *iximche'* or "corn tree" in Quichean languages, was an important source of food in times of famine. This suggests that Quicab's problems with unrest among his subjects were caused, at least in part, by hunger.[61] If so, it would have been in desperation that they decided to "travel the roads" with a rebel.

Much of the route Cawek describes himself as following runs through territory that once belonged to the Cakchiquel and Rabinal nations but was occupied by the Quiché during the reign of Quicab. In effect, the story he tells is that of the origin of the linguistic and political boundaries that have separated these peoples ever since that time. The westernmost place he mentions is *Cholochik Juyub'* / *Cholochik Chaj*, "Mountains in a Row / Pines in a Row," which is inside the boundaries of the present-day Quiché town of Santa Catarina Ixtahuacán and very near the western limit of Cakchiquel territory. Next he comes to *Pan Tzajaxaq* or "Thunderclap," the location of the present-day village of Xajaxac. This place lies between the Quiché town of Chichicastenango and the Cakchiquel town of Sololá, on the Cakchiquel side of the present political and linguistic boundary between them (see map 2). Then comes *Chi Nimche'* or "Big Tree," corresponding to the K'iche'-speaking hamlet of Panimaché. Today it is claimed by Chichicastenango but controlled by Sololá.[62]

At this point on his itinerary Cawek made a temporary turn to the north, going to the site of the Cakchiquel capital at Lord's Place. In the script of the play it is called *Panaraweno* or "Mint Place," a scrambled and shortened version of the K'iche' name *Pan Ajawarem,* which (like the Kaqchikel name *Chiawar*) means "Lord's Place." Cawek makes no mention of meeting with opposition when he arrived there. This is consistent with the story told in the *Annals of the Cakchiquels,* which is that the Cakchiquel lords abandoned the place when Quicab warned them of an impending attack. They moved about thirty kilometers to the southeast and founded a new citadel they called *Iximche'* or "Corn Tree," a name which again suggests that this was a time of hunger. Meanwhile their old citadel was occupied by speakers of K'iche', who renamed it *Chuwila',* "Nettles Heights." At the time of the Spanish invasion it acquired the additional name Chichicastenango, a Nahuatl translation of its K'iche' name.

When Cawek and his rebel horde arrived at their next stop, *Kab'raqan* or "Earthquake," they "came within a very short distance" of the Quiché capital at Old Camp and Whisker Place. They were less than a day's walk from the capital, in the Quiché hamlet called Chicabracán today. The implication seems to be that they now posed a direct threat to the Quiché establishment, but then "they turned in this direction," which is to say eastward toward Rabinal, "taking by force / the length and breadth / of the mountains and valleys." Again there is a suggestion of famine: "With their bellies grumbling / since the worms in their bellies were grinding away / they turned this way."

The next two stops on Cawek's route are well to the east of Earthquake. First comes *Pan Cha'lib'* or "Bountiful," and then *Xol Chaqaj* or "Between the Wasp Nests." The former place is three kilometers southwest of the center of the present-day Quiché town of Joyabaj, while the latter lies a short distance east of there. It is known from other sources that Joyabaj (or *Xoyab'aj*) was a Rabinal citadel until it was taken by the Quiché during the reign of Quicab.[63] Today the inhabitants count themselves as Quiché, though they speak a version of the K'iche' language that is similar to the Achi dialect of Rabinal.

Cawek admits to attacking a number of Rabinal places that are even farther east, on or near the present-day border between the Quiché town of Joyabaj and the Achi-speaking town of Cubulco. This same border divides the Guatemalan Department of Quiché, which includes the ancient Quiché capital, from the Department of Baja Verapaz, which includes the town of Rabinal. On the ridge that marks the border is Workers, the place where the founding lords of the Rabinal nation first established themselves. In other words, the ancient seat of the Rabinal lords, whose domain once extended well to the west of there, ended up marking the western limit of their lands.

A few kilometers northwest of Workers, at a place called *Chi K'otom* and *Chi Tikiram,* "Pitted" and "Planted," Cawek caused the death of nine warriors who were afterward buried by Lord Five Thunder and other Rabinal lords.[64] Cawek went on to "finish off / two or three branches" of the Rabinal nation at a series of other places in the same general area. One of these, *B'alamwak* or "Standing Jaguar," is directly north of Workers and connected to it by a ridge. On the east side of this ridge there happens to be a place called Bath. If the story of Lord Five Thunder's bath was taken from his own life rather than that of Noble Bathhouse, this is a likely location for Cawek's attempted assassination, though there are many other highland places with the same name.[65]

Standing Jaguar heads a whole list of places attacked by Cawek, and though some of them have not been identified, they were probably in the same frontier area. By the time he attacked *Chi Kunu* or "Drumbeat" he had turned back toward the west, staying close to the line of the frontier rather than heading east toward Red Mountain (see map 2). The story of his participation in the eastern expedition leaves off here, but there is more to be told about the Quiché horde he brought along with him. Man of Rabinal complains that "even now / they have yet to return / inside their own fortress / inside their own walls." Instead, he says, "they have settled" at *Pan Amak'a'* or "Spilt Water," a town whose ruins are located two kilometers southeast of the center of the Quiché town known today as *Pamak'a'* or Zacualpa.[66] According to other sources, Spilt Water was a Rabinal town until it was taken by the Quiché during the reign of Quicab. It remains Quiché today.

By the time Man of Rabinal captures Cawek of the Forest People, Cawek is a worn-out warrior who no longer has an army of hungry people behind him. He has been lurking somewhere within earshot of the citadel on Red Mountain, trying to lure people outside the walls at night by making the cries of animals. The sources reveal nothing as to how the historical Father Fox came to the end of his career, but as a matter of theatrical fact Cawek becomes a prisoner of war and loses his head.

THREE

Under Spanish Rule

THEATER AND EVANGELISM

The European invasion of highland Guatemala first took the form of what Mayans called *nima kamik ch'aq,* "the great death of the flesh," or simply *yawab'il,* "the sickness."[1] This was a smallpox epidemic, arriving in 1520. Four years later came military forces led by Pedro de Alvarado, crossing the border that separated the easternmost province of the Aztec empire from the westernmost reach of the Quiché kingdom—the same border that separates Mexico from Guatemala today. At that time the rulers of the Quiché kingdom were Three Deer and Nine Dog, members of the same noble lineage as Cawek of the Forest People in the Rabinal play. When the massive army they sent to stop Alvarado was defeated, they invited him to a peace conference at their capital, the citadel of Old Camp. He turned the conference into a trial, taking them prisoner, torturing them until they confessed to plotting against him, and burning them at the stake.[2]

The Spanish conquest of the Quiché kingdom was completed in 1524, the same year in which it began, but the consolidation of Spanish rule throughout highland Guatemala took another twenty years. The invasion had come well after the reign of Quicab, at a time when the lords of the Cakchiquel and Rabinal nations were no longer subordinate to the Quiché. At first the Cakchiquel lords collaborated with the Spaniards against the Quiché, but when they realized that the Spaniards were the enemies of all the highland peoples, they turned against them and resisted until 1530.[3] The region where the Rabinals are located held out even longer, so much so that Spaniards gave it the Nahuatl name Tezulutlán, meaning "Land of War."

In 1537 the task of bringing the Land of War under control was taken out of military hands and given to missionaries of the Dominican order, under the leadership of Fray Bartolomé de las Casas.[4] They resettled hilltop fortress towns on valley floors, starting with Rabinal. By 1547 their experiment in nonviolent conquest was recognized as a success and the name of the region was officially changed to Verapaz, "True Peace."

In the Guatemalan highlands, as elsewhere in Mesoamerica, the early missionaries set about destroying the images and dismantling the temples of Mayan religion and replacing them with the images and temples of Spanish Christianity. In the case of the performing arts they took a different approach, seeking to reorganize existing productions according to the Christian calendar and transform them into celebrations of saints.[5] They trained Mayans as choirmasters and collaborated with them in composing Christian prayers, chants, and songs in local languages. These new works were inserted into the programs of festivities that included traditional productions. The long-range goal was to transform or supplant any features of public performances that might run contrary to Christian teachings.

In the field of drama the missionaries introduced the vernacular theater tradition of medieval Europe. In at least one major respect the imported dramas were like the indigenous ones: Acting and dancing were combined in the same performance.[6] Among the early productions were mystery plays with such themes as the fall of Adam and Eve, Noah and the ark, and the adoration of the Magi.[7] Miracle plays, which concerned the lives of saints, were also produced. In the town of Rabinal, a play performed until around 1950 told the story of the apostle Paul.[8] Locally called *Nima Xajoj* or "Principal Dance," it was offered on the feast day of the Conversion of St. Paul, January 25, which also serves as the main occasion for performances of *Rabinal Achi*. It happens that both plays concern a man whose military career has come to an end, and in both plays he meets his end by decapitation. It may be that in the thinking of the early Dominicans, *Rabinal Achi* served as a prelude to *Nima Xajoj* in the same way that readings of Old Testament prophecies serve as a prelude to readings from the Gospel in the mass. If so, this may help explain why *Rabinal Achi* survived a long period during which similar dances in other towns were repeatedly subjected to bans.

A miracle play that remains popular in Rabinal is the *Baile de San Jorge*. The characters include a dragon, of course, but with the sun and moon painted on its long reptilian body, recalling the celestial aspect of the cosmic Mesoamerican dragon widely known as the Plumed Serpent. Accompanying this character is a second monster with the horns of a goat and the wings of a bat. His horns are those of a Christian devil, but his bat nature is of Mayan origin. A parish priest of the mid-twentieth century reported his name as "Camán Xoch," which identifies him as *Kama Sotz'*, the "Snatch Bat" who appears in the Popol Vuh story of the hero twins named Hunahpu and Xbalanque.[9] His normal habitat is the Bat House of Xibalba, the Mayan underworld, and it is there that he suddenly snatches off the head of an unwary Hunahpu. That is probably why he also had a role in the Rabinal play about St. Paul.

The colonial missionaries composed handwritten scripts for the plays they introduced, in some cases collaborating with parishioners to produce translations of at least some of the speeches into the local Mayan languages. The actors— whether or not they could read or else had to be read to, and whether or not they knew much Spanish—memorized their parts. The use of scripts gave the mission- aries control over what was said in performances, but not over the meanings ascribed by the actors and playgoers. The problems of interpretation were so great that many plays eventually became targets for bans. Among other things, most of them, like the Rabinal plays about St. Paul and St. George, included a devil among their characters. This had the unintended effect of giving active roles to what seemed to Mayans to be members of their own forbidden pantheon.

One of the most successful plays scripted by missionaries was *La danza del venado* or "Deer Dance," which was based, in part, on indigenous hunting rituals.[10] Today it is among the most widely performed plays in Guatemala. In addition to deer, the cast includes pumas, jaguars, monkeys, dogs, hunters, and an elderly couple. To these the missionaries added Spanish military characters, but friendly ones with names like Understanding, Contentment, and Happiness, taken from the Golden Age allegories of Spanish theater. This change served to transfer the action into a time when Spanish and therefore Christian authority had already been established. All the characters, including the Indian ones, were scripted to speak in rhymed and metered Spanish verse, except when an Indian recited a Christian prayer or a statement of Christian doctrine that had been translated into the local Mayan language. The old couple, originally mountain deities who owned the deer and had to be asked permission to hunt them, became rustic country dwellers who knew how to pray for success in the hunt by appealing to heavenly rather than earthly powers.

Many plays involving deer are performed in present-day Verapaz. Those with scripted Spanish dialogue are called *Kaxlan Kej* or "Castilian Deer" in order to distinguish them from the others. The people of Rabinal no longer perform *Kaxlan Kej*, preferring alternative plays that go under such titles as *Xajoj Kej*, "Deer Dance"; *Ixim Kej*, "Corn Deer"; and *B'alam Kej*, "Jaguar Deer." The dialogue in these plays is improvised rather than scripted and mostly in Mayan laguages rather than Spanish. But the characters, as in the scripted plays, include animals, hunters, and an old couple.[11] The question as to whether these are Mayan dances that have resisted Hispanicization or Hispanicized dances that are being re-Mayanized is an open one.

The speeches in scripted deer dances, whatever the subject matter of the moment might be, often include oaths, blessings, or praises in which members of the Trinity, Joseph and Mary, or the local patron saint are named.[12] No doubt these passages were seen as serving a didactic purpose, but they also reflect long-standing habits of speech among Christian Europeans. They must have struck early audiences as bizarre, since there is no evidence that Mayans—or any other indigenous Americans, for that matter—peppered their conversations with invocations of divine powers before Europeans arrived. Even so, at some point in the writing and revision of scripts for the drama now known as *Rabinal Achi,* oaths and blessings were introduced into the speeches. The choice of words for such passages presented a two-sided problem. On the one hand, the use of Christian names would be anachronistic, since a dance of this kind reenacted a time in which Christians had yet to appear on the Mayan horizon. On the other hand, the invocation of Mayan deities would have the effect of keeping them alive.

The solution was a compromise, one that gave at least the illusion that there was a point where the theologies of Christians and Mayans intersected. The numerous divine names of Mayan prayers were set aside altogether, and the divine epithets were reduced to the two that remain in the *Rabinal Achi* script: *Kaj* and *Ulew,* "Sky" and "Earth." A listener who leaned toward Mayan tradition could have heard these words as a shortened version of *Uk'ux Kaj, Uk'ux Ulew,* "Heart of Sky, Heart of Earth," a couplet recorded in the Popol Vuh, and might have thought about thunderbolts and the divine power once wielded by Mayan lords. But a listener who leaned in the opposite direction could have heard the same words as a shortened version of a central tenet of Christian doctrine, namely, "There is only one God in heaven and on the earth."

CHARLEMAGNE AND THE TWELVE KNIGHTS OF FRANCE

Some of the plays introduced by missionaries had their source in the medieval struggle between the Christian and Islamic worlds. These plays, which most often go under the title *Moros y cristianos,* are performed in Rabinal and other towns all over Mesoamerica to this day.[13] In some of the early productions Indian actors were cast in the roles of Moors, while Spaniards played the Christians who conquered and converted them. The battle scenes in such plays combine physical combat with verbal arguments, alternating back and forth between the two. Like Cawek of the Forest People in *Rabinal Achi,* a Moor may admit to past acts of violence against the nation of his opponent, but unlike Cawek, he will also be pressed to admit his religious errors. By the time such a play draws to a close, all the Moors have either been killed or baptized. As for Cawek and his Rabinal captors, they stand on the same ground when it comes to matters of religion, from the beginning of their play right through to the end. In place of citations of the Bible there are allusions to the central narrative of the Popol Vuh, as when Cawek compares his head to a calabash and thus compares himself to the father of Hunahpu, whose head was transformed into the first calabash.

The fifteenth-century Spanish conquest of Granada serves as the source of inspiration for some of the dramas about Christians and Muslims, but the eighth-century expedition in which Charlemagne crossed the Pyrenees provides an alternative. His avowed purpose was to take Zaragoza from the Saracens, but he was unsuccessful. On his way back to France his forces were attacked by Basques at Roncesvalles, in Navarre, resulting in the deaths of Roland and other knights. As the story of his expedition was told and retold, the Basques became Saracens whose attack was made possible by the treachery of a knight with a grudge against Roland. The earliest written version, dating from the twelfth century, is the verse epic *Chanson de Roland.* A prose version, titled *Fierabras* after a warrior on the Saracen side, was among the earliest literary works to be disseminated by means of the printing press, appearing in France in 1486. A Spanish translation of *Fierabras,* retitled *Carlomagno y los doce pares de Francia,* was published in various editions beginning in 1521. Later in the sixteenth century numerous copies were shipped to the Americas. From Mexico and Guatemala all the way to Chile and Argentina, *Carlomagno* became the basis for poetic compositions, ballads, and dance dramas.[14]

In Guatemala, dramatic versions of *Carlomagno* have come down to the present in at least ten different manuscripts, all of them twentieth-century versions that are separated from the original printed text by an indefinite number of prior manuscript versions. Except for a few lines of church Latin, the dialogue is entirely in Spanish, and in all but one case the prose of the printed text has been rewritten as verse. The play continues to be performed in Quiché towns located near the city of Quetzaltenango and in the Pacific piedmont, together with a scattering of Cakchiquel and Pokomam towns. The versions of the script from the Quiché towns of Cantel and San Bernardino, which run to more than 3,500 lines of verse, are the longest of all known texts for plays performed in the Mayan towns of Guatemala.[15] *Rabinal Achi,* which ranks first in length among dramatic texts in Mayan languages, runs a little over 2,800 lines when it is broken into verse. In the length of its speeches it ranks first among all plays, including those with Spanish texts. In the opening dialogue between Cawek of the Forest People and Man of Rabinal the *average* speech runs a little over 90 lines, as compared with 57 lines for the *longest* of all the speeches in *Carlomagno*.

In both its details and its general structure, *Rabinal Achi* has more points of resemblance to *Carlomagno* than to any other play performed in Guatemala. It seems quite likely that at some period during the long history of composition and revision that lies behind the surviving scripts of these two plays, some of the individuals responsible for past versions of *Rabinal Achi* or similar dance dramas were familiar with past versions of *Carlomagno*. It is even possible that they saw themselves as creating an indigenous counterpart to *Carlomagno,* but if so, they did much more than merely change the names of the characters and places.

Many of the speeches in both plays begin or end with invocations of divine powers, but the dramatic implications are quite different from one play to the other. The divine names spoken by the Christians in *Carlomagno* include Dios, Espíritu Santo, Jesús, and Emperátriz María. At the broadest level, what that play is about is the triumph of the powers invoked by the *cristianos* over those invoked by their enemies. For their part, the *mahometanos, turqueos, moros,* or *paganos* (as the enemies are variously called) seek the aid of *dioses* (always in the plural), Mahoma Santo, and Apolín (Apollo). In *Rabinal Achi,* on the other hand, the two sides to the conflict are in agreement when it comes to invocations, calling upon Sky and Earth. By the end of *Carlomagno* all the infidels have either died or converted to Christianity, whereas the royal court of Rabinal and its Quiché counterpart begin the play with a single set of beliefs and end it in the same way. Plays similar to *Rabinal Achi* enjoyed great popularity during the early colonial period, and one of the reasons for this may have been that they recalled a time when not even enemies challenged one's beliefs.

A more particular point of comparison between the two plays is their use of the number twelve, which carries somewhat more cultural weight for Europeans than for Mayans. The emperor Carlomagno is served by *doce pares* or "twelve peers," meaning a dozen knights who include Roldán (Roland), while Lord Five Thunder is served by *kab'lajuj Uq'anal Kot, Uq'anal B'alam,* "twelve Golden Eagles, Golden Jaguars." Twelve turns up in a number of other passages in *Rabinal Achi,* as when Man of Rabinal refers to the "twelve lords" of the Rabinal nation. It has been argued, even without bringing the text of *Carlomagno* into the picture, that the presence of the number twelve in *Rabinal Achi* is a symptom of Europeanization, and that it replaced the number thirteen.[16]

In the matter of the twelve Golden Eagles and Jaguars, the point to consider is that Lord Five Thunder wonders whether Cawek "will help them reach perfection." It turns out that when Cawek "helps" them at the end of the play, he does so by joining them in a ritual that ends with his execution. Implicitly he becomes, in spirit, the thirteenth member of their company.

As for the twelve lords referred to by Man of Rabinal, their number is corroborated by another source. In 1537, when Fray Bartolomé de las Casas founded a mission at a valley site adjacent to the present town center of Rabinal, he persuaded the people of the Rabinal nation to move down from the surrounding hills. To do so, he had to deal with the lords of twelve different divisions of the nation. The archaeological evidence is consistent with his account. Overlooking the valley are two hilltop sites that date from the end of the pre-Columbian period. One of these is known today as *Chuwi Tinamit* or "Above the Town," and the other is the site called *Kaqyuq'* or "Red Mountain" in the play. Both sites have palaces and temples arranged around six separate plazas, for a total of twelve.[17] So whether or not the authors of *Rabinal Achi* intended an allusion to *Carlomagno* when they made use of the number twelve, they were able to do this without contradicting the facts of their own history and culture.

In both plays the action centers not around the hero (if heroes are supposed to be protagonists) but around a remarkably fierce warrior who happens to be on the wrong side. In *Carlomagno* this warrior is Fierabrás, who is in the service of a Turkish king and in some versions is his son. His counterpart in *Rabinal Achi* is Cawek of the Forest People, who is (or once was) in the service of the lords of the Quiché kingdom and is modeled, in part, on the son of a famous Quiché king. By chance the name of the Turkish king is Balán, which is close to *b'alam,* a K'iche' term for "jaguar." The composers of the *Rabinal Achi* script or one of its predecessors may have intended an allusion to Balán when they wrote the lines in which Cawek names his lords. Instead of having him name Quicab, Cauizimah, and Iztayul, who would have been served by Father Fox (his main historical counterpart), they substituted names from a remote era in which *B'alam* was a favorite choice. At one point they have Cawek saying that he serves lords named *B'alam Ajaw, B'alam Achi, B'alam K'iche',* "Jaguar Lord, Jaguar Man, Jaguar Quiché."[18]

Fierabrás is described as the strongest man in the world and is sometimes portrayed as a giant. This is not true of Cawek as he appears in *Rabinal Achi,* but he may have been depicted differently in other versions of the play that were once performed in towns other than Rabinal. In any case he has escaped the world of drama and now enjoys a second life in the realm of folktales, where he possesses superhuman strength. One of the phrases by which he is addressed in the play, *oyew achi* or "brave man," has become Yew Achi, the name by which he is known to storytellers. According to a tale told in both Cubulco and Rabinal, the people of Rabinal moved to their present location in order to escape the nocturnal attacks of Yew Achi.[19]

Both *Carlomagno* and *Rabinal Achi* open with a speech by the chief antagonist, who seeks to provoke a fight. Fierabrás addresses his challenge to Carlomagno
but is answered by Oliveros, one of the twelve knights who serve Carlomagno.
Cawek expresses his desire to chop through the root and trunk of the Lord of the
Cawuk and Rabinal nations, which is to say Lord Five Thunder, but it is Man of
Rabinal, a warrior in the service of Lord Five Thunder, who answers him. Both
challenges are followed by one-on-one conflicts, and in both cases the means of
expression alternates back and forth between the physical and verbal planes.

When Fierabrás questions Oliveros concerning his identity he gets an evasive
response at first, but Oliveros eventually gives him a straight answer. Cawek and
Rabinal play out an analogous exchange but in reverse, with Rabinal asking the
questions and Cawek evading them. Fierabrás, who makes no secret of his own
identity, brags about his past accomplishments as an enemy of Christianity, which
include destroying Rome, killing the pope, and making off with a collection of holy
relics. Cawek, on the other hand, speaks of his own deeds only in response to
accusations by Man of Rabinal, admitting to having invaded Rabinal territory with
an army of Quiché rebels, attacking Lord Five Thunder while he was bathing, and
robbing a fertile valley of its rich soil.

Finding himself defeated, Fierabrás is so impressed by the gallantry of
Oliveros that he insists on becoming his comrade-at-arms. The situation with
Cawek is reversed, in that he should have been acting as Rabinal's comrade in the
first place but chose instead to become his enemy. Fierabrás fervently desires to
accompany Oliveros to the court of Carlomagno, whereas Cawek proposes that
before he appears at the court of Lord Five Thunder, Rabinal should gallantly allow
him to pay a farewell visit to his homeland. When Fierabrás appears before
Carlomagno he asks to be baptized, whereas Cawek's behavior in the presence of
Lord Five Thunder is that of an unrepentant prisoner of war.

In an episode that takes place after the encounter between Oliveros and
Fierabrás, Carlomagno sends a knight named Ganalón to the Turks as an emissary.
Ganalón threatens them with war if the holy relics are not returned, but when they
offer him great riches he agrees to act as their secret agent. On his return he
persuades Carlomagno to send Roldán and other knights to Roncesvalles, where
the Turks will be waiting in ambush. The resultant battle is enacted in the course
of the play, but an analogous episode in *Rabinal Achi* is assigned to a time
preceding the events of the play. It took place when Cawek was an ally of the lords
of the Rabinal nation, who feared an attack by their Uxab and Pokomam enemies.
Cawek, as Man of Rabinal reminds him, accepted the task of going before the
enemy lords as an emissary, warning them to stay inside their existing territory.
While he was on this mission he failed to observe that their forces were numerous

and on the move, which resulted in disastrous Rabinal losses at places named Below the Cave and Under Ripe Yellow Corn.

Man of Rabinal stops short of accusing Cawek of conspiring with the Uxab and Pokomam lords, but he finds it hard to believe that their preparations for war could have escaped Cawek's notice. Instead of admitting to a conspiracy with the enemy lords, Cawek portrays them as making what could be interpreted as an attempt to bring him over to their side. He quotes them as contrasting their own easy life as wealthy growers of cacao with the constant struggles of Rabinal subsistence farmers. In his reply to the lords, as he recounts it, he interpreted their remarks to mean that they were threatened by the diligence of the Rabinal people, and that they wanted to see them greatly reduced in numbers and in territory. He does not say whether the discussion went any further, and Man of Rabinal does not pursue the matter. Whether Cawek failed to observe the enemy's true strength or else conspired to keep it a secret, Rabinal holds him responsible for the disaster that followed.

Both plays have an episode in which a prisoner of war interacts with an unmarried woman who is a member of the court of his captors. In *Carlomagno* this takes place at the court of the enemy king, Balán, while in *Rabinal Achi* it takes place at the court of Lord Five Thunder. The prisoners in question are Oliveros, who is captured (along with several other knights) after his defeat of Fierabrás, and Cawek. While imprisoned, Oliveros and his companions are secretly visited by Floripes, who is the daughter of Balán and (in some versions) the sister of Fierabrás. In the Rabinal play it is Cawek who makes the first move, and he does so openly. He asks Lord Five Thunder to allow him to dance with the Mother of Quetzal Feathers, who is (at least implicitly) the lord's daughter.

Floripes wants to free Oliveros and the other prisoners and take the holy relics to the court of Carlomagno. Once there, she plans to marry Guy de Borgoña, a knight she somehow met at the time of the destruction of Rome. In effect the relics will serve as her dowry, whereas the marriage of the Mother of Quetzal Feathers would mean a transfer of precious objects in the opposite direction, from the family of her husband to that of her parents. The Mother of Quetzal Feathers remains unmarried throughout the play, but she is named, as eligible daughters once were, after the green feathers and jade of the bride price she would bring.

In both plays there is an enemy who is defiant to the end, meeting death in the final scene. In *Carlomagno,* during a final battle in which the Christians are victorious over the Turks, Balán refuses baptism and dies from a wound inflicted by a sword or (in one version) hangs himself. In *Rabinal Achi,* when Cawek appears at the court of Lord Five Thunder, he passes up any chance he might have had for mercy and accepts death by decapitation.

Looking back over the various points of comparison, it would appear that the composers of *Rabinal Achi* may well have given some thought to the relationship between the story they set out to tell and the story told in *Carlomagno*. But if so, they were at least as interested in the contrasts as in the similarities. In this they resemble the authors of the Popol Vuh, whose biblical allusions often have the effect of highlighting differences between the story they have to tell and the story told in Genesis.[20] Their story of the origin of the world begins with air and water, but instead of a maelstrom they describe a calm sea beneath an empty sky. Their gods do not bring light and earth into this world by creating them but rather by revealing that they were already there. And when these gods attempt to get the human species started by making a single figure out of mud, it dissolves without leaving any descendants. As for the authors of *Rabinal Achi,* they script a confrontation between two warriors in which one is reluctant to reveal his identity to the other, as in *Carlomagno,* but it is the loser who is reluctant rather than the winner. The loser, rather than being an enemy who becomes an ally, is a former ally who has become an enemy, and instead of humbling himself before the winner's lord and beginning a new life, he proudly accepts death.

TWO VERSIONS OF THE CONQUEST

When plays representing the Spanish conquest were introduced they were modeled, in part, on plays in which Christians confront Muslims. The story they tell is one in which the primary purpose of the Spanish invaders is to bring Christianity to the Indians. They end when all the Indian characters, with one exception, have either been killed or baptized. Two different conquest dramas are known for Guatemala, both bearing the same two titles. In Spanish they are called *La conquista,* but speakers of K'iche' and Kaqchikel call them *Saq K'oxol* or "White Sparkstriker," thus placing the only character who escapes baptism in the title role. The older play, which dates from the colonial period, was performed in Rabinal and neighboring Cubulco as recently as the 1950s.[21] The newer play, which emerged several decades after the end of colonial rule in 1821, is performed in scores of towns today.

The play from the colonial period, which includes Cortés and Montezuma among its main characters, tells the story of the conquest of Mexico. Two of its secondary characters, Alvarado and a king named Quiché, replace Cortés and Montezuma in the newer play, which deals with the conquest of the Quiché kingdom.[22] The character who avoids becoming a Christian is represented as a sort of demon or evil sorcerer in both plays, but for many Quiché spectators he was and still is a beneficent deity—a gamekeeper, giver of wealth, and patron of diviners. In their interpretation he escapes into the woods at the end of the play, there to keep the ancient customs alive.[23]

All the characters in the post-independence play speak Spanish, but the Indians in the play from the colonial period speak K'iche' whenever they converse with one another. The surviving manuscripts for the older play, which go back as far as 1726, provide the earliest known documentation for dramatic dialogue in a Guatemalan Mayan language. In the case of *Rabinal Achi,* our direct knowledge of the text goes back no farther than an 1862 publication based on an 1850 manuscript whose fate is unknown.

Many of the speeches in the older *Saq K'oxol* play, like those in *Rabinal Achi,* open with exclamations that were probably taken from traditional formal oratory. Such openings are absent from the Popol Vuh and other narrative texts of the colonial period, perhaps because those texts, unlike the plays, were not composed with a large audience in mind. The commonest exclamation in both plays, which is used on both sides of a dialogue, is *Ye'ja!* It is spoken twice each time it is used in *Saq K'oxol,* but in *Rabinal Achi* it is usually spoken just once. Among its possible sources is the imperative verb *ye'ja',* "Make haste!"[24] But it also calls to mind *ye',* "yes," and *ja,* "What?" It is shortened to *E'ja!* in some passages of the version of *Rabinal Achi* that was published in 1862 and throughout the 1913 manuscript version. When José León Coloch trains actors or plays a role himself, he always says *E'ja!* He commented that this word exists only in the play, where "it means, 'Listen to me.' It is used to get the attention of the other person." In performance the vowels are drawn out, with a high pitch on the first one and a downward glide on the second.

In *Saq K'oxol,* as in *Rabinal Achi,* the exclamations that open speeches are often followed by invocations of divine powers. At the end of *Saq K'oxol* all the Indians except for the one in the title role accept baptism, but before that they often call upon *Unik'ajal Kaj, Unik'ajal Ulew,* "Center of the Sky, Center of the Earth," followed by *Cho, Palo,* "Lake, Sea." Lastly they pair *Inup,* "Ceiba Tree," with *Kaq Ja,* "Red House" (the term for a pyramid and the temple on top),[25] both of which reach from the earth toward the sky. All three of these couplets are epithets that could have been combined with the proper names of specific deities in actual prayers. In *Rabinal Achi* the invocations never go beyond "Sky" and "Earth," but they could have been longer at some time in the past. Even if no additional lines were actually uttered, the audience could have imagined how they would go.

None of the passages shared by the two plays runs longer than a pair of parallel lines. It is possible that some of the couplets in question were borrowed from one of the plays by the composers of the other, but they are probably older than either play, belonging to the stock-in-trade of traditional verbal artists. For example, references to *oxlajuwinaq q'ij* and *oxlajuwinaq aq'ab'*, "thirteen score days" and "thirteen score nights," would have their source in the prayers of Quiché diviners called *ajq'ij* or "daykeepers," who continue to use such lines today.[26] Both scripts have couplets based on the parallel terms *tz'aq*, "earthworks" or "fortress," and *k'oxtun*, "walled or fenced enclosure," and the same terms are paired in Quiché narratives written in the sixteenth century.[27] *Rabinal Achi* differs from *Saq K'oxol* and from the earlier texts in modifying both these terms with *nimal*, "great," nearly every time they occur.

The meaning of one of the couplets that occurs in both plays has been a source of controversy. Cawek uses it in his opening speech, calling Lord Five Thunder a *worom ajaw, k'aqom ajaw*. The primary meaning of *woro-* is "to pierce, bore a hole through," but it can also mean "to sodomize"; with the suffix *-m* it becomes "pierced" or "sodomized."[28] The term that runs parallel to *worom* is rendered as "cakom" in Brasseur de Bourbourg's version of the *Rabinal Achi* text and "kaqom" in Munro S. Edmonson's composite version of the *Saq K'oxol* texts. Both Brasseur and Edmonson take this word to be a form of *kaq* or *kaqo*, which literally means "red" and is used in various idioms expressing hate or envy. Brasseur translates the couplet as "prince infâme, prince odieux" and adds a footnote about sodomy in which he describes Cawek as a "perceur" rather than as "percé," thus treating *worom* as if it were active rather than passive. Anita Padial Gerchoux and Manuel Vázquez-Bigi, whose Spanish version of the script is based on Brasseur's French, chose the words "príncipe lascivo, príncipe odioso" and added a note glossing *worom* as "penetrador." Edmonson, who got the passive construction right, has "a pierced lord, a red lord."[29]

A problem shared by all these treatments of the couplet is that no dictionary of K'iche', whether colonial or modern, testifies to the use of the suffix *-m*, which is properly attached to verb stems, with *kaqo*, which is an adjective. The attested form that bears the closest resemblance to Brasseur's "cakom" and Edmonson's "kaqom" is *k'aqom*, in which *k'aqo-*, "to shoot with an arrow or dart" or "to lance," is suffixed to mean "shot" or "lanced."[30] As a term in parallel construction with *worom*, meaning "pierced," *k'aqom* makes infinitely better sense than the unattested form that has been taken to mean "odious" or "red." Georges Raynaud, who produced a revision of Brasseur's translation, went some distance toward this improved reading of the couplet. His unpublished manuscript has been lost, but it served as the basis for the Spanish translation of Cardoza y Aragón, who has "jefe perferador, jefe lanzador."[31] Thus the idea of lancing comes through, but the error of reading passive forms as active remains.

The most recent French translation of *Rabinal Achi* is that of Alain Breton, who rendered the couplet as *worom ajaw, k'aqom ajaw* and got the grammar right, arriving at "souverain transpercé, souverain perforé."[32] There remains the question of just what Cawek means when he describes Lord Five Thunder in this manner. If he means to be insulting, he might still be saying that his adversary has been sodomized. Or he might be saying that the lord has already been wounded—pierced by an arrow, dart, or lance—or that he is so unlikely to be the victor in an engagement that he might as well have been pierced already. The trouble with such interpretations is that these men are armed with axes, not with weapons that pierce.

An alternative interpretation, offered by Breton, is that the couplet is not insulting to Lord Five Thunder but rather refers to the pierced nose that was one of the markers of lordly status among the Quiché and their neighbors. This is consistent with the meaning of *k'aqo-*, which refers specifically to shooting or lancing by means of a projectile point made of stone. In the present context it would mean that the lord whose nose has been pierced *(worom)* has also been penetrated by a stone *(k'aqom)*. The stone in question would not be a projectile but rather an ornament of the kind Mesoamerican lords wore in their noses and lips.[33] Thus the "pierced" lord would also be a "bejeweled" lord.

The notion that the couplet honors Lord Five Thunder is confirmed by the *Saq K'oxol* script, where it is used in a context that clarifies its meaning. In that play a lord, speaking to his daughter, first addresses her by saying, *Witzitzil, at ixoq ajaw,* "Hummingbird, you are a lady," thus reminding her that she is of noble birth (literally a "female lord"). Then he adds, *at b'a ranab' worom ajaw, k'aqom ajaw,* "you are also the sister of a pierced lord, a lanced (or bejeweled) lord."[34] Given the context, he cannot mean this as an insult; rather, he is continuing to describe his daughter as a woman of high status. His point is that her brother is not only of noble birth like herself, but has achieved the status of a man whose septum and lower lip have been pierced so that he can wear the ornaments of a true lord.

To all of this it should be added that if the customs of highland Guatemala were like those of the Mexican plateau, then the piercing of noses and lips for the wearing of ornaments was not an automatic privilege of lordly birth but was restricted to men who had taken a captive in battle. In that case, Cawek would be recognizing Five Thunder both as a lord and as a successful warrior—in other words, as a worthy opponent.

DANCES OF THE TRUMPETS

From the late sixteenth to the early eighteenth century, plays similar to *Rabinal Achi* were performed in numerous Mayan communities. Their existence is revealed by the reports of Spanish officials, both civil and religious, who saw them as a threat to the colonial order. The identifying features of these plays include music played on wooden trumpets and a drum; characters costumed as a warrior, puma, jaguar, and eagle; and the representation of the sacrifice of a warrior.

References to these suspect plays nearly always include the word *tun* or *tum*, referring to the trumpets, and sometimes its meaning is specified, as in the phrase "el baile de trompetas tun."[35] The trumpets are described as making "a horrible and sad sound" that struck fear into those who heard it.[36] This is consistent with the way the sound is described by the prisoner in the Rabinal play, who speaks of hearing *uk'oq lotzo tun*, "the sorrowful sound of the blood-letter's trumpet." The phrase *lotzo tun* takes such forms as *Loj tum*, *Lox tum*, and *Ox tum* when it names plays in colonial documents. One of the Rabinal play's terms for a prisoner of war, *teleche'*, is also used, either by itself or in the title *Tum teleche'*. The word *ulew* or "earth," which the Rabinal characters use in countless invocations of divine forces, appears in the title *Ni ulew tum*, "Great Earth Trumpets." This particular play is reported for the province of Verapaz, where Rabinal is located. The Rabinal play itself still carries the alternative title *Xajoj tun*, "Dance of the Trumpets."

If the characters in colonial dances of the trumpets were organized in the same manner as in *Rabinal Achi*, they contrasted with the plays scripted by missionaries not only in their content, but in their overall structure. The characters in *Carlomagno* are equally divided between warring Christians and Moors, while in *Saq K'oxol* they are equally divided between Spaniards and Indians. In the deer dances the characters are on generally friendly terms, but they are equally divided between two groups whose members pair off when they participate in dialogues or dances, with deer and beasts of prey on both sides. The contrasting structure of *Rabinal Achi*, in which all the characters except the prisoner are on the same side, would seem to be a direct reflection of the play's roots in court rituals that were centered on a prisoner of war.

Nearly all the colonial documents that mention dances of the trumpets either argue that they should be banned, announce an actual ban, or deny a request to lift a ban that is currently in effect. Performances were first prohibited in 1593, with the next known prohibitions coming in 1624, the centenary of the Spanish conquest of the Quiché kingdom, and in 1625.[37] In 1631 a plea for a ban on a similar drama was made by a missionary outside Guatemala, who stated that the Chontal Maya of Tabasco were performing representations of human sacrifice in which one of the actors played a jaguar.[38] In Guatemala itself, new bans were issued or appeals to lift old ones were denied in 1632, 1650, 1678, 1679, 1684, 1748, 1749, and 1770. Behind some of the earlier bans was the worry that public representations of sacrifice might be masks for real sacrifices carried out in private. Later it was argued that Indians should be cut off from the memory of their pre-Christian mode of existence in general.

Several bans were aimed at Quiché towns along the Pacific piedmont, among them San Antonio Suchitipéquez, San Bernardino, Samayac, Mazatenango, San Martín Zapotitlán, and Retalhuleu. The ban of 1625 covered the entire province of Verapaz and thus applied to Rabinal. Cakchiquel towns affected by prohibitions included Patulul, in the Pacific piedmont, together with Alotenango and San Miguel (formerly San Juan) Milpa Dueñas, in the highlands. The latter pair of towns is located just outside of what was then the capital of Guatemala, known today as Antigua.

Efforts to suppress dances of the trumpets put the early missionaries in an awkward position, since they themselves had devoted a good deal of energy to the development of local theater productions. This was particularly so in the Verapaz region, where the Dominican order had made tactical compromises with local beliefs and customs. Most of the attempts to suppress dances of the trumpets were initiated by clerics, but the 1625 proclamation affecting Verapaz was addressed to Dominicans by a civil official. He complained that there were too many dances in general, and that the Indians who participated in them were wasting time that ought to be spent working for Spanish landowners and squandering money that ought to be saved for making tribute payments to the Spanish crown. However the Dominicans may or may not have responded to his proclamation at the time, present-day Rabinal surpasses all other Mayan towns in the number and variety of its dance productions.[39]

THE PRISONER OF WAR AS A PROPHET

Unlike mystery plays, miracle plays, the Deer Dance, *Moros y cristianos, Carlomagno,* and *La conquista,* dances of the trumpets represented a world in which Europeans had no role. Performances created a time and space, however brief and bounded, where characters could not be made to cite the Bible, recite Christian doctrine, or use Christian names to invoke divine powers. Not only that, but there could be no final scene in which they were all converted to Christianity. But even a setting of this kind left an opening for the construction of an explicit link to the Christian world, on the model of the prophecies that Christians interpret as linking the Old Testament to the New. No such link is present in the version of the dance of the trumpets now known as *Rabinal Achi,* but an eighteenth-century account of a different version has it ending with a prophecy of the Spanish invasion.

The writer who described the prophetic Dance of the Trumpets is Fray Francisco Ximénez, a Dominican who served as parish priest in Chichicastenango, Rabinal, and Sacapulas between 1701 and 1729. He is also the source of the oldest known text of the Popol Vuh, having made a copy from an earlier text during his stay in Chichicastenango. Shortly after leaving his next post, in Rabinal, he began writing his voluminous *Historia de la Provincia de San Vicente de Chiapa y Guatemala.*[40] In the early chapters of this work, which concern the history of the Quiché kingdom, he depends almost entirely on his knowledge of the Popol Vuh. But then, when he comes to the last generations before the Spanish invasion, he turns to a new source, a dance in which a warrior is sacrificed. True to the Dominican tradition, he tries not to make this dance sound alarming, stating that "the Quiché Indians…no longer do it with as much superstition and sorcery as formerly."[41]

The version of the play outlined by Ximénez seems more appropriate for an audience close to the ancient Quiché capital than for an audience in Rabinal, suggesting that he was relying, at least in part, on what he learned about it during his stay in Chichicastenango.[42] His renegade warrior is not a Quiché with a record of offenses against the Rabinal king, but rather a Cakchiquel with a record of offenses against the Quiché king, and the warrior who defeats this renegade is not from Rabinal but from Quiché. Ximénez titles his play "quichevinac" after the victor, a name whose equivalent in the Rabinal version, *Kaweq K'eche Winaq* (Cawek of the Forest People), belongs to the vanquished.

Like Cawek in the Rabinal play, the renegade of the Ximénez play causes a disturbance outside the fortress of those who eventually capture and sacrifice him: "He was coming at night to the buildings of Quiché, where the king was sleeping, and was letting out great yells and shouts, addressing many insults and affronts to the king." He called the king *mama k'aixon* or "sold-out grandfather," implying that the king's relatives had profited from the sale of his favors,[43] and named him *K'otuja,* "Noble Bathhouse," after the Quiché king who survived an attempt to assassinate him while he was taking a bath.[44] In the Rabinal play the king is called "grandfather" not only by the captive but by the captor as well, and without the attached insult. There is talk of a bath incident, but instead of being evoked by the name Noble Bathhouse it is openly discussed, with the king casting himself in the role of the bather and Cawek casting himself in the role of the attacker.

Ximénez describes the renegade of his play as a sorcerer who was magically "going by a single leap to another mountain." This is his fanciful version of what is described in the Rabinal play as a boundary-marking expedition carried out by Cawek, who progresses mountain by mountain. Ximénez writes further that the renegade's rival "was doing the same thing, and following him at a great distance," and "he had to seize him with great care, because he was breaking the cords with which he tied him." This is consistent with the Rabinal play except in the breaking of the cords. When the captive admitted to the king that "it was he who was making cries at night," the king told him, "Well then, you will see what a fiesta we will make of you." The king "organized a dance to celebrate the capture of that sorcerer," and the dancers "transformed themselves into eagles, lions, and jaguars," whose role it was to sacrifice the prisoner.

No women appear in the Ximénez version of the play, nor is there any discussion of the fact that it would have been better for the captive if he had become an in-law rather than an enemy. And when this captive makes an ominous speech to his captors at the end of the play, he does not maneuver them into the roles of lords of Xibalba, nor does he imply that his descendants will one day avenge him after the manner of the divine heroes who overcame the lords of Xibalba. Instead he makes a direct prophecy of a calamitous invasion by "very terrible and cruel men" who will be "clothed, not naked like ourselves." Ximénez comments, "There is no doubt that this was a prophecy of the coming of the Spaniards, and that God allowed it to be announced to them through the mouth of this sorcerer." Here he expresses the central paradox of clerical thinking about the invasion. On the one hand, it was a matter of Church doctrine that native diviners, interpreters of dreams, and readers of omens were false prophets whose messages originated with the devil. On the other hand, the Church's theory of history demanded that the invasion, as a major event in the progress of Christianity, must have been prefigured or prophesied in some way, even as the events of the New Testament are anticipated in the Old.[45] The solution was to allow one correct message, and one only, to pass through the mouths of native "sorcerers": the message that their world would end and that of Christianity would begin.

The notion that the European invasion fulfilled a prophecy receives more attention in European accounts than it does in highland Mayan ones. No aura of prophecy is conferred on the invaders by the Quiché authors of the Popol Vuh, who instead make a point of stating that diviners of the pre-invasion era made accurate predictions of future events in general, and that they did so by consulting a book of the kind Mayans had possessed since ancient times.[46] Further, the European imagination is at work in Ximénez' notion that the natives, who in fact possessed one of the oldest cotton-growing and textile-weaving traditions in the world, were naked until the coming of Europeans, whom he styles as "men of cloth." The same imagination is at work when he has his prophet saying that the invaders "will destroy all these buildings and leave them converted into the habitat of owls and foxes." There are analogous passages in the Rabinal play, but they are different in two ways. First, the depopulated places of the Rabinal script become the habitats not of literal owls and foxes but of metaphorical katydids and crickets, which contrast with the honey bees (productive subjects) needed to sustain the rulers of a fully-functioning hive. Second, the cause of abandonment is not an attack but a revolt, and the person responsible is not a Spaniard but a Quiché.

DANCES OF THE TRUMPETS TODAY

The dance dramas that were the objects of bans during the colonial period have present-day descendants in several Mayan communities other than Rabinal. Contemporary productions in which performers carry tall backpacks resembling those of Rabinal have been reported for the Guatemalan Mayan towns of Chichicastenango, where the language is K'iche'; Santa Cruz Verapaz, where Poqomchi' is spoken; Nebaj, Chajul, and Cotzal, all of which speak Ixil; Aguacatán, which speaks Awakateko, a language closely related to Ixil; and San Juan Ixcoy, which speaks Q'anjob'al.[47] For each of these dances the instruments include a slit drum, and the use of trumpets is reported for Chajul and Aguacatán. Except for Chichicastenango, all these towns are like Rabinal in being on or near the northern frontier of what was the Quiché kingdom and the southern boundary of the region whose Classic-period culture was that of the lowland Maya. Despite their language differences, they may once have been more closely linked than they are today. Chajul, together with the nearby K'iche'-speaking town of Cunén, is mentioned in the dialogue of *Rabinal Achi*.

In the Aguacatán dance there are two performers with backpacks, as in Rabinal, but they are masked rather than veiled, they carry an ax and shield rather than going empty-handed, and they have speaking parts instead keeping silent. In Chajul there are four carriers of backpacks. The dramatic aspects of these dances have not have been reported in detail, but at least two of them have a story line resembling that of *Rabinal Achi*. In the case of Santa Cruz Verapaz, the performance is said to concern a prince who was pursued into the forest by magicians who wanted to sacrifice him. In Chajul it is said to concern the death of a man named Oyeb, whose name suggests the many Rabinal speeches in which Cawek is addressed as *oyew achi*, "brave man." Oyeb, instead of being captured by a warrior, is shot by a hunter, and instead of dancing with a maiden who could be the sister of his captor or the daughter of his captor's lord, he is rescued by the hunter's daughter and becomes her lover. In the end, instead of being decapitated with axes, Oyeb is done in by the prayers of a priest-shaman hired by the hunter.

In Chajul, Oyeb has the power to transform himself into a hummingbird, and *Tz'unum* or "Hummingbird" is the title of the Aguacatán play.[48] In Rabinal, Cawek compares himself to a bird (though not a hummingbird), and he drinks a kind of pulque named *Ixta Tz'unun,* "Quick Hummingbird." When human beings were sacrificed in Mesoamerica they were given an intoxicating drink whose active ingredients included more than alcohol. Whatever may have been added to Quick Hummingbird, it had the effect of bringing dreams.[49] As for hummingbirds, they were widely regarded as the souls of dead warriors, and in pulque-producing areas today they are compared to the human tapsters who drain the sap from the stems of maguey flowers.[50] Such is the complex of ancient ideology and practice that lies behind the drink given to the condemned man in the Rabinal play, the hummingbird transformations of the hunted hero of the Chajul play, and the name, at least, of the Aguacatán play.

In both Chajul and Aguacatán the dancing alternates with intervals during which the performers engage in dialogue or sing songs, using both Spanish and the local language. The same may be true for the other plays in which some of the characters carry backpacks, but in no case is the present-day existence of a script reported.

On the Pacific piedmont, in the Quiché towns of San Bernardino and Samayac, there are dances that retain the use of a slit drum but not the trumpets, and in which no backpacks are carried. The performers do not engage in dialogue and their actions are not plotted.[51] Instead, they burlesque contemporary life by means of improvised mimes. The Samayac performance, however, includes at least one detail that could be a fragment from an ancient drama. When the dancers move through the streets in procession, they bring with them a model of a Mayan house of a kind now rarely seen along the Pacific coast, with wooden walls and a thatched roof. It is filled with fireworks, and they set fire to it when they reach the plaza.[52] This recalls the Popol Vuh episode in which Hunahpu and Xbalanque disguise themselves as vagabond actors. In one of their performances, they set fire to a house and then restore it.[53]

The present state of the dance dramas of San Bernardino and Samayac may not be the result of a replacement of tragedy with comedy, but rather of the survival of the comic aspects of what were once composite performances. In Rabinal the comic possibilities of *Rabinal Achi* are exploited by a separate group of performers called *Ajq'eq* or "Los Negritos."[54] At present this group appears during the Christmas season, a month ahead of the fiesta whose events include proper renditions of *Rabinal Achi,* but there could have been a time when comic interludes were intermingled with high seriousness rather than being relegated to a separate occasion, whether in this or in other dances of the trumpet in other places. Examples of composite productions, including satires of serious performers by clowns, abound among the Pueblo peoples of what is now the Southwest United States, where Spanish interventions had far less impact on dance dramas than they did farther south.[55] For that matter, even the European theater tradition drawn upon by Spanish missionaries had room for comic relief.

The satiric version of *Rabinal Achi* violates the boundaries between real life and rehearsals, between rehearsals and performances, between musicians and actors, and even between one character and another. It begins when an actor sleeps with the wife of a musician. Next, when both men attend a rehearsal, the musician pretends that he is the actor and the actor is the musician, and that it is he who has slept with the other's wife. Then they argue as to which of them is to act in the play and which is to play an instrument. Both of them end up acting, one taking the role of Cawek of the Forest People and the other that of Man of Rabinal, but in the process of quoting from one another's speeches, as happens in a proper performance of the play, they become confused as to which of them is playing which role. Their roles become clear to the audience only when Cawek lies dead, at which point Rabinal upbraids him for failing to keep on dancing.

Scripts and Voices

FROM MANUSCRIPT TO PRINT

It was Charles Étienne Brasseur de Bourbourg, a priest and antiquarian of Flemish descent, who first brought the text of *Man of Rabinal* into print, accompanied by a facing-page French translation.[1] As a traveler and sojourner in Mesoamerica, the interest that guided him was the acquisition of manuscripts bearing on the antiquities of the region. He arrived in Guatemala City on February 1, 1855, and by March he was writing letters to friends about his discoveries there. At the library of the University of San Carlos he found manuscript volumes containing the writings of Francisco Ximénez, the Dominican friar who had served as parish priest in Rabinal and other Mayan towns in 1701-1729.[2] What attracted Brasseur most was a volume in which Ximénez had included a grammar of the K'iche' language, written by himself, and the text of a major work by Quiché authors, to which he had added a Spanish translation. The title Ximénez chose for this work was *Las historias del orígen de los indios de esta provincia de Guatemala,* but Brasseur would one day make it famous under a K'iche' title: Popol Vuh *(Popol Wuj),* meaning "Council Book."

The original Popol Vuh was a hieroglyphic book, but the version that comes down to us, written between 1554 and 1558, is in the roman alphabet. Its authors were among the first Mayans to use this writing system for their own language. The first Spaniard to become aware of their work, in 1701 or shortly thereafter, was Ximénez, who saw it in Chichicastenango while serving as the parish priest there. He made a copy, but it was not until after he was transferred to a post in Rabinal, in

1704, that he assembled the volume in which his Spanish translation appears together with the K'iche' text. He left Rabinal in 1715, but the volume remained in the Dominican convent there. Later, on a page he had left blank, someone named E. Chávez wrote words of praise for the Dominican order, giving the date as August 14, 1734, and naming the place where he did this as Rabinal.[3] In 1829, with the coming of the liberal reforms that followed independence from Spain, monastic orders were expelled and their convents were closed. The contents of convent libraries were taken to the University of San Carlos, where, for the first time, they came to the attention of scholars whose agendas differed from those of missionaries. Brasseur happened to be a priest, but his research interests were secular.

After three months in Guatemala, Brasseur accepted a temporary post as parish priest in Rabinal. We do not know what his other options might have been, but given the research he had already done, he would have ranked Chichicastenango and Rabinal very high as places where he might be able to further his interests. Among other things, he wanted to learn the K'iche' language and retranslate the Popol Vuh into French. He took the Ximénez volume with him to Rabinal, and whatever the circumstances under which he removed it from the library at the University of San Carlos, he never returned it. He assumed his duties as parish priest on May 17, 1855, and he lost no time in continuing his pursuit of antiquities. On May 28 he was taken to the ruins on Red Mountain, the site of Lord Five Thunder's fortress in *Rabinal Achi*. By June 3 he had heard about the play and was on the track of a manuscript that was supposed to contain its text. Apparently he never came into possession of this manuscript, but by August 7 he had managed to take down the text of the play in his own hand. He was told that it had not been performed for some thirty years, but with his encouragement and financial support a new production was mounted in time for the town's 1856 fiesta. The main celebration fell on January 25, day of the conversion of St. Paul, but public performances of the play began on January 19, the eve of the day of St. Sebastian.

Brasseur left Rabinal in May 1856, and he departed Guatemala for Paris early in 1857. The manuscripts and notes he took with him became the basis of a series of publications under the general title *Collection de documents dans les langues indigènes.* The first volume, appearing in 1861, was *Popol Vuh: Le livre sacré et les mythes de l'antiquité américaine, avec les livres héroïques des Quichés.* The second volume, which appeared in 1862, was divided into two parts. First came *Grammaire de la langue quichée,* based almost entirely on Ximénez but bearing Brasseur's name, followed by *Rabinal-Achi ou le drame-ballet du tun.*[4]

There has been much discussion of what seem to be two different story lines in Brasseur's accounts of his acquisition of the text of the Rabinal play.[5] One story is that he took it down in dictation from Bartolo Sis of Rabinal, who had acted in the play and knew all the speaking parts from memory, and the other is that his source was a manuscript in the possession of this same Bartolo Sis. Whether one reads the letters Brasseur wrote while he was still in Guatemala or his 1862 publication, the same supposed contradiction appears.[6] In other words, it is not as though he said one thing in private correspondence and another in print. Partly for this reason I suspect that both stories are true, which is to say that they actually form two different threads in the same story.[7] My other reason is that both stories make sense in terms of my own experience as the collector of the text of a play in a Quiché town.

During October of 1976, while Barbara Tedlock and myself were doing field work in the Quiché town of Momostenango, we became curious about a play known locally as *Xajoj K'oy* or "Monkey Dance."[8] It was Andrés Xiloj Peruch, a priest-shaman who was tutoring us in the ways of a diviner at the time, who first brought the play to our attention. He arranged an interview with the owner of the script, who was responsible for teaching the performers their lines. At our first meeting this man opened the pages of his manuscript in front of us but did not let it out of his hands. It was typewritten on ruled paper and bound in a notebook. Yes, he had once been in possession of a handwritten version, but it had become so worn and stained that in 1950 he had asked the town secretary to transcribe it, after which he had thrown it away.[9]

After awhile the man consented to recite the script of the Monkey Dance so that we could make a tape recording. As he spoke he kept his notebook open and turned its pages, but I could see from my side of the table that he did not keep his eyes fixed on the text at all times, and that his recitation tended to run a little ahead of his page turning. When I asked him to repeat one of the speeches later, he did so without bothering to look it up. He obviously knew the entire text by heart. This was all the more impressive because it was mostly in Spanish, a language in which he was far from fluent. When I showed him a passage about monkeys from the Popol Vuh he turned out to be a slow reader, piecing it together word by word whether he was looking at the K'iche' text or its Spanish translation.

At a second meeting we tried to persuade this man to let us make a photocopy of his notebook in the nearest town that had a machine, almost two hours away. The answer was no, not even if we took him with us. But then Xiloj asked him if he would let us make a copy by hand. Now the answer was yes, on the condition that the work would be done then and there. For the first time he allowed me to handle the notebook, but he never let it out of his sight during the whole time I copied it out with pen and paper. He remarked that he never lets the actors have copies of their parts. Instead he reads their lines aloud at rehearsals and they repeat after him, on and on until they all have their parts memorized. Later, in Rabinal, I would learn that the director of *Rabinal Achi* follows the same procedure at his own rehearsals, reading to the actors while keeping the script to himself.

This is not a story about print culture, in which copies can be produced in any number, but rather about manuscript culture, in which the limit on the number of copies existing at a given time is more important than the issue of which copy is the "original." Further, in the case of the owner of the Monkey Dance script, it is not a story about the kind of literacy in which reading ability is readily transferable from one text to another, but rather about the kind of literacy that is transmitted together with the oral recitation of a particular text. He knew the names of his predecessors going back four generations, and what came down this line of transmission at every stage was not only written but spoken. If something ever happened to his notebook it would not be the words of the play that were lost. Rather, his authority as a transmitter of these words would be diminished. The present director of *Rabinal Achi* happens to be highly literate, but he, too, has come to his present state of knowledge not only by seeing the words of his play but by hearing and speaking them on multiple occasions.

Returning to the case of Brasseur, we can see him moving in on the manuscript of *Rabinal Achi* but encountering obstacles. It is easy to imagine that Bartolo Sis, the owner of this manuscript, was more willing to dictate the words to him than to let him handle the document itself. Judging from the cases of the present-day owners of the Monkey Dance and Rabinal scripts, Sis was handling Brasseur in the same way he would have handled actors at a rehearsal—with the difference that Brasseur was writing down what Sis said to him instead of memorizing it. When he asked Sis to repeat passages so that he could check his work for errors, it must have become apparent to him that Sis knew the play from memory. The fact that he was taking dictation rather than copying a text accounts for his claim that his work with Sis ran on for twelve days. Toward the end Sis may have relaxed his guard enough to allow Brasseur to check his transcription directly against the manuscript, but only while they were present together.

So great was Brasseur's talent for acquiring manuscripts that the existence of the Sis manuscript has been questioned on the grounds that no such item was found in Brasseur's collection after his death. Here I would point out that Brasseur never claimed to have acquired it. Not only that, but on the occasion when he finally got a close look at it, it would have lost much of its appeal to him as a collector. As he indicates in his 1862 publication, it was only a copy of the "original," a copy that Sis himself had made. It bore the date October 28, 1850, and thus was less than five years old when Brasseur saw it.[10] He doubtless inquired after the whereabouts of the original, but he may well have received an answer something like the one I got when I asked about the fate of the manuscript that preceded the 1950 typescript of the Monkey Dance.

Whether or not Brasseur got a close look at the Sis manuscript, the version of the play he published has a number of features that are consistent with other plays whose texts have been transmitted by manuscript in the Mayan towns of Guatemala. In his script there are only occasional stage directions in the facing-page French translation and even fewer in the pages with the original text; in other scripts stage directions are sparse or nonexistent. His dialogue is preceded by a list of characters that neither follows the order of their appearance nor reflects the size of their share in the dialogue or action, and the same is true of most other scripts. In the case of *Rabinal Achi,* either of these two ways of ordering characters would have meant a list headed by Cawek of the Forest People (Brasseur's "Queche-Achi") and Man of Rabinal, but instead it is headed by Lord Five Thunder, the character who ranks first in social status. In the same way, lists of characters for *Carlomagno* are not headed by Oliveros and his Turkish rival Fierabrás, who have leading roles but are mere knights, but by the kings they serve, Carlomagno and Balán.

Nearly all the labels for the speaking parts in Brasseur's script combine the name of the character with the verb *kach'aw,* "speaks," and an ordinal number. Thus the first speech of Man of Rabinal is labeled "U nabemul ca chau Rabinal-Achi," or "Man of Rabinal speaks for the first time"; his second speech is labeled "U camul ca chau Rabinal-Achi," or "Man of Rabinal speaks for the second time"; and so forth. In contrast, the parts in the script for the Monkey Dance of Momostenango are simply labeled with the names of the characters. The same is true for most Guatemalan scripts, but there are exceptions. In one version of the Deer Dance, one of *Carlomagno,* and at least one of *Saq K'oxol,* some (but not all) of the part labels follow the name of the character with Spanish verbs of speaking such as "habla" or "dice."[11]

No manuscript reported for Guatemala comes close to matching Brasseur's published version of *Rabinal Achi* in the extent to which its part labels include verbs. This could be the result of his editorial interventions, but it could also reflect the manner in which Bartolo Sis dictated the speeches to him. When Sis was about to begin a given speech, he may well have uttered a sentence in which the subject was the name of a character and the predicate was the verb *kach'aw,* "speaks." When a speaker of his language wishes to mark a statement as a quotation, this particular verb is the likeliest one to be chosen.

There remains the problem of the numbering of the parts in Brasseur's text. The numbers run in a separate series for each character, which has the effect of producing some passages in which the numbers assigned to one of the parties to a dialogue are strikingly divergent from the numbers assigned to the other. For example, when Lord Five Thunder speaks for the first, second, and third time, he is responding to the ninth, tenth, and eleventh speeches of Man of Rabinal. Later, when Lord Five Thunder speaks for the fourth, fifth, and sixth time, he is responding to the eleventh, twelfth, and thirteenth speeches of Cawek of the Forest People. The numerical organization of these speaking events into separate series, as contrasted with the option of placing them all on a single time line, suggests the multiple rhythms of the Mayan calendar. The scheduling of rituals by means of the contemporary Quiché version of this calendar, as Xiloj taught us, involves keeping track of several independent series of dates. For example, the first, second, and third in a series of visits to a shrine on a high hilltop in Momostenango respectively follow the fourth, fifth, and sixth visits to a lower shrine.[12] However long ago numbers were given to the parts in *Rabinal Achi*, it seems likely that this was done by someone from Rabinal rather than by Brasseur. In the manuscript Sis read from, the numbers need not have been spelled out as parts of sentences, as they are in Brasseur's text. Rather, they could have taken the form of marginal notations in arabic numerals. Otherwise, the parts in his manuscript need not have been labeled with anything more than the names of the speakers for Sis to introduce a part to Brasseur by saying something like, *Julajujmul kach'aw Rab'inal Achi*, "Man of Rabinal speaks for the eleventh time."

There are two gaps in the numbers in Brasseur's published text, but until now they have passed unnoticed (or at least unremarked) by non-Mayan readers. The numbers are all in place up through the exchange where the fourth speech of Cawek of the Forest People is followed by the fifth speech of Man of Rabinal. But the next two speeches after that are labeled as Cawek's sixth and Rabinal's seventh, so that Cawek has no fifth speech and Rabinal has no sixth.[13] The solution to this mystery lies in the part of the text labeled as the fifth speech of Rabinal, which is suspiciously long—in fact, if it really did belong entirely to him, it would be the longest single speech in the entire play. In the early part of this speech Rabinal reacts to Cawek's previous statement and then raises a new question about Cawek's past actions, which fits the general pattern of the ongoing dialogue between them. But then, instead of waiting for an answer as he normally would, Rabinal supplies the answer himself. Next, in the last part of the speech, he reacts to his own answer and then raises a further question. It seems more than likely that the answer once constituted the fifth speech of Cawek, and that the reaction to the answer and the further question once constituted the sixth speech of Rabinal.

However it came about that three speeches were collapsed into one, someone reversed the use of the first and second persons in Cawek's fifth speech so that its grammar, if not its content, would fit Rabinal. For example, where the text now has Rabinal saying to Cawek, *Mi xtzaq apana la yeb'al la, sik'ib'al la,* "You delivered your announcement, sir, your cry, sir," a prior version would have had Cawek saying to Rabinal, *Mi xintzaq apana la nuyeb'al, nusik'ib'al,* "I delivered my announcement, my cry." The changes would have been made by someone attempting to deal with a version of the text in which something was missing or unreadable. It could have been a copyist in Rabinal, whether Sis or one of his predecessors, or it could have been Brasseur. I am inclined to think it was Brasseur, trying to make sense of his imperfect field notes in faraway Paris. Failing to notice the gap in the numbers of the speeches, he used his grammatical knowledge to switch the first and second persons wherever their use seemed inappropriate for what he decided must be a single long speech by Man of Rabinal.

The failure of Brasseur, his publishers, and subsequent readers to notice the missing speech numbers is, in my opinion, an effect of the difference between Mayan and European thinking about temporal sequences. By chance, the loss of these numbers creates a pattern that fits European methods of numbering: a speech labeled "fourth" (Cawek's) is immediately followed by others labeled "fifth" (Rabinal's), "sixth" (Cawek's), and "seventh" (Rabinal's). This sequence camouflages the error for a European reader, but not, as we shall see, for a Mayan reader in the town of Rabinal.

Brasseur chose a prose format for his text and translation, though it happens that among all the major works that date from the colonial period of Mesoamerican literature, *Rabinal Achi* is unsurpassed in the degree to which it is versified. In failing even to comment on its poetic form he was following in the footsteps of his Dominican and Franciscan predecessors of colonial times, who treated all indigenous discourse as prose whenever they transcribed or translated it. When they taught indigenous pupils how to adapt alphabetic writing to indigenous languages, they transmitted the prose format along with it. Such was the format for the scripts of *Saq K'oxol,* and the same format would have been used for the scripts of *Rabinal Achi* and other dances of the trumpets, all the way down to the one Bartolo Sis used when he read to Brasseur in 1855.

In the openings and closings of speeches Brasseur sometimes ends a sentence or two with an exclamation point rather than a period. Today the loudest lines in a given speech are more likely to occur at the beginning and end than anywhere else, so he may have been expressing his memory of what he heard in performances rather than reading a heightened rhetorical force into the transcribed words he saw before him. His occasional use of a row of four or five periods to separate sentences may express his memory of full and deliberate pauses, but such pauses must have occurred, as they do today, in many more places than between sentences.

58. From page 26 of Brasseur de Bourbourg's *Rabinal-Achi*.

FROM PRINT TO MANUSCRIPT TO PHOTOCOPY

The story of what happened in Rabinal after the departure of Brasseur has been pieced together by Carroll Edward Mace,[14] who has been studying the dance dramas of Rabinal and other Guatemalan towns since 1957. In 1862 Brasseur sent an inscribed copy of the book containing the text of *Rabinal Achi* to Nicolás López, who had been his servant and guide during his stay in Rabinal. Whatever the fate of the Sis manuscript or its predecessor, this book became the vehicle for the transmission of the speaking parts of the play. The book was handled with circumspection in the same way a manuscript would have been, and it became stained with candle drippings and the smoke of incense. A story went around that a man had once taken the book from its place without first praying before it, with the result that his arm became paralyzed.

As of 1913, the current owner of the book was charging the producers of the play a fee each time they used it. But in that year he allowed Manuel Pérez, the

59. Page 5 of the manuscript of Manuel Pérez.

director of the play at the time, to make a handwritten copy. Pérez wrote out the text (but not the translation) on the ruled pages of a school notebook with images of the *Niña, Pinta,* and *Santa María* sailing across the front cover and a multiplication table on the back. He preserved Brasseur's labels for the parts, complete with the gaps in the numbering, thus leaving Rabinal's long speech undivided.

By 1940 the Pérez notebook, along with the directorship of the play, had passed to Esteban Xolop. He was illiterate, but he knew all the parts well enough to teach them to the actors. In 1952 his son, Eugenio Xolop, copied the Pérez version.[15] Esteban instructed his son to do this work only at night, since the events in the play took place before the present sun first rose. His son noticed the problem with the numbering, but instead of dividing the long speech of Rabinal he renumbered the subsequent speeches, writing arabic numerals in the margins of the Pérez notebook.[16] A transcription of four speeches from Xolop's copy of Pérez has been published by René Acuña.[17] From this it is apparent that Xolop followed

Pérez word for word and line for line, even to the placement of the hyphens in words that are broken between one line and the next. It is as if he had been trying to duplicate the exactness of mechanical reproduction. His copy was eventually acquired by Acuña.[18]

After Esteban Xolop died in 1987, the Pérez notebook passed to his daughter María and her husband, José León Coloch, who became the producer and director of the play. He has solved the problem of wear and tear on the script by reading aloud from a bound photocopy at rehearsals. He prayed over this copy before he opened it and recited passages for me in 1988. In 1989, when he recited a long passage running all the way to the end of the play, he closed the cover when he finished and prayed. He followed the same sequence that can be heard in every town where Quichean languages are spoken, first addressing *Tiox*, the ultimate celestial deity; then *Juyub' Taq'aj* or "Mountain-Valley," the ultimate terrestrial deity; and finally *qatit qamam*, "our grandmothers our grandfathers," meaning ancestors in general. It was not the script as a physical object he was treating as sacred, but the act of giving life to the voices of the play's characters, who are themselves ancestral beings.

The Pérez and Xolop manuscripts have stirred some speculation that they might have their own line of connection, independent of Brasseur, that runs back to the Sis manuscript or some other source that antedates Brasseur.[19] This is because they give the appearance of following orthographic conventions that date from colonial times and are absent in Brasseur's book. On careful inspection, however, the Pérez manuscript betrays an intimate connection with the book. The contents of the page on which the dialogue begins in Pérez match the contents of the page on which it begins in Brasseur, with the titles of the play at the top and the last line ending in the midst of a speech by Man of Rabinal. On Brasseur's page (figure 58) this line ends with the first syllable of the word "ca-kom," which is broken by a hyphen and continued at the top of the next page of text.[20] Pérez chose to omit the dangling syllable (along with two French footnotes not shown in figure 58) from his version of the page (figure 59). With one exception (to be discussed later), his only other changes on this page are matters of word breaks, spelling, and punctuation.

The dialogue in the Pérez manuscript continues on the back side of the page where it begins, but each and every word of Brasseur's next page of dialogue is missing. It seems obvious that Pérez must have been working from a copy of Brasseur's book that was missing a leaf. It would have been the one that carries page 27 of the translation on the front side and page 28 of the original text on the back. This happens to be the first leaf in a new signature, the most likely one to

cablahuh chi abauab, e r'ahaual huhun chi tzak, huhun
chi qoxtun?. . . . . ؛ . ؛ : . . .

...... Ma-pa x-cha ri quitzih chike. « Chi pet–an Alak,
» alah, cablahuh chi oyeu alah, cablahuh chi achihab

60. Blank spaces in the Brasseur (top) and Pérez (bottom) versions of a passage in the
fourth speech of Man of Rabinal.

come loose in a book whose paper has become brittle with age and whose stitching
has loosened with heavy use.[21] As it happens, the lines that end page 26 and begin
page 30 both belong to the same speaker, so the loss of page 28 did not create as
much of a problem as might otherwise have been the case. The fact that Pérez did
not supply the missing passage by consulting his own or someone else's memory
suggests that there may have been a hiatus in the oral transmission of the play at
some point between the generations of Sis and Pérez.

There is other evidence for Pérez' close dependence on the book. Where
he leaves lines of his notebook paper blank in the midst of a speech he does so
at precisely the same places where the typesetter inserted blank lines in the
printed text (figure 60).[22] The purpose of the typesetter's blank lines was to
create a better visual balance between pages of original text and the facing pages
of translation. The text always ran shorter than the translation, but he often chose
to insert blank space in the midst of a text page rather than letting all of it fall at
the bottom. To do this he broke into the text at the end of a sentence, using a
long series of periods to fill out the rest of the line of type in question and
following it with blank space. Pérez inserted such fillers not only in these lines

but in many others as well, seeking to create the general effect of a justified right margin (figures 59 and 60).

Instead of using single periods to end sentences, as Brasseur did, Pérez used them as small-scale fillers, inserting them into most of the spaces he left between words (see figures 59-61). In the case of Brasseur's exclamation points and short rows of periods, he simply omitted them, entrusting matters of loudness and pausing to the oral transmission of the speeches.

The part of the text that falls at the top of page 116 in Brasseur's book is headed with the number 116 in the Pérez manuscript (figure 61), where it happens to come in the midst of a page.[23] Pérez did not copy any other page numbers, but perhaps he included this one because he was coming near the end of his task. It belongs to the next-to-last page of text, which carries all but seven of the lines of type belonging to the play's final speech.

There remains the question of colonial elements in the orthography used by Pérez. As can be seen from the table on the next page, there is actually only one case, that of Ɛ, in which he follows a colonial usage that is absent in Brasseur. When he replaces colonial k with Ɛ, he departs from colonial usage where Brasseur does not, and the same is true when he replaces colonial z with tz. In other cases he departs from colonial practice in the same way that Brasseur does, as when he uses q instead of colonial 4 or ɡ, t instead of colonial tt, ch instead of colonial 4h, and tz instead of colonial 4, . In the case of qu, which normally substitutes for c before e and i, he follows a practice unique to himself, reducing it to plain q and frequently using it where c would be the normal choice.[24]

In using Ɛ for two different sounds, Pérez follows a practice that is common in the spelling of Mayan surnames in the parish archives of Rabinal.[25] For example, in the names that appear as "CagueƐ" and "Ɛohom" in those archives, the Ɛ stands for a plain back k sound in the former case and a glottalized back k in the latter (respectively *q* and *q'* in the spelling of the Academia de las Lenguas Mayas de Guatemala).

Clearly, there is no need to imagine that Pérez saw a prior manuscript version of the play in order to account for his use of Ɛ, the one and only sign he could not have seen in Brasseur's book. He was simply following a spelling practice known locally. Further, he made no attempt to conceal his reliance on the book. He reproduced some of its blank lines and noted one of its page numbers. And instead of looking for paper that might recapture the look and feel of an old manuscript, he wrote on the ruled pages of a contemporary school notebook. That Western scholars should have thought this manuscript was

— 116 —

QUECHE-ACHI

UTUQUEL CA CHAUIC.

Yx, Cot, yx, Balam. « X-elic! » qu'yx cha cami....
Mana x-in el-tah; xa mi-x-in pixabah chi uloc u vach nu
huyubal, u vach nu tagahàl avi x-i bin-vi mi-x-i zilab-vi

116

qui che achi

utequel chic qachauic

ix got. ixBalam. xelic. quixcha.
mana xinel tah. xamixinpixa...
bah. chiculoE. uvach nutuyubal.

61. The top of page 116 in Brasseur's book (top) and the corresponding passage in the
Pérez manuscript (bottom).

ORTHOGRAPHIC VARIATIONS

COLONIAL	BRASSEUR	PÉREZ	ALMG*
c or qu	c or qu	c or q	k
4 or g	q	q	k'
k	k	Ɛ	q
Ɛ	g	Ɛ	q'
h	h	h	j
x	x	x	x
tt	t	t	t'
ch	ch	ch	ch
4h	ch	ch	ch'
z or ç	z	tz	s
tz	tz	tz	tz
4,	tz	tz	tz'

*Academia de las Lenguas Mayas de Guatemala

bringing them closer to an "original" tells us more about them than it does about Pérez. His purpose was to create a copy of the script that was both useful and authoritative, and his tools were a notebook and pen. In the process, he modified the book's orthography according to local practice and adapted its dotted space fillers to his own needs.

In matters of wording Pérez followed the book rather closely, but he did make some emendations. Here and there he tried to clarify words he found obscure, and he also made changes that increased the consistency of the wording. In the play's opening speech, for example, he changed Brasseur's *k'u xere* to *xa k'u xere,* which is something like changing "even so" to "but even so." In all the rest of Brasseur's text there is only one other instance in which *xa k'u xere* lacks its initial *xa,* and that happens to be on the page that was missing from the copy of the book used by Pérez. He added his *xa* while he was writing the line in which it appears (see figure 59) rather than squeezing it in later, so he may have been guided by his memory of past performances rather than by something he remembered reading.

In Brasseur's text the exclamation that opens most speeches takes the form "Yeha!" *(ye'ja)* in some places and "Eha!" *(e'ja)* in others, but Pérez decided to use "eha" throughout. To know for certain whether changes of this kind have played a more general role in the history of the play we would have to examine some of manuscripts that preceded the one Brasseur saw in 1855, but if they were anything like the 1726 version of *Saq K'oxol,* they would have displayed a greater variety of exclamations. "Yeha!" is common in that script, but a character who is agitated may begin with "Acay!" *(akay)* instead. Visitors announce themselves with "Cula!" *(kula'),* "It's a guest!" and the hosts reply with "Uve!" *(uwe'),* "Very well!" A character who is about to leave may begin a final speech with "Alelele!" *(alelele'),* "Away that way!"[26] Each of these contexts exists in *Rabinal Achi,* but the exclamations that go with them are absent.

Despite the fact that Pérez retained Brasseur's prose format, he inserted words and phrases that intensified existing parallel verse patterns and extended parallelism into passages where it had been lacking.[27] In this first example, from Cawek's seventh speech, Pérez added a word *(unimal)* to the second line of a couplet but stopped short of making a further addition *(chupam)* that would complete the parallel relationship between the two lines:

chupam unimal tz'aq	inside the great fortress
unimal k'oxtun	the great walls

In other places Pérez made additions that brought a couplet up to the level of full symmetry, as in this passage from the thirteenth speech of Cawek (the added word is underlined):

chuxe q'ij	beneath the sun
chuxe saq	beneath the light

In both of these examples Pérez supplemented the second line of a couplet by means of an analogy with the first line. But there are other cases in which his addition created a couplet where there was none before, as in this passage from the sixteenth speech of Cawek:

are b'a wa' nuqajom	the one I have borrowed
nuchaq'im	I've been loaned

Analogy is still at work here, but the model for the parallel relationship between *nuqajom* and *nuchaq'im* occurs in a different speech (Cawek's fifteenth).

Even without the filling in of couplets by Pérez, *Rabinal Achi* surpasses all other lengthy texts in Quichean languages in the degree of its insistence on parallel verse, and in the degree to which couplets prevail over alternative forms. There are a few triplets, such as this one from the fourth speech of Lord Five Thunder:

roq'ib'al utiw	the cries of coyotes
roq'ib'al yak	the cries of foxes
roq'ib'al utuy	the cries of agoutis

Pérez did not attempt even out such passages by adding a fourth line, but neither did he make any changes that increased the number of triplets. As for quatrains, such as this one from the fourth speech of Man of Rabinal, he kept them intact:

laq'a chuq'a nima kinak'	quickly gathering large beans
laq'a ixtapakal	gathering white-winged dove beans
laq'a kaqix koruwach	gathering red-feathered quail beans
laq'a tzuleyuji	gathering striped quail beans

We do not know to what extent Pérez made his decisions on the basis of what *sounded right* in terms of what he remembered hearing, and to what extent he made them on the basis of what *looked right* in terms of what he remembered reading. Whatever the proportion might have been, he contributed to a process of crystallization that must have begun long before Brasseur arrived on the scene. He increased the internal consistency of the text's poetic structure by reducing asymmetries within parallel couplets and by increasing the total number of couplets without adding to the number of triplets and quatrains. Similar processes have shaped other works that underwent long periods of combined oral and written transmission, among them the Homeric epics.[28]

Like Bartolo Sis before him, Manuel Pérez undertook the task of preserving an ancient play that was unique, by then, to his own town. Both of them worked under very different conditions from those of the scribes who participated in the spread of dances of the trumpets from one town to another during the height of their popularity, which roughly coincided with the seventeenth century. A period of growth requires the creation of a greater number of new manuscripts and interactions among a greater number of directors and actors than the preservation of one play in one town. The post-independence version of *La conquista* went through such a period relatively recently. Today it is performed in more than forty towns, and the known scripts number more than sixty. A comparison of scripts that date from the years 1872 to 1958 reveals that several of their creators went so far as to insert new speeches and even new characters.[29]

Among the obstacles standing in the way of further changes in the composition of the *Rabinal Achi* script is the entrance of mechanical reproduction into the chain of transmission. The first time this happened it took the form of a printed book. With Pérez there came a return to manuscript transmission, but his manuscript already has a successor: the bound photocopy Coloch uses at rehearsals. For a second time, then, mechanical reproduction has entered the process of transmission.

When the present photocopy begins to wear out another will be needed—unless, that is, the text undergoes revision at the hands of one or more of the many native speakers of Achi or other dialects of K'iche' who has been trained in linguistics in recent decades. One possibility is a revision that would move the text toward Achi as it is spoken today. Another possibility, one that would require a thorough knowledge of texts that date from the same general period in which *Rabinal Achi* has its roots, would move the text closer to the way it might have been spoken in earlier times, cautiously adjusting or clearing away some of the accumulated changes, ambiguities, and obscurities. A high standard for work of this kind has been set by the 1999 edition of the Popol Vuh text, prepared by Luis Enrique Sam Colop and produced by Cholsamaj, a Mayan publishing house in Guatemala City.[30] But either kind of work, it seems to me, should be carried out with the full knowledge and cooperation of José León Coloch, who knows more about how the play's performers should *sound* and how and when they should *move* than any other living person. Moreover, when he performs without looking at the script he becomes an active participant in the composition of the speeches, as will become apparent.

REHEARSING FROM THE SCRIPT

The characters in *Rabinal Achi* make speeches about times of war, but the performance of the play requires a time of peace. This is not only a matter of civil order in the Rabinal town center but also involves the freedom to walk freely and safely in the surrounding mountains and valleys. When Barbara Tedlock and I first visited Rabinal in 1988, the townspeople had recently emerged from a period in which the play could not be given. As Coloch explained it, "There are places for sacrifices. We can see Red Mountain, Water Jar Point, Henequen Mountain, Belted House, and Worn-out Trumpet Point. These are the important places where sacrifices are made before the presentation of the Dance of the Trumpets." All of them are mentioned in the play's dialogue. Just a few years before it had been too dangerous to complete the necessary visits. Between 1980 and 1983 the Guatemalan army had carried out massacres of civilians in at least nineteen different locations within the municipality of Rabinal, all but one of them rural.[31]

The sacrifices require the services of a Road Guide, a specialist in the rites of the indigenous religion. "There is a whole collection of things that are burned," Coloch said, "copal incense, white sugar, brown sugar, cigars, cigarettes, liquor, wine, chocolate, bread, and so on." The Road Guide not only walks the paths that lead to the shrines where he burns these offerings and prays over them, but later accompanies the actors and musicians to the sites of their performances, leading them in prayer each time they complete the play.

Coloch complains that it is not easy to recruit the actors. "When I invite people to take part in the dance," he says, "I tell them what the dance is about, that it is a very nice play and is appreciated by people from other towns." There are other plays, with more action and less dialogue, that get a bigger local turnout, so his point about the outside interest in *Rabinal Achi* is important to his argument. When Barbara Tedlock and myself witnessed and videotaped two performances in 1998, one was attended by a dramatist from Montreal and by a reporter and cameraman from a television station in Guatemala City, while the other was videotaped by an ethnographer from Mexico City. The production expenses were paid, in part, by the International Red Cross, whose representatives saw the continuation of the play as a reassertion of the town's vitality in the wake of the massacres of the early 1980s. As this book goes to press, Coloch is applying to the Guatemalan Ministry of Culture for the funding of future productions.

Rehearsals normally begin in October and run until the full-dress presentations of January. They are held at night, in the patio behind Coloch's house.[32] Participants are fed on these occasions, and if they come from remote hamlets they spend the night and get breakfast the next morning. In January they receive meals from any confraternities that may invite them to perform the play.

On the subject of his training methods Coloch remarked, "Some people accept the invitation but they want a copy of the play, and that cannot be done. Copies have never been given to the dancers. The play has to be heard, only. It has to be memorized from what is heard. It's the memory that does the work."[33] At each meeting of the actors, he said, "we rehearse the entire dance at once. We do not learn a few lines at a time, but the entire book. Each rehearsal takes about two and a half hours—if people come on time, that is." As they run through the script, "the people who play each character should be alert to their roles." They not only need to learn their own lines, but to pay attention to cues in the lines spoken by their counterparts. When, for example, the actor in the role of Man of Rabinal ends a speech by saying, "So say my words / before Sky / before Earth / since we haven't many words / to speak with you. / May Sky and Earth be with you / prisoner, captive," these lines do more than provide a highly formal frame for the speech he is bringing to a close. They also serve as a step-by-step countdown for the actor in the role of the said prisoner, who will be the next to speak.

The longest speeches in *Rabinal Achi* are the longest of any play performed in the Mayan towns of Guatemala, and longer than the great majority of speeches in the Western dramatic literature. Coloch nearly always takes the role of Cawek for himself because "he is the one who talks most in the play," with nineteen speeches as contrasted with twelve for Man of Rabinal, nine for Lord Five Thunder, and five for Slave. "Once I instructed someone else for that character and he didn't learn it," he recalled. "When I asked him what had happened, he told me that he had a lot of work to do. I didn't believe him and I asked again whether the problem was that he couldn't memorize his whole part. 'That is true,' he said." Coloch had tried to anticipate this problem by giving the man an early start. "I had instructed him from August to November. At that point what could I do? I was happy that someone could help me, but it didn't work out." So he ended up playing the role of Cawek himself, as usual.

In the first two performances of 1998 the actor playing the role of Man of Rabinal dropped a good many of his lines. For those listening closely the effects on the play's narrative were reduced by the fact that when Cawek and Rabinal are in dialogue, they quote from one another's speeches before they give their replies.

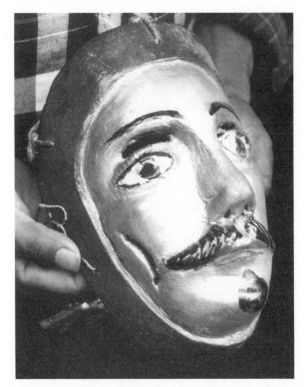

62. The mask of Cawek of the Forest People, held by José León Coloch.
Note the slot cut through the cheek.

Coloch, who knows Cawek's speeches quite well, was thus able to put some of the missing lines back in play simply by speaking his own part.

Before I had ever witnessed a performance of the play I asked Coloch whether the wearing of masks made it difficult for an audience to follow the dialogue. He insisted that "people can hear what is being said. I have been among the public, and I could hear what the actors were saying." This is because the masks for *Rabinal Achi*, unlike those for other plays, have crescent-shaped slots in the cheeks that let the sound out (figure 62). To demonstrate this Coloch brought Cawek's mask out of his house and stood opposite me in his patio (the same patio where rehearsals are held). Holding the mask over his face, he recited the play's opening speech, and he certainly proved his point. The space separating the mask from the face serves as a resonator, amplifying and deepening the voice, and every syllable comes out clearly. The effect on voice quality recalls that of the pre-electrical phonographs whose sound passed through a wooden resonating chamber.

Whatever the actors may say in public performances, what they say at rehearsals is subject to direct measurement against what their instructor says. He either has the current script open before him or has a reader available for consultation, as in the case of Esteban Xolop and his literate son Eugenio. When Coloch read sections of the play's dialogue aloud for me in 1988 (figure 63) and 1989, he kept track of where he was in his copy of the Pérez manuscript, but just as Pérez sometimes *wrote* what sounded right to him rather than following Brasseur's text word for word, so Coloch sometimes *said* what sounded right to him rather than following the Pérez text word for word. In the following passage *usachik* had already been added by Pérez, but Coloch crystallized the verse structure still further (his additions are underlined):

Chaya chire oyew	Give it to the brave
chaya chire achi	give it to the man
xa nima retalil	but only to mark the greatness
ukamik	of his death
usachik	his disappearance
waral chuxmut kaj	here at the navel of the sky
waral chuxmut ulew.	here at the navel of the earth.

Both of the changes involve the use of analogy to complete the symmetry of a couplet.

In some of his additions Coloch went beyond the use of ready-made material. Such was the case when he read Cawek's sixth speech, in which Cawek describes a journey that took him deep inside Rabinal territory to a place called *K'amb'a*. Cawek says that being at this place reminded him that his ambitions had been disappointed. He asked himself a question, and this, in Coloch's rendition, is the phrasing he quotes himself as having used:

"*La mana rokikam*	"Isn't it right
xchintaqijta ub'i	that I should be recognized
Ajaw K'amb'a Juyub'	as Lord of Water Jar Mountain
Ajaw K'amb'a Taq'aj?"	Lord of Water Jar Valley?"

The texts have Cawek calling himself *Ajaw K'amb'a,* "Lord of Water Jar," and nothing else. The place name *K'amb'a* occurs elsewhere, but without being followed by *Juyub* and *Taq'aj,* "Mountain" and "Valley." That pair of words partic-

63. At his home in Rabinal in 1988, José León Coloch examines his bound photocopy of the Pérez version of the *Rabinal Achi* text. He had just finished reading aloud from it. His voice was recorded on the tape machine at left.

ipates in a total of eighty couplets, but most of them contain no place names. The one prominent exception, occurring eleven times, is *K'iche' Juyub' / K'iche' Taq'aj,* "Quiché Mountain / Quiché Valley," referring to the capital of the Quiché kingdom and its immediate surroundings. In two cases the first of those two lines (but not the second) is prefaced with *Ajaw.*

Analogy is still at work in Coloch's rendition of this passage, but the change from "Lord of Water Jar" to "Lord of Water Jar Mountain / Lord of Water Jar Valley" involves more than filling out a blank in a couplet whose completed form already exists somewhere else. At the same time, it accomplishes more than an expansion of poetic sound patterning. It is also a rhetorical move, one that strengthens the play's characterization of Cawek. The title "Lord of Quiché Mountain / Quiché Valley" is a real one, belonging to the lord to whom Cawek owes fealty. To use it as a model for the title Cawek imagines for himself is to suggest that his frustrated ambitions are grand ones. What makes this passage still more intense, at least for playgoers who know local lore, is that Water Jar Mountain is said to bear visible marks of Cawek's visit. "When he went to Water Jar," as Coloch tells the story, "he disintegrated that mountain because he was angry, and as we can see now, it has been flattened out." Only in this negative sense did Cawek ever come to be "recognized" as the "lord" of that place.

Another change that did more than fill a blank with preexisting material occurred in Coloch's reading of Cawek's tenth speech. This is Cawek's first speech before Lord Five Thunder, which he delivers from a standing position despite a previous admonition to kneel. Toward the end of the speech he expresses his contempt for the idea of humbling himself. He closes with a sarcastic offer to go ahead and kneel anyway, then attempts to make an assault on the lord. As he comes to the point of making his move, Coloch has him speak these two lines:

| *are b'a numeb'al wib'* | well this is how I humble myself |
| *are nuxoq'olob'al wib' wa'* | this is how I get down in the mud |

The first line is present in the texts, while the second comes from Coloch. The verb stem *meb'a-*, "be humble," occurs elsewhere in the play, but *xoq'olo-*, "get muddy," does not.

The couplet "Lord of Water Jar Mountain / Lord of Water Jar Valley" and the line that goes "this is how I get down in the mud" may originate with Coloch, or they may have their source in his memory of past performances by other actors or their teachers. Either way, they give evidence that in the case of *Rabinal Achi*, the final step from script to scripture has not yet been taken. A script, even when the kinds of changes made by Pérez are on the point of being ended by mechanical reproduction, still leaves some room for small-scale recomposition during the act of performance, even when the performer is reading aloud. The words of a canonized text, on the other hand, can only be spoken correctly or incorrectly, completely or incompletely.

PLAYING VARIATIONS ON THE SCRIPT

An opportunity to take a close look at what happens to the words when the script has been set aside is presented by the speech that opens the play. The evidence considered here consists of four different sound recordings of Coloch's renditions. The first two, on audio tape, were made when he demonstrated the acoustic properties of the Cawek mask on August 10, 1989. The other two, on the soundtracks of videotapes, were made when he played the role of Cawek in public performances of the play on January 17 and 18, 1998. This particular speech is valuable for identifying variations that cannot be attributed to mere shifts in memory. For one thing, it is one of the shortest of the nineteen speeches that belong to Cawek. For another, Coloch has played the role of Cawek many times.

Here are two versions of the opening words. The first is that of Brasseur and Pérez, except that the orthography has been modernized and line breaks have been inserted. The second version is common to all four sound recordings of Coloch, which are the source of the line breaks. Here and in subsequent passages, the lines correspond to uninterrupted sound sequences that are separated from one another by clear-cut pauses:

Katel uloq, worom ajaw	Come on out, pierced lord
k'aqom ajaw	lanced (bejeweled) lord
Katel uloq uworom ajaw	Come on out, lord <u>who is pierced</u>
uk'aqom ajaw	lord <u>who is lanced</u>

The addition of *u-* may originate with Coloch, or it may have been transmitted orally from previous performers. It increases by one syllable the extent of the parallel between the two lines and thus contributes to the process of crystallization.

The next three lines are as follows, first according to Pérez and then as Coloch renders them on all four occasions:

xa k'u xere	but even so
chinab'e wa'e	I must be the first one
mawi kanuk'iso	I'm not finished
xa k'u xere	but even so
qi chinab'e wa'	<u>let me</u> be the first one
<u>*keje*</u> *mawi kanuk'iso*	<u>since</u> I'm not finished

Coloch's addition of the particle *qi* to the second line makes it tentative and more polite, while his shortening of *wa'e* to *wa'* (both translated here as "the...one") is a case of modernization. In the third line his addition of *keje* clarifies the argument of the speech: Though Lord Five Thunder is in a position of authority, he should let Cawek take the lead "since" Cawek has unfinished business, to be revealed in the lines that follow.

The wording of the first version of the next passage is shared by the texts and by the second of Coloch's 1989 demonstrations, while that of the second version is shared by his other demonstration and by both of his 1998 performances:

uch'ayik	chopping
uwixal	the root
ukutamil	the trunk
uch'ayik	chopping
uwixal	the root

This passage is repeated in the text of Cawek's fourth speech, and when Coloch performed that speech in 1998 he omitted *ukutamil* from his January 17 rendition but included it on the following day. The instability of this passage is at least partly accountable to the ambiguity of its structure. The full version constitutes a triplet in the sense that *uch'ayik* shares the third-person singular prefix *u-* with *uwixal* and *ukutamil*, but those two words constitute a couplet on their own in the sense that they alone share the *-l* suffix, which marks the "root" and "trunk" as being not just ordinary possessions of the lord who is about to be named, but intimate and permanent possessions—such as body parts, relatives, or vassals.

The root and trunk that Cawek has yet to finish chopping belong to the lord who rules the people he identifies in the next three lines, first naming them after two locations within their domain and then giving the names of the two nations to which they belong. The first of the three versions is that of the texts, the second is that of Coloch's first 1989 demonstration and both of his 1998 performances, and the last is that of his second (and more formal) 1989 demonstration:

Ajaw Chakachib'	of the Lord of Walkers
Samanib'	Workers
Kawuq Rab'inal	Cawuks and Rabinals
Ajaw Chakachib'	of the Lord of Walkers
Ajaw Samanib'	Lord of Workers
Kawuq Rab'inal	Cawuks and Rabinals

Lajaw Chakachib'	of <u>that</u> Lord of Walkers
<u>*Lajaw*</u> *Samanib'*	<u>that Lord of</u> Workers
Kawuq Rab'inal	Cawuks and Rabinals

In the second version Coloch's addition gives symmetry to a couplet, something Pérez chose to do in many passages but not in this one. In the third version Coloch's *Lajaw* is a contraction of *la'*, "that," and *ajaw*, "lord." Like his addition of *keje* (discussed earlier), this change is an interpretive clarification, based on an understanding of the wider context. Without the addition of "that," a listener with no prior knowledge of the play could easily make the mistake of thinking that the "Lord of Walkers / Lord of Workers" is the person standing before Cawek, namely Man of Rabinal, rather than a third party.

Cawek next marks everything he has said so far as a formal declaration, made before the very cosmos. The first version is that of the texts, together with the more formal of Coloch's 1989 demonstrations and both of his 1998 performances; the second comes from his less formal demonstration:

kacha' k'u ri nutzij	so say my words
chuwach Kaj	before Sky
chuwach Ulew.	before Earth.

<u>*mi xcha'*</u> *k'u ri nutzij*	<u>so have said</u> my words
chuwach Kaj	before Sky
chuwach Ulew.	before Earth.

There are later speeches in which wording like that of the second version is used to mark a quotation as something said on a past occasion. By using such wording in this particular speech Coloch departed from the corresponding passage in the text, but he was on solid ground as an interpreter of the story told in the text as a whole. In Cawek's fourth speech it becomes clear that he had indeed spoken the words of the present speech on a prior occasion.

Cawek's next lines are directly addressed to Man of Rabinal. First come the words of the texts, followed by those of three of Coloch's oral renditions. In the less formal of his 1989 demonstrations he simply omitted this passage:

| *keje mawi k'ia tzij* | since no more words |

| *kinch'aw uk' la* | am I saying to you sir |

| *keje mawi k'ia tzij* | since no more words |
| *kojtzijon uk' la* | <u>are we speaking</u> with you sir |

The first version is the only instance in which the texts follow the phrase *mawi k'ia tzij* with *in-* (the first person singular) and *ch'aw* (a relatively casual verb of speaking), rather than with the more formal *oj-* (first person plural) and *tzijon* of the second version. By choosing the latter wording (except when he omits this passage), Coloch forwards the process of crystallization. What disappears as a result is just a small detail, but it happens to be a detail that is consistent with one of the strands in Cawek's character: He is given to all sorts of improprieties, both large and small. In his own speeches, Man of Rabinal consistently makes the more formal choice when he uses these lines.

Here are the final words of Cawek's first speech, first according to the texts and then as Coloch renders them:

Kaj Ulew chik'oje uk' la	Sky and Earth be with you sir
Uq'alel Achi	Man of Glory
Rab'inal Achi.	Man of Rabinal.

Kaj Ulew ta chik'oje uk' la	Sky and Earth <u>then</u> be with you sir
Uq'alel Achi	Man of Glory
Rab'inal Achi.	Man of Rabinal.

The addition of "then," like the earlier addition of "since," increases the links between successive lines.

Out of the speech's maximum of nineteen lines, eleven are affected by Coloch's departures from the text and six of these are involved in variations among his performances. This leaves eight lines that are the same in the text and in all four oral renditions. Most of the variations seem minor when considered individually, but they add up to a surprising amount of fluidity for a short speech that is anchored in the reading of a text. A contrast is provided by the 1998 performances of the relatively inexperienced actor who took the role of Man of Rabinal. He alternated between following the text closely and dropping whole passages, making some of his lapses of memory obvious by pausing for a long time instead of covering them up by moving quickly ahead. Coloch's own variations arise not from problems of memory, but from the fact that he knows the play very well, both in terms of its localized sequences of words and its general argument.

TIMING, AMPLITUDE, AND INTONATION

What the actors learn, described in terms of conventional linguistics, is combinations of phonology and syntax that produce words, phrases, and sentences. Described in terms of conventional poetics, much of what they learn consists of groups of phrases, mostly in pairs, that are parallel in meaning and (nearly always) in their grammatical construction as well. But at the very same time and from the very beginning, they are also hearing and reproducing dimensions of sound that are usually ignored by text-based approaches to linguistics and poetics.

One of these dimensions is timing or pacing. The actors are not just learning what words to use in what order but how to articulate syllables slowly enough to be heard clearly at a distance in an outdoor space. At the same time they are learning when and how long to pause, segmenting the flow of sound into separate lines like the ones presented in the preceding discussion of the opening speech. This aspect of timing is not completely independent of linguistic or poetic structures, but neither can it be fully predicted from them. The actors' instructor did not learn his timing by seeing it in the script but by hearing it in the voices of a previous instructor and previously instructed actors.

Another dimension of the voice that actors hear and reproduce from the day of the first rehearsal is that of volume or amplitude, which in this case is most importantly a matter of speaking loudly enough to be understood in performance spaces. At the same time the actors are also hearing patterns of intonation, such as the high-to-low trends in pitch that unite words and phrases into longer statements and the similarities in pitch level that sometimes unite separate phrases across the gap of a silence.

What timing, amplitude, and intonation all have in common is that they operate on a larger scale than consonants, vowels, or syllables, which is why linguists sometimes call them "suprasegmental" features. They are more obvious than anything else in a speaking voice, so much so that they can be clearly perceived by a listener who has no knowledge of the particular language being spoken, or by a listener who is near enough to recognize the sound of human speech but too far away to catch any words. In conventional texts such as the one published by Brasseur, these features may be indicated, if only roughly and incompletely, by punctuation marks. Pérez, who saw no use for such marks other than as space fillers, entrusted timing, amplitude, and intonation to vocal transmission alone.

The large-scale features of the speaking voice can be explored by mapping its sound as a physical event occurring in real time. At the simplest level, representing a vocal performance as a physical phenomenon means distinguishing between the presence of sound and its absence and giving more visual weight to loud sounds than to soft ones. And it means plotting these sounds and the silences that separate them against a time scale. In the transcription of Cawek's opening speech that follows, this is accomplished by means of an oscillographic readout from the recording of the second of Coloch's demonstrations of the mask in 1989. Running beneath it is a time scale calibrated for half seconds. The horizontal line that connects the oscillating vertical marks generally registers silences, but where it is notably less than half a second long it corresponds to consonants that do not involve the use of the vocal cords, such as *ch* or *j*. The height of the vertical marks registers the relative volume of vocal sounds: The more these marks depart from the horizontal line, the louder the voice. The volume and pitch of the speaking voice rise and fall together most of the time, so that the general trends of intonation can be read from the swelling and shrinking of the oscillations over the course of whole phrases or groups of phrases.

The most remarkable thing revealed by the readout is that each of the pairs of parallel words or phrases in the speech participates in what is actually a three-part structure. Internally, each triad is loudest and highest at the beginning and softest and lowest at the end, and with one exception the boundaries between its three parts are marked by pauses. Externally, each triad is followed by a pause, and the next triad begins louder and higher than the end of the previous one. The exceptional triad, with only one of its internal boundaries marked by a pause, comes first:

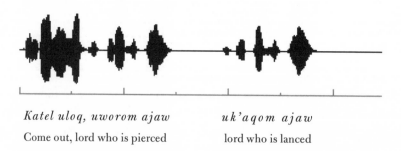

Katel uloq, uworom ajaw   *uk'aqom ajaw*

Come out, lord who is pierced   lord who is lanced

The two halves of the couplet *uworom ajaw / uk'aqom ajaw* are united across the gap of the pause not only by the parallels in the sounds of their syllables but also by sharing the same overall profile in their amplitude. What separates *Katel uloq* from this couplet is a sudden drop in amplitude accompanied by a drop in pitch, the vocal equivalent of a comma in a written composition.

Coloch has two different ways of delivering Cawek's next lines. The version that continues the same performance as the one graphed above takes the form of two triads, each divided into parts by pauses:

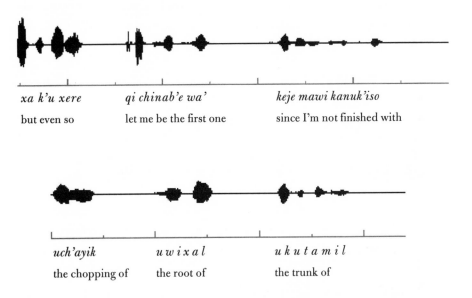

| *xa k'u xere* | *qi chinab'e wa'* | *keje mawi kanuk'iso* |
| but even so | let me be the first one | since I'm not finished with |

| *uch'ayik* | *u w i x a l* | *u k u t a m i l* |
| the chopping of | the root of | the trunk of |

Both of these triads are marked off by profiles with an overall trend from louder and higher to softer and lower, but the first one, which lacks any verse structure, is a triad solely by virtue of its profile and its pauses. Here is the alternative treatment, shown as it occurred in Coloch's other 1989 demonstration:

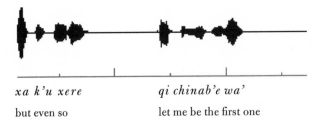

| *xa k'u xere* | *qi chinab'e wa'* |
| but even so | let me be the first one |

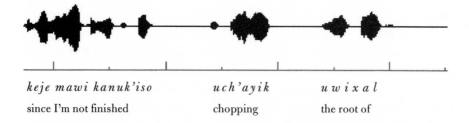

keje mawi kanuk'iso   *uch'ayik*   *uwixal*

since I'm not finished   chopping   the root of

Here the first two parts of the triad lacking verse structure in the other version are allowed to float as a dyad, while the third part is converted into the introductory element of a new triad. *Uch'ayik,* instead of serving as an unparalleled introduction to a couplet, now joins *uwixal* to form a couplet, while *ukutamil* is squeezed out of the picture.

In the next triad Cawek names the person whose "root" (and in some renditions "trunk") are the objects of his unfinished "chopping." It is shown here as it was delivered during the same 1989 performance with which we started:

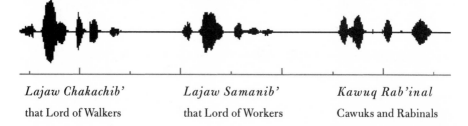

Lajaw Chakachib'   *Lajaw Samanib'*   *Kawuq Rab'inal*

that Lord of Walkers   that Lord of Workers   Cawuks and Rabinals

In this case the extra element in the triad follows the couplet rather than introducing it. In a sense it constitutes a second couplet, but on a smaller scale than the main one. *Kawuq* and *Rab'inal* are both proper nouns referring to nations, but they lack any parallel in their construction or their syllabic sounds, which may be why they are run together without a pause.

At this point Cawek marks everything he has said so far as a formal proclamation, made before the gods of the sky and earth. He and Man of Rabinal use the same or slightly different words, organized as they are here into a triad followed by a dyad, in many other speeches:

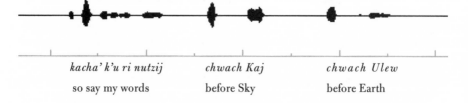

kacha' k'u ri nutzij   *chwach Kaj*   *chwach Ulew*

so say my words   before Sky   before Earth

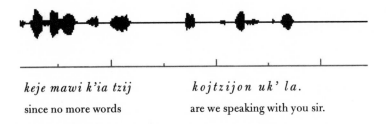

keje mawi k'ia tzij   *kojtzijon uk' la.*

since no more words   are we speaking with you sir.

The triad follows the predominate pattern, in which the unparalleled element introduces the couplet. The dyad that follows is like a triad in beginning louder than what immediately precedes it and ending softer than what follows, but its two parts are linked together as two parts of the same clause rather than by parallel construction. They do share *tzij,* but it occurs at very different locations in the two parts.

When Coloch follows the opening of this speech with a triad instead of a dyad, the dyad just presented constitutes the first full departure from the triadic pattern. It stands in the way of the established rhythm of the speech—and, appropriately enough, it announces that the message has come to an end. On top of that it comes at the end of a sentence, not only in grammatical terms but in those of intonation as well. The jump from the soft and low ending of the dyad (see above) to the loud and high beginning of the final triad is the steepest transition of the entire speech:

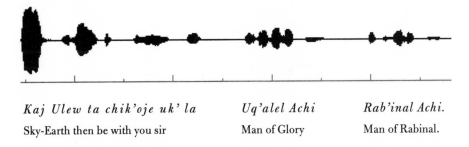

Kaj Ulew ta chik'oje uk' la   *Uq'alel Achi*   *Rab'inal Achi.*

Sky-Earth then be with you sir   Man of Glory   Man of Rabinal.

This return to full triadic form—with a couplet introduced by an unparalleled phrase, with two internal pauses neatly in place, and with an overall downward progression of amplitude and pitch—ends Cawek's speech. There is one small complication in the verse structure: The introductory phrase, like the unparalleled closing phrase of the triad that named a lord, contains its own small-scale couplet. *Kaj* and *Ulew* or "Sky" and "Earth," like *Kawuq* and *Rab'inal,* form a pair in their meaning but not in the sounds of their syllables.

In the range of its loud-to-soft voicing, the final triad echoes the full range of everything that has been said before it. Its opening *Kaj* is nearly as high and loud as *Katel uloq* in the first triad, and the final *-chi* of the last *Achi* scarcely makes a ripple in the horizontal line, whose flatness signifies silence. In terms of intonation this triad constitutes, all by itself, the second complete sentence in the speech, and it has grammatical completeness as well.

Looking back over the oscillographic transcription as a whole, one of its most remarkable features is the short duration of the individual sound events—or, to put it the other way around, the frequency of the silences. Out of the total elapsed time of the speech, 40 percent is taken up by pauses. The longest sound (1.8 seconds) is more than four times as long as the shortest (0.4 second), but the silences are much less variable, with the longest (0.7 second) less than twice as long as the shortest (0.4 second). The difference between any two successive silences is seldom greater than 0.1 second. This gives the listener an expectation, each time the voice falls silent, as to when it will be heard again. The biggest single contrast in successive pauses is between the one that precedes "so say my words" (0.7 second) and the one that separates that phrase from the rest of its own triad (0.4 second). In the absence of an abrupt change in loudness or pitch, this contrast gently reinforces the message sent by the words, which is that the part of the speech devoted to a formal declaration is now complete but that something more will be said.

When line breaks are determined by *scanning* a text rather than *listening* to a sound recording, the results can be rather different from the ones presented here. When Alain Breton scanned the Pérez text of the present speech on the basis of syntax and parallelism, he came up with fifteen lines. Of the nineteen pause-divided lines Coloch produces when he delivers the play's opening speech without deletions, only nine begin and end in the same places as Breton's lines. For example, in the case of *kacha k'u ri nutzij / chuwach kaj / chuwach ulew,* "so say my words / before sky / before earth," Breton runs the first two lines together as one, thus underestimating the internal cohesion of the parallel couplet. In the case of *Kaj Ulew ta chik'oje uk' la,* "Sky-Earth then be with you sir," he places a break between *Kaj* and *Ulew,* thus focusing on their parallel semantic relationship and leaving their lack of a parallel sound relationship out of consideration.[34]

In the play's later speeches dyads are in higher proportion than in the opening one, and there are intonational groups that run to four lines or (where lists of names or epithets are involved) even longer. In general, pauses are stable in their relationship to the words. Some of the lines defined by pauses may be changed in the details of their wording, regrouped by means of intonation, or simply dropped, but the pause between two lines never shifts in such a way that a fraction of one line is shunted into another. Occasionally the pace may be accelerated by omitting pauses, combining what would ordinarily be two or three separate lines into one. When Coloch reads the script aloud he has a tendency to accelerate when he reaches the passage that formally announces the end of a given speech, but in his full-dress performances he keeps to the same even pace as when he demonstrated the mask.

As compared with the actors in *Rabinal Achi*, the professional orators who practice their arts in highland Mayan towns enjoy a much greater latitude when it comes to variations in wording and voicing. Quiché performers such as Esteban Ajxup of Momostenango, who prays on behalf of the supplicants at the shrines of mountain gods, and Tat Justo Yac of Cantel, who speaks at the ceremonies where marriages are negotiated and completed, learn their art through lines of transmission that are strictly oral.[35] They improvise on a larger scale than actors, selecting material from a repertoire appropriate to a type of occasion, combining it with personal information provided by their clients, and adding touches that mark their personal styles. In their parallel phrasing they are much more likely than actors to run beyond couplets and even beyond quatrains, with correspondingly longer intonational groups. When they come to the final phrase in a parallel series, they are more likely to abbreviate or expand it than to make it fully symmetrical with the preceding phrases.

Hieroglyphic inscriptions are highly laconic, but skilled performers could have used them as a starting point for verbose improvisations similar to those of contemporary orators. It is not writing as such that limits the range of variation and elaboration available to a speaker but rather the use of writing to produce a script, which is to say a detailed prescription. In the case of *Rabinal Achi,* the double process of recopying the script and relearning the speeches has brought the formal structures of Quichean phrasing and voicing more and more to the surface. If orators playfully resist these structures, copyists and actors embrace them.

The Play Enacted

SITES

On the day of a performance, the participants in *Rabinal Achi* gather for costuming at the house of José León Coloch (figure 64). Those who live at some distance from the town center have spent the night there, sleeping in hammocks. The masks, the trumpets and drum, and the objects carried by the actors are laid out on the stone floor of the room where the household altar is located. There the Road Guide prays over them, lighting tall candles and swinging his incense burner.

The masks and costumes used in most of the dance dramas of Guatemala are rented from one of several specialized workshops that manufacture and refurbish them.[1] The tasks normally involved in producing a play include organizing expeditions to a town where a workshop is located. In the case of *Rabinal Achi,* however, the masks and most of the clothing are locally made. Items that cannot be found locally are purchased in other towns and reused in later years.

For at least part of the distance to the site of a public performance, the cast parades down a street or road in full costume. The first performance of 1998, like the first one Brasseur de Bourbourg witnessed in 1856, was given in honor of St. Sebastian. On both occasions it took place on the Saturday preceding his day, which is January 20. In 1856 the Saturday in question fell on January 19, while in 1998 it fell on January 17. The latter performance was carried out in the patio of the house that was currently hosting the confraternity of St. Sebastian, beginning at dusk and lasting into the evening. When it got dark the patio was lit by a few scattered light bulbs. The performers with masks removed them so that they could see what they

64. On the morning of the 1998 performance in front of the cemetery chapel,
the finishing touches are put on the costume of the Mother of Quetzal
Feathers. At right is María Xolop, wife of José León Coloch and
the daughter of his predecessor as director of the
play, Esteban Xolop.

were doing. They placed their masks in front of the image of the saint (figure 65), which is where they would have put them after the performance in any case.

When the play was over the entire cast knelt before St. Sebastian and prayed, after which everyone present was served atole (corn gruel) and tamales. The next morning the first fully public performance was given, the one on which the account that follows is largely based. Other performances, some of them at confraternity houses and others in the town's main plaza, were given later in the week, culminating (as they did in 1856) on January 25, the fiesta of the conversion of St. Paul. Each performance lasts about two and a half hours.

The main plaza and public market are at the east end of the town's main street. The parish church stands on a rise on the east side of the plaza, facing west. Looking west from its steps, past the ceiba tree that shades the plaza and over the tops of the market stalls, one can see straight down the main street to the chapel that stands at the entrance to the cemetery. In front of the chapel is a stone terrace, reached

65. The floor in front of the altar of St. Sebastian on the evening of a performance of *Rabinal Achi*.
In the background are bouquets of flowers and bundles of aromatic herbs; pine needles have
been scattered across the nearer part of the floor. In the basin at right are tamales that will
later be served to the performers and spectators; behind and to the right of the basin
is the Road Guide's pottery incense burner. Two actors have chosen
to remove their masks so as to see better.

from the street by a broad stairway, that gives the opposite view. The street
becomes a dirt road at this point, swerving to the right around the terrace and
chapel and continuing to Cubulco, the next town west. The January 18 performance of *Rabinal Achi* took place on the terrace. It was a Sunday, the principal
market day in Rabinal, so there was a good deal of traffic going by, both vehicles
and pedestrians. The spectators consisted mostly of people who lived nearby or
happened to be passing by, together with men who had come to the chapel to pray
and make offerings of incense to the dead on behalf of households or lineages. Some
people watched and listened for a few minutes and others stayed longer. One small
boy and one old man moved in close and stayed for the entire performance, trying
to follow every word and movement.

ROLES

Man of Rabinal and Cawek of the Forest People wear face masks that are wooden,
carved, coated with gesso, and painted with human features. Their clothing is

identical except for contrasting colors. Both of them wear velvet capes, sleeved tunics, and pants, bordered with gold braid and gold fringes. These items are distantly modeled on full-dress military uniforms of the eighteenth or nineteenth century, but the tunics are cinched with locally handwoven cotton sashes. Formerly both men wore black street shoes; today they wear handmade leather sandals of a type that is widely available in the public markets of Guatemala. On the present occasion Rabinal wears a headdress shaped like the head of a coyote, while Cawek's headdress is shaped like the head of a jaguar. Both are festooned with multicolored feathers. These headdresses, introduced during the 1990s, were inspired by images of pre-Columbian Mayan warriors. Formerly both characters wore two-cornered boat-shaped hats front-to-back, crowned with feathers.[2]

Rabinal and Cawek are both armed with a wooden hatchet, carried in the right hand, and a small round shield, carried in the left. The ax and shield are tied to their wrists so they can let them dangle whenever they need to do something else with their hands. Both items are always visible, like the attributes held by images of saints; Cawek remains in possession of his ax and shield even when he kneels to have his head cut off. Formerly the shield was a silver plate with a handle welded to the back; today it is a brass cymbal.[3] Fastened to its center are several strings with hole-punched coins dangling from the loose ends. When a performer takes a step or turns, the coins tinkle; when he shakes the shield, they rattle against it.

Lord Five Thunder's mask is like Rabinal's in having a blue border and like Cawek's in lacking a frown. Instead of a helmet in the shape of an animal head he wears a two-cornered hat front-to-back, crowned with plumes, but otherwise his costume contrasts with theirs only in its color scheme. Like them he carries an ax and shield, but his shield is a silver plate with a handle, smaller than their cymbals and closer in size to the shields carried by Classic Maya lords.

The role of the wife of Lord Five Thunder, who is simply called Lady, is played by a woman, while that of their daughter, the Mother of Quetzal Feathers, is played by a girl in her early teens. Neither of them speaks during the play, and the role of Lady is often left unfilled (as it was in 1998).[4] Formerly they wore veils, but today their faces are uncovered. Both wear a cloth headband, trimmed with gold braid, which holds a bunch of feathers upright at the back of the head; a cotton blouse (huipil) of a type that is worn only on ceremonial occasions, brocaded with designs that are specific to Rabinal; a sarong of a type widely worn by Mayan women in Guatemala, woven from tie-dyed threads that produce streaked or marbled designs; and leather sandals. Both carry an ax, but not a shield. Tied by a string to the left wrist of the girl is a carved calabash drinking vessel produced by the local crafts industry. It does not figure in the action.

66. The framework for the backpack to be worn by Jaguar, under construction
for a 1980 performance. Photo by Carroll Edward Mace.

Slave is played by a man whose mask is similar to those worn by Rabinal,
Cawek, and Lord Five Thunder, complete with a mustache, but who wears a wig
of long, black hair and is dressed like the girl and her mother. The actor holds an
ax in his right hand, and tied to his left wrist is a carved calabash like the one carried
by the girl. In the scripts this character is addressed by Lord Five Thunder and
referred to by Cawek as "man slave / woman slave," but in performance the word
for slave, *mun*, becomes *muy*, an interpretation that focuses attention on the
mustache. *Muy* is a term for a small fish with barbels like those of a catfish, but it is
also a figure of speech for a woman with facial hair.[5]

The last two characters are addressed as "Eagle" and "Jaguar," but when
they are talked about they are called "twelve Golden Eagles, Golden Jaguars." This
could mean that a total of twelve (or even twelve of each) once appeared in the play,
but it is unlikely that more than one Eagle and one Jaguar participated in the
execution of Cawek. The men who play these roles are veiled rather than masked.
Today they wear feathered cylindrical hats; formerly they wore brimmed hats.
Their capes, tunics, and pants are like those of Cawek, Rabinal, and Lord Five
Thunder, except for variations in the color schemes, and they wear the same
sandals (formerly street shoes) as everyone else. Each of them carries on his back

a carved and painted wooden plaque that announces his identity, a pair of eagles for one and a pair of jaguars for the other.

Each carved plaque is set against a backdrop of the sort that is constructed for the image of a saint carried in procession, made of strips of cloth, ribbons, and feathers mounted on a framework of lashed sticks (figure 66). Seen from the front, this device forms a backdrop for the head and trunk of the performer. From the center of each plaque rises a wooden pole, topped by a basket-like object made of cloth wrapped around a framework of sticks that radiate outward and upward from the pole like the spokes of an inverted umbrella. The rim is decorated with feathers. Together, the pole, basket, and feathers reach almost a yard higher than the head of the dancer.

The musicians, consisting of two trumpeters and a drummer, wear white cotton shirts and pants, long red sashes with brocaded ends, brocaded head scarves whose main colors are red and white, and the usual sandals. When they are in procession they are assisted by a man in street clothes, who carries the drum with a tumpline. Also accompanying the performers on each of their appearances is the Road Guide, who is costumed in the same way as the musicians.

SCENES

When the performers first enter the stage, it has no front and no back. But this is not theater in the round—rather, it is a theater of four sides and four corners, like the four sides and corners of the Mayan world. Members of the audience take up positions on any side where there is room for them. The only visible scenery is outside the stage. From the point of view of a spectator on the terrace in front of the cemetery chapel, the actors play against a backdrop that combines walls covered with whitewash, roofs of red tile, broadleaf and coniferous evergreens, glimpses of the pale blue ridges that enclose the town, and, over all of this, a hazy bright sky that softens all the shadows.

Before the play begins all the performers, already in full costume, take their opening positions. The Road Guide stands on the steps that lead from the terrace to the chapel, outside the space where the action will take place. The musicians stand in front of a masonry bench on the south side of the terrace, again outside the space of the action. The actors line up in single file along the west side of the terrace, defining the western boundary of that space. They face south, with Eagle in front, at the southwest corner of what will become a square, and Jaguar in the rear, at the northwest corner. In between are Man of Rabinal, Cawek of the Forest People, Lord Five Thunder, Mother of Quetzal Feathers, and Slave, in that order. If someone were playing the role of Lady, she would stand behind Quetzal.

All the actors remain on stage throughout the play, whether or not they have a role in the current sequence of events. It is possible to divide these events into four scenes, but only by listening to what the actors say about where they are or where they intend to go, and then watching their movements.[6] In the opening dialogue Rabinal and Cawek repeatedly describe themselves as being "here at the navel of the sky, navel of the earth," meaning that they are somewhere in the vicinity of the town of Rabinal. Each time they speak this line they join the place represented in the play with the place of its performance, at least in a general way, thus uniting themselves with their audience.

Rabinal focuses the scene somewhat by speaking as if he had found Cawek "outside the great fortress, outside the great walls." About halfway through their dialogue Cawek names this fortress, calling it "Red Mountain / Shaker / Dressed in Red / Tepecanic." Red Mountain stands two kilometers north of the center of Rabinal, rising 300 meters above the valley floor on which the town is situated. Its shape can be glimpsed through the trees on the north side of the terrace, and with an open view it is possible to discern the steep-sided platforms of earth and stone on its summit, topped by what remains of the walls of palaces and temples. "Outside the great fortress" could be anywhere on the slopes around those ruins, or down here in the valley below, where the performance is taking place.

Throughout the first scene Rabinal and Cawek make their speeches in the physical presence of Lord Five Thunder and the members of his court, but in the world constructed by their words they remain outside his presence. The shift to the second scene occurs when Rabinal leaves Cawek in the keeping of Jaguar, on the north side of the stage, and then goes before Lord Five Thunder and his court, who are seated on a wooden bench on the west side, in front of the chapel. In effect, the chapel stands in place of the main palace on top of Red Mountain.

In the second scene, while Rabinal engages in dialogue with Lord Five Thunder, it is Cawek who is physically on stage and yet outside and invisible so far as the words are concerned. For the third scene Rabinal, joined by Slave, goes back to where he left Cawek and engages in a further exchange of words with him. The fourth and final scene begins when Rabinal and Slave bring Cawek before Lord Five Thunder and his court. The final dialogue takes place between Cawek and the lord.

EVENTS

The first sound to be heard is a fanfare from the trumpeters. For this Rabinal and Cawek turn their backs to each other and lift their faces and axes, staring toward distant mountain ridges. Cawek joins his voice to that of the trumpets, letting out a long, high, fading cry: *Eeeiiiiiiii.* After the fanfare comes dance music, combining the two trumpets with the drum to make what Cawek will later call "the sorrowful sound of the bloodletter's trumpets / the bloodletter's drum." The actors dance counterclockwise around the four sides of the stage, turning in a small counterclockwise circle when they start out and when they reach one of the four corners. Eagle turns by himself, Cawek and Rabinal turn together, Five Thunder turns with Quetzal and Slave, and Jaguar turns by himself. In dividing themselves in this way, they foreshadow the pattern of the positions they will take up when the play's opening dances are over.

The first dance is interrupted three times by further fanfares. For the first two Rabinal and Cawek turn their backs to one another, as before, and everyone else stops where they happen to be. For the last fanfare the dancers break into a rapid walk, following a circular path around the stage. Rabinal walks behind Cawek, as if pursuing him. At the end they stop at the middle of the west side and reverse positions, with Cawek to the north and Rabinal to the south, and face each other. The two of them stand far enough apart to be well out of one another's reach.

Now the time has come for the dialogue to begin. Just as there is no front to the stage when Cawek and Rabinal dance or promenade, so there is none when they talk. Whichever one is speaking at the moment paces up and down continuously, taking three or four steps before he stops for a moment and turns around; his counterpart meanwhile paces on a parallel path. Their gazes meet only randomly. Cawek's first speech is really meant for Lord Five Thunder rather than Man of Rabinal, who is blocking his path. Rabinal paces with his own rhythm rather than following Cawek's every move, but they are separated by an invisible line that Cawek cannot cross.

In the world inside the play Lord Five Thunder is currently inside his fortress, out of earshot. It is almost as if Cawek were engaged in a monologue at the moment when Rabinal confronts him. He uses the second person familiar (marked by the pronoun *at*), telling his imaginary listener to "come on out," meaning outside the fortress. Next, if he were following the script, he would call Five Thunder a "lord who's been pierced / lord who's been fitted with gems," referring to the nose and lip ornaments that once served as markers of lordly status, now transformed into the mustache and goatee that decorate the lord's mask. But when Cawek is played by Coloch he instead calls Five Thunder a "lord who has pierced / lord who has lanced," referring to his skills as a warrior.[7] Either way, Cawek honors his opponent. But then, without actually uttering Five Thunder's name, he comes to the point: "I'm not finished / chopping through / the root / the trunk / of that Lord of Walkers / that Lord of Workers / Cawuks and Rabinals." Commenting on these words, Coloch said, "It's as if someone said they would kill me and all my sons."

After stating his desire to cut Lord Five Thunder's tree, Cawek gives it the force of an oath by saying, "So say my words before Sky / before Earth." He will invoke Sky and Earth in nearly every speech he makes, and so will Rabinal. For audience members of the early colonial period these words would have summoned the memory of whole lists of divine names and epithets that could no longer be uttered in a fully public way. They could easily imagine Cawek as saying "Heart of Sky / Heart of Earth," thus invoking the patron deity of lordship, and going on to invoke the power of his ax scepter, saying, "Newborn Thunderbolt / Sudden Thunderbolt."[8]

At the end of his opening speech Cawek switches to polite address and speaks directly to the man in front of him, saying, "I'll have no more words with you, sir" (in which "sir" translates the polite second-person pronoun *la*). He ends by calling his counterpart "Man of Glory, Man of Rabinal" for the first of what will be many times. These words are followed by a fanfare, for which the two men turn their backs to each other. Music and dance follow, with everyone moving around the four sides of the stage as before. Again, the dancers stand still for a second and third fanfare, then walk a circular path around the stage for the fourth and final fanfare. Rabinal and Cawek end up where they started, at the middle of the west side.

Again the two men pace up and down on either side of an invisible line, but now it is Rabinal who speaks. Instead of calling Cawek a lord he calls him *oyew achi,* "brave (or angry) man," and instead of talking past him to an unseen opponent, he addresses him from the outset as "Cawek of the Forest People," thus recognizing him as a member of the Cawek lineage of the Quiché nation. Then, after quoting Cawek's opening words verbatim, he answers them with a warning, saying, "You spoke them in range of my weapon / in range of my shield / and my upraised ax blade / and my bracelet / my armband / my white paint / my gourd of tobacco." These items are all emblems of Rabinal's status as a lord; not a single one of them, not even his ax or shield, is a practical weapon of war. Not only that, but except for the ax and shield, they exist only in words. Cawek is "within range"— or, more literally, "inside the power"—of these emblems, whose ultimate source is divine. The only physical force Rabinal proposes to use comes from a different source: "I shall catch you / with my henequen rope / my henequen cord," he says. The specification of henequen ties the play to the town of Rabinal, where the traditional crafts include making ropes from the fibers of locally grown henequen plants.[9]

Like Cawek, Rabinal backs up his threat with an invocation of Sky and Earth. He treats Cawek as if he had already defeated him, calling him "prisoner, captive."

The enactment of the capture has been handled in various ways over time. According to Brasseur's script, Rabinal's first and second speeches were separated by an interval of silence, during which he lassoed Cawek by the head. But the Pérez script, which has been in use since 1913, combines the opening lines of Rabinal's first speech with closing lines of his second, omitting everything in between. The part of the original first speech in which Rabinal threatens to use a rope has disappeared, though the idea of a capture is still there, since he ends the original second speech (like the first) by calling Cawek his "prisoner, captive." During the middle of the twentieth century these words were followed by an enactment of the capture, but the visible link between Rabinal and Cawek was no longer a rope. Instead, they took hold of opposite ends of a long sash. In recent productions the rope has reappeared, but it does not serve to bind Cawek until much later in the play.[10] In the present translation the lines that Pérez left out have been restored and the binding of Cawek has been moved back to its original position between Rabinal's first and second speeches.

In Rabinal's second speech (or what is now the latter part of his first), he demands to know more about his antagonist's identity than his membership in the Cawek lineage of the Forest People. He begins by asking, "Where is your mountain? / Where is your valley?" Cawek could answer this by naming his birthplace, but Rabinal does not wait for him to do so. Instead he insults Cawek, saying, "Weren't you born of clouds? / Weren't you born of mist?" Coloch explained this figure of speech by saying, "He's treating him as if he had no parents. And he's not from here, but has come from outside to impose his laws."[11] As if that were not enough, Rabinal accuses him of being "on the run / in the face of violence / in the face of war."

Cawek's response to these insults, today as in the past, comes after an interlude of alternating fanfares with standstills and music with dancing.[12] While all this is going on, a wooden bench is placed at the center of the west side of the stage, facing east. When the music stops, the drum carrier sets the drum down in front of the drummer, who will henceforth play in a sitting position, and retires. Eagle goes to the southwest corner and begins walking back and forth along the southern border of the stage, while Jaguar stays behind on the northern border and begins walking back and forth on his own path there. Lord Five Thunder sits on the south end of the bench, while the Mother of Quetzal Feathers sits to his left and Slave sits to her left.[13] Cawek and Rabinal end up in front of the bench, close to center stage. The Road Guide, who has been standing offstage to watch the action, sits on the steps of the cemetery chapel, which rise from the west side of the stage.

Now, for the first time, the stage could be said to have a front and back—if, that is, we count Lord Five Thunder and his court as being seated at the back and looking toward the front. But it continues to be the case that those attending the play may choose to stand on any of the four sides, and it happens that the least favored side, at least in this particular performance space, is the so-called front. As Cawek begins his reply to Rabinal, they pace up and down as before. Their parallel east-west paths define the scene of their confrontation. The members of the royal court, though they have already assembled, belong to a scene that has yet to be enacted.

Cawek takes offense at Rabinal's words, saying, "The words you have spoken are hurtful right on their face, sir." In response to the demand that he reveal his identity, he asks, rhetorically, "Am I brave? / Am I a man? / Yet I should reveal the face / of my mountain / my valley?" Rabinal responds to this refusal by threatening to bring Cawek before Lord Five Thunder, where, if he wants to, he can "just shriek" and "just shout" instead of revealing who he is. Beginning with this exchange the interludes that separate their speeches are brief, each consisting of a single fanfare during which the two men turn their backs to one another. The dropping of the longer interludes with dancing signals the beginning of a series of verbal exchanges that will move them away from the anger of their initial confrontation and toward a mutual understanding of what must happen next. But each time they turn their backs between speeches, they make their distance visible once again. Among other things, their respective mountains and valleys lie in opposite directions.

Rabinal's threat to take a shrieking Cawek before Lord Five Thunder elicits an evasive response. Cawek agrees to reveal his identity, but first he protests his unimportance, calling himself "this little house wren, this bird." This is not quite as modest a comparison as it might sound, since a male house wren, though small, is loud and clear in his voice and never stops moving.

Next, instead of answering the demand that he reveal the names of his birthplace, Cawek names two of the remotest places ruled by the Quiché lord he serves, saying, "I am the brave / I am the man / of the lord of foreign Chajul / foreign Cunén." He goes on to give names to this lord, but instead of using names that belong to the period of the events of the play, he goes back to a time before the present sun and moon first rose and invokes the founders of the Quiché kingdom. The names and the sequence in which he mentions them have undergone some changes, having been copied and recopied for a century and a half longer than the corresponding passages in the Popol Vuh manuscript. Instead of saying "Jaguar Quitzé / Jaguar Night / Not-Quick," Cawek says "the Jaguar Lord / Jaguar Quiché / the quick one."[14]

At one level, Cawek's use of names that predate the dawn of the present world can be interpreted as an expression of veneration for his ancestors. At a more subtle level, he is twisting Rabinal's questioning of his parentage into a positive statement. What the Popol Vuh says about the founding lords is that "they had no mother and no father," but were rather "made and modeled" by the very gods.[15] Cawek, by using their names, offers an ironic acceptance of Rabinal's insult, and he follows it by saying, "I'm just a drop of water fallen from clouds and mist."

Rabinal, despite the lack of a straightforward answer from Cawek, now realizes who he is. "What I terrible joke you're someone I ought to help out," he says, and he goes on to invoke the comrades-at-arms relationship they ought to enjoy by calling Cawek both his elder brother and his younger brother. He says this because the Rabinal and Quiché nations had a long history of fighting on the same side of any conflict and because Cawek himself once came to Red Mountain as an ally.

Having recognized who his prisoner is, Rabinal proceeds to berate him for his recent actions. Among other things, he has been making the cries of wild animals outside the fortress of Lord Five Thunder. His purpose, as Rabinal describes it, is to lure "the children, the sons of light," meaning the subjects of Lord Five Thunder, into an ambush. The Popol Vuh describes the use of the same ruse by the founders of the royal houses of the Quiché nation, including the house of Cawek:

> They would get up on the mountain peaks, just crying out with the cry of the coyote
> and the cry of the fox. And they would make the cries of the puma and jaguar.... They
> did it just as a way of decoying [other] nations.... And then, when they saw just one
> or two people out walking, they intended to overwhelm them.[16]

The simplest way to interpret the animal cries is to suppose that they are mere imitations, and that the physical shapes of those who make them are those of human beings, lying in wait for any hunters they may be able to decoy. An alternative reading is that the human beings in question are shape-shifters who take on the forms of animals when they make the cries, or that the animals embody their personal spirit companions. A third reading, and the one that best fits the thinking of contemporary Quiché priest-shamans, is that the action in question should not be understood as taking place in the physical or waking world. Instead, the guardian spirits of powerful human beings are attempting to lure the spirits of other human beings into a trap, with physical illness and death awaiting those who fail to resist. This interpretation is supported by later speeches in which Cawek is described as "he who is the dream from which we cannot awaken." If correct, it would mean that at the time of his capture by Rabinal, he had been acting not so much as an enemy warrior as an enemy shaman.

The animal cries in the Popol Vuh account are those of the coyote, fox, puma, and jaguar, but Rabinal substitutes the agouti, a timid rodent, for the puma. In so doing he makes a joke at Cawek's expense. The joke is easily missed today, but in earlier times it would have been caught by playgoers who remembered that there had been a renegade member of the Cawek lineage whose nickname was *Tata Yak,* "Father Fox," and whose noble title was *Chituy.* [17] By following his mention of the fox *(yak)* with the agouti *(utuy),* Rabinal evokes the nickname and makes a pun on the title.

Rabinal does not pursue the question of Cawek's recent actions but rather demands that he explain his past deeds as a rebel, asking, "What about those braves, those men / who became restless, agitated / after you incited them, sir?" In this way he opens a long interrogation, accusing Cawek of what will turn out to be a whole series of belligerent actions. He begins by recalling a time when the rulers of the Quiché kingdom summoned Cawek and himself to the capital, expecting both of them to help put an end to a rebellion among nearby subjects. But then he turns to Cawek's more recent role as an invader of Rabinal territory, leading an attack instead of rendering aid. He blames Cawek for the deaths of nine warriors at a place called Pitted and Planted, a short distance from the site of the ancestral Rabinal town of Workers.

It is in this same speech that Rabinal first names the lord he serves: *Mama Ajaw Job' Toj,* "Grandfather Lord Five Thunder." He plays on the day name *Toj* in the same way contemporary diviners do, telling Cawek, *Are na k'u katojo ri sanaj la,* "So now you will pay *[katojo]* for your deeds, sir." He goes on to describe what the payment will be by turning Cawek's own words back on him, saying, "this is where we chop clear through / *your* root / *your* trunk, sir."

Cawek ignores Rabinal's threats, but he does respond to Rabinal's demand that he explain his deeds as an enemy warrior. Going deep into the past, he brings up an episode that occurred before the call for help went out from the Quiché rulers. On this earlier occasion it was Lord Five Thunder who was in trouble, and he sent a message to the Quiché capital asking for help. His enemies were not rebels among his own subjects but rather the former occupants of Red Mountain and its valley, the Uxab and Pokomam nations. He wanted Quiché warriors to come and help him make war on them, and he promised to grant them arable land in return.

Cawek gets far enough in his account of the call for help from Red Mountain to say that it was passed on to him by the lords at the Quiché capital, who urged him to arouse his strength and weapons and "traverse the length and breadth / of the mountains and valleys." But then he uses these words to change the subject, remarking (with irony) that he happens to be in the midst of a long journey right now. He proceeds to narrate the itinerary that has brought him inside Rabinal territory in his current role as an invader.

Describing the purpose of his journey, Cawek says, "I'm working the soil / I'm resetting the boundaries of the land," which has two different meanings. On the one hand, he speaks as if he were collecting on Lord Five Thunder's earlier promise of arable land. On the other, he is claiming a role in a much grander project than the measurement of mere cornfields. He has been resetting the boundaries of the lands ruled by the lords at the Quiché capital, following a path whose main trajectory runs eastward. The first three places he mentions—Pines in a Row, Thunderclap, and Big Tree—all lie south of the capital, close to the present-day boundary between speakers of the K'iche' and Kaqchikel languages. Next he turned north to Lord's Place, which was the seat of the Cakchiquel lords until it became the Quiché town of Nettles Heights (later known as Chichicastenango). He continued northward to Earthquake, which was in Quiché hands even then, but then he resumed his eastward trajectory. By the time he got to Bountiful, roughly halfway between the Quiché capital and Red Mountain, he had entered what was then Rabinal territory.

Continuing eastward, Cawek came to a town called Between the Wasp Nests. It is only when he tells the story of what happened there that he gives any hint that his expedition might have encountered resistance. He says that as he approached the town, "I heard, already in progress / the sorrowful sound of the bloodletter's trumpets / the bloodletter's drum / played for the twelve Golden Eagles / Golden Jaguars." The music could have been read as a sign that a sacrifice was under way, possibly involving prisoners taken from his own party, or perhaps it was meant to signal that his further advance into Rabinal territory would result in such sacrifices. In any case Cawek says that it was then, when he heard the music, that he first declared his devotion to the project of "chopping through the root / the trunk" of the Rabinal lord.

Cawek says nothing more about what happened at the town called Between the Wasp Nests, but it will later come out that he was less than a day's march from places where he would inflict great losses on the Rabinal nation. Instead of telling that story, he ends the present speech on a note of frustration at never having completed his chopping project. He asks himself, "Now, what's to be done / about that oh-so-respectable lord? / I've yet to dismay him / I've yet to teach him a lesson."

Man of Rabinal begins his reply by taking up the first of Cawek's two subjects, Lord Five Thunder's call for help in making war on the Uxab and Pokomam. Rabinal notes that when Cawek answered that call, he was sent on an errand that had to be carried out before an attack could be launched. His job was to visit the lords of the enemy nations as a combined emissary and spy, assessing their military strength and looking for any evidence that they might be on the move. His performance was unsatisfactory, to put it mildly. Rabinal uses sarcasm to describe what happened: "You, sir, did not succeed / in seeing / observing / the Uxab / the Pokomam / because they transformed themselves / into gnats / into flies / into ants / into conqueror ants." He starts off this list of insects with a pun, playing off Uxab to get *uxil,* the term for "gnats." His implication is that Cawek failed to observe (or at least failed to report) a large-scale troop movement that was going on right under his nose. Man of Rabinal learned the truth only later, when he sent out a second spy.

Man of Rabinal blames Cawek's incorrect report for the fact that the Uxab and Pokomam regained some of the territory from which the Rabinal nation had previously banished them. He demands to know just what was said when Cawek met with the Uxab and Pokomam lords, implying that he might have agreed to collaborate with them. The first thing the lords did at the meeting, according to Cawek, was to portray themselves and their nations as prosperous and harmless. They told him that even if they did venture outside their present territory it would not matter, since they were not numerous. Besides, they were enjoying an easy life. All they had to do was to tend their orchards, picking and cutting pataxte and cacao (pataxte being the lesser of two grades of cacao). They were "shaded by quetzal feathers / shaded by glistening green," as they put it, referring to the shiny leaves of the trees in the orchards and, at the same time, alluding to the fact that pataxte and cacao seeds, like quetzal feathers, carry a high value. Indeed, these seeds served the peoples of Mesoamerica as a currency, a fact that is the ultimate source of European lore about money that grows (or doesn't grow) on trees.

Having described their own comfortable lives, the Uxab and Pokomam lords portrayed the people of the Rabinal nation as "burning with pain" and "burning with anguish" in pursuit of their sustenance. Cawek claims that he turned their words against them, interpreting their statement as meaning that in reality, they were "simply dismayed / simply astonished" by the "persistence" and "determination" of the Rabinal people. He thus portrays himself as loyal to those who sent him to meet with the Uxab and Pokomam lords, but he offers no explanation of his failure to discover that their subjects were strong in numbers and on the march.

Now Rabinal reminds Cawek, once again, of the losses that resulted from his shortcomings as an observer. The consequence for Cawek himself was that "you did not plant crops / in the bright mountains / the bright valleys." He was not granted the land that Lord Five Thunder had offered in exchange for his services, even though "you spent the power of your weapon, sir / the power of your shield, sir / and you also spent the strength / of your elbow, sir / your shoulder, sir." Rabinal almost seems to be sympathizing with Cawek at this point, but then he draws a line: "Since you know, sir / where the boundaries of the land are / why must your run, sir / crossing the length and breadth / of the mountains and valleys?"

Rather than answer Rabinal's question, Cawek takes up the story of what happened after he was denied land. He headed for home, he says, but he began this journey by surveying the perimeter of the valley commanded by Red Mountain. He proceeded as if he were staking a claim to ownership, measuring the distance from one boundary marker to another in cords (a Mayan unit of measurement equivalent to twenty strides or twenty meters). Starting from Red Mountain itself, he followed a path that traced an arc connecting the eastern, southern, and western sides of the valley. Today, the five places where he stopped are the sites of shrines that consist of hearths for the burning of offerings. During the period when the play is being rehearsed, the Road Guide goes to each of these five places on five successive days, saying prayers and making offerings. His prayers are addressed to the divine lords of the mountains and valleys, including the lords of these very places, and to the spirits of the characters named in the play, who once walked the earth in the flesh. There was a time when his predecessors would have scheduled these rites for auspicious dates on the Mayan divinatory calendar, but Rabinal is not among the towns where this calendar remains in use today.

The first place Cawek came to was Water Jar Point, on a hilltop three kilometers southeast of Red Mountain and two kilometers east of the Rabinal town center, overlooking the Rabinal valley.[18] He says that when he got there he asked himself, "Isn't it right / that I should seek to be / Lord of Water Jar Mountain / Lord of Water Jar Valley / by planting my sandals / on the heads of the children / the heads of the sons / of the Man of Glory / Man of Rabinal?" By saying this at a shrine, he was doing more than imagining himself as the owner of land and vassals that belonged, in reality, to Man of Rabinal. Shrines like these can be used by people who feel wronged to ask for justice before the court of the gods. Even petitioners who make no complaints about anyone in what they actually say can do unintentional harm if resentments happen to well up in their minds while their offerings are still burning on the hearth. Negative words or thoughts, together with the ashes of the offerings that accompanied them, remain at a shrine like a deposition on file at a court. As Coloch put it, Cawek "was very upset and so he cursed our place." The play keeps the memory of his curses alive, but it also reenacts his capture and sacrifice by those who were cursed. Each performance raises his angry ghost, then lays it to rest once again.

From Water Jar Point Cawek went three kilometers south to his second stop at Henequen Mountain, Henequen Valley, a place consisting of a hill and the valley at its foot. At the shrine on the hill he lamented never having planted crops in the area he was surveying. Then he went on to his third stop, Healing Waters, in a bottomland one kilometer west of Henequen Mountain and three kilometers south of the Rabinal town center. "When I looked out over the land," he says, "the yellow-colored, white ears of ripe corn / yellow sustenance, white sustenance / bird-footed bean shoots / spread out ahead of me / spread out behind me." As he walked along, "I left the prints of my sandals / on that land." Coloch, following local tradition, understands these lines to mean that "he collects the richness of this place. He puts some of the soil in his sandals, and where pieces of that richness are dropped the land becomes fertile." In this case, instead of registering a complaint at a shrine, he took a small sample of the arable land that had once been promised to him.

Leaving Healing Waters, Cawek went a kilometer and a half northwest to Croaking Frog Point at Belted House, the location of a fourth shrine. From there he went another seven kilometers northwest to the fifth and final shrine, at Worn-out Trumpet Point. This is directly west of the Rabinal town center, on a ridge that defines the boundary between the towns of Rabinal and Cubulco. According to local lore, it is the place where the play's Eagle and Jaguar first took up the burdens they carry on their backs.[19] This suggests that their movements along the boundaries of the performance space are to be understood as marking out Lord Five Thunder's whole domain, not merely his royal court.

To describe what he did at Worn-out Trumpet Point, Cawek plays on the word for "trumpet," *tun,* to get *xintunan,* "I trumpeted." He says, "I trumpeted there / because of my troubled heart." Trumpeting, as a figure of speech for what he said there, means that it sounded sorrowful. He was in pain, he says, "because I did not plant crops / here at the navel of the sky / navel of the earth / in the bright mountains / bright valleys." For one last time before leaving the Rabinal mountains and valleys, he was putting his feelings on record at a shrine.

Cawek states that he was at Worn-out Trumpet Point "for thirteen score days / and thirteen score nights." These two lines refer to the divinatory calendar, which runs through all possible combinations of thirteen day numbers and twenty day names to generate a total of 260 dates. Here, as when the same lines occur in later speeches, they are spoken at moments when dates on the divinatory calendar would have played a role in the events represented in the play. It could be that early versions of the script included specific dates but that they were replaced by generalized references to thirteen score days and nights in the same way that the names of the ancient gods were replaced by generalized references to Sky and Earth.

When Cawek moved on he headed straight west, back into Quiché territory. According to Coloch he returned to his home at Red Earth, a place he mentions in his next speech.[20] It is located sixty kilometers west of Worn-out Trumpet Point, inside the boundaries of the present-day town of Chiché and around fifteen kilometers east of the Quiché capital at Old Camp and Whisker Place. Coloch says that when he got there, "he untied his sandals and left the soil he had taken from the navel of the earth, the navel of the sky, here in Rabinal. He left the soil there so the land would produce plentiful food for his people."

When Man of Rabinal gets his next turn to speak he returns to the subject of Cawek's more recent boundary-setting expedition, the one that brought him back into Rabinal territory by way of Bountiful and Between the Wasp Nests. What concerns Rabinal is an issue Cawek has been evading all this time, namely, that he used this expedition as an occasion for stirring revolt among the subjects of the very lords he was supposed to be serving. Rabinal notes that he himself was on a boundary-setting expedition when he received news of the revolt. He had reached a place called Look-See Point, which may have been one of the many spots that provide spectacular views of Lake Atitlán. His next stop was at Panajachel or "Sculpture Tree," a Cakchiquel town on the north shore of the lake.

By the time Rabinal arrived at Sculpture Tree, Cawek was at Big Tree, just a few kilometers away. Rabinal sent him a message questioning his actions, but he ignored it, moving on to Lord's Place and Earthquake. There, as Rabinal notes, Cawek's forces "came within a very short distance / of Quiché Mountain / Quiché Valley." The implication seems that they now posed a danger to the very capital of the Quiché kingdom, which lay a half day's march west of Earthquake. What happened instead, says Rabinal, is that "they turned in this direction," meaning eastward toward his own nation, "taking by force / the length and breadth / of the mountains and valleys." Later he will give details of their easternmost advance into Rabinal territory, but here he does a flash-forward to one of the outcomes of their invasion. "Even now," he says, "they have yet to return / inside their own fortress / inside their own walls." They did turn around, but instead of going all the way home they settled at Spilt Water, still inside what was then Rabinal territory. And they are still there, in the Quiché town known as Zacualpa.

Now Rabinal returns to the subject of Cawek's eastward advance, describing events that occurred after Cawek moved beyond Between the Wasp Nests and before the Quiché vassals he brought with him turned back. The account begins with an incident that occurred while Rabinal continued his boundary-marking work, arriving at House Point by the Rocks that Face Each Other. While he was there he learned that Cawek had ambushed Lord Five Thunder at a place called Bath, which may have been on a slope a short distance below the ancestral Rabinal town of Workers. He found this all the more objectionable because Lord Five Thunder's only reason for being there (as Cawek later admits) was to bathe.

At this point Rabinal abandoned his survey work and went to investigate the situation in his homeland. It was a long journey, and by the time he arrived on the scene he found Five Thunder trapped inside a "plastered hive" or walled enclosure, where he had taken refuge. "I got him safely out of there," says Rabinal, and "if it were not for me / and this is certain / then the trunk, the root / of my lord, my liege / would have been chopped clear through." He goes on to accuse Cawek of attacking a series of places near Bath. In an earlier speech he mentioned the loss of nine Rabinal warriors at Pitted and Planted; in this one he charges Cawek with attacks that resulted in losses on a larger scale, saying, "Didn't you, sir, finish off / two or three branches of the nation / down in the canyons / up on the heights?" He then lists Standing Jaguar, Sparkling Dust, Reed Rattles, Drumbeat, Mace Valley, and Sapota Tree, which are like Pitted and Planted in being on or near mountain ridges that mark the present-day eastern limit of people who identify themselves as Quiché.

In his answer to Rabinal's latest charges, Cawek begins by admitting that "these are true words / not false words." Then he takes the story back to the moment when the lords at the Quiché capital asked both him and Rabinal for help in putting an end to unrest among their subjects. For the first time he gives the place names of the capital, having previously referred to it only as "Quiché Mountain / Quiché Valley." Following the script, he runs the two names together as *Q'umar-machi*, thus combining *Q'umarka'j*, "Old Camp," with *Chi Ismachi'*, "Whisker Place."[21]

Cawek describes a whole hierarchy of lords, but instead of dividing them into ranked lineages and naming the ranked titles within each lineage, as the Popol Vuh does, he uses figures of speech to sketch the general outlines of their world. First he uses a calendrical metaphor, calling them "our lords / our lieges / from the rank of Lord Thunder / to the rank of Lord Knife."[22] *Toj* and *Tijax*, or "Thunder" and "Knife," are day names from the divinatory calendar, each of whose twenty names has a corresponding lord with a particular sphere of influence in human affairs. If we read Cawek's choice of the lords of Thunder and Knife as a diviner would, he is referring to a sequence of authorities that runs from a lord in charge of payments to a lord in charge of disputes.[23] The question of how many lords it takes to get from Thunder to Knife has two answers, since diviners have two methods for getting from one day to another. One way is to count each successive day, in which case the number required to get from Thunder to Knife is nine. The other way is to hold the day number constant, which means counting each thirteenth day. The number of same-numbered days required to get from Thunder to Knife is itself thirteen, so that the total elapsed time between (for example) One Thunder and

One Knife is thirteen times thirteen days.[24] We need not think there is some one correct solution to the problem, since nine and thirteen are both key numbers in Mayan numerology. The main point is that each lord has a place in a hierarchy with multiple grades.

Continuing his description of the lords, Cawek uses metaphors to evoke the dispersed domains they represent in their meetings. First he calls them *Kuchuma Aj*, "Gathered Cane Plants." *Aj* is a day name whose corresponding lord looks after the affairs of households, so perhaps this is a reference to the fact that before all else, each lord is the head of his own noble house. At the same time, the stalks of cane plants growing in the same body of water are joined together at the root. When a council of lords meets at the capital, it is as if the whole kingdom became a single stand of cane plants. Amplifying this same metaphor, Cawek speaks of the lords as *Kuchuma Cho*, "Gathered Lakes." They come from every part of the Quiché world, which has a sacred lake for each of the four directions and a fifth lake at the center, near Old Camp and Whisker Place.[25] He also calls them *Kuchuma Tz'ikin*, "Gathered Birds," comparing them to birds that flock together on lakes and wetlands.

When Cawek calls the lords *Kuchuma Siwan*, "Gathered Canyons," he is probably referring to relatively low-ranking lords with low or exposed dwelling places rather than high and fortified ones. The contrasting term (which does not occur in the play) would be *Kuchuma Tinamit*, "Gathered Citadels."[26]

In a later speech Man of Rabinal describes the lords at the Quiché capital with all these same metaphors and adds one more: *Kuchuma Kab'*, "Gathered Honey." This refers to the people both he and Cawek otherwise call "the creatures / of yellow honey, fresh honey," who bring "sustenance" (tribute payments) to the hives where higher lords dwell, or in this case the hive of all hives.

Cawek admits that he knew about the summons sent out by the gathered lords and says he thought about going before them. But he had another matter on his mind—namely, the crops he had never planted on the land he was never given by Lord Five Thunder. He had "a little bit of land" of his own at Red Earth, not far from the capital, but he left it "because / this heart of mine went away / with the children of light / the sons of light," which is to say with the vassals who were rebelling. He acknowledges receiving the message Rabinal sent him from Sculpture Tree but says that he simply continued with what he was doing. He moved on to Earthquake, coming very close to the capital before he turned eastward. After that came the incident at Bath, followed by the attacks on Standing Jaguar, Sparkling Dust, Reed Rattles, Drumbeat, Mace Valley, and Sapota Tree.

Having accepted the blame for all these actions, Cawek now begins to say things that betray his fear of retribution. In a show of humility, he calls himself "a mere squirrel / a mere bird." Then he suddenly brings up the notion of brotherhood, though he had failed to respond when Rabinal mentioned it earlier. He proposes "to work here, to serve / your children, sir / your sons, sir," but says he should first go home to settle his affairs. "It would be a mark of greatness," he says, "to let me go away, sir / to my mountain / my valley."

Rabinal responds to Cawek's proposal by wondering how, if he went along with it, he could possibly explain such a decision to Lord Five Thunder. He rehearses the speech he would have to make, beginning with a description of Cawek. He would say, "Well, perhaps this is the brave / perhaps this is the very man / with whom we've been concerned / outside the great fortress / the great walls," referring to Cawek's recent efforts to lure Five Thunder's subjects (or their spirits) into ambushes. And he would go on to describe Cawek as "he who is the dream from which we cannot awaken," a dream that had been happening "for thirteen score days / and thirteen score nights." Here we have another instance where a general reference to the divinatory calendar occurs in a context where specific dates would have played a role in the events being described. If people had been having bad dreams because of Cawek, they would have asked diviners to interpret them, and the diviners would have taken the dates of the dreams into consideration when formulating their interpretations.

Having rehearsed the words he would use to describe the trouble caused by Cawek, Rabinal imagines himself as having to continue his speech to Lord Five Thunder by saying, "I have let him go away / to his mountain / to his valley." But this is not a scenario Rabinal finds acceptable. Instead, he now says, he must let Lord Five Thunder decide whether Cawek should be allowed to go home before appearing at the royal court. He then goes off to consult with the lord, leaving Cawek behind.

The staging of Rabinal's departure from Cawek, like that of his capture of Cawek, has been handled in different ways over time. In the middle of the nineteenth century, when Rabinal threatened to rope Cawek in his first speech and then did so, he tied his end of the rope to a tree—provided that a tree was available, that is. Such would have been the case when performances were held in the patios of the houses of confraternities, as some of them continue to be. In recent performances staged by Coloch, Rabinal carries a rope looped around his waist from the moment the play begins, but it does not figure in the action until his departure. The rope is branched like a Y, and a stage hand ties the ends of the branches around Cawek's upper arms while Rabinal holds the other end. Meanwhile, Jaguar stops pacing at the middle of his path along the northern border of the stage and turns to face south. Rabinal takes Cawek to that spot and gives his end of the rope to the stage hand, who ties it around Jaguar's waist. In the stage directions for the present translation the initial binding of Cawek has been restored to a position following

Rabinal's first speech, as noted earlier, while the transfer of one end of the rope from Rabinal to Jaguar has been kept where it is.

Now, with a fanfare, Rabinal goes before Lord Five Thunder on the west side of the stage. He paces up and down before the bench while he delivers the news of his capture of Cawek. He begins by greeting both the lord and lady, whether or not the character named Lady is present in a given production. Then he tells the story of how he captured and questioned Cawek, describing his initial difficulties by saying, "I had to pry open the mouth / of the brave / the man / since it wasn't quick and easy / to get him to reveal the face / of his mountain / his valley." Next he offers a brief review of Cawek's misdeeds, starting with his recent attempts to lure people outside the safety of the fortress with animal cries and then going back to the time of the incident at Bath and the attacks at Standing Jaguar and Sparkling Dust. He reminds Lord Five Thunder that these attacks were preceded by a warning, sent by "our lords, our lieges" at the Quiché capital. He makes no mention of Cawek's desire to go home before appearing at court, declaring that "this is where / we shall chop clear through / his root, his trunk / here at the navel of the sky / navel of the earth." There is no fanfare when he finishes speaking, and in fact none of the changes of speaker that take place at court are marked by fanfares.

Lord Five Thunder now speaks for the first time. He thanks Sky and Earth for the capture of Cawek and tells Rabinal to "bring him in here." He cautions Rabinal to advise the prisoner that "he must not howl / he must not shriek" when he enters the fortress. At one level, Five Thunder is simply saying that Cawek should speak like a human being rather than making the cries of animals and otherwise behaving the way "Forest People" do. At another level, he is saying that Cawek must not attempt to use the powers of his animal guardian spirits.

With Rabinal still before him, Lord Five Thunder reviews the various resources his court has for dealing with the prisoner. First on his list are twelve "workers in jade / workers in metal," whom he describes as Cawek's elder and younger brothers. He wonders whether Cawek "will help them reach perfection / completion." Implicitly, Cawek would become the thirteenth member of this brotherhood, but not in the flesh. As will become clear later, what they need to complete their work as craftsmen is Cawek's bones.

Next on Lord Five Thunder's list of possibilities are the "twelve Golden Eagles / Golden Jaguars." Again, Cawek might "help them reach perfection," which is to say that he might become the thirteenth member of their company. At the end of the play he does join them, dancing with the one Eagle and one Jaguar who appear in today's productions, after which the two of them participate in his execution.

Third on the list are "the bench adorned with metal / raiment adorned with metal." With apparent irony, Lord Five Thunder wonders whether Cawek "will come to be enthroned." Perhaps he is referring to the unlikely possibility that Cawek will emerge as the victor in his encounter with his executioners.

The fourth item is the "mead that burns / bites / sweetens / delights," which is the drink of lords. "Mead" translates the ambivalent term *ki'*, which can mean either "poison" or "sweet." It is also the term for maguey plants in general and for pulque, the alcoholic drink made by tapping the sap of maguey flower stalks. Pulque recipes, apparently including the one followed at Lord Five Thunder's court, commonly included honey. It was probably standard practice among the Maya, just as it was in central Mexico, to give an alcoholic drink to a condemned prisoner of war. The particular drink that awaits Cawek bears the name "Quick Hummingbird."[27] There was a widespread notion in Mesoamerica that humming-birds, which are attracted to maguey flowers, are the souls of dead warriors.

Fifth on Lord Five Thunder's list is "the double warp / the tamped weft / the weaving tightly done," which he calls "the work of my mother / my lady." This is a newly woven piece of cloth, brocaded in a pattern that is specific to the weavers of Rabinal. Cawek will later become the first person to wear it, displaying it to the court while he dances.

The sixth and final place on the list is occupied by the girl who sits to the left of Lord Five Thunder. He is the first to mention her, calling her "the Mother of Quetzal Feathers / Mother of Glistening Green." He wonders whether Cawek might be "the first to show / her mouth / her face," dancing her "round and round." He even wonders whether Cawek "could become a father- or son-in-law / a brother-in-law." Both of the kin terms used here are reciprocal: *jiaxel* covers both sides of the relationship between a woman's father and her husband, and *b'alukixel* (like English "brother-in-law") covers both sides of the relationship between a woman's brother and her husband. Five Thunder does not say whose in-law Cawek would become, but given the fact that he is talking to Man of Rabinal about the Mother of Quetzal Feathers, the implication is that she is a daughter to him and a sister to Rabinal, and that Cawek could become his son-in-law and Rabinal's brother-in-law. Such relationships create links between individual males from separate patrilineages and form the basis of alliances between the patrilineages themselves, with givers and takers of daughters and sisters on both sides.

The kind of reciprocity by which the men of allied lineages marry one another's daughters and sisters has an opposite, and that is the reciprocity by which the men of enemy lineages kill one another's sons and brothers. This is what gives the play its tragic twist. In the normal order of things, as Lord Five Thunder and Man of Rabinal understand it, the Quiché and Rabinal nations are allies. Cawek, as a member of a Quiché lineage, ought to be like a brother on the battlefield, as Man of Rabinal suggested earlier. In the royal court, on the other hand, he should comport himself as a potential son-in-law or brother-in-law. Lord Five Thunder states that he would consider an in-law status for Cawek "if he gave praise / if he were respectful / if he bowed / if he lowered his face / when he entered here." But what has already happened is that Cawek has acted as an enemy on numerous occasions, vowing to cut the tree of Lord Five Thunder's lineage at its root and finishing off whole branches of the Rabinal nation. Moreover, Man of Rabinal, Cawek's captor, has already called him a doomed man. Lord Five Thunder, by speaking of an in-law relationship, is not so much raising the possibility of turning his present enemy into a future ally as he is alluding, with deep irony, to a marriage that has been made impossible by the past. When the time comes for his face-to-face dialogue with Cawek, he will make no mention of a possible in-law relationship.

Having heard Lord Five Thunder's description of the courtly respect he would expect from a potential son-in-law, Rabinal makes his own display of respect, that of a man who has come before his lord in the role of a returning warrior and should disarm himself. "Since this strength of mine / this manhood of mine / was your gift, sir / your present, sir, to me," he says, "I must therefore leave / my weapon here / my shield here." He then hands them to Lord Five Thunder and says, "Guard them, sir / put them away, sir / inside their box / upon their shelf / so that they may rest now / just as I may rest."

In his reply to Man of Rabinal, Lord Five Thunder wonders what would happen if he accepted the surrender of the weapon and shield and put them away. He asks, rhetorically, "What then would be the name of your means of defense, sir / in the course of ascending / descending / the highlands / the lowlands?" And he wonders further who would defend "our children / our sons," meaning the vassals belonging to himself and Rabinal. At the end of this speech he hands the ax and shield back to Rabinal.

Man of Rabinal now takes his leave of Lord Five Thunder, who sends him on his way with good wishes. There is a fanfare while Rabinal walks to the spot where he left Cawek bound to Jaguar. His message to Cawek, which he delivers while pacing up and down, consists mostly of a long quotation from Lord Five Thunder, with variations in the original wording. The topics that come first are the admonition not to shriek or howl, the workers in metal and jade, the twelve Golden Eagles and Jaguars, and the throne adorned with metal, in the same order as before. The order of the remaining topics is reversed, with the Mother of Quetzal Feathers followed by the lord's drink and the brocaded cloth. The notion that Cawek could become an in-law, which is now separated from the passage about the Mother of Quetzal Feathers, comes at the end of the quotation. To admonish Cawek to behave properly, Rabinal speaks for himself rather than quoting Lord

Five Thunder. He says, "You must bow, sir / you must kneel, sir / when you enter there, sir / before my lord, my liege."

At the end of Rabinal's speech Slave rises from the bench and goes to Rabinal and Cawek, pacing back and forth to the west of them while they continue their dialogue. He never takes his eyes off Cawek. In replying to Rabinal, Cawek addresses himself only to the demand that he behave in a respectful manner. "If I must simply bow / if I must lower my face," he says, "well then, this is my way of humbling myself / well then, here is my weapon / here is my shield." What he wants to do when he comes before Lord Five Thunder is to bring down his day of birth, which is to say the destiny that was given to him by the divine Lord Five Thunder, who rules his day of birth. To this he adds, "Would that I could just bind / his lower lip / to his upper lip," and then, making a move on Man of Rabinal, he says, "How about it? / You try it first, sir." Slave steps between him and Rabinal and the three of them walk in a small counterclockwise circle, as if Cawek's move and Slave's intervention had combined to produce a curved trajectory. Jaguar, still joined to Cawek by the rope, walks a wider circle. When they stop, Slave, with Rabinal at his right, faces east toward Cawek, who has Jaguar at his left. At this point Slave speaks for the first time, telling Cawek not to kill Rabinal, who then takes the rope that binds Cawek to Jaguar and stands behind Cawek. Jaguar goes back to pacing the northern border of the stage.

During a long fanfare Cawek, followed by Rabinal and Slave, walks a counterclockwise circle around the stage. When he arrives at the east side he turns west, followed by the others, and walks straight to the west bench, standing in front of Lord Five thunder as the music ends. Rabinal unties Cawek and stands a short distance south of the bench, facing north toward Cawek. Slave stands near the north end of the bench, keeping his eyes on Cawek.

Cawek now addresses Lord Five Thunder, pacing back and forth in front of the bench as he does so. From his opening lines, his manner is different from that of Man of Rabinal. Where Rabinal said, "It's a clear day, lord. / It's a clear day, lady," he says instead, "It's a clear day, man." He then reviews what he was told by Rabinal before coming, focusing on the admonition that he should bow down and lower his face when he came before the court. In answer, he raises his ax and shield and attempts to make a move on Five Thunder. Slave grabs Cawek's right arm and circles him clockwise, telling him not to kill the lord, and then returns to his seat on the bench.

At this point Cawek accepts the hopelessness of his situation, but he rejects the notion that he was destined to come to such an end. "My day has been turned upside down," he says, "my birth has been turned upside down." In effect he is claiming that his capture is the opposite of his original fate, as determined by the date of his birth on the divinatory calendar. He ends this speech by addressing the man who sits in judgment over him properly, calling him "Grandfather Lord Five Thunder," and then kneels.

In his first speech to Cawek, Lord Five Thunder invites him "to go ahead and *speak,* sir / go ahead and *talk,* sir," rather than make the cries of animals. He recites Cawek's past wrongs, mentioning the rebel force that passed close to the Quiché capital; the incident at Bath; the attacks on branches of the Rabinal nation at Standing Jaguar, Sparkling Dust, and other places; and the brave men who ended up buried at Pitted and Planted. Near the end of his speech he says, "Truly you are dead, sir / you are lost," thus seeming to pass sentence without considering any other possible outcome.

Cawek rises for his reply, in which he readily admits to the deeds of which he is accused. "Truly it is I / who am to blame," he says, but then he shifts the blame, bringing up the issue of the land he never received from Lord Five Thunder. He states that he acted as he did "because of my troubled heart," meaning the regret he felt "because I did not plant crops / in the bright mountains / in the bright valleys." He is not in a position to demand land now, having already extracted a great price for what he was denied. All he can do in his present condition is to ask for such favors as may be granted to a condemned man. He starts with the drink called Quick Hummingbird. "I have yet to taste it," he says, "yet to mark the greatness of the manner of my death / my disappearance / here at the navel of the sky / navel of the earth."

The drink Cawek asks for is granted by Lord Five Thunder, who orders Slave to give it to him. Slave unties the calabash from his-her left wrist and presents it to Cawek, who lets his ax and shield dangle from his wrists and takes it with both hands. Then comes a fanfare while Cawek walks a counterclockwise circle around the stage. When he comes back to the bench, on the west side, he turns his back to it and takes a couple of steps eastward as the music stops. In silence he takes four long draughts from the calabash, holding it in his right hand and tilting his head back. He faces east for the first draught, west for the second, north for the third, and south for the fourth. Then he returns to his position in front of Lord Five Thunder and speaks to him, gesturing with the calabash instead of the ax. He starts off by denigrating the drink he was given. "But then," he continues, "you, sir, have yet to taste / what I have at my mountain / my valley," which is "amazingly delicious / delectable." This is full of irony, the implication being that if Five Thunder did have the opportunity to taste the drink with Cawek in the role of host, he would be doing so as a condemned prisoner.

Now Cawek turns his attention to the calabash, holding it higher as he asks, "Could this be / the skull of my grandfather? / The skull of my father?" He then wonders whether his hosts might make his own skull into a drinking vessel, "carved in front / and carved in back" like a calabash from Rabinal. He imagines that his own relatives might purchase such a drinking vessel some day, and if they did, his sons and grandsons might hear it described as the skull of their own father or grandfather. In this way he turns his personal story into an allegory of the myth of the hero whose head was turned into a calabash and whose twin sons avenged him, as told in the Popol Vuh. Given that the very identity of the Rabinal nation is tied to the making of carved calabash vessels, there is no way Cawek's sons or grandsons will be able to see such a vessel without remembering who cut his head off. For them it will be as if the calabash carried an inscription recording that event. In this sense his head will survive his death, no matter what the fate of his actual skull.

It is not only the future of his head that Cawek wonders about. He also imagines that a bone from his arm will become the handle of a rattle, and that a bone from his leg will become a stick for playing a slit drum. People will marvel at the sound of these instruments "as long as there's a sky / as long as there's an earth for them / here inside the great fortress / inside the great walls." It is not known whether he means long bones from his own skeleton, or whether references to such bones served as metaphors for rattle handles and drumsticks. Either way, he is inscribing the musical instruments of his captors with the memory of himself.

Cawek hands the calabash back to Slave and makes a further request for something that will "mark the greatness" of his death, this time the brocaded piece of cloth Rabinal told him about. Lord Five Thunder grants it, once again ordering Slave to hand it over to Cawek. Slave rises from the bench, unfolding a large piece of brocade in the same local style as the head scarves worn by the musicians and the Road Guide. He-she gives Cawek a warning, telling him not to abuse the cloth, and ties it around his waist in such a way that it serves as an apron. Cawek then speaks in the direction of the musicians, telling them that if they were using his instruments rather than theirs, "the very sky would tremble / the very earth would tremble" with a sound that would reach all the way over to his own mountain and valley. "But we would hang our heads / hide our faces," he says, "at the prospect of promenading / dancing / with this man slave / woman slave." A fanfare sounds, followed by music. Cawek and Slave dance around one another in front of the bench and then dance a square path around the sides of the stage, turning a circle at each corner. When they come back around to the bench, a fanfare sends them into a circular walk around the stage. At the end Slave returns to his-her seat on the bench and Cawek resumes his position in front of it.

Before making his next request of Lord Five Thunder, Cawek says, "Get on with my breaking / my beating. / The time has come for me to be divided / the time has come for me to be parceled out." He acknowledges that so far, he has been granted all his requests. Removing his apron, he hands it back to Slave. Then, despite his remarks about being divided and parceled out, he asks for the maiden at Lord Five Thunder's side, the Mother of Quetzal Feathers, saying, "I must dance her round and round / I must dance her on and on." As with his other requests, he makes this one "only to mark the greatness / of my death / my disappearance."

Again Lord Five Thunder grants Cawek's request, ordering Slave to present Quetzal to him. She rises and Slave, standing behind her, puts his hand on her shoulder and guides her to a position in front of Cawek. He admonishes Cawek not to wear her out. Again, a fanfare is followed by music. Cawek and Quetzal turn a circle in front of the bench and then dance the usual square. They face one another, never touching, while Slave dances behind Quetzal. At the end comes a fanfare while the three of them walk a circle. Quetzal and Slave return to their places on the bench and Cawek gets in position to make another speech.

Cawek begins by acknowledging the granting of his latest request, and for the first and only time he says nothing to detract from what he has been offered by Lord Five Thunder. Instead, he says of the Mother of Quetzal Feathers, "Guard her, sir / shelter her, sir / inside the great fortress / great walls." But then he goes directly from his happiest moment in the court of his captors to a request for a dance with two of the characters who will participate in his execution. What he wants to have presented to him now is the "twelve Golden Eagles / Golden Jaguars / who will be my companions / on the last day / the last night." He goes on to say, "I'm going to play a game here," striking his shield with his ax. Lord Five Thunder then orders Eagle and Jaguar to come and join Cawek in his game. With a fanfare, Jaguar leaves his path on the north side of the stage and moves in behind Cawek, who meanwhile moves to a position behind Eagle. As the music begins, the three of them dance the square, turning a circle separately at each corner. When Cawek comes back around to the bench a fanfare sounds and they break into a circular walk. When Jaguar reaches his northern path he stays there, while Cawek stops in front of the bench and Eagle returns to his southern path.

After this dance Cawek speaks of having "played out a game" with Eagle and Jaguar, using the power of his ax and shield. Whatever the power of Eagle and Jaguar might consist of, they are unarmed and do not enter into visible combat with Cawek while dancing with him. He ridicules them, asking Lord Five Thunder, "Is that an *eagle* standing there, sir? / Is that a *jaguar*, sir?" As far as he is concerned, the Eagle and Jaguar of Rabinal are harmless, unlike the ones he has at his own mountain and valley. "They are devastating when they stare / they are devastating when they gaze," he says, and "they are devastating when they scream / when they click their teeth, their claws." Lord Five Thunder answers Cawek's braggadocio with a put-down, saying, "We have yet to see the teeth / of the eagle / the jaguar / that live on your mountain."

Now Cawek makes his final request, asking for something that has not been mentioned in previous discussions of what he might be granted. "Now give me / thirteen score days / thirteen score nights," he says, referring to the divinatory calendar. By way of explanation he adds, "I have yet to say farewell / to the face of my mountain / the face of my valley / where I walked / on all four sides / to all four corners." In some present-day highland communities, these words would be understood as referring to the timing of ritual visits to the four directional mountains that stand on the boundaries of the lands belonging to an ideal town, and to the four directional hills that stand closer to its center. Visits to the shrines on these mountains or hills are timed in such a way as to divide 260 days into four quarters of 65 days each.[28]

No one speaks in answer to Cawek's request for time to say farewell to his mountain and valley. Instead all the characters join him in a dance around the four sides and four corners of the stage. In effect, the perimeter of the stage becomes the perimeter of the mountains and valleys of his home. First the dancers form a file running north to south along the west side of the stage. Rabinal rises and goes to the head of it, followed by Cawek, Lord Five Thunder, Mother of Quetzal Feathers, and Slave. Eagle then goes to a position in front of Rabinal, while Jaguar falls in behind Slave. Then they all dance the square; after two circuits a fanfare sounds when Cawek reaches the bench. There he turns east, stopping at center stage. The others walk a circular path until they come to the east side of the stage, where they form a straight line and face west.

Now, pacing up and down before the assembled cast, Cawek of the Forest People makes his final speech. He "speaks alone," as the script has it, which is to say that he does not expect to enter into a dialogue with anyone. "Little Eagle, little Jaguar," he says, "perhaps you thought, 'He's leaving!' / but I didn't leave. / I merely said farewell from here / to the face of my mountain / to the face of my valley." He expresses the spiritual nature of his farewell by saying, "I've returned to the meadows / I've returned to the barrens / but my courage / my manhood / didn't come with me." *Achijilal,* here translated as "manhood," is a matter of physical power. Not only did Cawek not go home with his weapon and shield, but he did not go home in his body.

If it were not for the long period of missionary interference, the play might represent Cawek as saying prayers at the four corners of the stage, addressing his mountains and valleys by name and burning incense. But even without that, anyone familiar with the rituals that are performed in the present-day world of mountain and valley shrines knows that he could indeed say farewell "from here." The spirit familiars of these sacred places are all in communication with each other. Standing at one place, Cawek could call upon any other places whose names he might know. In such a prayer he would explain why he was so far away, thus excusing himself from appearing in person and, at the same time, lodging an implicit complaint against his captors. That all the characters move around the four sides and corners of the stage with him makes it clear that unlike the Christians and Moors or conquistadors and Indians of other plays, Cawek and his Rabinal hosts are in agreement about the way the world works.

As Cawek continues speaking he ponders his end, invoking Sky and Earth and asking, "Can it be true / that I'm dead here / I'm lost / here at the navel of the sky / navel of the earth?" He then speaks to his ax and shield, together with his clothes and sandals. "You then!" he says, using familiar address, "Go to our mountain / go to our valley / then tell our story / before our lord / our liege." He imagines that his personal effects, having been delivered to his lord, would speak in his own voice and say, "The road is closed / for my courage / my manhood / searching / striving / for our meals, our morsels." He goes on to compare himself to a squirrel and a bird, as he has done before, but now he says that this is a squirrel or bird "who died in the branch of a tree / in the flower of a tree." This would seem to be an extension of the metaphor that makes a lineage into a tree, transforming its members into creatures that live and die in its branches.

Finally Cawek speaks to Eagle and Jaguar again, telling them to do their work with their teeth and claws. He warns them that "you certainly won't stand my hair on end / in the blink of eye / because / I am truly brave / coming as I do / from *my* mountain / *my* valley." Then he wishes them well with one last invocation of Sky and Earth. A fanfare sounds and everyone walks a counterclockwise circle around the stage, with Cawek falling in behind Eagle and Jaguar bringing up the rear. When Cawek nears the bench on the west side he begins to spiral inward toward stage center with the others behind him (figure 67). He reaches the center at the same moment his spiral brings him into position to face west, then kneels with his head bowed. At that moment the music begins and the others begin to dance, forming a tight circle around him.

With each left step the dancers swing their right arms toward Cawek, and those who have axes aim them toward his neck whenever they pass close to it, never actually touching him. Eagle and Jaguar hold the right hand flat, as if to make a chopping blow, when they swing it toward him. Nothing is done to represent the separation of his head from his body, or his blood or any other physical detail. His

67. Cawek follows an inward-spiraling path that takes him to stage center, followed by the other actors. He is first shown heading south (top left, at the extreme left), then heading east (top right, at center right), then beginning to kneel facing west at center stage (bottom left, center), then kneeling with the other actors closing in around him (bottom right). From the 1998 performance at the cemetery chapel.

end is a matter of the words already spoken, his kneeling position, and the gestures of the dancers.

Once Rabinal has danced a full circle around him, Cawek rises with a fanfare and steps into place behind him. Everyone breaks into a walk, spiraling outward until Cawek, who starts his walk facing west, has come around to the middle of the east side of the stage. Then the music resumes and everyone dances the square. This has the effect of returning the actors to the timeless point from which they started. It is not that Cawek has undergone a resurrection but that all the characters have returned to their status as the ghosts of people who lived and died in ancient times.

When Eagle reaches the east side of the stage he goes to the northeast corner and stays there. The rest fall in behind him, forming a line across the east side with Jaguar at the south end. They all turn to face east and continue to dance in place for a few measures, keeping the left foot forward and shifting their weight back and forth between left and right, swinging the right arm forward when shifting to the left foot. After a fanfare they do an about face and dance westward, staying in line except when Cawek does one turn with Rabinal while Lord Five Thunder turns with Quetzal and Slave. As they approach the west side a fanfare sounds and they stop. By this time the bench has been removed by the stage hand. Road Guide, who has stayed outside the stage all this time, now enters it. He stands in front of the dancers facing west, toward the door of the cemetery chapel. When the fanfare stops the musicians also face in that direction.

Now everyone kneels and prays to the ancestors whose graves lie in the crowded enclosure behind the chapel. They all speak at the same time but independently, creating a collective murmur.

Notes

INTRODUCTION

1. For more on the play's roots in ancient Mayan culture, see chapter 1.
2. For more on theater in Mayan towns during the colonial period, see chapter 3.
3. The historical sources of the play's characters and narratives are explored in detail in chapter 2.
4. *Carlomagno* is discussed in detail in chapter 3.
5. J. Eric S. Thompson (1960:66), for example, used the term "predestination" when writing about the Mayan calendar. Schele and Freidel (1990:84), on the other hand, point out that ancient lowland kings took an active role in their relationship to the forces of time.
6. "Capital punishment" takes its name from the same Latin source as "decapitation."
7. For the names of K'iche' and other Mayan languages of Guatemala I follow the official spellings of the Academia de las Lenguas Mayas de Guatemala (1988). I have kept traditional spellings for the Quiché nation or kingdom and for other Mayan nations or kingdoms.
8. Enrique Sam Colop, a K'iche'-speaking linguist and literary scholar from Cantel, accompanied me on a visit to Rabinal in 1989. No dialect of K'iche' is more widely separated in space from Rabinal than his, and yet he was able to engage in a lengthy conversation with José León Coloch, the director of *Rabinal Achi*.
9. The full story of the scripts and the manner in which the play's dialogue is actually performed is told in chapter 4.
10. See the first section of chapter 4 for a detailed discussion of Brasseur.
11. The interaction between the memories of performers and the editorial interventions of copyists is discussed in more detail in chapter 4, in the section titled "From Print to Manuscript to Photocopy."
12. For Luis Cardoza y Aragón's Spanish version of Georges Raynaud's unpublished French translation, see Raynaud and Cardoza y Aragón (1929-30), Raynaud (1953), and Cardoza y Aragón (1972). The Spanish version of Monterde (first published in 1955 and since reprinted) is a light revision of Cardoza y Aragón. The Spanish version of Antonio C. Villacorta (1942) is based on Brasseur. Anita Padial Guer-choux and Manuel Vázquez-Bigi (1991) based their Spanish version on Brasseur and Cardoza y Aragón. Sacor's Spanish version (1991) repeats errors that stem from

previous Spanish versions and directly contradict the original texts. The Spanish version in Breton (1999:141-293) was translated from the French of Breton (1994:153-319) by Jorge Mario Martínez.

13. The English version of Richard E. Leinaweaver (1968), which is complete, is based on Cardoza y Aragón. Nathaniel Tarn's English version of what Brasseur treated as the last of four scenes is based on Brasseur and Cardoza y Aragón. Abridged English versions of Brasseur have been published by Eleanor Wolff (1977) and Thomas Ballantine Irving (1985).

14. Breton (1994:319).

15. Pérez has "maqu" in place of mata, which Breton reads as "ma k'u"; this does not change the fact that the sentence is negative.

16. The verb stem -itzma- is prefixed to make the action incomplete (k-) and to give it a first-person singular object (-in-) and a second-person plural familiar subject (-wi-); the suffixes indicate that the action is beginning (-r-), that the subject of the verb is causing it to happen (-isa-), and that the verb is active rather than passive (-j). See the notes to Cawek's final speech for more on this passage.

17. See the section titled "Timing, Amplitude, and Intonation" in chapter 4 for a full discussion.

18. Soto and Fox engaged in "cultural translation," which goes beyond the substitution of translated dialogue for dialogue in an original language. As Soto (1998) described this process, "We have converted every language—sound, visual, movement, lights, and set—into something different from the original representation performed annually in Rabinal." In reviewing this production for Guatemala's largest daily, Enrique Sam Colop (1998) noted with approval that the actors, unlike the performers in some of the shows put on by Guatemalan tourist agencies, were not trying to pass themselves off as Mayans. The participants included a Cuban, an Australian, two African Americans, an Italian, and a Chinese.

19. For a translation of this play, whose title is *Atsumori*, see Waley (1976:35-44).

20. See Stephen Sondheim's discussion of musicals as "presentational plays" in which "numbers go out front" (1997:277).

21. Except for Coloch, who usually plays the role of Cawek, the actors have no direct access to the script. Once on stage they are, in effect, engaging in oral formulaic composition. For details of their departures from the script see chapter 4.

PART ONE

Rabinal Achi or Dance of the Trumpets

CHARACTERS

The list of characters published by Brasseur and copied by Pérez contains descriptions of characters and alterations of their names that appear to have been authored by Brasseur. His interventions contradict the play's dialogue on a number of points, as detailed below.

Cawek of the Forest People: This translates *Kaweq K'eche Winaq,* which is what the prisoner is consistently called by all the other characters. Brasseur, however, calls him "Cavek-Queche-Achi" in his list of characters and labels his speaking parts "Queche-Achi," following the model of the name of his opponent, "Rabinal-Achi." He thus takes *K'eche* to be synonymous with *K'iche',* which it is not. Pérez, following his lead, goes a step further and uses "quiché" or "qiché" *(k'iche'),* not only in the labels of Cawek's speeches, but within the speeches of the other characters as well. When Coloch reads from Pérez he says *K'ache',* and that is what he calls this character in conversation.

When *K'eche* is used instead of *K'iche'* in sixteenth-century documents written in Quichean languages, it is nearly always followed by *Winaq,* specifying that the reference is to people; in contrast, most terms for nations (such as *K'iche'* and *Rab'inal)* do not require such modification. This is probably because *K'eche* is shortened from *k'echela'j,* an ordinary term for "forest," and *K'eche Winaq* is to be understood as "Forest People." In a context such as that of the Popol Vuh, written by Quiché authors, *K'eche Winaq* calls up a proud heritage of emergence into glory from the depths of a great forest (see D. Tedlock 1996:150-62, 181). But in the context of the Rabinal play, where these same words name a prisoner of war, they may have called up the same meaning as *k'echela'j winaq,* which is "rustic, gross, foolish person" (FV, TC).

Man of Rabinal: The other characters consistently call this one *Rab'inal Achi,* nearly always prefacing these words with the noble title *Uq'alel Achi,* "Man of Glory," in which *q'alel* carries the sense of something clear or manifest. According to the Popol Vuh, this title was created as a reward for military achievement after successful Quiché military campaigns during the reign of Quicab, the most famous of Quiché kings (D. Tedlock 1996:190, 348).

Brasseur lists Man of Rabinal as "Rabinal-Achi" but then adds "Ahau-Galel-Rabinal," though none of these three words is ever combined with any of the others in the dialogue. He then identifies Rabinal as *uk'ajol* or "the son of" Lord Five Thunder. This is plausible, though the two of them neither address one another as "father" and "son" nor are identified as having such a relationship by other characters.

Lord Five Thunder: When the lord served by Man of Rabinal is addressed with full formality he is *Mama Ajaw Job' Toj. Mama* is "grandfather" or "old man," and *Job' Toj* is this lord's birth date on the 260-day divinatory calendar. He shares his day name (but not his day number) with the patron deity of the Rabinal nation, who is named in the Popol Vuh as *Jun Toj,* "One Thunder" (D. Tedlock 1996:162). In its origin the day name *Toj* shares its meaning with such forms as *tojojil,* "thunderer" (ibid.:296), but its divinatory associations run by way of the verb stem *toj-,* "to pay" (B. Tedlock 1992:115). Tribute payments to lords were due on days with this name.

Pérez, except in his list of characters, changes *Job'* to *Ojob',* meaning "Cough." I take this to be an error, resulting from his unfamiliarity with the divinatory calendar and with ancient naming practices.

Lady: She is greeted as *xoqajaw,* literally "woman lord." Brasseur lists her as the wife of Lord Five Thunder, a reasonable inference. He is the only character in the play who bears the title *ajaw,* "lord," and when the casting of a production includes her part (which is not always the case) she sits where he sits and dances where he dances. But rather than referring to her as his wife he calls her *nute,* "my mother," presumably meaning that she is the mother of his children. She does not have a speaking part.

Mother of Quetzal Feathers, Mother of Glistening Green: The other characters refer to this girl as *ri Uchuch Q'uq', Uchuch Raxon,* but these are not her names, properly speaking. Rather, they constitute a figure of speech for a daughter who will bring a high bride price (see the entries for "ƐuƐ" in FV and "doncella" in TC). Brasseur identifies her as the wife of Man of Rabinal, but her role is always played by a maiden around ten to twelve years old. Moreover, Lord Five Thunder implies that she is his unmarried daughter and that Cawek is (or could have been) a candidate for her husband (see the "son-in-law" note to his first speech). *Raxon* refers to bright green things, especially quetzal feathers and jade (FT).

Slave: This character, who is represented as androgynous (see the entry in the list of characters that prefaces the play), is always addressed as *achij mun, ixoq mun,* "man slave, woman slave." It is not clear whether he-she has always been androgynous, or results from combining two slaves into one. In his cast of characters,

Brasseur lists "Mun" and "Ixok Mun," translating the former as "Un Esclave" and treating the latter as the proper name of a character he describes as "esclave favorite de Rabinal-Achi" (1862:24-25). Of the five speeches made by a slave, he attributes the first two to Ixok Mun (pp. 90, 92) and the other three to Mun (pp. 102, 106, 110), even though Mun makes each of his three speeches in response to being addressed as "achih mun, ixok mun." Pérez follows Brasseur except for assigning the third Mun speech to "ixoℇ mun."

Eagle and *Jaguar:* When these two characters are the subject of conversation they are always referred to as being twelve in number, but when they are addressed no number is mentioned. Only one Eagle and one Jaguar have ever been reported in eyewitness descriptions of performances. But there are references to multiple "Aigles et Tigres" in Brasseur's stage directions, and there could have been a time when there were twelve (see the note on "those twelve lords" in the fourth speech of Man of Rabinal and the notes for the first speech of Lord Five Thunder). In the gladiatorial sacrifices of the Mexica (Aztecs) there were two eagle and two jaguar priests (Sahagún 1951:51).

Road Guide: This translates *k'amol b'e,* the title of a ritual specialist whose prayers and offerings are required for the production of the play. He is not listed by Brasseur or Pérez, but he dresses in the same costume as the musicians and accompanies the cast in all its public appearances.

The last item in Brasseur's list of characters reads as follows: "Quïatak ahlabalib ruq quïa munib, alahil chic, achi vepu ixok, e xahel chire Xahoh-Tun." His authorship of this statement is given away by his awkward handling of the language, his vision of emancipated slaves, and his well-known penchant for exaggeration: "A great many warriors along with many slaves, now free, men as well as women, they are the dancers of the Dance of the Trumpets."

Ahead of the play's opening speech and in three other places Brasseur inserted headings that divide the play into four scenes or acts, all of them copied by Pérez. No other texts for plays performed in Guatemalan Mayan towns have such divisions. Moreover, when *Rabinal Achi* is performed all the actors are on stage at all times, and there are no interruptions. On Brasseur's text pages the headings are in K'iche', but it is clear that he translated them from French rather than the other way around. In the case of the first heading, "U Nabe Banbal" is as close as it is possible to get to a literal rendering of "Premier Acte," though he has "Scène Première" on the facing page. In actual usage *b'anb'al,* which combines *b'an-,* "do, make" with the instrumental or locational suffix -*b'al,* means "tool" (PG) or "place where something is done or made" (DB, FT), and its commonest contemporary application is to latrines and toilets (see the entries for *kuk'oto* and *xo'j rilik* in AG).

Cawek of the Forest People speaks for the first time.

Come on out, lord who's been pierced / lord who's been fitted with gems: This translates *Katel uloq, worom ajaw / k'aqom ajaw.* The verb *katel* is in the second person familiar *(-at-)*, which is why I have introduced "you" into the translation of two of the lines that follow. *Ajaw* is "lord" and *-m* makes the verb stems *woro-* and *k'aqo-* into substantives. For the second stem Brasseur has "cako-," but the form that best fits with *woro-*, "to drill or bore a hole through" (DB, MX), is *k'aqo-*, which, because spearheads and arrowheads were made of stone, covers not only shooting and lancing, but also stoning (FT, FV, TC; see also the entries for "cacoqueh" and "cacomqueh" in DB). The reference is to the fact that a lord who had taken a captive in battle was entitled to have his own nose and lower lip pierced *(worom)* for the insertion of a stone *(k'aqom)*, in this case not a weapon but an ornament.

however that may be / let me take the lead: Brasseur has "Cuxere chi nabe vae" and Pérez has "xacuxere chinabe vae," while José León Coloch performs this passage as *xa k'u xere / qi chinab'e wa'*, dividing it into two distinct lines by means of a pause. The first line is a common phrase meaning "however" or "even so." In the second line *qi* is a particle that conveys an effort to be polite or correct (FV); *ch-* is imperative and *i(n)-* is "I," a combination that carries the sense of "let me"; *nab'e* is "be first, be ahead"; and *wa'e,* shortened to *wa'* in contemporary speech, is "this one" or "the one who," referring to the subject of the preceding verb. A literal translation of *chinab'e* would be intransitive: "Let me be the first one."

since I'm not finished / chopping through / the root / the trunk: Here Coloch remarked, "It's as if someone said they would kill me and all my sons." He treats the words *mawi kanuk'iso,* "I'm not finished," as belonging together in the same line, but Breton puts *mawi* at the end of the previous line and (unlike Brasseur) misses the fact that it makes the present line negative.

of that Lord of Walkers / Lord of Workers: When Coloch recites the present lines from memory he says *Lajaw Chakachib' / Lajaw Samanib',* in which *Lajaw* is a contraction of *la',* "that," and *ajaw,* "lord." The texts have a plain *ajaw* in the first line and omit it in the second. Pérez renders the "Zamanib" of Brasseur as "tzamanib," but this need not be taken as an emendation, since he uses "tz" whether he is transcribing a "z" or a "tz." Both names carry the pluralizing suffix *-b',* which is used only for nouns referring to persons. The *Annals of the Cakchiquels* uses "Çamaneb" as a place name (Brinton 1885:110), but otherwise the adjectival suffix *-l* replaces *-b'* when these two names refer to places, as in the "Chacachil" of the *Annals* (Brinton 1885:88-89) and the "Tzamaniel" (probably an error for "Tzamanil") of Ximénez (1977:213). *Chakach* is a noun for "basket" (DB, FT, FX) or a verb stem for standing on four legs or walking in a tentative, step-by-step manner (DB, FX, FV). *Sama-,* which here carries the action-focus suffix *-n,* is to work, practice, or do exercises (TC); *tzama-* would mean "to adorn with jewels" (FX, FV, TC), while *tzamal* is "diligent" (TC). I have chosen "Walkers" and "Workers" as translations for the two names, partly in order to preserve a similarity of sound between them.

A place named "Chacachil" is included in the itinerary of highland lords who went on a pilgrimage to a lowland lord named Nacxit in order to receive emblems of rulership, as described in *Annals of the Cakchiquels* (Brinton 1885:88-89). The pilgrims stopped there not long before reaching Fish in the Ashes *(Karchaj),* which would place it somewhere northeast of Rabinal. Van Akkeren (1999:287n) asserts that it is the place known today as *Kachil* or Plano Grande, a mountaintop seven kilometers north of Salamá, though Arnauld (1993:59) does not report an archaeological site for that location. The *Annals* names "Çamaneb" as the place where the Rabinal nation saw its first dawn (Brinton 1885:110-11). What may be its ruins, known today as Tres Cruces (Ichon 1982:72-77) or Los Cimientos Patzaj (Arnauld 1993:90-91), are located on a ridge nine kilometers south-west of the Cubulco town center, on the boundary between the lands of Cubulco and those of Joyabaj.

Cawuks and Rabinals: Brasseur has "Cauk Rabinal" and Pérez has "cavuƐ Rabinal," while Breton reads "kawuq rabinal" and takes "kawuq" to be the name of a Rabinal lineage. *Kawuqeb'* and *Rab'inaleb',* names for two closely related nations *(amaq'eb'),* appear together in the Popol Vuh (D. Tedlock 1996:187, 324) and two other sixteenth-century documents (Carmack and Mondloch 1989:84, 179). The former name, variously spelled "Caoqueb," "Caokeb," and "CavoƐeb" in these documents, becomes Caoqué in Spanish. It belongs to the nation that once controlled the citadel of *Saqkab'aja* or "Plaster House," which was conquered by the Quiché during the reign of Quicab. The town of San Andrés Sajcabajá is located fifty kilometers west of Rabinal, and its dialect is similar to that of Rabinal (Campbell 1977:14-15). After the Spanish invasion some Caoqués were resettled in the towns of Santa María Caoqué and Santiago Caoqué, a short distance northwest of Guatemala City; the name Caoqué has been officially replaced by Sacatepéquez, the name of the department in which they are located (D. Tedlock:1996:324).

since I haven't many words / to say to you, sir: In the texts this is *keje mawi k'ia tzij / kinch'aw uk' la,* literally "since not many words / am I saying with you sir." Coloch's rendition of the second line, which is consistent with later passages that are analogous to the present one, is *kojtzijon uk' la,* "are we speaking with you sir."

May Sky and Earth be with you, sir: This invocation of the divine, *Kaj Ulew chik'oje uk' la,* is modeled on Spanish blessings and oaths, as are most of the similar expressions occurring later. They are the products of compromises between missionary goals and indigenous realities, with Christian forms and the mention of "Sky" (which could be taken as an allusion to God) compensating for the heterodox "Earth." At a deeper level, mentions of *Kaj* and *Ulew,* "Sky" and "Earth," are an abbreviation of *Uk'ux Kaj, Uk'ux Ulew,* "Heart of Sky, Heart of Earth," a divine epithet used in the Popol Vuh (D. Tedlock 1996:223-24, 343). It refers to *Tojil,* "Thunderer," the patron of lordship and the deity who would have been offered the blood of Cawek of the Forest People.

Here and elsewhere, "sir" is my way of translating polite address in K'iche', which is marked by *la* or *lal* (singular) and *alaq* (plural).

Man of Rabinal speaks for the first time.

Listen!: This cry varies between "yeha" and "eha" in the Brasseur text, but in Pérez it is always "eha." "Yeha" is used extensively in the script for *Saqi K'oxol,* a Quiché play about the conquest of Mexico (Edmonson 1997:8-72). In Coloch's pronunciation the word is *e'ja'.* Its original form may have been *ye'ja'* (FV), in which *ye'j-* is "to hasten" and *ye'ja'* (with an imperative suffix) is "make haste." Another source glosses "yeh" as a "way of mocking" (FX). Coloch, who says the word *e'ja'* is used only in the play, explains that "it means, 'Listen to me.' It is used to call the attention of the other person." In performance the vowels are drawn out, with a higher pitch on the first one. Both the Brasseur and Pérez texts omit this cry at the start of Cawek's third and Rabinal's fourth speeches, but since Coloch uses it in his own renditions of those speeches, even when he reads from the Pérez text, "Listen!" has been inserted in the present translation.

Brave man: Oyew means "brave" (DB) or "angry" (FX).

"Come on out, lord who's been pierced": Beyond this line, the text of Rabinal's quotation of Cawek is missing from Pérez, along with the remainder of Rabinal's first speech, the label for Rabinal's second speech, and the first three lines of type from his second speech (corresponding to the first eight lines of the present translation). Breton (1994:159n.) unjustly calls this "une erreur" on the part of Pérez. The omitted material coincides exactly with page 28 of the Brasseur text, filling the reverse of a leaf that was obviously missing from the copy of Brasseur's book available to Pérez. The absence of the obverse of this leaf (page 27) did not matter, since it carried the French translation of page 26 of the original text.

...in range of my weapon / in range of my shield: The literal meaning of *chupam ral nuch'ab' / chupam ral nupokob'* is "inside the weight (or power) of my weapon /

inside the weight (or power) of my shield," and in other contexts I have chosen "power" or "strength" instead of "range." *Al* is "weight" (DB, FX, FV, MX, AG) or "power," as in "the power of God" (DB); *ralib'al* is "lasso" and *ralim* is "tied together" (FT). "Weapon" translates *ch'ab'*, which is "arrow" or "dart," while *ch'ab'ij* is to shoot with the same (FX, FV, TC).

and my snail-shell bracelet / my armband / my white paint / my gourd of tobacco: These are all emblems of the lordly status of Man of Rabinal. Equivalent emblems appear in the Popol Vuh, but with different names (D. Tedlock 1996:316). In the play the first two items are *chinku*, "bracelet of bone for dancing" (DB), in which *chin-* could be from *chinik*, referring to a small snail (TC); and *k'alq'ab'*, "armband" (DB, FX). In place of these terms the Popol Vuh has *t'ot' tatam*, "snail-shell rattle," and *makutax*, from Nahuatl *macuetlaxtli*, referring to a leather armband (RS). Instead of the play's *saqkab'* or "white paint" (literally "white earth"), the Popol Vuh has *q'an ab'aj*, "red ochre" (literally "red stone"). In the play the gourd of tobacco is called by the K'iche' term *salme't*, which combines a variant of *sel*, "painted gourd" (FV), with *me't*, "tobacco," but the Popol Vuh uses a Yucatec Maya name, *k'us b'us*. For other emblems of lordship, see "upraised ax handle" and "upraised ax blade" below.

with my henequen rope / my henequen cord: The term translated as "henequen" is *saqki'*, which is "the maguey whose leaves they make into ropes" (FV; see also DB). Brasseur has "zaki" (changed by Pérez to "tzaɛi"), meaning "white," but *saqki'*, which later occurs in a place name (see Henequen Mountain / Henequen Valley below), makes better sense. Numerous species and varieties of maguey or century plant *(Agave)* are cultivated in Mesoamerica, with the most important distinction being between those used for fiber, including henequen *(Agave fourcroydes)*, and those whose sap is tapped to make pulque (see "the twelve drinks" below). The present-day crafts of Rabinal include the making of ropes from henequen fibers.

Man of Rabinal speaks for the second time.

Pérez omits the beginning of this speech and runs the rest of it on with Rabinal's first speech; see the note headed "Come on out, lord who's been pierced," above.

and my upraised ax handle / my upraised ax blade: This couplet, which translates *nuyakim wit / nuyakim ikaj*, refers to the ax carried by the speaker. It is never referred to in any other way, except for one instance in which the second line is used alone. *Wital ikaj* is "ax handle" (FV); *wit* is "the oak from which ax handles are made" (PG); and *ikaj* is specifically an ax blade for cutting wood (FX, DB, FV). The ax in question here is an emblem of lordship equivalent to the manikin scepter held by Classic Maya lords (see chapter 1).

Where is your mountain? / Where is your valley?: Here Man of Rabinal is asking for the
names of the places where Cawek's lineage has the shrines that serve its members and their wives as the *warab'al ja* or "foundation (literally sleeping place)
of the house" (see B. Tedlock 1992:77-83). These would be the places where
his birth was first announced to his ancestors and the gods.

on the slope of a mountain / on the floor of a valley: This is *tzala juyub' / tzala taq'aj,* in
which *tzala* is translated as "slope" and "floor" on the basis of such forms as
tzalam, which refers to boards and other things with flat surfaces (DB); *tza-
lanem,* "slope of a mountain" (DB); and *tzalan,* "slope," especially a slope
whose surface is even (FV).

Weren't you born of clouds? / Weren't you born of mist?: Man of Rabinal uses familiar
rather than polite address throughout this speech, and he means these two
questions as direct insults to Cawek. They imply that Cawek, like an orphan
or foundling, might not be able to give a substantial account of his place of
birth and parentage.

Cawek of the Forest People speaks for the second time.

Alas, O Sky! / Alas, O Earth!: This invocation of the divine, *Aqaroq Kaj / Aqaroq Ulew,*
is unlike others occurring in the play in that it is not based on a Spanish exclamation. *Aqaroq* seems to consist of the verb stem *aqar-,* "to stop" (FV), with
the imperative suffix *-oq,* and is said to express both pain and admiration (in
the entry for "acaoc" in FX). In the Popol Vuh it combines a tone of despair
with an attempt to gain attention from a distance (D. Tedlock 1996:276), and
it is used to open a prayer addressed to the god whose epithets include "Heart
of Sky, Heart of Earth" (ibid.:192) and whose icon is the upraised ax discussed above.

in my teeth, in my face: Literally, *chi nuchi', chi nuwach* is "in (or at) my mouth" and
"face." In some contexts I have kept "mouth," but in the present one "teeth"
provides an appropriate English expression.

"Now reveal the face / of your mountain / your valley": In this context "face," which translates *wach,* has the sense of "identity." Cawek is interpreting what Man of Rabinal said rather than repeating his exact words, but he nevertheless phrases his
interpretation as a direct quotation. In the Popol Vuh, whose characters frequently quote one another, the same practice is followed (D. Tedlock
1998:180). Pérez moves the script of the play a step closer to the norms of prose
narrative in European languages by recasting this sentence as indirect discourse
(see Breton 1994:164, lines 114-15).

Man of Rabinal speaks for the third time.

Pérez labels this as *uroxmul,* "his third," even though he omits the part of Brasseur's text
where the label for Rabinal's second speech appears. Written in the margin, in a
different hand, is "2°R.," an abbreviation for "segundo de Rabinal." Similar
notations accompany Rabinal's later speeches, in each case assigning an arabic
numeral that is lower by one than the number whose name is written in the text
proper. Coloch told Breton (1994:73) that these numbers were inserted by
Eugenio Xolop, the son of Coloch's predecessor as director of the play.

then Sky willing / Earth willing: "Willing" translates *karaj,* "wants, desires." This pair of
phrases, which is based on Spanish "si Dios quiere" (the equivalent of English
"God willing"), postdates sixteenth-century texts such as the Popol Vuh.

you'll just shout / you'll just shriek: This is *xa at wajim / xa at perajim,* translated on the
basis of *waj,* "cry of war" (DB), and *perere-,* "cry" (AT).

inside his great fortress, inside his great walls: "Fortress" and "walls" translate *tz'aq* and
k'oxtun. The former term covers earthworks, together with buildings whose
principal materials are stone or earth; the latter refers to the walls or stockade
enclosing a fortress (TC).

Cawek of the Forest People speaks for the third time.

of this little house wren, this bird: "Little house wren" translates "ix tapicholon" in Brasseur and "ixtapichol on" in Pérez. "Tipicholol" is "a small bird famous for its
song" (FT); *tapich'olol* (PG) or "tapicholol" (FT) is the bird called "cur-
ruchiché" in Guatemalan Spanish. It is the Southern house wren *(Troglodytes
musculus),* whose song is similar to that of the house wren of eastern North
America *(Troglodytes aedon).* Like Cawek, who compares himself to this wren, it
is loquacious and constantly on the move as it forages. *Ix,* which is frequently
used in references to birds, is diminutive.

In this same passage Enrique Sam Colop (personal communication)
hears a sound play on *pich'o'l,* a term for ears of corn that are overlooked
when a field is harvested (AT). If Cawek is to be understood historically as
one of Quicab's younger sons, the one known as Father Fox, he may have felt
overlooked (see the notes to "who makes the cries of foxes" and "who makes
the cries of agoutis and jaguars," below).

of the lord of foreign Cunén / foreign Chajul: The present-day towns of Cunén and Chajul
are on the northern frontier of the ancient Quiché kingdom and due north of its
capital. "Foreign" translates *yaki,* which often refers to speakers of Pipil, a lan-

guage closely related to Nahuatl that was once spoken in Guatemala on the Pacific coast and the middle Motagua valley, but it has a broader reference to foreign languages in the general term for an interpreter, *ajyakichi'* (DB), in which *aj-* is occupational and *chi'* is "mouth." Chajul speaks Ixil, which, in terms of the overall structure of the Mayan language family, places it on the opposite side of a deep divide from K'iche'. Cunén speaks K'iche' today, but before it came under Quiché rule it may have spoken Ixil. Its lands are bordered on the north by speakers of Ixil and on the west by speakers of Awakateko, the language most closely related to Ixil.

the Lord Jaguar Man / Jaguar Quiché / the quick one: These lines and similar ones occurring in Cawek's fourth speech and Rabinal's fifth are treated as the names and epithets of a single lord in the texts, but behind them are the names of the founders of the lineages that held the top titles in the hierarchy of Quiché lords (D. Tedlock 1996:289; 146-49; 194-97). In rank order they are *B'alam K'itze* ("Balam Quiche" in the play texts), founder of the *Kaweq* or Cawek lineage; *B'alam Aq'ab'* or "Jaguar Night" ("Balam Achi" in the play), founder of the *Nijayib'* or Great House lineage; and *Majukutaj* or *Majukotaj*, "Not-Right-Now," founder of the *Ajaw K'iche'* or "Lord Quiché" lineage. The last name is "lahucutah" in Brasseur and "la hucutah" in Pérez; *la'* is "that" and *juqutaj* or *juqotaj* means "instantly" (DB).

Man of Rabinal speaks for the fourth time.

What a terrible joke you're my elder brother. / What a terrible joke you're my younger brother: "What a terrible joke" translates *xa pe xa lal*, which is a worn-down version of the phrases *xa petze* and *xa alaj*, both of which refer to a joke or jest (PG). By itself *alaj* can have the same meaning, but *petze* carries a sense of distrust, fear, and even terror (FX).

There is no generic term for "brother" in Quichean languages; elder brother is *atz* and younger brother is *chaq'*. What Man of Rabinal is telling Cawek is that they should not have found themselves in the position of being enemies.

who makes the cries of foxes: The particular member of the Cawek lineage on whom the Cawek of the play may be modeled was a rebellious son of Quicab, the most famous of Quiché kings. Whatever name this son may have preferred, his enemies knew him as *Tata Yak*, "Father Fox" (Recinos and Goetz 1953:94).

who make the cries of agoutis and jaguars: Man of Rabinal follows normal practice when he pairs coyotes and foxes, but here he produces an insult by altering the expected pair of animals, which would be *koj* and *b'alam*, "pumas" and "jaguars" (see D. Tedlock 1996:66-67). For the puma he substitutes *utiw*, "agouti"

(PG), which is a rodent *(Dasyprocta punctata)* about twice the size of a rabbit. It is easily startled and shrieks loudly as it flees.

If Cawek is modeled on Father Fox (see the previous note) then the insult is double, since *utuy* plays on the sound of *Chituy,* the noble title held by Father Fox (Recinos and Goetz 1953:94). It ranked sixth among the titles held by the Cawek lineage and thus placed him fifth in the line of succession (see "Councilor of the Stores" in D. Tedlock 1996:322, 340).

...the children, the sons of light: This is *saqil alk'ajol,* in which *alk'ajol* is compounded of *al,* referring to a woman's children of either gender, and *k'ajol,* referring to a man's sons. In most contexts, as here, the combination of these two terms refers to the vassals or subjects of lordly persons (PG, TC). *Saqil* refers to the fact that such people were born and begotten in the "light," which is to say when the present sun and moon had already risen. Lords and ladies, on the other hand, trace their ancestry back to a time when the earth was dark, as told in the Popol Vuh (D. Tedlock 1996: part 4).

the providers, creatures / of yellow honey / fresh honey: Vassals or subjects are here compared to worker bees, bringing nectar back to the hive. In the case of subjects who are warriors, the Popol Vuh uses the metaphor of yellow jackets and wasps, which (unlike the honey bee native to Mesoamerica) sting people who threaten their nests (D. Tedlock 1996:172-73).

...my lord, my liege: This is *wajawal, nuwinaqil.* In other contexts *winaqil* refers to human persons in general, but in this couplet it is short for *nima winaqil,* literally "great person," another term for nobility (DB).

...those twelve lords: During the period immediately prior to the Spanish invasion the Rabinal valley was ruled from two hilltop sites, each of them with palaces and temples organized around six plazas (Fox 1987:220). One of these sites was Red Mountain (see below) and the other was the site known today as *Chuwi Tinamit* or "Above the Town," eight kilometers northeast of Red Mountain (Arnauld 1993:65). When Fray Bartolomé de las Casas founded a mission on the site of the present-day Rabinal town center in 1537, he had the task of persuading the leaders of twelve different divisions of the Rabinal people to move down into the valley (Ximénez 1977:214). These twelve lords may have been the owners of the twelve workers in jade and metal, twelve Golden Eagles and Jaguars, and twelve drinks mentioned by Lord Five Thunder in his first speech (see below).

...the food in each bowl / the drink in each jar: This translates *upam jujun chi waib'al / chi uk'ib'al.* For the last word Pérez follows Brasseur's "oqobal," but later (in the seventh speech of Cawek) he changes it to "oqibal." *Way* is any solid food made of maize and *uk'iy* is atole (maize gruel); when paired, these terms become comple-

mentary metonyms for all food and drink, and with the instrumental suffix -*b'al* they become terms for all containers of food and drink. In the texts these lines follow the verbs discussed in the next note, which is perfectly good form in the original language but calls for reversal in English translation.

was dissolved / tasted / freshened / and absorbed: The subject of these verbs is the food and drink in the previous note, but in each case Pérez changes the completed action prefix *x-* to the second-person plural prefix *ix.* The first verb is *xja'rik,* "softened" (FT), "melted, liquefied" (DB, AG), "aged" (DB), or "taken apart" (MX). The second, for which the "xtaamic" of Brasseur is changed to "ix tuanic" by Pérez (not only here but in the seventh speech of Rabinal), is *xt'amik,* "tasted" in the sense of "sampled" during the process of preparation (FV, TC). The third is *xtuxarik* (whose *tuxa-* form is attested by AT), "began to bud, sprout, reappear"; in the present context, it presumably carries a figurative connection to the preparation of food (perhaps dried food) that has been in storage. The fourth verb is *tzarajmaqirik,* translated on the basis of *tzarajmaq,* "sponge" or (because it is absorbent) "pumice" (DB, FX, FV, AT).

…we must finish the farm work: This translates *chiqatanab'ataj utik,* in which *tanab'a-* is "cease work," *-taj* puts the focus on the result, and *utik* is "their plantings," referring to the plantings of the vassals (the children and sons of light) mentioned in the following line. The shortening of *tik* from the more familiar *tikon* is attested in colonial sources (FX, FV, TC). Brasseur has "tiic," a form not attested in any dictionary of K'iche' or Kaqchikel, and gives it the cannibalistic translation "mordre" (bite), as if the text read "tionic" *(tionik).* Pérez changes Brasseur's "tiic" to "tihic" *(tijik),* a common verb for "eat," and Breton, who translates this as "consommer," cites it as evidence for the existence of cannibalism among the ancient Quiché (Breton 1994:175). The fact is that the narrative in which this passage occurs moves from the consumption of a supply of ordinary food and drink (see the previous two notes) to the harvesting of a bean crop (see the next note), and there is nothing in the oldest version of the text (Brasseur's) that demands a cannibalistic reading.

"quickly gathering large beans / gathering white-winged dove beans / gathering red-feathered quail beans / gathering striped quail beans": "Large beans" is a literal translation of *nima kinaq'.* The remaining three terms refer to varieties of beans that are named for the resemblance of their coloration to that of birds. The second item, "xtapacal" in Brasseur and "ixtapaqal" in Pérez, appears in dictionaries of Quichean languages as *xtapakal* (AT) or "xtacapal" (see the entry for "friçol" in TC) and is glossed as a term for a variety of beans. Its source is Pipil, in which *istakehtapal,* "white-winged," refers to a species of dove (LC), presumably the white-winged dove *(Zenaida asiatica)* whose range extends from the southern

United States through Central America (Howell and Webb 1995:324). The third item is "cakix-coruvach" in Brasseur, shortened to "ixqorovach" in Pérez. The generic term for quail is *saq korowach* (FT, FV, TC), in which *saq* is "white," here replaced by *kaqix*, "red-feathered."

The fourth item on the list, "tzuleyuhi" in both texts of the play, appears as "zuleyuchi" in a K'iche' dictionary source that identifies it as a kind of bean (DB). This term comes from Pipil, in which *sulin* is "quail" and *iyuh* is "stripe" (LC); Coloch describes the bean in question as striped. Among the Nahuatl terms for beans is *soletl*, "quail beans," referring to a variety that is "painted the color of a quail" (Sahagún 1951:63).

Weren't there nine clenched fists / nine forearms: The "fists" are *moq'ol* (PG); *moq'ej* is "to hold something in a fist" (FT). The "forearms" are *chumay*, "the arm from the elbow to the hand" (DB, PG). I take these fists and forearms to be metonyms for the "braves" and "men" mentioned in the following lines. Nine fists or forearms would refer to nine warriors (not four and a half), following the pattern of *aqan* or "leg," which is used in counting animals ("three legs of cow" or "of chicken" means three cows or chickens).

Brasseur interprets this passage (and a later one with the same words) as naming a place, and Breton follows suit. Such a reading is implausible because none of the phraseology used for place names elsewhere in the text is used here, and because the location of the event partially described here is accounted for (complete with standard phrasing) in the very next sentence (see the next note).

there at the place called / Pitted / and Planted: Literally, *Chi K'otom / Chi Tikiram / chuch'a'xik* is "at Pitted / at Planted / as it is called," which is ordinary Quichean phrasing for the introduction of proper names in a narrative. Here and elsewhere I have substituted ordinary English phrasing.

K'otom is "hole" (FX) or "excavation" (MX), while *tikiram* refers to something planted in the ground. This place may have received its names from what took place there, or Man of Rabinal may be fitting his narrative to preexistent place names. There is a place known today as *Chi K'otom* three kilometers west of Standing Jaguar, near the northeast corner of the lands of the town of Joyabaj (Arnauld 1993:89).

How could your heart's desire / not be fulfilled, sir / over those braves / those men?: Literally, *Naqipa mawi chik'owik / rajab'al k'ux la / chirech wa' oyewal / wa' achijilal* is "How could it not be fulfilled / the desire of your heart, sir / over these brave ones / these manly ones?" In the text these lines precede "Weren't there nine clenched fists / nine forearms (see above), but I have moved them here for consistency with later occurrences of the same four lines, where they follow accounts of the losses inflicted by Cawek rather than preceding them.

Cawek of the Forest People speaks for the fourth time.

Alas, O Sky! / Alas, O Earth!: Coloch adds these lines, which are the same as the ones that
begin Cawek's second speech (see above).

Red Mountain / Shaker / Dressed in Red / Tepecanic: Originally these four names may have
referred to the four major sections of the ruins that lie three kilometers north of
the Rabinal town center (Fox 1978:255), perched on a hill that rises 300 meters
above the valley floor. These would have been the sections labeled by Smith
(1955:44-48) as groups A, C, D, and E (B appears to be on a boundary between
sections). In a similar manner, the Popol Vuh gives four names to the four-part
ruin known today as Cauinal, 20 kilometers northwest of Rabinal (D. Tedlock
1996:317).

  "Red Mountain" translates *Kaqyuq'*, which is "Cakyug" in Brasseur
and "qaԐyuԐ" in Pérez. This is a Poqomchi' name, in which *kaq* is "red" and
yuq' is "mountain" (OS). In the *Annals of the Cakchiquels,* a list of places
brought under the control of the Quiché kingdom during the reign of Quicab
includes *Chi Kaqyuq'* (Brinton 1885:132-33), in which the addition of *chi*
simply means "at." In everyday Rabinal speech the name has become *Kajyub'*,
in which *jyub'* is shortened from *juyub'*, "mountain." It is commonly applied
to the entire ruin, but it may once have referred to the main group of buildings
(A), which is much larger than the others. The second of the four names,
Silik, is translated on the basis of the verb *sili-,* "to move, shake" (DB, FX),
and Coloch's own gloss, "it moves"; in Poqomchi' *sili-* is "to slip, slide" (OS).
The third name is *Kaqokawunik,* in which *kaqo* is "red" and the rest means
"ornamented" or "prepared" (FT, TC). The last name is of Pipil origin, from
tepe, "mountain," and *kumit,* "jar" (LC).

...ten score seeds of pataxte / five score seeds of cacao: "Ten score" and "five score" are
lajuk'al and *ok'al,* in which *-k'al* is a numeral classifier used for counting cacao
seeds by the score (see the entries for "ocal" or "ogal" in DB, FX, FV).
"Pataxte" (a Spanish word derived from Nahuatl) is *peq,* the K'iche' term for a
lower grade of cacao (from the tree *Theobroma bicolor*) than cacao proper (from
Theobroma cacao); "cacao" is *kakow.* In European languages, the words
"cacao" and "cocoa" ultimately stem from a Mayan source (S.D. Coe and M.D.
Coe 1996:35).

*Since the Uxab / the Pokomam / desire the death / of the Lord of Walkers / Lord of Workers /
Cawuks and Rabinals:* These lines translate *rumal taseq karayix ukamik / ri
Ajaw Chakachib' / Ajaw Samanib' / Kawuq, Rab'inal / chuwach Uxab' / chu-
wach Poqomam,* literally, "because since it is desired his death / the Lord of
Walkers / Lord of Workers / Cawuk, Rabinal / in front of the Uxab / in front of
the Pokomam." It is clear from the syntax that the person referred to by *u-* (his)

in *ukamik* (his death) is the *ajaw* (lord) who is named here, which is made even clearer in Rabinal's fifth speech. Even so, Breton makes this lord into the desirer of someone else's death, as if the text read *karayix ukamik* rumal ri *Ajaw,* which would indeed mean "sa mort est désirée *par* le roi" (1994:181, emphasis added).

Pérez changes the "Pokomam" of Brasseur to "Poℰomab" throughout, thus matching its ending to "Uxab," the name with which it is always paired. Pérez uses "ℰ" for both the "k" and "ℰ" of proper colonial orthography, equivalent to today's *q* and *q';* in the present case the evidence of colonial documents and the official spellings of the Academia de las Lenguas Mayas (1988:25) favor *Poqomam,* but Breton uses *q'.* The pairing of the names *Uxab'* and *Poqomam* may reflect the dual ethnic and linguistic identity of the people whose territory lay north, east, and south of Rabinal and once included the Rabinal valley (see Miles 1957). A sixteenth-century Quiché document describes a war against enemies whose double identity is given as *e Yaki, e Poqomam,* "those who are Mexican, those who are Pokomam" (Recinos 1957:108-109), suggesting that Uxab was a term for the speakers of Pipil (closely related to Nahuatl) who lived among speakers of Poqomam (a Quichean language), some of them immediately east of Rabinal. Today the Pokomam people of the script are split into speakers of Poqomam, south of Rabinal, and Poqomchi', to the north.

In the *Annals of the Cakchiquels, Uxa* and *Nimpoqom* appear two positions apart in a long list of the names of places said to have been brought under the control of the Quiché kingdom during the reign of Quicab (Brinton 1885:132-33). The putative ruins of *Nimpoqom,* now known as *Pakaqja,* are located five kilometers northwest of the Rabinal town center (Ichon 1982:68-71). According to the *Title of the Lords of Totonicapán* (Carmack and Mondloch 1983:195), the war Quicab waged in order to recover the bones of his father was directed against the *Uxajayil,* "those of the House of Uxa," and the "4gohayil," which (judging from other sources) is a misspelling of "Cohayil" *(Kojayil),* "those of the House of the Puma." Another source says the object of his campaign was a town called *Koja* (Recinos 1957:140-45), and the *Annals* lists *Koja* among the places conquered by Quicab, placing it immediately after *Chi Kaqyuq',* "At Red Mountain" (Brinton 1885:132-33), which was a Pokomam town at the time. All of the names involving *koj,* "puma," point to the people called *ajkaqkoj,* "those of the Red Puma," located in the present-day Pokomchí town of San Cristóbal Verapaz (Recinos 1957:104-105).

...*Quiché Mountain / Quiché Valley:* This is an epithet for the principal town of the Quiché kingdom and its environs; in later speeches it is referred to by the names of the twin citadels at its heart, Old Camp and Whisker Place.

to come and cultivate: "Cultivate" translates *echab'entaj,* which in some later contexts is rendered as "plant crops." In the present passage the spelling is "echabenatah," but later it is mostly "echabentah." Dictionary forms such as *echb'ej,* "inherit, own" (AG), and *echb'enik,* "inherit, take possession of" (MX), suggest an invitation to take possession of land. On the other hand, such forms as *echa',* referring to stored crops and all types of vegetal food (FV, FT), and *echa'laj ulew,* "fertile land" (FT, FX), suggest that *echab'entaj,* with its processual *(-b'en)* and result-of-action *(-taj)* suffixes, could mean an invitation to make land productive, which is consistent with the context.

then all the sprouts of our squash vines... / will travel their roads: The spreading out of squash plants *(k'um)* seems to be a metaphor for territorial expansion.

I'm going step by step right now / I'm working the soil: In both texts the first of these lines is "in hintantah." Here and in two later passages my literal reading of this is *in,* "I"; *jin,* "I'm going," which is used in taking leave (DB, PG, FV); and (since it fits the place-to-place narrative that always follows these lines) *tanataq,* "steps" or "stairs" (DB). The next line, as Enrique Sam Colop has pointed out to me, should be read as *in kintaji'nik,* in which *taji'nik* is to cultivate land (AG). Breton translates the first line as, "Moi, je n'entendis rien" (1992:185), as if it began with the negative particle *mana* (which is absent) and as if *taj* were the negative particle that ends phrases beginning with *mana;* further, he ignores the *j-* before *in* and treats *tan* as if it were the verb *ta-,* "hear, understand," with the action-focus suffix *-n,* a usage that occurs only rarely (see Mondloch 1978:117).

I'm resetting the boundaries of the land: The verb stem here is *k'ojo-,* translated on the basis of *k'ojoj,* "to reseed a plant that didn't sprout" (FV) or "to mend," as when splicing a broken cord back together (TC). At the smallest scale, a phrase like this might be used for setting the boundaries of a cornfield. But Cawek's itinerary takes him along the boundary of the Quiché kingdom, from a point southwest of its capital to a point due east—or, as he states the matter, "from the place where the day goes out / to the place where the night enters"—and it takes him ever closer to Rabinal.

Mountains in a Row / Pines in a Row: These names, *Cholochik Juyub'* and *Cholochik Chaj,* are treated in the text as referring to a single place. The place in question is the westernmost one in the west-to-east itinerary of Cawek and thus should be mentioned first, but in the play's texts it has been reversed with Thunderclap, the next place east (see the following note). In a generally west-to-east list of places in a sixteenth-century document, "Cholochic Chah" comes immediately after "Ciha," which corresponds to the present-day Quiché town of Santa Catarina Ixtahuacán, and it is followed by places in the vicinity of Chichicastenango (Recinos 1957:101-102). There is a mountain still known today as *Cholochik*

Chaj in the territory of Santa Catarina (AT), near the boundary between people who speak K'iche' and those who speak Tz'utujil or Kaqchikel.

Thunderclap: This is *Pan Tzajaxaq;* today there is a village named Xajaxac east of Santa Catarina Ixtahuacán, about halfway between the centers of the Quiché town of Chichicastenango and the Cakchiquel town of Sololá. *Tzajaj* is "to thunder" (FX).

Big Tree: This is *Chi Nimche',* known today as Panimaché, a hamlet located eight kilometers east northeast of the center of the Cakchiquel town of Sololá. Like the places in the previous two notes, it is near the boundary of Quiché territory, and in fact its lands are disputed between Sololá and the Quiché town of Chichicastenango (McBryde 1947: map 20). It is connected with Lord's Place and Earthquake (see below) by a major footpath running northward.

Lord's Place: This translates *Pan Ajawarem,* which is an emended version of "Paraveno" and "Panaraveno," spellings that appear in both texts. *Pa* or *pan,* "in," is a preposition commonly used with K'iche' and Kaqchikel place names, but *araweno,* a K'iche' term for "mint" derived from Spanish "hierba buena," does not belong in a pre-Columbian place name. It would appear to have originated in a mishearing or misreading of *ajawarem,* which means "lordship" or "domain" in both K'iche' and Kaqchikel. In the *Annals of the Cakchiquels,* this place is the subject of the following statement: *Xeok na chi ajawarem qa mama k'ate k'a oq xkilaq'ab'ej tinamit Chiawar,* "Our grandfathers entered into lordship then, when they established the town of Chiawar" (Brinton 1885:132, translation mine). The author of this sentence is making a move that is characteristic of writers in Quichean languages, suggesting an etymology for the place name by inviting the reader to compare *chi ajawarem* with *Chiawar. Chi,* "at," is like *pan* in being frequently used with place names, while *awar* is probably shortened from *ajawar,* "to become a lord."

Lord's Place (or Chiawar) would be north of Big Tree (see above) and south of Earthquake (see below), putting it inside the territory of the present-day Quiché town of Chichicastenango. As Recinos has suggested, Chiawar was probably at the site of what is now the Chichicastenango town center (Recinos and Goetz 1953:91n). When Cakchiquels fled from Chiawar during the reign of Quicab it was occupied by Quichés, who gave it what the writers of the Popol Vuh treat as a new name: *Chuwila'* or "Nettles Heights" (D. Tedlock 1996:187, 349). The name "Chichicastenango" is a Nahuatl translation of *Chuwila',* made by the Tlaxcalan allies of the Spanish invaders.

Earthquake: This is *Kab'raqan,* corresponding to the present-day Quiché hamlet known as Chicabracán, which is spread out on a tableland between San Sebastián Lemoá and Chiché and lies inside the present boundaries of the town of Santa Cruz Quiché. In the text this place name is reversed with the previous one, but Cawek's journey from Big Tree (see above) to Earthquake would have taken him through Lord's Place before he got there. Beyond Earthquake he resumes his mainly eastward course, following a trajectory that keeps him inside the territory of K'iche' speakers but with speakers of Kaqchikel a short distance to the south.

Bountiful: This is *Pan Cha'lib',* rendered "Panchalib" in the texts, which is located three kilometers southwest of the center of the Quiché town of Joyabaj (Acuña 1975:114; Breton 1994:328, 334). To get there Cawek would have traveled eastward from Earthquake. According to two sixteenth-century Quiché documents, Joyabaj (or *Xoyab'aj*) was a Rabinal citadel until it was taken by the Quiché during the reign of Quicab (Carmack and Mondloch 1989:84, 179). The inhabitants still speak a dialect of K'iche' similar to that of Rabinal (Campbell 1977:14-15). *Cha'l* is "abundance" (FX, TC).

my fourth announcement, my cry: Coloch repeats *ukajmul,* "fourth," in front of *nusik'ib'al,* "my cry."

Between the Wasp Nests: This is *Xol Chaqaj,* which appears as "Xol-Chacah" in Brasseur and "xolchaεah" in Pérez. It is located a short distance east of the center of the Quiché town of Joyabaj (Acuña 1975:114; Breton 1994:328, 334). *Aqaj* is "wasp nest" (FT, FX, MX).

...the bloodletter's trumpets / the bloodletter's drum: These instruments are *lotzo tun* and *lotzo q'ojom. Lotzo* is "to let blood" (DB, FX, FV). In Guatemalan Spanish and in much of the scholarly literature on Mayans, *tun* is used as a term for the slit drum, but this usage is not attested in colonial sources for Mayan languages. In K'iche' and Kaqchikel, *tun* (DB, FX, PG) or *tum* (FT) was the term for "trumpet," while *q'ojom* was the term for "slit drum" (DB, FX, FV). The meaning of the Yucatec cognates was reversed, with *tunk'ul* serving as the term for "slit drum" and *jom* for "trumpet" (BV). In contemporary K'iche' *tun* or *tum* is still used for the trumpet (AG, AT, MX); its use as a term for the slit drum, reported by only one source (AT), may be a product of Spanish-K'iche' bilingualism. Otherwise the slit drum is still known as *q'ojom* (Morales 1988a:137), a term that now includes the marimba and can be extended to musical instruments in general (FT, AG, AT, MX). The slit drum used in recent productions of the play is made from the trunk of a *sanik che'* (PG, AT) or "ant tree" *(Platymiscium dimorphandrum),* a lowland species that is also the main source of the wood for marimba keys (Camposeco M. 1992:36).

Coloch commented that Cawek "knew he was reaching Rabinal because of the sound of the *tun.*" Pérez, apparently fearing that future directors of the play might think this passage called for actual music, wrote a stage direction in the top margin of the page on which it appears: *chama tun,* "the trumpets are quiet."

...*twelve Golden Eagles / Golden Jaguars:* For this first mention of the Eagles and Jaguars, both texts have the equivalent of *kab'lajuj Uq'anal Kot / B'alam,* but later they repeat *Uq'anal* in front of *B'alam.* Here and everywhere else Coloch produces two fully symmetrical lines, repeating both *kab'lajuj* and *Uq'anal* in front of *B'alam.* The prefix *u-,* meaning "his," makes sense in Lord Five Thunder's first speech, where it serves to connect the twelve Golden Eagles and Jaguars to Cawek (see the notes to that speech) and in Man of Rabinal's twelfth speech (where he quotes Five Thunder), but it appears in all other contexts as well, as if *Uq'anal* had become an immutable proper name.

...*as if the very sky were beating like a heart / the very earth were beating like a heart:* The verb is *lanau,* whose agent-focus suffix *-u* is translated by prefacing "sky" and "earth" with "very." The closest dictionary forms are *lanalik,* "thing that throbs like a heart," and *lanalot,* "palpitate like a heart" (FX).

along with the woman slaves / man slaves: The term for "slave," which is *mun* in both texts, is well attested in colonial and modern dictionaries but appears to be obsolete in contemporary K'iche', though it is survived by a homonym meaning "glutton" (MX, AT). Coloch, when asked for a term for "esclavo," said *taqo'n,* which can be applied to anyone who is sent on an errand. When he reads the written word *mun* aloud or speaks it during a performance he says *muy,* apparently referring to the fact that the character called *Mun* is dressed as a woman but wears a mask with a mustache. *Muy,* a term for a small fish called "bagrecillo" (DB) or "barbirrojo" in Spanish (PG), is a figure of speech for a woman with facial hair.

...*oh-so-respectable lord:* This is *la' lal ajaw,* in which I take *lal,* which is normally a term of polite address (translatable as "sir") rather than of reference, to be sarcastic. This reading is supported by dictionary entries that gloss *lal* and *lalanik* as "make fun of" (FX), and it fits Cawek's attitude toward the lord in question.

Man of Rabinal speaks for the fifth time.

here at the navel of the sky, navel of the earth: Throughout the play the term for "navel" is *xmut,* which is specific to Rabinal. It is a metathesis of *muxt,* the Rabinal term reported for the seventeenth century (DB). The usual term in both K'iche' and Kaqchikel was and still is *muxu'x.*

we advised you in vain, sir / we instructed you in vain, sir: The first verb is "qulelebeh" in Brasseur and "qelebeh" in Pérez; what makes the most sense is *k'ulub'ej,* "advise, give notice" (DB, FV). For the second verb, "hulkahibeh" in Brasseur and "Ɛahibeh" in Pérez, the best lead is *k'aji-,* "give to understand, teach a lesson, correct" (FX, FV, TC).

Bird's Drinking Water / Pieces of White Lime in a Row: These names, *Ruq'ab'a Ya'*
Tz'ikin and *Cholochik Saq Chun,* have yet to be plausibly traced to a place or
places. A sixteenth-century Quiché document mentions a place named
Ruq'ab'ala' Tz'ikin (Recinos 1957:105), but it is included in a list of other
places that are known to be in the territory of Chichicastenango, well outside
the Pokomam context of the present passage.

Don't let them get loose, sir: The verb used here is usually rendered as "yutzcopih" in the
Brasseur text and "yutzcupih" in Pérez. *Yusq'upij* is "untie, take out of prison"
(FX, FV) or "set loose" (TC).

you, sir, did not succeed: "Succeed" translates *xuch'ak,* which is "xuchak" in Brasseur and
illegible in Pérez. *Ch'ak* is "to win" (FX, FV).

because they transformed themselves / into gnats: Here Man of Rabinal uses sound play to
give the name of an enemy a negative meaning, turning the people called *Uxab'*
into *uxil,* "gnats." The verb is *tzolq'omij,* whose meanings include translation
from one language to another (FX). On the transformation Coloch commented,
"It seems that by an enchantment they walked away from where he [Cawek] was
watching them. He was supposed to stop them and make them go back to their
valleys. Suddenly, these people became ants and conqueror ants and walked
away beneath his feet. They did it as a mockery."

There is a parallel narrative in the *Annals of the Cakchiquels,* in which
pilgrims returning from the northern lowlands make two attempts to spy on
the Pokomam (Recinos and Goetz 1953:66). The first attempt fails, but the
second one brings the news that the Pokomam are numerous.

…conqueror ants: These are *ch'eken sanik,* a term glossed in dictionaries as "flying ants"
(FV) or else as a large ant called "sampopo" or "zompopo" (a Nahuatl-derived
word meaning "voracious") in Guatemalan Spanish (FT, PG, AT). *Ch'akan-* is
"to triumph" (MX).

Now they go through scene after scene / episode after episode: This is *xa nim kelememik /*
kechololik, in which *xa nim* is "just long." *Lem-* is "narrate" (FX) or (literally)
"to mirror," while *chol-* is "tell" (FX) or (literally) "put in order" or "in a row."
Both stems are reduplicated *(lemem-, cholol-)* to indicate repetitive action.

Below the Cave / Under Ripe Yellow Corn: These place names are *Ekem Pek* and *Xe Q'ana*
Jal. Jal is the term for ripe (hard) ears of corn, as contrasted with *aj,* referring to
green (soft) ears. Location unknown.

we had banished them: Literally, this is "we had caused them to leave it behind," which translates *mi xeqoq'ob'en kanoq,* an emended version of "mi-xe c'ocoben" in Brasseur
(the apostrophe is his way of separating the aspect marker c- from the verb stem)
and "mixecocoben canoε" in Pérez; *oq'otaj* is to "separate" (FV) or "banish" (TC).

Just what did they say in reply?: This is *Janpa na wi xkecha uloq,* in which *janpa* is "how much" or "how many" (MX). "In reply" translates *uloq,* "hither" (toward the speaker) and fits the context.

Cawek of the Forest People speaks for the fifth time.

The texts do not include a change of speakers here, but the next time Cawek speaks his part is labeled as his sixth (as it is in the present translation), there having been no fifth part for him. Moreover, Man of Rabinal's next part is labeled as his seventh (as it is here), there having been no sixth part for him. I have carved the two missing speeches out of what Brasseur ran together as one continuous speech by Man of Rabinal (the longest speech in the entire play), inserting appropriate openings and closings borrowed from other speeches. At the present transition between speakers the insertions are the seven closing lines of Man of Rabinal and the fifteen opening lines of Cawek. In its content the main body of the latter speech makes perfect sense as something Cawek would say, but it would appear that Brasseur, having lost track of the succession of speakers, reversed the use of the first and second persons in an attempt to make the syntax (if not the content) fit Man of Rabinal. I have restored the first and second persons to what I believe to have been their original state.

"Listen! Listen! / You Uxab / you Pokomam": Just before these lines both texts have a passage that runs *Chiri k'ut mi xkitzaq uloq kiyeb'al, kisik'ib'al,* "And then they sent back their announcement, their cry." I have omitted this sentence from my translation because it causes confusion. It refers not to the message that begins here but to the reply, which is quoted several lines later and is clearly identified as a reply by a sentence similar to this one.

"shaded by quetzal feathers / shaded by glistening green": Coloch recites these lines as *xe umujib'al q'uq' / xe umujib'al raxon,* but the texts omit the word *q'uq',* "quetzal feathers." The ordinary term for "green" or "blue" is *rax* or *raxa; raxon* (occasionally spelled "raxom" by Brasseur but not Pérez) is used only for an intense green like that of quetzal feathers or jade. Here the feathers are a metaphor for the leaves of pataxte and cacao trees (see below) and the taller trees that form the canopy under which they are planted.

"under the golden money / under the silver money": In these lines we have a three-way convergence between the frequent pairing of *q'ana* and *saqi* ("yellow" and "white") in Quiché ritual poetry, which evokes variety; the ancient use of cacao seeds for *pwaq* ("money"); and the post-Columbian introduction of money in the form of gold and silver coins.

"Here the only things that need care": This is *Xa e tz'ulik kok uloq,* in which *tz'ulik* is translated as "care" on the basis of *tz'ulej-,* "embrace, protect, clothe, sleep intertwined."

"as long as there are days / as long as there is light": Chuxe q'ij / chuxe saq is literally "beneath the day (or sun), beneath the light." Andrés Xiloj of Momostenango, commenting on a similar expression in the Popol Vuh, said, "This is the time that goes forward...or the number of times there will be until the end of the world" (D. Tedlock 1996:294).

because of their troubled hearts: In this line, *rumal uk'oqob'al kik'ux,* Cawek creates an indirect play of sound and meaning between the name *Poqomam,* which (whatever its etymology may be) suggests *poqom,* "pain, hurt," and *k'oq,* which has a similar meaning but is closer to "sorrow" or "regret" (TC, "coƐoh" in DB). To make the point more directly he could have used a parallel expression: *upoqom kik'ux,* "the hurt in their hearts."

...all four edges / all four corners: This is *chi kaj pa / chi kaj xukutal,* in which the first line is specific to Rabinal and the second is widely used. *Pa* is the term for the eaves of a roof (AT), and *kaj pa,* literally "four eaves," suggests a conception of the sky as a four-shed roof. In the Popol Vuh *kaj tz'uk,* "four sides," is used with *kaj xukut* (D. Tedlock 1996:220).

at a day's journey / or two days' journey: Literally, *pa jun warab'al / pa kay warab'al* is "in one place to sleep, in two places to sleep."

And these children and sons of yours, sir / . . . are simply dismayed: "children and sons of yours, sir," translating *ri alk'ajol la,* has been supplied on the basis of a similar passage occurring earlier in this speech.

Man of Rabinal speaks for the sixth time.

Here, as in the case of the beginning of the fifth speech of Cawek, no change of speaker appears in the texts. In the preceding speech the sixth line from the end and the final three lines have been interpolated. In the present speech a line that was probably added by Brasseur—"Mi-x-cha chi curi nu tzih" (1862b:52), which translates as "And then my words said"—has been deleted. The remainder of the speech makes perfect sense as a reply by Rabinal to what Cawek has just said.

...you used up / all the strength of your arms, sir / the strength of your shoulders, sir: This is *xul k'isa la uwach chuq' / uwach teleb' la.* "Used up all" translates *xul k'isa uwach,* literally "came to finish its face"; *k'isa uwach* means to completely consume something (FT). *Chuq'* is shortened from *chuq'a* or *chuq'ab',* "strength, force" (DB, FV, MX, AG), and is based on *q'ab',* "arm." *Teleb'* is "shoulder," while *teleb'aj* is to "carry on the shoulders or head" (DB, FV).

Cawek of the Forest People speaks for the sixth time.

In the margin of the Pérez text Eugenio Xolop wrote "5°q," an abbreviation for "quinto de

Quiché" (referring to Cawek). Unlike Brasseur, Breton, and others, Xolop noticed that Brasseur gave Cawek no speech labeled *uwakmul* ("his sixth") and so annotated this and subsequent Cawek speeches with arabic numerals that run one lower than the numbers appearing in the text proper.

I measured the distance in cords: The *k'a'm* or "cord" is a unit of land measurement equivalent to twenty strides (ten paces). Its ordinary use is for measuring off individual cornfields, but Cawek's itinerary takes him along the edge of an entire valley.

Water Jar Point: Tzam K'amb'a is a hilltop two kilometers east northeast of the Rabinal town center and three kilometers southeast of Red Mountain, overlooking the Rabinal valley (Arnauld 1993:65; Breton 1994:327, 329). Coloch suggested "water jar" as a translation for *k'amb'a*. He remarked that this place was "crumbled" by Cawek "because he was upset; and, as we can see now, it is not a mountain anymore."

that I should gain recognition / as Lord of Water Jar Mountain / Lord of Water Jar Valley: This translates *xchintaqijta ub'i' / Ajaw K'amb'a Juyub' / Ajaw K'amb'a Taq'aj.* The first line combines a variant of *taqej*, "to honor, obey" (FV), with *-ta(j)*, which makes the verb passive and places the focus on the result of action; *ub'i'* is "name of." A more literal translation would be, "I should receive the honor of being named." For *-taqijta* Brasseur has "takih-ta," correctly reading the final "ta" as a suffix, but Pérez writes "taqih" and moves the "ta" to the beginning of the next word. Breton then reads "taqih" as *t'akij*, "hit with a fist" (TC), and ignores the passive voice. The next two lines come from Coloch's oral performance; the texts are limited to a simple *Ajaw K'amb'a*, "Lord of Water Jar," mentioned once.

to Henequen Mountain / Henequen Valley: These names are *Saqkijel Juyub'* and *Saqkijel Taq'aj;* the mountain in question is a hill three kilometers south of Water Jar Point and three kilometers southeast of the Rabinal town center (Breton 1994:327, 329). Brasseur has "zaktihel," but the "zaεqihel" of Pérez makes more sense. *Saqki'* is the term for a kind of maguey (henequen) whose leaves provide fiber for ropes (see "henequen rope" above); the Poqomchi' equivalent is *sajkil* (OS).

to Healing Waters: Chi Tzalya' is located in a bottomland one kilometer west of Henequen Mountain (Breton 1994:327, 329). *Tzala ja'* is "salubrious water" (DB; *ya'* and *ja'* are synonymous). As Coloch sees it, Cawek is on his way back to his home at Red Earth (see below) when he comes to Healing Waters, where "he collects the richness of this place. He puts some of the soil in his sandals, and where pieces of that richness are dropped the land becomes fertile, as it does at Red Earth."

bird-footed bean shoots: Literally, *rixk'aq tz'ikin* is "claw of a bird." The reference, according to Coloch, is to a stage in the growth of a small ground bean when the plant looks like bird feet.

Croaking Frog Point at Belted House: This is *Tzam Xtin Q'urun chuwach Ximb'al Ja.*
Belted House is a kilometer and a half northwest of Healing Waters and the
same distance south of the Rabinal town center, at the edge of the valley (Breton
1994:327, 329). *Ximb'al* is "belt" (AT) and *ja* is "house." In the other name the
exact meaning of *xtin* is unknown, but most Quichean words beginning in *xt-*
are terms for lizards, frogs, and toads, while *q'uru* is onomatopoeic for the vocal
sounds of frogs or toads (MX, AG).

Worn-out Trumpet Point: This is *Tzam K'isin Tun,* six kilometers west of Belted House
and the Rabinal town center, on the ridge that separates Rabinal lands from
those of the town of Cubulco (Breton 1994:327, 329). *K'isin* is translated on
the basis of *k'isinaq,* "spent, worn-out" (FT, TC); Brasseur has "quezen" and
Pérez has "qizin."

I trumpeted there: In saying *mi xintunan wi,* Cawek creates a metaphor for what he did
(or how he felt) at Worn-out Trumpet Point, playing on the *tun* or "trumpet" of
the place name by using the verb *tunan,* "to trumpet."

for thirteen score days / and thirteen score late nights: "Thirteen score" translates *oxlajuwi-*
naq. Taken literally, this would mean a complete run through the thirteen day
numbers and twenty day names that combine to form the dates of the 260-day
divinatory calendar. "Late nights" translates *aq'ab saq,* shortened from *aq'ab*
saqirik, literally "night getting light," which is "very early in the morning" (DB).

Man of Rabinal speaks for the seventh time.

In the margin of the Pérez text Eugenio Xolop wrote "5°R," an abbreviation for "quinto
de Rabinal." The arabic numerals in the preceding notations for Rabinal's speeches are
lower by one than the numbers whose names are written in the text proper. The present
numeral is lower by two because Xolop, realizing that Brasseur had failed to give Rabinal
a sixth speech, lowered this and subsequent notations by two rather than one.

What about the children of light / the sons of light?: Here and three lines later the texts have
wal, nuk'ajol, "my children, my sons." If this were correct, it would mean that
the people who were incited to revolt in the narrative that follows were the vassals of Man of Rabinal. This is implausible, since the event in question took
place far from Rabinal and close to the Quiché capital. The present translation
is based on the assumption that the wording should be the same as it is later in
this same speech: *ri saqil al, saqil k'ajol,* "the children of light / the sons of
light," referring to the vassals of the lords at the Quiché capital.

Look-See Point: The exact location of *Tzam Muqutzu'm* is unknown, but since Man of
Rabinal visited this place shortly before arriving at Sculpture Tree (see below),

it could be one of many spots that provide spectacular views of Lake Atitlán. *Muqu* and *tzu'm* both mean "to see, look" (DB, FX, FV).

Sculpture Tree: This is *Pan Ajachel,* a present-day Cakchiquel town on the north shore of Lake Atitlán. *Ajache'* is the term for the tree *Casimiroa edulis,* known in Spanish as "matasano," whose plum-like fruit is edible and whose wood is used for carving; *ajamche'* is "woodcarving."

With their bellies grumbling / since the worms in their bellies were grinding away: These lines are *Taseq tz'ajtz'at kipam / k'a xirxotileb' ukoq kipam. Tz'ajtz'a* is the sound of thunder, while *xirixot* is that of a cricket or cicada; *koq rupam,* literally "grinding of the belly," is a term for an intestinal worm (TC).

Spilt Water: This is *Pan Amak'a',* whose ruins are located two kilometers southeast of the center of the Quiché town of Zacualpa. According to the Popol Vuh (D. Tedlock 1996:187, 357) and two other sixteenth-century documents (Carmack and Mondloch 1989:84, 179), all of which call it *Pamak'a',* it was a Rabinal citadel until it was taken by the Quiché during the reign of Quicab. *Mak'-* is "to spill" (MX).

Bath: This name, *Chatinib'al,* serves to designate various places in the Guatemalan highlands, one of which is on the slopes below Standing Jaguar, on the east side of the ridge connecting that place with the ruins of Workers (Arnauld 1993:89; Breton 1994:326, 330). Later passages treat the incident at Bath as if it took place somewhere near Quiché Mountain, Quiché Valley, but that may be an error introduced at some point during the history of the script. In each of the play's various retellings of the Bath episode, it always comes after Cawek has already turned eastward, away from Quiché Mountain, Quiché Valley, and just before the episode in which he attacks Standing Jaguar and other places in what was then Rabinal territory. A similar incident took place during the reign of the Quiché king known as *K'otuja* or "Noble Bathhouse," who survived an attempt to assassinate him at his bathing place (Chonay and Goetz 1953:187; Carmack and Mondloch 1983:142-43, 194).

House Point / by the Rocks that Face Each Other: These names are *Tzam Ja* and *K'ulawach Ab'aj.* The translation of the latter is based on Coloch's explanation of its meaning. Location unknown.

just a large drop of water from a cloud: "Large drop" translates *raqanib'al,* which is literally the "means of taking a step" or "leaving a footprint" of the *sutz'* or "cloud." A dictionary entry for *raqan jab',* literally the "leg or foot (or footprint) of rain," defines it as "the drops of a rainstorm when it begins or ends" (FV), a clear reference to the large drops that begin and end thunderstorms. Van Akkeren (1999:293), unaware of this figure of speech, argues that this passage refers to a tree that holds up the clouds.

when I reached / my lord, my liege: Three lines that immediately precede these in both texts have been deleted from the translation for reasons given in the note on Bath (above). The deleted lines read, "I got close / to Quiché Mountain / Quiché Valley."

inside the plastered hive: "Plastered hive" translates *chunaqam.* Brasseur has "akamchun," Pérez has "aƐam chun," and Breton keeps their word order, but Coloch prefers the reverse order, in which he is consistent with *chunaqaj,* "enclosure" (PG). *Chun* is "plaster," specifically lime according to Coloch, and *aqaj* is the term for a hive or nest of bees or wasps (FT, FX, MX).

There was a terrible silence: This is *Xa nim loloxinaq; lolo* is "a great silence in a house or a town" caused by "sickness or hunger" (FX). This recalls other allusions to famine, as in the line "with their bellies grumbling" (see above).

you would have chopped clear through / the root / the trunk / of my lord / my liege: Two lines that immediately follow these in both texts have been deleted from the translation for reasons given in the note on Bath (above). The deleted lines read, "at Quiché Mountain / Quiché Valley."

down in the canyons, up on the heights: When *siwan* and *tinamit* or "canyon" and "citadel" are used together, the former refers to the lower parts of a town or city and the latter to a group of palaces and temples located on a defensible hilltop or headland (D. Tedlock 1996:319-20).

Standing Jaguar: This is *B'alamwak,* a mountaintop seven kilometers southwest of the Cubulco town center, on the boundary between its lands and those of Joyabaj (Arnauld 1993:86; Breton 1994:326). Three kilometers to the south are the possible ruins of Zamaneb (see the notes to Cawek's first speech).

Sparkling Dust: This name is *Chi T'int'ot wi Poqlaj.* The texts have "tintot"; *t'it'oj, t'ijt'oj,* and similar forms are used for the shine or glitter of a light or the color white (see "sak-ttittoh" and "sak-ttihttoh" in FV, "zactetoh" in DB). Location unknown.

Reed Rattles: This is *Chi K'alqa Raxaj,* which is "Chi-Calcaraxah" in Brasseur and "chi-carcaraxah" in Pérez. *K'alaqan* (FV) or "Calocan" (DB) is "bells" or (in DB) "a construction of reeds used in place of bells" in a dance called *Wuch',* "Opossum." *Raxaj* is "reeds" (DB). Location unknown.

Drumbeat: This is *Chi Kunu,* which may be the place now known as Xeknup, nine kilometers west of Standing Jaguar and at the northern edge of the territory of the Quiché town of Joyabaj (Arnauld 1993:89; Breton 1994:326, 331). *Kunuluj* is the sound of a drumbeat (TC).

Mace Valley / Sapota Tree: These names are *Chi Q'osib'al Taq'aj* and *Tulul. Q'osib'al* is literally "instrument for giving blows." The sapota is a fruit tree *(Manilkara zapota).* The latter place could be *Chwatulul,* four kilometers north of Standing Jaguar and the same distance southwest of the Cubulco town center (Arnauld 1993:86), or *Patulul,* five kilometers east of Standing Jaguar and six kilometers south of Cubulco (Breton 1994:326).

...I must take your story, sir: "Story" translates *tzijoxik.* As a noun, *tzij* means "word"; as the transitive verb *tzijo-,* it takes on the sense of "tell, relate." The addition of *-xik* makes the verb passive, puts the focus on the object—and, if it carries no verb prefixes, turns it back into a noun. The literal meaning is something like "that which is put into words."

In Pérez this speech ends at the bottom of a page. Below it, in the margin, is the signature of Eugenio Xolop (see Breton 1994:111).

Cawek of the Forest People speaks for the seventh time.

Orders were given for a second time: Instead of *ukaib',* "second time," the texts have *nab'e,* "first time," thus following the pattern of the earlier line translated as "The first time orders were given" in the fourth speech of Cawek. This is an apparent error, since the orders described in that speech were issued at an earlier time and concerned a different matter than the orders in question here.

from the rank of Lord Thunder / to the rank of Lord Knife: This couplet, *Ajaw teq'en Toj / Ajaw teq'en Tijax,* constitutes an expression whose effect is something like saying "all the lords from number one through number ten." *Toj* and *Tijax* or "Thunder" and "Knife" are day names from the 260-day divinatory calendar, and each day has its *ajaw* or "lord." A period lasting from Thunder through Knife (inclusive) spans ten days and thus covers half the twenty day names. Thunder may have been chosen as the starting day for the expression because tribute was paid to lords on that day. Knife is a day on which people are apt to enter into verbal conflicts (B. Tedlock 1992:122-23).

   Teq'en, which is "Teken" in Brasseur and "tequen" in Pérez, combines *teq'e,* "to stack" (FV), with the substantive suffix *-n.* This reading fits with the reference to "each level" and "each layer" two lines later.

at Old Camp and Whisker Place: These two names, *Q'umaraqa'j* and *Chi Ismachi',* are reduced to "Gumarmachi" in Brasseur and "Ɛumarmachii" in Pérez. When they appear together in the *Title of the Lords of Totonicapán* they are rendered as "chi Ɛumarcaah chi yzmachi" (Carmack and Mondloch 1983:150-51). The *Annals of the Cakchiquels* has "Ɛumarcaah chi yzmachii" (Brinton 1885:128), while the "Títulos de la Casa Ixquin-Nehaib" (a Quiché document) has "Ɛumarcaah Izmachi" (Recinos 1957:77). *Q'umar* means "rotted, tattered, old, used, worn down by age" (FX, MX, FV, TC), while *ka'j* is "camp, cabin, farmhouse" (FX, TC); *izmachi',* literally "hairy-mouth," is "beard" or "bearded"

(DB, FX, AG). The names refer to two citadels that were built on adjoining headlands at the heart of the principal town of the Quiché kingdom. The town as a whole is referred to as Quiché Mountain, Quiché Valley (see above). Its ruins are located two kilometers west of the town center of Santa Cruz del Quiché, and its story is recounted in the Popol Vuh (D. Tedlock 1996:54, 181-86, 191, 337, 355).

on each level / on each layer: In this couplet, *taq tasib' / taq tasimaj, taq* is a distributive particle (FV) and the rest is translated on the basis of *tas,* "put in order" (DB, FX); *tasil,* "schist," a finely layered stone (DB); and *tesena'j,* "put between" (DB).

Gathered Cane Plants / Gathered Lakes / Gathered Canyons / Gathered Birds: This quatrain is *Kuchuma Aj / Kuchuma Cho / Kuchuma Siwan / Kuchuma Tz'ikin.* Brasseur has "Cuxuma" all four times, which Pérez changes to "quxuma." Breton changes Pérez to "k'oxoma," which he translates as "observatoire." It seems clear to me that these four phrases are analogous to *Kuchuma Kik'* in the Popol Vuh (D. Tedlock 1996:251), a lordly title in which *kuchu* is "gather, join together" (FT, DB, FX, MX, AG).

The meaning of the gathered *aj* or "cane plants" lies in a Mesoamerican metaphor whereby a sacred city is likened to aquatic plants that grow in clusters and have interconnected roots. The lakes would be the five sacred lakes of the four directions and center of the Quiché kingdom (see D. Tedlock 1997:87-88, 243-44); the canyons would be those of the expression "down in the canyons, up on the heights" (see above); and the birds would be relatively low-ranking nobles such as Cawek claims to be when he compares himself to a bird. In the ninth speech of Man of Rabinal, *Kuchuma Kab'* or "Gathered Honey" is added to this list, referring to the activities of "the creatures / of yellow honey, fresh honey" (discussed in the notes to Rabinal's fourth speech).

twelve braves / twelve men: Coloch repeats *kab'lajuj,* "twelve," a second time, but the texts do not.

so said their words: The texts modify *tzij,* "words," with *nab'e,* "first," thus repeating the error made in the phrase that introduced the subject of this message from the lords (see the note for the line "Orders were given for a second time," above).

inside the great fortress / great walls: Pérez adds *unimal,* "the great," before Brasseur's *k'oxtun,* "walls," and Coloch completes the symmetry by adding *chupam,* "inside," in front of that.

the creatures of yellow honey / fresh honey / were buzzing / in the breadnut trees / over their sustenance: The translation of the verb, *ketzerukutiaj,* is based on *tzeren,* a kind of bee (DB), and *tzerer,* the sound of a swarm of bees (FX). "Breadnut trees" translates *iximche',* literally "maize trees," referring to a broadleaf evergreen

(Brosimum alicastrum) called "ramón" in Spanish (Recinos and Goetz 1953:17, 97); the Q'eqchi' term for this tree is the same (EH). Its fig-like fruit was an important food in times of famine (Roys 1967:122n); for the Huastec Maya a heavy yield of this fruit portends a low maize yield (Alcorn 1984:566). Van Akkeren (1999:292) bypasses the question of botanical identification in favor of a symbolic "maize tree" to which the play's prisoner would be tied for sacrifice by arrows.

Breton (1994:228-29n) dismisses the possibility that the mention of this tree has anything to do with Iximché, the Cakchiquel capital, but there could well be an allusion to the famine that afflicted that town shortly after it was founded (Recinos and Goetz 1953:101). It is even possible that the famine provided the occasion for the name Iximché, whatever the town might have been called before the famine struck.

Red Earth: Coloch speaks this place name as *Pan Kaqil,* which is literally "in redness" and probably refers to the color of the earth there. Brasseur has "Pan-Cakil," Pérez has "pancaƐil," and Breton has "Pank'aqil." Acuña (1975:10-11, 114-15) locates this place near Joyabaj and Breton (1994:326, 330) follows suit. But Eugenio Xolop, the son of Coloch's predecessor as director of the play, located Cawek's home in the town of Chiché (Rodríguez 1962:48). Five kilometers east of that town's center is a hamlet labeled Tierra Colorada on maps. This location makes for a better fit with the other place names listed in the present passage, which include Earthquake, immediately west of the Chiché town center.

even though bathing was his only concern: Here I read *rumal xa katin ukoq,* following Brasseur's "rumal xa c'atin ucok." Pérez changes this to "rumal qaxacac ucoƐ," but Brasseur's version is consistent with a later passage in which Lord Five Thunder says, *Mapa xa kinatin ukoq,* "Wasn't bathing my only concern?"

There I raised / the power of my weapon / the power of my shield / and brought him down: This passage is immediately followed in both texts by four lines that have been deleted from the present translation for reasons given in the note on Bath (above). The deleted lines read, "at my mountain / my valley / Quiché Mountain / Quiché valley."

I whitewashed him in back / I whitewashed him in front: For the "tzahcabih" of the texts I read *saqkab'ij,* "to whitewash."

Isn't this what has been said / in my teeth / in my face / a mere squirrel / a mere bird?: Pérez skipped the text corresponding to these five lines plus three more, then entered the text for the next fifteen lines in his notebook. When he got as far as the passage translated here as, "But isn't it right / that we should do what is good / what is beautiful?" he noticed his error and recopied the passage he had abbreviated, beginning with the skipped material and continuing with the lines he had copied too soon (see Breton 1992:115-16). He did not go back to strike out the earlier copy of these lines, which have found their way into Breton's transcription and translation of his work, and into Coloch's oral rendition as well.

We are elder and younger brother / one to the other: Literally, *Atz in qib' / chaq' in qib'* is, "Elder brother I am to ourselves, younger brother I am to ourselves." Broadly speaking, this statement is true regardless of whether Rabinal or Cawek is the elder or younger of the two men; the point is that they should not be finding themselves, as they are in their present encounter, in the relationship of enemies.

...my golden metal / my silver metal: "Golden" and "silver" translate *q'ana* and *saqi*, literally "yellow" and "white," the standard combination for evoking varied coloration in Quiché poetry. For pre-Columbian audiences a statement like this would have covered the whole range of colors produced by various combinations of copper, tin, gold, and silver; for present-day audiences it simply calls up gold and silver. Excavations at the Quiché capital have revealed an area where metalworking was conducted (Weeks 1977) and grave goods in the form of gold jewelry (Carmack 1981:262, 287).

likewise all my clothes: Brasseur has "ruq xquetak v'atziak," while Pérez has "ruq ixqetaᴇ vatziaᴇ." I read *ruk' ixkej taq watz'iaq,* literally "along with same all my clothes"; *ixkej* is "the same" (FX) and *taq* is "all."

Man of Rabinal speaks for the eighth time.

Would I go before my lord, my liege / without taking those things?: Literally, *La jin ma xkinchapa k'u ri' / chuwach wajawal, chuwach nuwinaqil* is, "Am I going not taking those / before my lord, before my liege?"

Cawek of the Forest People speaks for the eighth time.

Take it, sir: The texts have *kinyopisaj la,* "Take me, sir," which is an obvious error for *kayopisaj la,* "Take it, sir," since Rabinal does not take Cawek anywhere on this occasion.

Ahead of the next speech Brasseur inserts "U Cab Banbal" in his text and "Scène Deuxième" in his translation. Below this heading is one of the three stage directions appearing in his text pages: "C'u yopisah chuvach Ahau Hobtoh," meaning, "He arrives before Lord Five Thunder." Pérez retains both the heading and the direction. As stated earlier, the division of the play into sections is Brasseur's invention; the same is probably true of the stage directions, which occur only rarely in the manuscripts of the plays performed in Mayan communities.

Man of Rabinal speaks for the ninth time.

It's a clear day: Brasseur has "cala," while Pérez has "qala"; in the Popol Vuh manuscript (folio 24v) this greeting is "cala ta." The correct form would be *q'alataj,* "it's getting to be cleared."

he who is the dream / from which we cannot awaken: Literally, *K'o qawaram / majab'i qayakalem ruk'* is, "He [is] our dream / there is not our rest from it." *Yakalem* is "rest" (DB).

since it wasn't quick and easy: This is *mawi k'u jujik jusuk',* in which *jujik* is "with brevity" (FX) and *jusuk'* is "right away" (DB, FT).

a fiction: Brasseur has "halou" and Pérez has "halau"; I read *jalow.* "Halouh" is "raise false testimony" (FX). In performance Coloch treats this as the first word of a new line, but Breton puts it at the end of the previous line and speculates that it is an alternative term for "agouti."

So how could his heart's desire / not be fulfilled: Here I read, *La janikpa mawi k'ut k'isowik / rajab'al uk'ux.* The heart in question is clearly that of Cawek, since Rabinal used the same phrasing (but in the second person polite) when questioning Cawek in his seventh speech, and since Cawek is the person Rabinal is discussing in the present speech, which is addressed to Lord Five Thunder. Nevertheless, Brasseur and Pérez repeat the earlier second-person polite wording *(rajab'al uk'ux la),* which makes the present passage refer to the heart of Lord Five Thunder rather than that of Cawek.

Lord Five Thunder speaks for the first time.

his twelve elder brothers / his twelve younger brothers / workers in metal / workers in jade: This is the first of three instances in which Lord Five Thunder gives the number *kab'lajuj,* "twelve," to persons or items that will be available to Cawek when he arrives before the royal court. In the present case twelve is to be understood as the total number of brothers, whether elder or younger (there is no generic term for "brother"), though the number is repeated for both kinds of brothers in the text. They are *ratz* and *uchaq',* "his elder brothers" and "his younger brothers," by virtue of the third-person singular possessive prefixes *r-* and *u-.* "His" means they are Cawek's, provided that he helps them "reach perfection" by becoming the thirteenth brother.

... *his twelve Golden Eagles / Golden Jaguars:* The second group of twelve on Lord Five Thunder's list is composed of *Uq'anal Kot, Uq'anal B'alam.* The *u-* prefix makes them "his," again meaning they are Cawek's but again with the provision that he helps them "reach perfection" by becoming the thirteenth. *Q'ana* or *q'anal* is "yellow," "ripe," or "glorious." When *q'ana* is combined with *b'alam*, a term that can be used for any spotted cat, the reference is to a proper jaguar *(Felis onca);* in contrast, when *b'alam* is modified by *saq,* literally "white" but also meaning "plain" or "ordinary," the reference is to an ocelot *(Felis pardalis)* or margay cat *(Felis wiedii),* both of which are much smaller than a jaguar (FV, FX, DB). The *kot* or "eagle" in question here would be the crested eagle *(Morphnus guianensis),* about the same size as a bald or golden eagle, or the even larger harpy eagle *(Harpiya harpyja),* which also has a crest.

...his twelve drinks / his twelve poisons... / the mead that burns / bites / sweetens / delights: These drinks comprise the third and final twelve on Lord Five Thunder's list; again, "his" means they will be Cawek's. "Poison" translates *matul* (DB, FX, PG), but according to Coloch this word can also mean "what one feels when one has a little bit of a drink, savoring it." "Mead" translates *ki',* a term for maguey and for pulque, the alcoholic drink made from the sap of the maguey flower stalk; pulque recipes (apparently including the one used here) commonly included honey. *Ki'* can also mean either "poison" or "sweet," a contradiction explored here in the contrast between "burns / bites" and "sweetens / delights." In Yucatec *ki* is "maguey" and *ki'* is the term for an alcoholic beverage made from the bark of tree (AB).

In the Popol Vuh the preparation and consumption of *ki'* twice marks the death of heroes (D. Tedlock 1996:83, 131, 245), just as it marks the death of Cawek. It was probably standard practice among the Maya, just as it was in central Mexico, to give an alcoholic drink to a prisoner of war before he was sacrificed. During the colonial period the production of pulque was licensed and later banned in the Quiché town of Almolonga (Camposeco M. 1994:26).

Quick Hummingbird: This is *Ixta Tz'unun,* in which *tz'unun* is a nearly universal Mayan term for "hummingbird." *Ixta* is translated on the basis of *xtah,* "quick, fast" (DB) or "rebound, bounce like a ball" (FX), glosses that fit the motion of a hummingbird; in the present passage this word may allude to the effects of the drink.

The link between the hummingbird and the pulque Cawek eventually receives from his hosts is twofold. First, among the Ñähñu (Otomí) of central Mexico (and probably more widely), hummingbirds are the avian counterparts of human tapsters who collect the sap of maguey flower stalks to make pulque (Bernard and Salinas Pedraza 1989:110, 234). Second, there is a widespread Mesoamerican notion that hummingbirds are the souls of dead warriors (Hunt 1977:63).

When I drink it / it brings me dreams: This translates *kantijo / ul k'ama war.* Brasseur has "can tihol ca ma var" here, but "tihol," judging from a similar passage in the twelfth speech of Cawek, is an error for "tiho ul." Pérez changes "ca ma var" to "qamavar." At the beginning of a phrase, *ul* has the effect of "it occurs" (TC). *K'ama* is "bring" and *war* is "sleep" or "dream."

the tamped weft: This is *k'oxaj uwa; k'ox* is "hit one thing hard against another" (FV); *wa* is "weft" (FT). This interpretation agrees with Coloch's understanding of the line.

the weaving tightly done / the work of my mother / my lady: Brasseur repeats all three of these lines a second time, an error corrected by Pérez. For the first line Brasseur has "ri qui calatz ca banic" and Pérez has "riquiqalatz qabaniic," difficult to sort out in either case. The best clue is that *latz'*, meaning "tight" or "packed" (PG, DB), can be used with respect to weaving (FV). This suggests, in turn, that the "ca" or "qa" prefixed to "latz" should be treated as a separate word, the most appropriate clues being *k'al*, "to tie" (FV, TC), *k'alanik*, "to arrange" (with a load of firewood as an example, MX), and "Ɛalo" (probably *k'alo*), "to align" (with carding as an example, DB). The emended line would read *ri kik'al latz' kab'anik*, literally "that whose arrangement tightly is done."

...Mother of Quetzal Feathers / Mother of Glistening Green / goods that come from / End of the String at Fish in the Ashes: In all later contexts "Glistening Green" is followed by references to jade and precious beads (see the notes to Rabinal's twelfth speech). The line translated as "goods that come from" is *ri petenaq*, which is ambiguous. In the present context and in all but one of its later occurrences I take it to refer to quetzal feathers and jade, and to clarify this meaning I have added the word "goods." But the same line can also be taken to mean "who comes from," referring to the girl who is said to be the "mother" of the objects in question—and that, I think, is what Cawek wants it to mean in his fifteenth speech.

"End of the String" translates *Tzamk'a'm*, a place corresponding to the present-day Kekchí hamlet known as Tzancanijá (listed in Gall 1976), which is two kilometers southwest of the San Pedro Carchá town center and forty-five kilometers north of Rabinal. "Fish in the Ashes," as a translation for *Karchaj* (*Karcha* in Q'eqchi'), follows Kekchí tradition as to the meaning of this name, as recounted to me by Marcelo Cho of San Pedro Columbia, a Kekchí village in Belize. *Kar* is "fish" (in both Q'eqchi' and K'iche'), while *chaj* (*cha* in Q'eqchi') is "ashes." A sixteenth-century Quiché document states that the tribute paid to Quiché lords by the people of Carchá consisted of quetzal feathers and jade (Recinos 1957:102-107).

who will come to dance her round and round: This is *xchulo mesesej*. According to Coloch, *mesesej* is "to make a turn in a dance"; "round and round" is my way of translating the reduplication in this verb *(-eses-)*.

who could become a father- or son-in-law / a brother-in-law: The kin terms employed
here are *jiaxel* in the first line, which covers either party to the relationship
between the father of a woman and her husband, and *b'alukixel* in the second
line, which covers either party to the relationship between the brother of a
woman and her husband. Given the conversational context, the Mother of
Quetzal Feathers (who was mentioned just before this) could be the daughter
of Lord Five Thunder (who is speaking), the sister of Man of Rabinal (who is
being spoken to), and the potential wife of Cawek (who is the main topic of
their conversation). As Coloch describes this situation, Cawek "could
become an in-law who gives or an in-law who takes. As a giver he would have
to give his sister in marriage, and as a taker he would marry the sister of Rabinal. Or a giver could be someone who has a daughter ready for marriage, and
a taker would be the one to marry her."

if he were respectful / if he were dignified: The terms translated as "respectful" and "dignified" are respectively *nimanel* and *okesanel,* in which -*n* is the active voice
and -*el* is agentive. Both texts have "octizanel" for the second term, but *nima-*
normally forms couplets with *okesa-.* Examples are *nimaxel, okesaxel,* "worthy
of obedience, worthy of credibility" (FT), and *nimab'al, okesab'al,* "reverence
and solemnity" (FV).

Lord Five Thunder speaks for the second time.

What then would be the name / of your means of defense, sir: Literally, *Naq ub'i' k'u ri' /
to'b'alil la* is, "What (is) its name then the means of defense of yours (polite)?"
Brasseur has "Nakubi chi curi ri toobalil la," which Pérez changes to "naɛabich-
icuri ritotobal la." *To'l* is "defense" (AG), *to'b'al* is "aid" (DB), and Coloch
glosses *to'b'alil* as "something with which to defend oneself."

in the course of descending / ascending: Brasseur has "chuvach la x-ulan uloc pahal uloc,"
while Pérez has "chuvach laxulanuloɛ lapaɛal uloɛ." I agree with Breton that
the pairing of *xulan,* "go down slope," and *pakalik,* "go up slope" (DB) makes
sense here, but I find his retention of the twice-repeated "la" of Pérez to be awkward. My reading is *chuwach xulan uloq / pakal uloq.*

Ahead of the next speech Brasseur inserts "Rox Banbal" in his text and "Scène Troisième"
in his translation.

Man of Rabinal speaks for the twelfth time.

Below this label Brasseur inserts his attempt at a back-translation from "Il va prende
Queché-Achi au bois où il est attaché" on the opposite page: "C'u qama Queche-Achi
ximilic che," meaning something like, "He takes Queche-Achi tied-to tree." Pérez changes

this to "qu qama qiche achi ximilic qiche achi," which eliminates the tree and means something like, "He takes Man of Quiché, Man of Quiché is tied."

of jade / of precious beads: "Jade" translates *yamanim; yamanik* is reported in virtually all colonial dictionaries of K'iche' and Kaqchikel as a term for "precious stones," but one of them (PG) specifies "esmeralda," an apparent reference to jade. "Precious beads" translates *xteq'oqib'*, which appears as "xtecokib" in Brasseur and is glossed as "precious stones" in dictionaries that variously render it as "xte-coc" (DB), "xtekok" (TC), and "xteϾoϾ" (in a source cited by Breton 1994:431). I interpret these stones as beads on the basis of the verb stem *teq'o-*, "to open a hole through something" (AG).

who will be the first to show its face: This translates *xchul sa wa' uwach,* following Brasseur; Pérez adds *uchi',* "its border," ahead of *uwach,* "its face," thus matching the corresponding passage in Lord Five Thunder's first speech.

Cawek of the Forest People speaks for the ninth time.

and his words say this: The text actually reads *kacha ri tzij la,* "so say your words, sir," referring to the quotation of Rabinal's words that precedes this line, but in order to clarify the passage I have translated it as if it referred to what follows, which is a quotation of Lord Five Thunder's reply to Rabinal.

the day of birth: Here Cawek is wishing that he could change the destiny of Lord Five Thunder, which is partly bound up in the birth date that gives him his name. A diviner might predict that an ordinary person born on a day named *Toj* or "Thunder" would be chronically ill or in debt, constantly in need of the help of diviners to straighten things out (B. Tedlock 1992:115-16). But in Lord Five Thunder's case, his birth date could give him special access to the power of *Tojil,* the patron deity of lordship.

Would that I could just bind / his lower lip / to his upper lip: This is *Karaj xa xchinkewij / rekem uchi' / rajsik uchi'.* The only good clue to the meaning of the verb *kewij* is a dictionary entry for "quevequic u chi," glossed as the term for the cheek strap in a bridle (DB). The other two lines, literally "below his mouth" and "above his mouth," are terms for the lower and upper lip (PG).

Slave speaks for the first time.

Brasseur labels this as an unnumbered speech of *Ixoq Mun,* "Woman Slave," but in present-day productions there is only a single androgynous Slave. Xolop wrote "1°," an abbreviation for "primero," in the margin of Pérez.

Ahead of the next speech Brasseur inserts "U Cah Banbal" in his text and "Scène Quatrième" in his translation.

Cawek of the Forest People speaks for the tenth time.

Below this label Brasseur inserts the last of the three stage directions in his text pages: "Ca qulun chuvach Ahau-Hobtoh," meaning, "He approaches in front of Lord Five Thunder." Pérez includes this in his version.

It's a clear day, man: Cawek begins his first speech to his host with a slight, addressing him simply as *achi* or "man" instead of "Lord Five Thunder"; he then moves on to mockery, talking about how his host is an honored man.

Such was your announcement, sir / your proclamation, sir / as it was delivered / by your brave, sir / in my teeth, in my face: This translates *mi xcha apanoq / ri yeb'al la, ri sik'ib'al la / rumal ri achijilal la / chi nuchi', chinuwach,* following Pérez and Coloch. Brasseur's version lacks the second line of text and has *oyewal la,* "your brave, sir," in place of *rumal ri,* "by."

my way of kneeling: This is *nuxukub'al wib',* omitted by Pérez and Coloch.

this is how I get down in the mud: Here Coloch says *are nuxoq'olob'al wib' wa',* which is lacking in both texts. *Xoq'ol-* is "get muddy" (DB).

oh lord: This translates *lal ajaw,* "you (polite) lord"; Coloch adds *Job' Toj,* "Five Thunder."

Slave speaks for the second time.

Brasseur labels this speech as the second by *Ixoq Mun* or "Woman Slave," though he did not number the first one. Xolop wrote "2°," for "segundo," in the margin of Pérez.

my lord, my liege /…/ where he stays, where he sits: When Coloch read this passage aloud for Sam Colop and myself he temporarily abandoned his oratorical mode of delivery for a storytelling mode. Expressing the urgency of Slave's intervention, he ran all five of these lines together in a single line. In public performances the actor in the role of Slave speaks with the same deliberate pace that pervades the rest of the dialogue.

Cawek of the Forest People speaks for the eleventh time.

my day has been turned upside down / my birth has been turned upside down: This is *pak'ab'am nuq'ij / pak'ab'am walaxik,* literally "on its back (is) my day, on its back (is) my birth." The implication is that fate can be reversed.

Lord Five Thunder speaks for the fourth time.

in front of the great walled fortress: This translates *chuwach unimal tz'aq k'oxtun,* following both texts, but Coloch separates *tz'aq,* "fortress," and *k'oxtun,* "walls," between two different lines and uses *chuwach unimal,* "in front of the great," in both lines, thus intensifying the parallelism.

...*nine or ten:* In some contexts this pair of numbers seems to be an estimate of a number in the range of nine or ten, but the action referred to here would have involved a much larger number of people. Multiples of nine or ten may be implied, with the possibilities starting at *b'elej k'al, laju k'al,* "nine score, ten score," and including multiples of *much',* "eighty," and *chul,* "eight thousand."

...*reaching Quiché Mountain:* Here Coloch adds a line, *K'iche' Juyub',* "Quiché Valley," thus making a couplet.

Likewise it was you, sir / who came to draw me out, sir: This translates *Xawi qi lal / mi xinul elesaj la,* following Brasseur's text, but Pérez changes the second line to *mi xul elesaj ri wajawal ri nuwinaqil,* which would mean "who came to draw out my lord, my liege," as if this were Man of Rabinal talking about what Cawek did to Lord Five Thunder rather than Lord Five Thunder himself.

in range of your weapon, sir: Here Coloch adds a line, *chupam ral pokob' la,* "in range of your shield, sir," thus making a couplet.

You, sir, whitewashed my back / my face: Coloch repeats *sajkab'ij la,* "you, sir, whitewashed," in front of *nuwach,* "my face," and treats the expanded phrase as a separate line. This passage is followed in both texts by two lines that have been deleted from the present translation for reasons given in the note on Bath (above). The deleted lines read, "there at Quiché mountain / Quiché valley."

you did your best, sir / to chop clear through / my root, my trunk: This passage is followed in both texts by two lines that have been deleted from the translation for reasons given in the note on Bath (above). The deleted lines read, "at Quiché mountain, Quiché valley."

you, sir, would be chopping through: Brasseur has *kech'ay,* as if "they" (Lord Five Thunder's own men) would be the attackers, but Pérez corrects this to *kach'ay,* so that the chopping is done by "you" (Cawek).

inside the great walled fortress: Here and in subsequent cases, this line translates *chupam unimal tz'aq k'oxtun,* following both texts. In each case Coloch separates *tz'aq* and *k'oxtun,* "fortress" and "walls," between two separate lines, preceding each with *chupam unimal,* "inside the great."

We are the ones who buried them: This translation clarifies the texts, which simply say *mi xqab'ano,* "we did it."

inside each fortress / inside each set of walls: Both texts have *upam jujun chi tz'aq / chi k'oxtun,* but this translation follows Coloch, who repeats *upam jujun,* "inside each," in front of *k'oxtun,* "walls."

Cawek of the Forest People speaks for the twelfth time.

Your words, sir, also say: / "Did you, sir, finish off / two or three branches of the nation / … ?" / So say your words, sir. / And truly it is I / who am to blame / because of my troubled heart: These fourteen lines are translated from the text of Brasseur. Pérez omits them, as do Breton and Coloch.

When I drink it: This translation follows Pérez, who has *kantijo,* "I drink it"; Brasseur has *katij la,* "you drink it, sir." The change to the first person makes for a better fit with the next two lines.

It serves to glorify my mother / my lady: Literally, *unimab'al* is "her means of being great"; *nimab'al* carries a sense of reverence (FV, FT). This is may be a reference to the goddess of the maguey plant, from which the drink requested by Cawek was made (see the earlier notes on "the twelve drinks" and "Quick Hummingbird"). The name of the Mayan maguey goddess is not known, but the Mexica goddess, shared with the Huastec Maya, is Mayahuel, who had four hundred breasts flowing with maguey sap (Anawalt 1993). Her day on the divinatory calendar was the equivalent of the K'iche' day named *Q'anil* or "Ripeness," coming the day before *Toj.*

I have yet to taste it: Brasseur has *katij la,* as if Cawek were wanting "you, sir" (Lord Five Thunder) to "taste" the beverage, but Pérez corrects this to *kintijo,* so that the would-be taster is "I" (Cawek).

Lord Five Thunder speaks for the fifth time.

Man slave / woman slave: This is *achij mun / ixoq mun,* used by Lord Five Thunder each time he calls upon the single character who responds.

Offer it to the brave man: Coloch repeats *chayaka' chire,* "offer it to," for *achi,* "man," and treats the resultant phrase as a separate line.

Slave speaks for the third time.

Brasseur labels each of the unnumbered parts of the character who obeys Lord Five Thunder's orders with *Mun,* "Slave," apparently referring to the man slave he lists as *Mun* (as contrasted with *Ixoq Mun*) in his cast of characters. Xolop wrote "3°," for "tercero," in the margin of Pérez.

I give it to the brave / to the man: Coloch repeats *kanuya'o chire,* "I give it to," for *ri achi,* "the man," thus increasing the symmetry of the couplet.

Cawek of the Forest People speaks for the thirteenth time.

it shouldn't be counted as a meal: This is *mawi wa k'o chiretalij,* in which *-etalij* is translated as "counted as" on the basis of *etal,* "sign, mark," and *ech'etalij,* "to measure up" or "come up to the mark" (FX, FV). Pérez and Coloch omit this line.

Could this be / the skull of my grandfather? / Could this be / the skull of my father?: This translates *Tase are' / ujolom numam / tase are' / ujolom nuqajaw,* following Brasseur's version of the text. *Tase* (sometimes *taseq*) is a particle described by DB as conditional (see his entry for "taseƐ"). It is often translatable as "if" or "since," marking the first part of an if/then sequence of conditions and consequences. But since the present sentences are embedded in a series of questions I have treated them as posing questions as well, expressing the consequential nature of a later question by beginning it with "then." Pérez recasts and reduces the present passage to *qatz are' / ujolom nukajaw,* "truly this is / the skull of my father," divided into two lines by Coloch as he reads the Pérez text aloud.

Coloch understands Cawek to be talking about a calabash vessel here (see the next note). Calabashes (not to be confused with gourds) grow on trees of the genus *Crescentia.* In the Popol Vuh the first calabashes grew when the Lords of Death, rulers of an underworld domain called Xibalba, sacrificed a hero named One Hunahpu and placed his head in the fork of a tree that had been barren until then (D. Tedlock 1996:97, 259-60). Cawek's question evokes this story, shifting the scene from Rabinal to Xibalba and casting his captors as evil lords. It also recalls the story of the Quiché king Quicab, who is said to have avenged his father's death by recovering his skull and bones from those who had slain him (Recinos 1957:140-45).

carved in back / and carved in front: Here Coloch remarked, "He's comparing himself to a calabash." The drinking vessel is a carved Rabinal calabash in Coloch's productions of the play. Rabinal has long been famous for the production of calabash vessels that are lacquered and then carved (Morales 1981; Luján and Toledo 1986:189-221). In a sixteenth-century description of tribute owed to the Quiché kingdom, the people of Rabinal are listed as making a portion of their payments in *tzima rob'enal,* "Rabinal calabashes" (Recinos 1957:106-107).

ending up as an even trade for / five score seeds of pataxte / five score seeds of cacao: For the first line Brasseur has "tzakibal-ta re," which is hard to make sense of, but Pérez changes this to "tzaƐatitzabal tare," combining *tz'aqatisab'al,* "replacement, substitute" (TC), or (literally) "instrument for causing to be complete"; *ta (taj),* which marks the trade as the result of previous action; and *re,* "for them," referring to the pataxte and cacao mentioned in the succeeding lines. Coloch repeats the first line before the cacao line, thus increasing the parallelism.

"This is the skull of our own grandfather / our own father": Now Cawek is implicitly casting his descendants in the roles of Hunahpu and Xbalanque, the twin sons of

One Hunahpu, who defeated the Lords of Death and avenged the death of their father (D. Tedlock 1996:138-39).

this remembrance of me: The term translated as "remembrance" is *k'uxtub'al,* which is specific to Rabinal (listed under "cux" in DB).

"as long as there are days / as long as there is light": This translates *chuxe q'ij / chuxe saq,* as in Cawek's fifth speech. Brasseur drops the second *chuxe* here, but Pérez and Coloch restore it.

for a toponowos, a slit drum: The first of these two terms is "toponowos" in Brasseur and "toponowotz" in Pérez; the equivalent term in colonial dictionaries is *tepunawas* (PG, FV) or *tepanawas* (TC). It is borrowed from Pipil *tepunawas* (LC), equivalent to Nahuatl *tepunaztli* or *teponaztli* (RS). The second term, *q'ojom,* is the usual K'iche' one for the same instrument (see the note for "the bloodletter's drum" above).

give it to me, sir: This couplet-completing phrase, *chiyata la chuwe,* is added by Pérez and rendered as a line by Coloch.

This must be done for me right now: The urgency is conveyed by the verb stem *iqikij,* "do something in haste" (FV).

Lord Five Thunder speaks for the sixth time.

the work of my mother, my lady: This translates *ub'anom nu te, nu ixoq ajaw,* following Coloch; his expanded version makes more sense than the "banom La" of Brasseur or the "ri ubanom la" of Pérez. Brasseur takes "La" to be the second person polite pronoun, addressed to "Madame" (the silent character he lists as "Xokahau") even though Lord Five Thunder is in the midst of addressing Slave.

Give it to the brave / to the man / only to mark the greatness / of his death / here at the navel of the sky / navel of the earth: This translation follows Brasseur, who has the equivalent of *chaya chire oyew / chire achi / xa nima retalil / ukamik / waral chuxmut kaj / chuxmut ulew.* Pérez, following the model of a couplet that appears in other speeches, adds *usachik* ("his disappearance") after *ukamik.* Coloch increases the symmetry of two other couplets by inserting a second *chaya* ("give it") in front of *achi* and a second *waral* ("here") in front of *chuxmut ulew.*

Slave speaks for the fourth time.

Neither Brasseur nor Pérez nor Xolop numbers this part.

Cawek of the Forest People speaks for the fourteenth time.

Neither Brasseur nor Pérez numbers this part. Written in the margin of Pérez is "13°," an

abbreviation for "décimotercero," which continues Eugenio Xolop's independent numbering of Cawek's parts.

Well sirs, you who are flutists: "Flutists" translates *ajsu';* the dictionaries agree in glossing
   su' as "flute" and *ajsu'* as "flutist," though the present reference, as Coloch
   interprets it, is to the trumpet players of the play. There may be irony here, given
   that flutes, unlike trumpets, were played in contexts other than war and sacrifice. But it could also be that *su'* was actually a generic term for wind instruments and not for flutes alone; in any case, it is commonly extended to cover the
   shawm (chirimía) introduced by Spaniards.

my Mexican flute / my Mexican slit drum: The term translated as "Mexican" here is *yaki,*
   which can have the more general meaning "foreign."

But we would let our hair fall forward / we would hang our heads: This translation follows
   Coloch, who says *chiqajta qawi' / chiqajta qajolom,* literally "let it be lowered
   our head hair, let it be lowered our head." Both texts omit *chiqajta* in the second
   line.

Pérez added "musica" in the right margin of the next part label, referring to the music that
separates the above speech from the next one.

Cawek of the Forest People speaks for the fifteenth time.

Brasseur and Pérez label this speech, which follows an interlude of dancing, as Cawek's
   fourteenth, having failed to give a number to what he said just before dancing.
   In Pérez, where Xolop's marginal notations reckon the pre-dance speech as his
   thirteenth, the post-dance speech becomes his fourteenth. In the present translation both speeches have been numbered because that is consistent with the
   play's opening scene, where the speeches Man of Rabinal makes just before and
   just after an interlude of dancing are both given numbers by Brasseur.

...the things I have borrowed / the things I've been loaned: This translates *ri nuqajom / ri
   nuchaq'im.* Brasseur has "cahom" and "chaim" for the nouns, which Pérez
   changes to "Єohom" and "chaЄim." Breton arrives at *qajom* and *chaq'im* as the
   only likely pair of words with parallel meanings; *qajom* is "borrowed" (AG,
   FV), while the translation of *chaq'im* is based on *chaq'imaj,* "ask for a loan"
   (FV, TC). Brasseur probably heard the *q'* in *chaq'im* as a plain glottal stop,
   which in his orthography called for writing "chaim," with the two vowels
   directly juxtaposed, not "chayim."

The time has come for me to be divided / the time has come for me to be parceled out: Literally, *mi xchul nujacha / mi xchul nupere* is "it must come my division / it must
   come my being taken apart." *Jach-* is divide, apportion (DB, FX, MX); *pere-* is
   "take bread or fruit apart" (FV) or "break in small pieces" (FX). The reference

may be, in part, to the things Cawek has been loaned for his dances, but more to the point is his impending dismemberment. In his thirteenth speech he anticipated not only losing his head but having his arm and leg bones made into artifacts.

Guard these things, then / put them away, then: This translates *chik'uta b'ala / chitz'apijta b'ala,* in which the third-person object of the verbs is not specified. "These things" has been supplied on the basis of the preceding lines, in which Cawek speaks of the things he has borrowed and then foresees that his own body will be taken to pieces. In using the verb stem *tz'api-* he may be alluding to the five unlucky days at the end of the Quiché year, which are called *tz'api q'ij,* "days that enclose" or "imprison." The rest of the year is composed of eighteen periods of twenty days each, and Cawek makes eighteen speeches before he comes to his final soliloquy.

I have danced them on and on: This is *mi xinjikikij uloq,* in which *jik-* refers to movement in a straight line (see the entries for "hiquil" in FX and "hiquic" in FV) as contrasted with the curved movement of *mes-* (see "dance her round and round" above). "On and on" translates the reduplication *(-ikik-).*

who comes from / End of the String at Fish in the Ashes: In other contexts I have translated *ri petenaq* as "goods that come from," referring to quetzal feathers, jade, and precious beads (see the notes to Lord Five Thunder's first speech), but here it seems appropriate to shift to "who comes from," referring to the girl who is the "mother" of these things. In his thirteenth speech Cawek put her father in the mythic role of a lord of the underworld; the girl's underworld role is implied by the place name *Karchaj* or "Fish in the Ashes," which, according to the Popol Vuh, is the location of the entrance to that world (D. Tedlock 1996:36, 94, 255).

Slave speaks for the fifth time.

Neither Brasseur nor Pérez numbers this part, but in the margin of Pérez it is reckoned as fifth.

Cawek of the Forest People speaks for the sixteenth time.

In Brasseur, Pérez, and the Pérez margin, this is Cawek's fifteenth speech. Pérez added "musica" in the right margin, referring to the music that separates the previous speech from this one.

The one I have borrowed / the one I've been loaned: Following Coloch, this is *are b'a wa' nuqajom / are b'a wa' nuchaq'im.* The second line is omitted by Brasseur, while Pérez has only *nuchaq'im* for that line.

has been given to me by both ends: The texts have *mi xya k'ula chuwe.* For *k'ula chuwe* Brasseur has "c'ul ach ve" and Pérez has "qula chuve"; *k'ula* is "by both ends" (FV) and figures in various words having to do with marriage, such as *k'ulanik,* "married." Cawek's statement is doubly ironic: for one thing, "borrowed" and "given" are in contradiction; for another, he seems to be alluding, by means of sound play, to his lost chance to become Lord Five Thunder's son-in-law through marriage to Mother of Quetzal Feathers (see the "Mother of Quetzal Feathers" and "father- or son-in-law" notes above).

before the helmet / before the lance: "Helmet" is *to'j,* which appears as "too" in the texts (indicating *o* followed by a glottal stop); my reading is based on a dictionary entry for *to'j,* "helmets of war" (DB). "Lance" translates *ch'amiy,* which is usually glossed as "staff" but also means "lance" (PG).

Lord Five Thunder speaks for the eighth time.

"Give them to me now, sir / lend me something you have, sir": The first line, *Chiyata b'a la chuwe,* is missing from both texts but is added by Coloch, who thus forms a couplet.

You then, my eagle / you then, my jaguar: The texts do not repeat *Ix b'ala,* "You then," but Coloch does. The resultant verbal symmetry fits the symmetry of Lord Five Thunder's gestures toward the eagle and then the jaguar in actual performance.

Pérez added "musica" in the right margin of the next part label, referring to the music that separates the above speech from the next one.

Cawek of the Forest People speaks for the seventeenth time.

In Brasseur, Pérez, and the Pérez margin, this is Cawek's sixteenth speech.

the Golden Eagle / Golden Jaguar: This translates *Ruq'anal Kot / Ruq'anal B'alam,* following Coloch; the texts omit *Ruq'anal* for *B'alam.*

There are some with nary a tooth / some with nary a claw: This is *K'o jinta re' / k'o jinta rixk'aq.* A seventeenth-century source notes that *jintaj,* "nothing, not even one thing," is specific to the Rabinal dialect (see the entry for "humervachil" in DB). Speakers of the central dialect of K'iche' might say *mawi jun,* more like "without a single," instead.

Lord Five Thunder speaks for the ninth time.

that live on your mountain / live in your valley: The second of these lines, *ri k'o cha taq'ajal,* is added by Coloch to make a couplet.

Cawek of the Forest People speaks for the eighteenth time.

In Brasseur, Pérez, and the Pérez margin, this is Cawek's seventeenth speech.

to the face of my mountain / the face of my valley: In earlier contexts Cawek's mountain and
valley are his birthplace (see "Where is your mountain?" above). Here he is
about to pray, a context in which the meanings of "my mountain" and "my valley" extend to the petitioner's own body (B. Tedlock 1992:235, 263 n.3). He
may be alluding to this meaning when he says, a few lines later, "Just now you
were saying, 'He left!' / But I didn't leave," meaning that his body didn't leave.

where I walked / where I moved: This translates *awi xinb'in wi' / mi xinsilab' wi*, following
Pérez and Coloch; Brasseur omits the second line.

Ahead of the next speech Pérez inserted the number 116. In Brasseur's book the same
speech starts at the top of page 116.

Cawek of the Forest People speaks alone.

In both texts the label on this part carries the words *utukel kach'awik,* "he speaks alone,"
instead of a number. By Xolop's reckoning in the margins of Pérez this is Cawek's
eighteenth speech, but by the more consistent count used here, Cawek has already given
eighteen speeches by this time. A numerological consideration based on the Maya calendar
could have entered into the organization of some earlier version of the play. As was
commented earlier (see the notes to Cawek's fifteenth speech), the Quiché year is divided
into eighteen parts of twenty days each, plus five extra (and unlucky) days at the end.

"'The road is closed'": Literally, *Q'atajin ulo wa'* is, "It is cut off here this." *Q'ata-* (FV,
MX) or "catah" (FX) is "to cut," and can be used to express the idea of "not
letting someone continue on a road" (FV); *-n* places the focus on the action.
Both texts have "qatahin," which is very unlikely to be an error for "catahin,"
but Breton transcribes it as *ka-tajin* (with *ka-* as the prefix for the incomplete
aspect) and translates the phrase as, "Il est en route," thus reversing its meaning.

"Say this / to our lord / our liege." / Isn't that what you'll say: The inclusion in the message of the instructions given to the messenger is standard practice in the
Popol Vuh, where the embedding of quotations within the version of the message that is finally delivered runs up to as many as four layers (D. Tedlock
1996:93, 115-16, 270-71). If Cawek's equipment and clothing actually spoke
when they were delivered to his lord, they would say something like this to
him: "'"The end has come for my bravery, my manhood, searching, striving
for our meals, our morsels." Say this to our lord, our liege,' so said your brave,
your man to us, oh lord."

Then I shall resemble / that squirrel / that bird / who died on the branch of a tree / ... / here at the navel of the sky / here at the navel of the earth: This points up the irony of the location of Cawek's impending death. When he was born his umbilical cord would have been placed high up in a tree near his home, which is very far away from where he is now.

Do it now with your teeth / your claws: Coloch repeats *chib'ana b'ala,* "do it now," for the second of these two lines.

But you certainly won't stand my hair on end / in the blink of an eye: Literally, *Mata qatz jumerwachil / kiniwitzmarisaj* is, "Not certainly at one glance you are causing me to become hairy." For the verb stem Brasseur has "izma-" and Pérez has "itzma-"; *-r* is inchoative, *-isa* is causative, and *-j* is active transitive. The closest dictionary form is *itzmaijik* (with a passive ending), glossed as "have one's hair stand on end" (DB). Van Akkeren (1999:281), following Breton, offers "you cause my hair—or feather—growing" as a literal translation and then suggests "cover me with arrows" as a free translation, this in support of his notion that Cawek is expecting to be shot with arrows. But having one's skin shot full of holes would seem to be the opposite of having it break out in goose bumps, not to mention the fact that the only weapons carried by the play's characters are axes, not arrows. *Jumerwachil* is "in an instant" but more literally "at one blink" or "at a glance" (DB).

　　　　Other translators, ignoring the fact that *mata* (or "maqu" in Pérez) puts this whole statement in the negative, have made it appear that Cawek wants to get things over with quickly. The negative reading is perfectly obvious to Coloch, who commented, "He's saying they won't defeat him."

PART TWO

Mayan History Onstage and Behind the Scenes

CHAPTER ONE

KINGS AND CAPTIVES

1. The readings of the names inscribed on these vessels were provided by Stephen Houston (personal communication 1999).

2. See Coe (1978:124), Schele and Miller (1986:153), and Reents-Budet (1994:257-59, 346-47) for discussions of these vases and their provenance.

3. The use of a sash is reported by Mace (1967:30).

4. The famous scene depicting prisoners at Bonampak (room 2, north wall) is exceptional in showing them naked or clad only in loin cloths. They may have been fresh from the battlefield and not yet ready for formal presentation.

5. For a discussion of this panel see Schele and Miller (1986:226) and Miller (1986:104). I thank Stephen Houston for bringing it to my attention and for the interpretation of the inscriptions (personal communication 1999). He interprets the marks on the prisoners' clothing as cuts or rips that mark their degraded status, but I suspect the marks merely represent designs in the weaving. The marks on the cloth draped over the middle prisoner's arm are the same as the marks on his captor's clothing, and the zigzag marks on the prisoners' head scarves appear to leave these pieces of cloth intact rather than dividing them into tatters.

6. All of the shields carried by the warriors in the battle scene of the Bonampak murals are rectangular (Miller 1986:96-112 and plate 2).

7. Standing figures with scepters and shields are on Quiriguá Stele E (Sharer 1994:327); on Naranjo Stele 13 (Graham and von Euw 1975: fig. 2:37); on Seibal Stele 21 (Graham 1996: fig. 7:53); on Jimbal Stele 1 (Schele and Freidel 1990:391); on Yaxchilán lintels 1, 3, 32, 52, and 53 (Tate 1992:172, 220-21, 262-63); on Dos Pilas stelae 1 (Schele and Miller 1986:77), 11, 14, and 15 (Houston 1993:88-94); on Itzimte stelae 3, 8, and 10 and Lintel 1 (von Euw 1977: figs. 4:11, 21, 25, 31); on Uxmal Stele 2 (Graham 1992: fig. 4:87); and on the walls of the crypt in the Temple of the Inscriptions at Palenque (Robertson 1983: figs. 234, 254-55, 261,

268-69, 287, 296-300, 318-19). Two of these figures (Naranjo Stele 13 and Dos Pilas Stele 14) stand on the backs of captives.

8. Seated figures with scepter and shield are on the lintels inside Tikal temples I and IV (Sharer 1994:162, 170-71); on Pixoy Stele 5 (Von Euw 1977: fig. 4:43); on the walls of the crypt in the Temple of the Inscriptions at Palenque (Robertson 1983: figs. 238, 245, 280); and on the side of the south bench in the Temple of the Chac Mool at Chichén Itzá (Schele and Freidel 1990:370).

9. On the lowland Maya scepter or ax god, often called God K in the literature, see Baudez (1992), Taube (1992:69-79), and Grube (1992:210-11); his Quiché equivalent is discussed in D. Tedlock (1996: 296-97). The image is called *k'awil* in hieroglyphic inscriptions and *k'ab'awil* in sixteenth-century documents written in K'iche' and Kaqchikel; in both cases, the name of the god it represents varies according to the kin group and/or location to which it belongs.

10. The face on the shield is that of the god often designated as GIII in the Mayanist literature, identified as a god of fire by Stuart (1999). In standing figures it can be seen most clearly on Yaxchilán Lintel 3 and in the Palenque crypt figures; in seated figures it is clearest in the case of the Palenque crypt and Tikal Temple IV. A Chak figure in the Dresden Codex (page 66a) has a lightning-striking ax in one hand and holds a shield bearing a logogram that reads *ix,* "jaguar," in the other.

11. The Quiché book known as the Popol Vuh gives the fullest picture of *Tojil;* see D. Tedlock for his story (1996:45-49, 152-72) and for the meaning of his name (pp. 296, 319). The scepter term appears in the *Title of the Lords of Totonicapán* (Carmack and Mondloch 1983:149).

12. The source for the name of the Rabinal deity is the Popol Vuh (D. Tedlock 1996:162, 352); for the Cakchiquel deity it is the *Annals of the Cakchiquels* (Recinos and Goetz 1953:52).

13. For the full argument that the city of the pilgrimage was Copán, see D. Tedlock (1997:12-14, 236-37). In the art of Copán, images of the god of the scepter do not take the form of a scepter as such, but there is a sixth-century text (on Stele 15) that refers to the display of the scepter (Fash 1991:83).

14. On the reference to dancing in the accompanying inscriptions at Yaxchilán and Dos Pilas, see Grube (1992); the reading of the glyphs in figure 9 is that of Stephen Houston (personal communication 1999). In the case of Yaxchilán lintels 32 and 53 the bearer of the scepter and shield is dancing opposite a woman. A dancing figure similar to the Palenque example illustrated in figure 10 may be seen on Stele 3 at Tzum (Von Euw 1977: fig. 4:55).

15. According to the *Annals of the Cakchiquels,* the rulers of the Cakchiquel kingdom performed this ritual in 1504 and again in 1517, at a time when their power was on the rise and the Quiché kingdom was in decline (Brinton 1885:162-63, 168-69; Recinos and Goetz 1953:111, 114).

16. "Pokob" *(poqob'),* which means "column, pillar, post" (PG, FV, TC), appears as the name of a dance drama in the *Annals of the Cakchiquels* (Brinton 1885:162, 168),

the Totonicapán document (Carmack and Mondloch 1983:146-47), and the *Título C'oyoi* (Carmack 1973:295). The spelling in all these sources is more reliable than in the Popol Vuh, whose "pocob" *(pokob'),* if correct, would mean "shield." Nevertheless, van Akkeren (1999:284-87) changes the spelling in the Totonicapán source to agree with the Popol Vuh. I chose "shield" in translating the Popol Vuh (D. Tedlock 1996:181, 318), but that was plainly in error. The *Título C'oyoi* has *Poqob' Chanal;* a colonial dictionary whose spelling of "k" sounds is as bad as that of the Popol Vuh defines "Chanal Pocob" as "an ancient dance" (DB). By itself, *chanal* means "merriment, festival" (FX). The passage in the Totonicapán document (Carmack and Mondloch 1983:146-47) has "nima pokob upoɛob tohil" *(nima poqob', upoq'ob' tojil),* in which the contrast between "pokob" and "poɛob" in two successive words is clearly deliberate; *poq'o-* is to "come to light, bloom, hatch, burst forth, explode, thunder, abound" (DB, MX, AG), and *-b'(al)* is causal. A passage coming a page later (ibid.:148-49) makes the same contrast: "xpoɛobaxic upokoba" *(upoq'ob'axik upoqob'a).* The first of the two passages translates literally as "the great post, the means of bringing Tohil to light," and the second as "it was brought to light, his post."

17.   D. Tedlock (1996:181).
18.   In K'iche' these two quotations are respectively *jun nima k'utb'al, ilb'al,* and *xb'ina'j* (Carmack 1973:277, translation mine). According to the Popol Vuh, it was the gods themselves who originally asked to be hidden (D. Tedlock 1996:163).
19.   On the recovery of the skull and bones see Recinos (1957:140-45).
20.   This statement is based on an analogy with Aztec ceremonies of kingship, at which nonattendance was taken as a sign of disloyalty (Hassig 1988:189, 200).
21.   Descriptions of this occasion appear in the *Título C'oyoi* (Carmack 1973:277, 295) and the Totonicapán document (Carmack and Mondloch 1983:146-49, 195-96). Both sources mention that it took place during *Tz'ikin Q'ij.* This was the eighth division of the solar calendar, as is made crystal clear in pages 1-22 of the K'iche' Codex, an anonymous 1722 document otherwise known as "Calendario de los Indios de Guatemala" (see B. Tedlock 1999 for an introduction). A correct list of the divisions of the Quiché year is presented by Edmonson (1988:237), but the version given by Carmack (1981:88) is muddled. *Tz'ikin Q'ij* ran concurrently with the Yucatec Maya division known as *Xul.* In 1722 it began on September 20. In 1410, a year likely to have come during Quicab's reign, it would have run from December 5 through 24 (by retrospective Gregorian reckoning).
22.   This and all further details of the event come from the Totonicapán description. Carmack and Mondloch (1983:196) translate *ch'ab'i q'aq'* as "flaming arrows," but *ch'ab'i* covers all projectiles and *ch'ab'i q'aq'* is the term for meteors (B. Tedlock 1992:180).
23.   The description of *kaq tijax* as an iguana is given by FV, who notes that he has seen one himself. The Huave, in the Isthmus of Tehuantepec, describe meteors (not comets) as the tail of an iguana, and the Telleriano Remensis and Vaticanus A codices

represent large meteors as reptilian creatures with serrations on their backs (Köhler 1989:295-96).

24. The Andromedid meteor shower (also named Bielid after the associated comet) was last reported as a notable one in 1741 and is extremely weak today, but in ancient times large showers occurring in November or December found their way into Old World records, beginning in 524 A.D. (Lovell 1954:249, 349-50). In modern times the strong December shower has been the Geminid one, but it may be of relatively recent origin, given a lack of datable ancient reports in Old World sources (Lovell 1954:308). The dates of the two known Cakchiquel ceremonies analogous to Quicab's—April 30, 1504, and February 8, 1517 (Gregorian)—are unlikely ones for meteor showers. But it seems worth noting that on both occasions Venus was near to being as high in the eastern sky as it can get, rising hours before dawn. On those same occasions, Mars was near the zenith at sunset.

25. I thank Karl Taube for pointing this out to me.

26. D. Tedlock (1996: 224).

27. The full argument for this reading is given in the section "Two versions of the Conquest" in chapter 3.

28. Here it is assumed that the sumptuary laws of the highland Maya were like those of central Mexico; on the piercing of noses, lips, and ears there see Durán (1994:147, 209, 234).

29. According to the Popol Vuh only members of the three top-ranking Quiché lineages went on the later pilgrimage (D. Tedlock 1996:179), but *Annals of the Cakchiquels,* which offers a more detailed description of the itinerary, says that Cakchiquel lineages were represented (Recinos and Goetz 1953:64-66).

30. For other emblems of lordship with foreign names in the Popol Vuh see D. Tedlock (1996:316); for the Totonicapán document see Carmack and Mondloch (1983:150-51, 196). In two cases *Rabinal Achi* and the Popol Vuh offer terms that contrast but are nevertheless K'iche' in both cases. The "snail-shell bracelet" of the play is *chinku,* but the Popol Vuh has *t'ot' tatam,* "rattling snail shells"; *chinik* and *t'ot'* are both terms for "snail." Instead of the play's *saqkab',* "white paint" (literally "white earth"), the Popol Vuh has *q'an ab'aj,* "yellow ochre" (literally "yellow stone").

31. Nacxit is one of the names or epithets of the legendary king named "Quetzal Serpent" *(K'uk'ulkan),* who, according to the Chilam Balam books, arrived in Yucatán in the tenth century (Roys 1967:83n, 204).

32. For the full text of the relevant passage see Brinton (1885:90); he misinterpreted its meaning, as Recinos and Goetz point out (1953:64). The stem *or-,* referring to piercing, is equivalent to K'iche' *wor-,* as in *worom ajaw,* "lord who's been pierced."

33. For the full story of Eight Deer see Byland and Pohl (1994:137-76).

34. One figure of a Quiché lord wearing a nosepiece appears in a painted mural at Old Camp *(Q'umarka'j)* or Utatlán (D. Tedlock 1997:99); three figures of Cakchiquel lords wear nosepieces in incised murals at Iximché (Schele and Mathews 1998:303).

35.   The mustache and small goatee are not direct borrowings from the masks worn by
      Spanish characters in other dramas, which have gold mustaches and beards that are
      curly and more abundant. The Slave mask lacks the goatee, as does an older Cawek
      mask (fig. 2), but the Cawek mask currently in use has it (figs. 17, 46).

36.   On the past and present Mayan use of powdered tobacco and lime kept in gourds,
      see Thompson (1970:110-12).

37.   The penance undergone by Aztec lords on assuming high office is described in
      Sahagún (1954:61-65). On Quiché shamanic performances and fasts, see D. Ted-
      lock (1996:186, 192).

38.   On the Holmul style of vase-painting see Reents-Budet (1991); for the full story of
      the particular vase discussed here see Reents-Budet (1994:294-305).

39.   This reading of the name of the lord of Naranjo was supplied by Stephen Houston
      (personal communication 1999).

40.   The large raptors of Guatemala are the Crested Eagle *(Morphnus guianenis)*, Harpy
      Eagle *(Harpia harpyja)*, Black-and-White Hawk Eagle *(Spizastur melanoleucus)*,
      Black Hawk-Eagle *(Spizaetus tyrannus serus)*, and Ornate Hawk-Eagle *(Spizaetus
      ornatus vicarius)*, all of them crested (Howell and Webb 1995:206-211).

41.   McArthur (1966:140).

42.   See Miller (1999:179-82) for a cogent discussion of the Cacaxtla murals.

43.   This is an example of the so-called serpent bar, held by kings at such sites as Tikal,
      Naranjo, and Copán; see Schele and Freidel (1990:68-69, 415-16).

44.   For detailed descriptions of this kind of combat, see Durán (1971:178-79;
      1994:272-75). Van Akkeren (1999:281-88), in arguing that the Rabinal play
      originally ended with an arrow sacrifice, ignores the fact that no such sacrifice was
      performed by eagle and jaguar knights.

45.   Brasseur (1862b:113) calls this "une danse guerriere" but offers no description.

46.   See Mace (1981a:98, 98n, 108). He argues that the sacrifice Brasseur describes at
      the end of his 1862 translation of the play is an invention, given that in an 1859
      description of the play's ending he had simply said, "Ils le mettent à mort."

47.   On the vocabulary of Classic Maya politics, see Grube and Martin (1998, 2:55).

48.   See Schele (1984) and Houston and Stuart (1998:85). This is not to say that heart
      sacrifice did not exist among the Classic Maya. A sacrificial body with a large opening
      just below the rib cage is shown on Piedras Negras stelae 11 and 14 (Robicsek and
      Hales 1984: fig. 5).

49.   For the episodes in which gods lose their heads to the lords of death in the Popol
      Vuh, see D. Tedlock (1996:97, 126).

50.   See Houston and Stuart for an extensive discussion of personal identity among the
      Classic Maya (1998:83-92).

51.   See McAnany (1995:60-63), who argues that burials without skulls are at least as
      likely to be evidence of veneration as they are of sacrifice. The contemporary Itzá
      veneration of skulls is reported for San José Petén (Reina and Hill 1978:249 and
      plates 412-413).

52. Prisoners with names on their thighs appear on Toniná Monument 122, Yaxchilán Lintel 8, and Piedras Negras Stele 12 (Schele and Miller 1986:212, 218-19). See B. Tedlock (1992: chap. 6) for a full discussion of the divinatory symbolism of the human body.

53. The Tikal ruler in question was Hasaw Chan K'awil (Harrison 1999:133-37); for an example of a Tikal burial missing both the skull and femurs, see Harrison (1999:60).

54. This and similar uses of emblem glyphs and place names are reported by Stuart and Houston (1994:57-58, 61).

55. I judge the trophies in figure 23 to be representations of heads rather than real ones because the upside-down trophies worn by warriors on the south wall of Room 2 of the Bonampak murals are foreshortened in such a way as to show that they are flat rather than spheroid. I thank Mary Miller for calling my attention to the carved femur, which is illustrated in Miller (1999:220).

56. On the Maya king as cosmic tree, see Schele and Freidel (1990:90-91); on the entering of the tree by designated heirs, see Schele (1992:187).

57. On the role of the apron in a king's tree costume, see Schele and Miller (1986:77) and Tate (1992:56-59). The face on the trees and the apron, which has long been labeled as God C, is now interpreted as a generalized sign of divinity.

58. In Tate's interpretation (1992:46), the Classic apron was a sign that its wearer had let sacrificial blood from his penis. Obviously, this rite was the male equivalent of menstruation.

59. The drawing fills a page in a collection of Xiu family documents known as the Crónica de Oxkutzcab (n.d.); for a discussion see Morley and Brainerd (1956:148-49).

60. Mace (1967:30) describes a production by Coloch's predecessor in which the drinking vessel was a small pitcher.

61. In a sixteenth-century description of tribute owed to the Quiché kingdom, the people of Rabinal are listed as making a portion of their payments in *tzima rob'enal*, "Rabinal calabashes" (Recinos 1957:106-107). The most thorough treatment of calabash vessels in Mesoamerica is that of Luján Muñoz and Toledo Palomo (1986), which includes a chapter on Rabinal (pp. 189-99) and an autobiographical statement by calabash carver Julio Sis Pérez (pp. 201-21), a great-grandson of Bartolo Sis, who dictated the text of *Rabinal Achi* to Brasseur. See also Morales Hidalgo (1978a, 1981).

62. D. Tedlock (1996:91-98).

63. Carchá paid tribute to the Quiché rulers in quetzal feathers and jade at the time of the Spanish invasion (Recinos 1957:102-107).

64. For the full story of Blood Moon see D. Tedlock (1996:98-102).

65. See the entries for "ƐuƐ" in FV and "doncella" in TC. Brasseur (1862b:24-25) took this woman to be the wife of Man of Rabinal, which fits neither the internal structure of the play nor the meaning of her name.

66.   For the twins' full story see D. Tedlock (1996:104-139).

67.   For a discussion of this vase painting see Reents-Budet (1994:356-57).

68.   For the full story of the attempted resurrection see D. Tedlock (1996:141).

69.   In arguing that the prisoner in the Rabinal play should be understood as meeting his
       end by arrow sacrifice rather than decapitation, van Akkeren (1999:281-88) ignores
       the evidence for decapitation by sacrifice among the Maya. He also ignores Cawek's
       references to the heads of his ancestors, his descendants, and himself, and he
       overlooks Cawek's allusion to the origin story of decapitation, which is told in the
       Popol Vuh.

70.   The term translated here as "father- or son-in-law" *(b'alukixel)*, like the term
       rendered as "brother-in-law" *(jiaxel)*, is reciprocal. In previous translations of the
       play the former term has always been rendered as "son-in-law" or its Spanish or
       French equivalent, as if the meaning were limited to the notion that the lord might
       give his daughter to the prisoner.

CHAPTER TWO

HISTORY AS A PERFORMING ART

1.   I thank Stephen Houston for calling my attention to this stairway. A description and
      a drawing of the text on the added riser are included in Houston (1993:108, table
      4-1, and figure 4-11). A carved lintel in Temple I at Tikal shows Jasaw Chan K'awil
      riding in a litter in a procession that may have been part of a larger pageant
      dramatizing the story of a recent military victory in the year 695 (Martin and Grube
      2000:45).

2.   I originally made this argument in connection with an oral performance of a
      translation of the tablet in the Temple of the Cross at Palenque (D. Tedlock 1990),
      given by Bruce Frumker, Martha Mentch, Loa Traxler, and myself at the 1987 Maya
      Hieroglyphic Writing Workshop at the University of Texas.

3.   When Classic inscriptions deal with the capture of a prisoner of war, they often state
      nothing more than the date and the names of the captive and the captor, as in the
      cases of Yaxchilán lintels 8, 16, 44, and 45, and stelae 15, 18, and 20 (Tate
      1992:275-80). For suggestions as to how almanacs in the Dresden Codex might have
      been expanded when read aloud see D. Tedlock (1998:190-91).

4.   For the Popol Vuh toast see D. Tedlock (1996:91, 249-50). There are numerous
      passages in the *Title of the Lord of Totonicapán* in which the Quiché authors appeal
      to their descendants (Carmack and Mondloch 1983:144-45, 195) or ask them to
      listen (ibid.:98-99, 104-105, 182, 184). The author or authors of the *Annals of the*

Cakchiquels address their readers/hearers as *ix nuk'ajol,* "you, my sons," or *ix qak'ajol,* "you, our sons" (Brinton 1885:66-67, 104-5).

5. For the version of this chapter that appears in the *Book of Chilam Balam of Chumayel,* see Roys (1967:43-46, 125-31).

6. The Popol Vuh only quotes brief excerpts, one of which includes questions but stops short of giving the answers (D. Tedlock 1996:157, 162, 305); the Chilam Balam quotation, which is much longer, is clearly dialogical in form (see Roys 1967:38, 114-15).

7. These generalizations are based on Stevenson (1968:88-119), who necessarily relied largely on early colonial sources for central Mexico. On Aztec court songs see Durán (1971:299); for two Yucatec songs see Roys (1967:114-16; 139-40); on dialogue see Bierhorst (1985:45-46).

8. For a detailed discussion of the musicians in the Bonampak murals, see Miller (1986:82-85). One additional musician is depicted as standing outside the group discussed here, playing an upright, hide-covered drum.

9. The slit drum was first identified by Martí (1968, see figure between pp. 68 and 69), who illustrates a contemporary player of such a drum squatting on his haunches (ibid.:324).

10. See Stevenson (1968:63-73) for a full discussion of the slit drum.

11. Ximénez (FX) mentions the use of wooden trumpets in the early eighteenth century. On the music and musical instruments of the Dance of the Trumpets see Yurchenco (1990:177-82). Features that mark indigenous Quiché music are sorted out by Horspool (1982: chap. 7 and 282-83).

12. On the ant tree *(Platymiscium dimorphandrum),* see Camposeco M. (1992:36).

13. Francisco Antonio de Fuentes y Guzmán reported the use of rubber-tipped sticks to strike a slit drum in seventeenth-century Guatemala (quoted in Toledo Palomo 1965:54). The slit drums of central Mexico were also played with such sticks (Martí 1968:29).

14. See Horspool (1982:147, 227, 267-70) for a description of indigenous features of the music of the Quiché Maya and Yurchenco (1990:177-82) for a discussion of the music of *Rabinal Achi.*

15. Staff notations of its music have been published by Brasseur (1862b: 7 pages following 122), Yurchenco (1990:179), and Anleu (1991:123-26). Brasseur Westernized the relationship between the three voices, bringing them closer to a harmonious relationship, but Horspool (1982:269) makes it clear that there is a Quiché preference for loose synchronization and for dissonance. For a sound recording of a portion of the 1945 performance see Yurchenco (1978). Anleu seems to have produced a composite notation, based partly on previous performances and partly on what he heard in 1986. In the 1998 performance, which I recorded on videotape, the drum phrases typically began with four beats on the low tone rather than the two recorded by Yurchenco.

16. See B. Tedlock and D. Tedlock (1985) for an extensive exploration of this aesthetic as it is expressed in multiple arts.

17. It was Mary Miller who first interpreted these figures as a chorus (1986:89-90); the subsequent interpretation of the caption, which is not accurately reproduced here, was made by Stephen Houston. The generalized description of Mesoamerican music is based on Stevenson's survey of early accounts, most of which concern central Mexico (1968:88-119).

18. Among the Mexica, dance formations that moved in a circuit were closely associated with the slit drum (Kurath and Martí 1964:145-46); for illustrations of counterclockwise movement see Kurath and Martí (1964: figs. 93, 100-102). This is also the dominant direction of movement among the Pueblos of the Southwest U.S.

19. On ceremonies at 65-day intervals see B. Tedlock (1992:71, 192-94).

20. Brasseur, followed by Pérez, omits the number from Cawek's fourteenth speech, thus lowering the numbers of the subsequent speeches. For details on the numbering see the notes to the script that deal with Cawek's fourteenth and later speeches.

21. For the Nahuatl exclamations see Bierhorst (1985:188 et passim); for the Yucatec song see Roys (1967:114-116); for the songs in which *Aqaroq!* (translated as "Alas!") occurs and a discussion of its meaning see D. Tedlock (1996:157, 162, 276).

22. Garibay (1968:vii-xiv) argued that some of the songs in the *Cantares* give evidence of a pre-Columbian Nahuatl theater with dialogue; see also León-Portilla (1969:106-15). The present retranslation of one of these songs takes into consideration the Spanish of Garibay (1968:13-14) and the English of Bierhorst (1985:226-29). The song in question is included in a longer section of the manuscript that is headed *Nican ompehua teponazcuicatl,* "Here begin slit-drum songs" (Bierhorst 1985:218-19). The notation of drumbeats is omitted by Garibay but included by Bierhorst.

23. Garibay (1968:xxvii) interpreted the jade and quetzal feathers of the Nahuatl poem as metaphors for warriors.

24. *K'uxtub'al* and *jinta* are identified as specific to Rabinal in a seventeenth-century dictionary of K'iche' (DB). The same source gives the Rabinal term for navel as *muxt,* which suggests that *xmut* is a metathesis that developed later.

25. See Bricker (1981: chap. 10) for an exploration of the historical stratigraphy in several Mayan ritual dramas of Chiapas, Guatemala, and Yucatán.

26. For a reading of the tablet on the Temple of the Cross at Palenque, see Schele and Freidel (1990:246-47). On Calakmul dynastic vases, see Martin (1997). Martin and Grube (2000) offer a detailed survey of Classic Maya historical texts. For the dynastic passage in the Popol Vuh, see D. Tedlock (1996:194-97). For the part of the *Annals of the Cakchiquels* that is thickest with dates, see Brinton (1885:141-94) or Recinos and Goetz (1953:98-159).

27. Burkhart (1996:91-92) reports an analogous organization of time in a sixteenth-century Nahuatl translation of a Spanish drama whose subject is the passion of Christ. In the Spanish original, past events predict the future and serve to move it forward; in the translation, the past interrupts the flow of the present.

28. Pérez, except in his list of characters, changes *Job'* to *Ojob'*, meaning "Cough." I take this to be an error, one which he would not have made if he had been familiar with the divinatory calendar. Van Akkeren (1999:288), on the other hand, takes the change to be a correction and concludes that there was a *Toj* lineage in Rabinal, connecting it to the *Ajtojil* ("Keeper of Tohil") of the Popol Vuh. But *Ajtojil* is a title, not a lineage name; it is no more evidence of a *Toj* lineage than the existence of a title such as *Ajpop* is evidence of a *Pop* lineage.

29. On the auguries of the day named *Toj* see B. Tedlock (1992:115-16).

30. On the figure of speech for a marriageable daughter, see the entries for "ɛuɛ" in FV and "doncella" in TC. In the present-day wedding oratory of the Ixil Maya town of Cotzal, one of the metaphors for the bride is *q'uq'*, "quetzal" (Townsend et al. 1980:4). In the text that prefaces the script of the play the girl is mistakenly identified as the wife of Man of Rabinal (Brasseur 1862b:24-25, copied in Pérez), which directly contradicts the choice of a maiden to play her role. Moreover, the rest of the present speech implies that she is Lord Five Thunder's own daughter and that Cawek is (or could have been) a candidate for her husband.

31. According to the Popol Vuh, where the title appears as *Uq'alel Achij*, it was created as a reward for military achievement during the reign of Quicab (D. Tedlock 1996:190, 348).

32. None of the characters ever addresses or refers to Cawek by any other name than *Kaweq K'eche Winaq*, "Cawek of the Forest People." Even so, Brasseur labeled each of Cawek's speaking parts "Queche-Achi," which Pérez modified to "quiche achi." This has the effect of reducing the asymmetrical relationship between Cawek and his opponent, "Rabinal-Achi," to a simple opposition between men who represent the Quiché and Rabinal nations.

33. When *k'eche* is used instead of *k'iche'* in sixteenth-century Quichean documents, it is nearly always followed by *winaq*, specifying that the reference is to people; in contrast, most terms for nations (such as *rab'inal*) do not require such modification. This is probably because *k'eche* is shortened from *k'echela'j*, an ordinary term for "forest," and *k'eche winaq* is meant to be understood as "forest people." The common meaning of *k'echela'j winaq* is given in FV and TC.

34. For the Popol Vuh account of the generations see D. Tedlock (1996:194-95); the *Title of the Lords of Totonicapán* offers a variant account, increasing the number of early generations and decreasing the later ones (Carmack and Mondloch 1983:181, 184, 192-196).

35. Cawek also describes his adversary as the lord of *Chakachib'* or "Walkers," a town of the Cawuk *(Kawuq)* nation, which is named together with the Rabinal nation in the play and in several historical documents. The exact location of Walkers is unknown, but the pilgrims who went to the court of Nacxit (as described later) passed through it before they got to Fish in the Ashes. As for the Cawuk nation, its lands once included those of the present-day Quiché town of San Andrés Sajcabajá,

northwest of Workers. See the notes to Cawek's first speech for sources on Walkers, Workers, and the Cawuks.

36.   If the city in question was Copán, as suggested in the previous chapter, then the pilgrimage could not have taken place any later than the ninth century.

37.   In a similar fashion the authors of the "Título Real de Don Francisco Izquin Nehaib," a 1558 Quiché document, use the names of the founding lords as if they belonged to recent lords (Recinos 1957:107). See the Popol Vuh for the fullest account of the founders (D. Tedlock 1996: part 4). In the script, the first and second ancestors are mentioned in reverse order. The name first given as *B'alam Achi* in the script later appears as *Ajaw B'alam* and *B'alam Ajaw*. I interpret these names as equivalent to the *B'alam Aq'ab'* of the Popol Vuh and other sources by a process of elimination.

38.   The Popol Vuh says one generation (D. Tedlock 1996:179), while the *Title of the Lords of Totonicapán* says four (Carmack and Mondloch 1983: 184, 195). For more on the insignia see the notes to Man of Rabinal's first speech. The Popol Vuh only lists members of the three top-ranking Quiché lineages as participants in this pilgrimage (D. Tedlock 1996:179), but the *Annals of the Cakchiquels*, which offers a more detailed description of the itinerary, says that Cakchiquel lineages were represented as well (Recinos and Goetz 1953:64-66).

39.   For details on the identity of the Uxab and Pokomam, see the notes to Cawek's fourth speech.

40.   See Recinos and Goetz (1953:64-66).

41.   On the location of *Chatinib'al*, see the notes to Man of Rabinal's seventh speech.

42.   The fullest account of this incident is in the *Title of the Lords of Totonicapán* (Chonay and Goetz 1953:187; Carmack and Mondloch 1983:142-43, 194); it is also mentioned in the Popol Vuh (D. Tedlock 1996:181-82). The reign of Noble Bathhouse ended when he was killed in battle (Carmack and Mondloch 1983:195, 251n).

43.   This incident is depicted in the Zouche-Nuttall, Colombino-Becker, and Bodley codices (Boone 2000:119-20; see also Byland and Pohl 1994:163).

44.   See the notes to Cawek's seventh speech for more on the history of the capital and its names.

45.   For details on these names see the notes to Cawek's fourth speech.

46.   This comparison between Quicab and Alvarado is made in the *Title of the Lords of Totonicapán* (Carmack and Mondloch 1983:160-61, 199). According to this source Quicab came only one generation after Noble Bathhouse. The estimate of the time and duration of Quicab's reign is based on king lists, which present a tricky problem. At Palenque, nine securely dated reigns ending in 683 A.D. lasted an average of 20 years (based on Mathews 1992:116), while at Copán, eight reigns ending in 822 A.D. lasted an average of 34 years (based on Schele 1989:66-67). But among the Aztecs, nine reigns ending in 1520 lasted an average of only 16 years (based on Townsend 1992:12). The authors of the Popol Vuh place the rule of Quicab *(K'iqab')* and his viceroy, Cauizimah, five generations before those who were ruling when Alvarado arrived in 1524 (D. Tedlock 1996:195, 353). The *Annals of the Cakchiquels* is in

close agreement, placing Rajamun and Xkitzal, in the first of two generations of Cakchiquel lords who ruled concurrently with Quicab, five generations before Kaji Imox and B'eleje K'at, who ruled in 1524 (Recinos and Goetz 1953:91-92, 117). Carmack (1981:122) telescopes the lists of lords given in Quiché documents by eliminating all duplications of name—thus going against royal naming practices shared by the Classic Maya, the Aztecs, and Europeans—and moves Quicab three generations closer to the Spanish invasion in the process. I prefer the greater depth given by the Popol Vuh and would place the beginning of Quicab's reign, which was by all accounts a long one, near the end of the fourteenth century.

47. For a Quiché version of Quicab's quest see Carmack and Mondloch (1983:195); for a Cakchiquel version see Recinos (1957:140-45). The latter source tells of Cakchiquel participation; I infer Rabinal participation from the itinerary and from the evidence of the play. For evidence that the itinerary included the territory of the Uxab and Pokomam, see the notes to Cawek's fourth speech.

48. The quotation is from Carmack and Mondloch (1983:160-61, 200). There is no one source that describes all four of Quicab's expeditions; it is only when they are considered together, and in light of this quotation, that the scheme becomes clear.

49. The Cakchiquel list of Quicab's conquests, which focuses on the northern and eastern expeditions, totals thirty-six towns (Brinton (1885:132-33; Recinos and Goetz 1953:93-94), but some of these would have been places where Quiché rule was being reasserted rather than imposed for the first time. The lists in the Popol Vuh are shorter but more diverse (D. Tedlock 1996:187-89).

50. The western expedition is best described in the *Title of the Lord of Totonicapán* (Chonay and Goetz 1953:190-92; Carmack and Mondloch 1983:198-99). It expanded the area ruled by Quicab at the expense of the kingdom of Mam Maya, whose capital was at *Saq Ulew* or "White Earth," near present-day Huehuetenango.

51. These towns probably came under Quiché rule when Quicab conquered nearby Cumatz and Tuhal (Sacapulas) (Recinos 1957:146-47; Recinos and Goetz 1953:93-94). The "Título C'oyoi," a sixteenth-century Quiché document, includes a people called "xjil" (probably the Ixil) and a place called Cunén in a general list of Quiché conquests (Carmack 1973:276, 293). Chajul, though its primary language is Ixil Maya (only distantly related to K'iche'), has rural districts whose language is K'iche', and the same is true of the nearby town of Nebaj (Ajpacaja Tum et al. 1996:538). Cunén, though it may once have been an Ixil town, speaks only K'iche' today.

52. The Quichean branch of the Mayan family includes K'iche', Kaqchikel, Tzutujil, Poqomam, Poqomchi', and Q'eqchi'.

53. What I reckon as Quicab's southern expedition is described in the Popol Vuh (D. Tedlock 1996:52-53, 188, 326) and the *Title of the Lords of Totonicapán* (Carmack and Mondloch 1983:199-200).

54. Recinos and Goetz (1953:94).

55. The story of *Tata Yak* and his brother is told in the *Annals of the Cakchiquels* (Recinos and Goetz 1953:94-95). The *Title of the Lords of Totonicapán* mentions

that Quicab had five sons and gives their real names; the fifth one bore the day name *Q'anil* or "Ripeness," but without any number prefix (Carmack and Mondloch 1983:199). *Q'anil* is followed by *Toj,* Lord Five Thunder's day name.

56. The term for agouti (*Dasyprocta punctata*) is *utuy* in Quichean languages (FX, PG) and *cotuza* in Central American Spanish. Agoutis are about twice the size of a rabbit.

57. The authors of the Popol Vuh, writing from the perspective of the ruling Quiché lineages, make no mention of a revolt and treat the internal expansion as if it were a part of Quicab's own grand design (D. Tedlock 1996:187-88).

58. Recinos and Goetz (1953:96-97).

59. See the ninth speech of Man of Rabinal.

60. The additional Cakchiquel source is the "Testamento de los Xpantzay" (Recinos 1957:162-63)

61. For more on breadnut trees see the item on "the creatures of yellow honey" in the notes to Cawek's seventh speech.

62. For more on Mountains in a Row / Pines in a Row, Thunderclap, and Big Tree, see the notes to Cawek's fourth speech.

63. For more on Bountiful, Between the Wasp Nests, and Joyabaj, see the notes to Cawek's fourth speech.

64. For more on Pitted and Planted and its location, see the notes to Man of Rabinal's fourth speech.

65. For more on Standing Jaguar and Bath, see the notes to Man of Rabinal's seventh speech.

66. For more on Drumbeat and on Spilt Water (Zacualpa), see the notes to Man of Rabinal's seventh speech.

CHAPTER THREE

UNDER SPANISH RULE

1. These designations are from the *Annals of the Cakchiquels* (Brinton 1885:170-73).

2. See D. Tedlock (1999) for an analysis of Alvarado's treatment of the Quiché kings.

3. The story of the Cakchiquel lords and the Spanish invaders is told in the *Annals of the Cakchiquels* (Recinos and Goetz 1953:120-29).

4. On the missionary effort in Verapaz, see Ximénez (1977:214).

5. See Mace (1970:31-38) for a general discussion of these efforts.

6. In Europe it was not until the seventeenth century that acting and dancing were definitively separated between two different kinds of drama (Savarese 1991:165).

7. For a description of the types of drama introduced by early missionaries in Mesoamerica, see Horcasitas (1974:68-69).

8. See Mace (1970:50; 1981a:109).

9. The *Baile de San Jorge* at Rabinal is described by Teletor (1955:165-68) and further discussed by Mace (1970:62-64). Teletor (1955:182) notes that the bat character also appears in *Nima Xajoj,* the play described by Mace (see the previous note) as concerning St. Paul. For the story of Bat House see D. Tedlock (1996:125-28).

10. For multiple examples of the Deer Dance, including scripts, see Paret-Limardo (1963).

11. The deer dances of Rabinal and the rest of the Verapaz region are discussed by Mace (1970:57-62).

12. For examples of Deer Dance speeches that end with invocations of patron saints, see the scripts from the Tzutuhil town of San Pedro de la Laguna and the Quiché towns of Nahualá and Santa Catarina Ixtahuacán (Paret-Limardo 1963:50-64, 71-95, 105-136).

13. As Morales (1988b:1) points out, *Moros* or *Moros y cristianos* is commonly used as a title for a number of different plays, among them *Carlomagno y los doce pares de Francia,* whose origins go back to a thirteenth-century confrontation between Christians and Muslims rather than to the expulsion of the Moors from Spain in 1492. Four versions of *Moros y cristianos* have been reported for Rabinal (Mace 1970:39-40), but it is unclear whether any of them corresponds to *Carlomagno.*

14. On *Carlomagno* in Mexico, see Rubio (1996). The principal source for Guatemala is Morales (1988b).

15. For the San Bernardino version, which was copied from the Cantel manuscript, see Morales (1988b:136-97). My subsequent description of *Carlomagno* is based largely on Morales (1988b), which includes three complete scripts and discussions of the other seven versions reported for Guatemala.

16. Raynaud, writing in 1928, went so far as to call the use of twelve in the text of *Rabinal Achi* a "mutilation," replacing what should have been thirteen (see Cardoza y Aragón 1972:13).

17. An account of the Rabinal missionary efforts of Las Casas is given by Ximénez (1977:214). On the two archaeological sites see Fox (1987:220); Above the Town is six kilometers northeast of Red Mountain. For other examples of the use of the number twelve, see the *Title of the Lords of Totonicapán* (Carmack and Mondloch 1983:197-99; Chonay and Goetz 1953:173, 191, 193).

18. In the Popol Vuh, the jaguar names are concentrated in the founding generation of the ruling Quiché lineages; Quicab and his contemporaries were in the seventh generation (D. Tedlock 1996:194-96).

19. The folktale reported here is known in both Cubulco (Shaw 1971:55-56; Arnauld 1993:94), which borders on Rabinal, and Rabinal itself (Arnauld 1993:94); other Yew Achi stories are told in Momostenango (recorded by myself) and Zunil (Weisshaar and Hostnig 1995a:30 and 1995b:33). In Momostenango, as in Cubulco, he is defeated by Santiago, who is the patron saint of both towns.

20.   See D. Tedlock (1983: chap. 11) for a discussion of the manner in which the authors of the Popol Vuh alluded to Christian teachings in such a way as to differ with them.

21.   See Mace (1970:51), who notes that the Rabinal version was abbreviated.

22.   For a script of the older play see Edmonson (1997); for the newer play see Bode (1961), who discusses many versions and includes the Spanish text of its oldest known script, and *El baile de la conquista* (1981).

23.   See B. Tedlock (1986) for a full discussion of *Saq K'oxol.*

24.   *Ye'j-* is "to hasten"; adding *-a'* makes it imperative (FV).

25.   The first character to use the invocation discussed here is Montezuma (Edmonson 1997:6-7). On the meaning of "red house" see the note headed "on top of a great pyramid" in D. Tedlock (1996:302) and the entry for "otero" in TC, which reports that vassals addressed a lord with the words *at nu inub', kaq ja,* "thou my ceiba, my pyramid."

26.   This pair of phrases occurs four times in *Rabinal Achi;* for *Saq K'oxol,* see Edmonson (1997:6).

27.   This pair of terms occurs numerous times in *Rabinal Achi* and *Saq K'oxol;* for fifteenth-century occurrences see the "Títuto C'oyoi" (Carmack 1973:282) and the *Title of the Lords of Totonicapán* (Carmack and Mondloch 1983:118-19).

28.   For *worom* see DB; the analogous form in TC is *orom.*

29.   For the four cited readings of this passage, see Brasseur (1862b:26-27); Raynaud (1953:35); Gerchoux and Vázquez-Bigi (1991:239, 281n), whose repetition of Brasseur's grammatical error has been pointed out by Enrique Sam Colop (1993:34) and Edmonson (1997:16).

30.   For *k'aqom* see TC and, in DB, "caƐo" and forms beginning with "caco." TC distinguishes "k" sounds accurately but DB does not; the two sources must be read in combination.

31.   See Raynaud (1953:35) or Cardoza y Aragón (1972:31) for the latter's Spanish translation of the former's lost French manuscript.

32.   Breton (1994:156).

33.   On nose-piercing see Breton (1994:156n), who cites an example in the *Annals of the Cakchiquels* (Recinos and Goetz 1953:64), and Edmonson (1997:79n). On the piercing of noses, lips, and ears in central Mexico see Durán (1994:147, 209, 234).

34.   The source of this passage is Edmonson (1997:16); I have emended his text and revised his translation.

35.   For discussions of reports of dances involving the *tun,* a war captive, and/or representations of sacrifice during the colonial period, see Toledo Palomo (1965), Acuña (1975:127-56), and Mace (1981a:93-103). For the texts of some of the Guatemalan colonial documents in which such dances are mentioned, see Chinchilla-Aguilar (1963:9-19).

36.   Toledo Palomo (1965:63), translation mine.

37. These and the Guatemalan dates listed later are taken from the sources mentioned in the previous two notes.

38. This document has been published by Navarrete (1971).

39. For descriptions of Rabinal plays other than *Rabinal Achi*, see Teletor (1955:155-85), Stöckli (1997), and the superb accounts of Mace (1970; 1981a; 1981b; 1985).

40. According to Recinos (in Recinos et al. 1950:32-33), Ximénez was in Rabinal from 1704 to 1715 and wrote his *Historia* (Ximénez 1977) afterward.

41. All quotes concerning this early eighteenth-century dance drama are translations from Ximénez (1977:84-85).

42. Acuña (1975: chap. 17) argues that Ximénez based his account on what he learned about the Rabinal version of the play while he was the priest in Rabinal (1704-1714), and Mace (1981a:93) agrees.

43. The term *k'aixon* ("caixón" in the spelling of Ximénez) is composed of *k'ai-*, "to sell"; *-x*, passive, and the nominalizing suffix *-on*. When the verb *k'ai-* had persons as its object, it referred to the marketing of their services by third parties; thus Indians whose services had been allotted (without their consent) to colonists were called *k'aixel winaq* or "sold people" (FV).

44. This story is told in the *Title of the Lords of Totonicapán;* see Chonay and Goetz (1953:186-87) and Carmack and Mondloch (1983:194).

45. For the standard arguments against Mayan diviners, dream interpreters, and readers of omens, see the colonial K'iche' catechism published by Chinchilla Aguilar (1963:65-76). On the Church's theory of history as applied in Mesoamerica see Browne (2000:85).

46. D. Tedlock (1996:192).

47. For a general discussion of these dances see Mace (1981a:103-104); for details on the Aguacatán version, which is called *Tz'unum* or "Hummingbird," see McArthur (1966, 1977). Other possibilities, less clearly described, have been reported for San Juan Ixcoy (a Kanjobal town) and Chichicastenango by Lothrop (1927). Lothrop (1927: fig. 27) illustrates a pair of the carved wooden plaques that serve as the center of backpacks, but he does not say which town or towns they come from. Where the Rabinal carvings have a pair of eagles and a pair of jaguars, his display a pair of monkeys and a pair of human figures with spotted arms.

48. Yurchenco (1958, 1978) gives the fullest description of the Chajul version. She mistakenly translates "tzunun" *(tz'unun)* as "sparrow" (1958:283), not realizing that in Guatemalan Spanish the term "gorrión," which elsewhere means "sparrow," is used for hummingbirds.

49. The drink Aztecs gave prisoners to prepare them for sacrifice was called *teooctli*, "divine wine" (Durán 1971:178). It was a variety of pulque, which is made by fermenting sap from the flower stalk of a maguey plant (also called agave), but it had added ingredients whose sources may have included a plant of the genus *Datura* or closely-related *Solandra* (Furst 1976:136-37).

50. On dead warriors as hummingbirds see Hunt (1977:63); on pulque tapsters among the contemporary Ñähñu (Otomí), see Bernard and Salinas Pedraza (1989:110, 234).

51. Morales (1978b, 1988a).

52. Morales (1978b:59, 1988a:135). In the former source, Morales notes that Landa reported a Yucatec ceremony involving the burning of a "building" constructed for the purpose. This was a structure made by stacking firewood in such a way as to make an interior space with doorways; it was burned to the ground in a ceremony whose participants then walked on the coals (Tozzer 1941:148-49).

53. D. Tedlock (1996:132-35).

54. This is described by Mace (1981a:130; 1981b:49-50).

55. See, for example, the detailed scenario of the Tewa "Raingod Drama" provided by Laski (1958:34-59).

CHAPTER FOUR

SCRIPTS AND VOICES

1. For an account of Brasseur's life and works, see Mace (1973).

2. For accounts of the life and works of Ximénez, see Recinos et al. (1950:30-19) and Sáenz (1977).

3. Brasseur calls attention to this page in the introduction to his *Popol Vuh* (1861:xiv).

4. See the bibliographical entries for Brasseur (1861, 1862a, 1862b). In the case of the *Grammaire,* Brasseur did not even bother to translate Ximénez into French.

5. For discussions of the known versions of the text of the play, including Brasseur's accounts of how he obtained his version, see Mace (1967:31-35; 1981:105-107), Acuña (1975:29-55), and Breton (1994:23-37). Brasseur's published account is in his preface to the play (1862b:17-19). I agree with other commentators that the brief "Prologue de Bartolo Ziz," which Brasseur inserted after the list of the cast of characters (pp. 24-25), was composed by Brasseur himself. For one thing, the "Ziz" spelling is his own, meant to add an antiquarian touch; Sis himself used the "Sis" spelling when signing his name (see the frontispiece in Acuña 1975). For another, the prologue violates idiomatic usage and contains at least one made-up word, "nabe-bibal," with "prologue" appearing as the French translation on the facing page. In general the prologue reads like a literal back-translation from French to K'iche'. In my opinion it is simply Brasseur's way of communicating what he learned about the Sis manuscript when he saw it, including the date Sis had written on it.

6. It should also be noted that in an early publication, in a passage in which he discusses Rabinal history without mentioning that the play is his source, he cites "traditions écrites et orales" in the same sentence (Brasseur 1858:132n.).

7.   Breton (1994:28) also takes the position that both stories are true.

8.   For brief discussions of the Monkey Dance see D. Tedlock (1987; 1996:267, 302). I have Mace to thank for identifying it as the drama more widely known as the Deer Dance.

9.   In 1969 Mace (1970:132-33) had the experience of being shown a manuscript that turned out to be typewritten, this one in Rabinal. As in the present case, its owner had thrown the handwritten version away.

10. See Brasseur (1862b:24).

11. Labels with verbs appear in the manuscripts for the Deer Dance in the Quiché town of Nahualá (Paret-Limardo 1963:75, 81-83, 87, 89, 92), *Carlomagno* in the Quiché town of San Bernardino (Morales 1988b:46-136), and *Saqi K'oxol* in the Kekchí town of Cobán (Chun 1870). In a script of *La conquista* from Mexico, all the labels carry the verb "habla" (Jáuregui and Bonfiglioli 1996).

12. On the scheduling of overlapping sequences by the Quiché calendar, see B. Tedlock (1992:59-71, 203-6) and D. Tedlock (1997:81-86).

13. Brasseur (1862b:38-58).

14. Mace (1967:32-35; 1981a:105-108).

15. Mace, who generously provided me with a photocopy of the Pérez notebook in 1987, correctly describes it as based on Brasseur's book (1967:35; 1981a:106). A copy of his copy is in the Latin American Library at Tulane University.

16. Xolop signed his name on two different pages of the Pérez manuscript (see Breton 1994:80, 111); the marginal numbers are in the same hand. In his copy of Pérez he left intact the numbers named in the part labels.

17. This transcription, which is set in type but reproduces the lines of the manuscript original, appears in Acuña (1975:181-84, partially quoted on p. 53 of the same source).

18. Breton (1994:33) states that Acuña acquired this manuscript, and I have been told the same thing by Mace. Breton cites one of Mace's publications (1981:106) on this point, but the article in question states only that Acuña acquired the copy of Brasseur's book that served as a source for Pérez (see page 107).

19. René Acuña set forth such a hypothesis in his monograph on the play (1975:19-20, 50-53). He had seen the Xolop manuscript in Rabinal in 1959 but knew of the Pérez version only from Mace's 1967 report. He argued, as a corollary to his hypothesis, that Mace had been misled by Esteban Xolop as to the genealogy of these manuscripts. But Acuña backed away from his position in an introduction and footnote that were added shortly before his work went to press (1975:vii, 52n). He did so because he had meanwhile taken a second look at the Xolop manuscript, concluding that its ultimate source was indeed Brasseur. At the same time he discovered that the last page of this manuscript carried an acknowledgment of the Pérez version as its source, but even so he clung to the idea that the Pérez version (which he had never seen) might somehow have direct ties to a pre-Brasseur manuscript. Alain Breton, quoting from Acuña's original argument and ignoring his later misgivings, advocates

an independent lineage for the Pérez manuscript (1994:30-37) and uses it as the basis of the emended text he places opposite his French translation.

20.   The Brasseur page under discussion here (1862b:26) corresponds to page 5 in the Pérez notebook, which Breton labels as folio 2 (1994:87). In the present work citations of the Breton reproduction are given in terms of the page numbers of his monograph rather than the separate numbers he assigns to the notebook pages, which involve multiple errors. As if he were dealing with a colonial manuscript, he uses the term *folio* rather than *page* for his numbers, thus leading the reader to expect both sides of a given leaf to carry the same number. In the case of the notebook's first leaf he correctly labels the recto side as folio 1 (corresponding to page 1 in the numbering used here). In the notebook the verso of this folio (page 2) is blank (except for ink stains), as is the recto of the second folio (page 3). The text resumes on the verso of the second folio (page 4), but Breton prints this on the verso of his folio 1 and labels it folio 1 (1994:85-86). The recto of the notebook's third folio (page 5) then becomes folio 2 in his numeration, but he goes on to label its verso (page 6) as folio 3 (1994:87-88). From this point all the way to the end, his "folio" numbers follow the pattern of page numbers, ending with 64. The original notebook text actually ends on the recto side of folio 34 (or page 67).

21.   The gap falls between pages 5 and 6 of the manuscript, or between the recto and verso of folio 3. Breton attributes the missing passage to the carelessness of Pérez and uses Brasseur's text to fill the gap in his emended text (1994:73-74, 159n).

22.   On pages 10, 14, 15, 17, 19, 20, 21, 24, 26, 29, 31, and 52, Pérez skips a line in the same places where lines were skipped by Brasseur's typesetter (1862b:36, 42, 44, 46, 48, 50, 52, 56, 60, 62, 66, and 96).

23.   This is reproduced by Breton without comment (1994:147).

24.   In some places Pérez does the reverse, leaving Brasseur's "c" where he should have changed it to "q." For example, where Brasseur renders the common conjunction *k'ut* as "cut," Pérez fails to recast it as "qut."

25.   For transcripts of some of the parish records of Rabinal, see Acuña (1975:169-80).

26.   The *Saq K'oxol* exclamations discussed here are from Edmonson (1997:5-73, 75-78). On "Acay!" see FV. "Cula!" apparently consists of *k-*, the incomplete aspect, and the verb *ula-*, "arrive"; *ula'* is "guest" (MX, AG). *Uwe'* is attested by MX, but the more usual form is *we'*, which is the word closest to "yes." "Alelele!" is close to *jalele'*, "over there" (AG).

27.   Examples of changes in addition to the ones discussed here may be found in the notes to the translation.

28.   My use of the term "crystallization" is inspired by the classicist Gregory Nagy (1996:108-109, 143, 145), though he seems to use it only for the oral side of transmission. He traces increasing rigidity in Homeric texts through four centuries of parallel oral and written transmission.

29.   These changes are described by Bode (1961:221-22).

30. This version of the Popol Vuh text (Sam Colop 1999) is by far the truest to the original language of any that has ever been published.

31. According to the Equipo de Antropología Forense de Guatemala (1997), whose investigations included the excavation of clandestine cemeteries, more than 2,000 men, women, and children were killed in twenty separate incidents in 1980-83.

32. Mace (1981a:127) and personal communication.

33. Mace (1981a:107) reports that in 1953, Eugenio Xolop, the son of then-director Esteban Xolop, gave one of the actors a handwritten copy of his part.

34. In constructing his lines Breton (1994:156) applied a method similar to the one I had used to demonstrate the fluctuation between parallel and nonparallel phrases in the Popol Vuh text (D. Tedlock 1985:244, 248-49). He did not consider the pattern I had described for line breaks in spoken K'iche' discourse (D. Tedlock 1983b:143-45), and he says nothing about how the lines of the play are actually spoken.

35. For examples of the work of Esteban Ajxup, see D. Tedlock (1987:149-53, 159-60); for Tat Justo Yac, see Sam Colop (1994: chap. 4).

CHAPTER FIVE

THE PLAY ENACTED

1. On the workshops, which are called "morerías" in Spanish, see Luján (1987).

2. "Today" means the 1990s, and "formerly" means around the middle of the twentieth century. No descriptions or photos of costumes earlier than the 1950s are available.

3. For a description the play's costumes and properties as they were in the 1950s, see Mace (1967:30).

4. Lady appears in the list of characters in both Brasseur and Pérez, who identify her as the wife of Lord Five Thunder, and in a photograph of the cast of a production that took place in Rabinal in the mid-1990s. But there was no such character in a 1955 production in Antigua (Rodríguez Rouanet 1962:49) or in the 1998 production in Rabinal.

5. See the entry for "Slave" in the notes to the script.

6. Brasseur divided the text of the play and his translation into four scenes, but no such divisions are marked in other scripts for the dramas performed in Guatemalan Mayan towns, nor do performances stop and then start again as they do for the scene or act changes in modern Western theater.

7. See chapter 4 for a discussion of this and other changes Coloch makes when he plays this role.

8. For an alternative set of additional lines, see the discussion of the conquest drama in chapter 3.

9. For more on henequen see the notes to Rabinal's first speech.

10. Brasseur (1862b:29) specifies lassoing in his stage directions, while Mace (1967:30) was told by Esteban Xolop, Coloch's predecessor, that the two characters held a sash. In more recent productions the effect of moving the use of the rope to a much later position is to make Rabinal's power over the man he calls his captive seem even less a matter of physical force than ever.

11. The metaphor of cloudy origins is also present in Nahuatl (Aztec) oratory; see D. Tedlock (1999) for a discussion.

12. In 1998 this interlude followed the same general pattern as the previous one, except that the fanfares were shortened to three.

13. In the view of Coloch's predecessor, only Lord Five Thunder should be seated, though the Mother of Quetzal Feathers might occasionally sit down to rest herself from standing too long (Mace 1967:30).

14. See chapter 2 for a fuller discussion of these names.

15. See D. Tedlock (1996:146).

16. This translation is from D. Tedlock (1996:164).

17. See chapter three for further discussion of Father Fox, his title, and the agouti.

18. See the notes to Cawek's sixth speech for details on Water Jar Point and the places he visited subsequently.

19. This is reported by Teletor (1955:207).

20. On the subject of Red Earth see the notes to Cawek's seventh speech.

21. See the notes to Cawek's seventh speech for details on these names.

22. See the notes to Cawek's seventh speech for the reasons behind this translation.

23. On the divinatory meaning of the day *Tijax* or "Knife" see B. Tedlock (1992:122-23).

24. The thirteen days numbered One beyond the starting point at *Toj* would be *Iq'*, *Tz'ikin, Q'anil, Imox, Ix, Kej, Junajpu, Aj, Kame, Kawuq, E, Kan,* and *Tijax,* in that order (see B. Tedlock 1992:78).

25. On the five lakes, which remain a part of present-day Quiché cosmology, see D. Tedlock (1997:87-88, 243-44)

26. This would be on the model of the expression *siwan tinamit,* which is translated as "down in the canyons, up on the heights" in the seventh speech of Rabinal.

27. See the notes to Lord Five Thunder's first speech for more on maguey, pulque, and hummingbirds.

28. For a description of four-directional rituals timed by the divinatory calendar in Momostenango, see B. Tedlock (1992:192-93).

Glossary

agouti *Utuy,* a rodent *(Dasyprocta punctata)* about twice the size of a rabbit, hunted for its meat. It is easily startled and screams loudly as it flees.

Bath *Chatinib'al,* the place where Lord Five Thunder was bathing when Cawek of the Forest People attempted to lure him out into an ambush. It may have been located a short distance from Standing Jaguar.

Below the Cave, Under Ripe Yellow Corn *Ekem Pek, Xe Q'ana Hal,* two names for a mountain taken by the Uxab and Pokomam. Location unknown.

Between the Wasp Nests *Xol Chaqaj,* a place visited by Cawek of the Forest People when he was resetting boundaries. It lies east of the present Quiché town center of Joyabaj and southwest of Standing Jaguar.

Big Tree *Nimche',* a place visited by Cawek of the Forest People when he was resetting boundaries. Today it is the location of a hamlet known as Panimaché, eight kilometers east northeast of the Cakchiquel town center of Sololá. Its lands are disputed between Sololá and the Quiché town of Chichicastenango. It is connected with Lord's Place and Earthquake, also visited by Cawek, by a major north-south foot trail.

bird-footed bean shoots *Rixk'aq tz'ikin,* a stage in the growth of a small ground bean when the plant looks like bird feet.

Bird's Drinking Water, Pieces of White Lime in a Row *Ruq'ab'a Ya' Tz'ikin, Cholochik Saqchun,* two names for a place where Man of Rabinal once sent Cawek of the Forest People to deliver a message to the Uxab and Pokomam. Location unknown.

Bountiful *Pan Chalib',* a place visited by Cawek of the Forest People when he was resetting boundaries. A short distance southwest of the present Quiché town center of Joyabaj.

breadnut tree *Iximche',* a broadleaf evergreen *(Brosimum alicastrum)* called ramón in Spanish, with a fig-like fruit. It was an important food in times of famine.

cacao *Kakow,* the seeds or seed pods of *Theobroma cacao,* a tree domesticated by Mesoamerican peoples in ancient times. They formerly used the seeds as money and continue to use them to make chocolate beverages.

Cawek of the Forest People *Kaweq K'eche Winaq,* the warrior captured by Man of Rabinal. The Cawek lineage held the two top-ranking lordships of the Quiché kingdom.

Cawuks and Rabinals *Kawuq* and *Rab'inal,* the two nations ruled by Lord Five Thunder. Cawuk (or Caoqué) towns once included the present Quiché town of San Andrés Sajcabajá, forty kilometers west of Rabinal.

children of light, sons of light *Saqil al / saqil k'ajol,* a figure of speech used by lords when referring to vassals, referring to the notion that vassals were born after the rising of the present sun and moon, whereas lords have an earlier origin.

conqueror ants *Ch'eken sanik,* large ants called *zompopo* in Guatemalan Spanish, notorious for stripping plants of their leaves.

cord *K'a'm,* a unit of measurement equivalent to twenty strides (or ten paces), approximating twenty yards.

Croaking Frog Point at Belted House *Tzam Xtin Q'urun chuwach Ximb'al Ja,* a place visited by Cawek of the Forest People when he measured the perimeter of the valley ruled from Red Mountain. Belted House, known today as *Ximb'aja,* is a kilometer and a half south of the present town center of Rabinal.

Cunén and **Chajul** The northernmost towns ruled by the lord of Quiché Mountain, Quiché Valley. They are called "foreign" by Cawek because of a language difference. Today Chajul speaks Ixil, a Mayan language whose relation to K'iche' is a distant one. The present language of Cunén is K'iche', but it may once have been Ixil. Both places are sixty kilometers northwest of the present town of Rabinal.

Dance of the Trumpets *Xajoj Tun,* one of the play's two titles, referring to the two trumpets played by its musicians. In the dialogue they are referred to as *lotzo tun,* "trumpets of sacrifice."

Dressed in Red *Kaqo Kawunik,* the name of one of the four parts of the fortress of Lord Five Thunder (see Red Mountain).

Drumbeat *Kunu,* one of the places where branches of the Rabinal nation suffered losses at the hands of Cawek of the Forest People. It may be the place now known as Xeknup, nine kilometers west of Standing Jaguar and at the northern edge of the territory of the present Quiché town of Joyabaj.

Eagle and **Jaguar** *Kot* and *B'alam,* two sacrificial priests of Rabinal (see also Golden Eagles, Golden Jaguars).

Earthquake *Kab'raqan,* a place visited by Cawek of the Forest People when he was resetting boundaries. This is the present-day Quiché hamlet known as Chicabracán, spread out on a tableland between San Sebastián Lemoá and Chiché. It is connected with Lord's Place and Big Tree, also visited by Cawek, by a major north-south foot trail.

End of the String at Fish in the Ashes *Tzamk'a'm Karchaj,* a place named as a source of quetzal feathers and jade beads. Today it is the site of the Kekchí hamlet known as Tzancanijá, two kilometers southwest of the town center of San Pedro Carchá and forty-five kilometers north of the town of Rabinal.

Five Thunder See Lord Five Thunder.

Gathered Birds *Kuchuma Tz'ikin,* an expression comparing the lords who gathered at Old Camp and Whisker Place to birds that flock together.

Gathered Cane Plants *Kuchuma Aj,* an expression comparing the lords who gathered at Old Camp and Whisker Place to a clump of cane stalks.

Gathered Canyons *Kuchuma Siwan,* an expression comparing the lords who gathered at Old Camp and Whisker Place to the canyons surrounding the citadels there.

Gathered Honey *Kuchuma Kab',* an expression comparing the lords who gathered at Old Camp and Whisker Place to worker bees.

Gathered Lakes *Kuchuma Cho,* an expression comparing the lords who gathered at Old Camp and Whisker Place to the five lakes that marked the center and four sides of the Quiché kingdom.

Golden Eagles, Golden Jaguars *Uq'anal Kot, Uq'anal B'alam,* described in the dialogue as being twelve in number even though the characters on stage include only one Eagle and one Jaguar.

Healing Waters *Tzalya',* a place visited by Cawek of the Forest People when he measured the perimeter of the valley ruled from Red Mountain. It is in a bottomland with rich soil, one kilometer west of Henequen Mountain.

henequen *Saqki',* a variety of maguey *(Agave),* a yucca-like plant with spine-tipped leaves whose long fibers are used to make ropes like the one referred to by Man of Rabinal. The present-day crafts of Rabinal include rope-making.

Henequen Mountain, Henequen Valley *Saqkijel Juyub', Saqkijel Taq'aj,* a place visited by Cawek of the Forest People when he measured the perimeter of the valley ruled from Red Mountain. Henequen Mountain is a hill three kilometers south-east of the present town center of Rabinal.

House Point by the Rocks that Face Each Other *Tzam Ja chuwach K'ul Uwach Ab'aj,* a place visited by Man of Rabinal when he was resetting boundaries. Location unknown.

house wren *Tapich'olon,* a small bird to which Cawek of the Forest People compares himself. It is the Southern house wren *(Troglodytes musculus),* which, like the house wren of eastern North America, is loquacious and constantly on the move as it forages.

Jaguar Lord *Ajaw B'alam,* one of the names Cawek of the Forest People and Man of Rabinal give for the principal lord of Quiché Mountain, Quiché Valley.

Jaguar Man *B'alam Achi,* one of the names Cawek of the Forest People gives to the principal lord of Quiché Mountain, Quiché Valley, described by Cawek as ruling Cunén and Chajul as well. This name is a modification of *B'alam Aq'ab',* "Jaguar Night," founder of the *Nijayib'* or "Great House" lineage, which held the third-ranking title in the hierarchy of Quiché lords.

Jaguar Quiché *B'alam K'iche',* one of the names Cawek of the Forest People and Man of Rabinal give to the principal lord of Quiché Mountain, Quiché Valley, described by Cawek as ruling Cunén and Chajul as well. This name is a modification of *B'alam K'itze',* founder of the *Kaweq* (Cawek) lineage, which held the top two titles in the hierarchy of Quiché lords.

Lady *Xoqajaw,* literally "woman lord," the wife of Lord Five Thunder.

Look-See Point *Tzam Muqutzu'm,* a place visited by Man of Rabinal when he was resetting boundaries, just before he reached Sculpture Tree (Panajachel). The exact location is unknown, but it could be one of many spots that provide spectacular views of Lake Atitlán.

Lord Five Thunder *Ajaw Job' Toj,* ruler of the nations known as Cawuks and Rabinals, with Man of Rabinal in his service. His name is his birth date on the Mayan divinatory calendar. The day name (but not the number) is that of the patron deity of the Rabinal nation, who was known as *Jun Toj* or One Thunder.

Lord Thunder and **Lord Knife** *Ajaw Toj* and *Ajaw Tijax* are named in the expression "from the rank of Lord Thunder to the rank of Lord Knife," referring to a series of ten ranked titles whose actual names are unspecified. Thunder and Knife are two of the twenty day names of the Mayan divinatory calendar, each of which has its lord. A period running from Thunder through Knife (inclusive) would span ten days. Thunder may have been chosen as the starting day for the expression because tribute was paid to lords on that day.

Lord's Place *Pan Ajawarem,* a place visited by Cawek of the Forest People when he was resetting boundaries. It was known by this name until it was abandoned by the Cakchiquels and seized by the Quichés, who built their own town on the site and named it Nettles Heights *(Chuwila').* Today its official name is Chichicastenango. A major foot trail connects this location with two others visited by Cawek, Big Tree to the south and Earthquake to the north.

Mace Valley *Q'osib'al Taq'aj,* a place where branches of the Rabinal nation suffered losses at the hands of Cawek of the Forest People. Location unknown.

Man of Glory *Q'alel Achi,* the noble title held by Man of Rabinal. It was one of various titles that were bestowed on successful warriors by the lords of Quiché Mountain, Quiché Valley.

Man of Rabinal *Rab'inal Achi,* a warrior of the Rabinal nation, in the service of Lord Five Thunder.

Mother of Quetzal Feathers, Mother of Glistening Green *Uchuch Q'uq', Uchuch Raxom,* the unmarried daughter of Lord Five Thunder. These are not her personal names but rather figures of speech for a daughter whose marriage will bring rich gifts to her parents, including quetzal feathers and jade.

Mountains in a Row, Pines in a Row *Cholochik Juyub', Cholochik Chaj,* two names for the westernmost of the places visited by Cawek of the Forest People when he was resetting boundaries. A mountain known today as Cholochik Chaj is located in the territory of the present Quiché town of Santa Catarina Ixtahuacán, near the western limit of speakers of Kaqchikel.

Old Camp and **Whisker Place** *Q'umarka'j* and *Chi Ismachi',* twin citadels at the heart of the principal town of the Quiché kingdom. The town as a whole is referred to in the play as Quiché Mountain, Quiché Valley. Its ruins are located two kilometers west of the present town center of Santa Cruz del Quiché.

pataxte *Peq,* the seeds or seed pods of the tree *Theobroma bicolor,* a lower grade of cacao than *kakow* or cacao proper, which comes from *Theobroma cacao.*

Pieces of White Lime in a Row See Bird's Drinking Water.

Pines in a Row See Mountains in a Row.

Pitted and **Planted** *Chi K'otom* and *Chi Tikiram,* two names for a place where warriors who are described as "nine clenched fists, nine forearms" end up buried because of Cawek of the Forest People. This event may have given the place its name. It is on a mountain slope three kilometers west of Standing Jaguar, near the northeast corner of the lands of the town of Joyabaj.

Pokomam *Poqomam,* a nation that made war on the Cawuks and Rabinals after its people were driven from the valley where the town of Rabinal now stands. Today they are divided into speakers of Poqomam, located to the south and southeast of Rabinal, and Poqomchi', to the north. See also Uxab.

quetzal *Q'uq',* also known as the resplendent quetzal *(Pharomachrus mocinno).* The most spectacular bird in the New World, found in cloud-forest habitats ranging from Chiapas to Panama. Mayans valued the two-foot-long tail coverts of the male, which shine with a bright metallic green and iridescent blue.

Quiché Mountain, Quiché Valley *K'iche' Juyub', K'iche' Taq'aj,* an epithet for the principal town of the Quiché kingdom, otherwise referred to by the names of the twin citadels at its heart, Old Camp and Whisker Place.

Quick Hummingbird *Ixta Tz'unun,* also called "the lord's drink," was an alcoholic beverage whose ingredients included the sap of the flower stalk of a species of maguey *(Agave)* and honey.

Rabinal *Rab'inal,* a name that refers to people rather than a place in the play, possibly extending to all speakers of the Achi dialect of K'iche'. Today they are located principally in the towns of Cubulco, Rabinal, and San Miguel Chicaj, in valleys that drain into the Río Chixoy, but before the wars described in the play they extended farther west, in the areas of the present Quiché towns of Zacualpa (see Spilt Water) and Joyabaj (see Bountiful, Drumbeat, and Between the Wasp Nests).

Red Earth *Pan Kaqil,* a place where Cawek of the Forest People had some land he abandoned. Called Tierra Colorada on maps, it is located within the territory of the present Quiché town of Chiché.

red-feathered quail beans *Kaqix korowach,* named for the resemblance of their coloration to that of a species of quail.

Red Mountain *Kaqyuq',* the name of the main section of the citadel of Lord Five Thunder; the other three sections are named Shaker, Dressed in Red, and Tepecanic. The ruins of the citadel—consisting of temples, palaces, plazas, platform mounds, and terrace walls—are on a hilltop three kilometers north of the present town center of Rabinal.

Reed Rattles *Chi K'alqa Raxaj,* one of the places where branches of the Rabinal nation suffered losses at the hands of Cawek of the Forest People. Location unknown.

Sapota Tree *Tulul,* a place where branches of the Rabinal nation suffered losses at the hands of Cawek of the Forest People. It could have been the place now known as Chwatulul, four kilometers north of Standing Jaguar and the same distance southwest of the Cubulco town center, or else Patulul, five kilometers east of Standing Jaguar and six kilometers south of Cubulco. The sapota is a fruit tree *(Manilkara zapota).*

Sculpture Tree *Pan Ajachel,* a place visited by Man of Rabinal when he was resetting boundaries. It is the site of the present Cakchiquel town of Panajachel, on the north shore of Lake Atitlán. *Ajachel* is the term for a fruit tree *(Casimiroa edulis),* known in Spanish as matasano, whose wood is used for making carvings.

Shaker *Silik,* the name of one of the four parts of the fortress of Lord Five Thunder (see Red Mountain).

Sky, Earth *Kaj, Ulew,* an invocation of the gods of heaven and earth, spoken by the play's main characters. In its original form it would have been *Uk'ux Kaj, Uk'ux Ulew,*

"Heart of Sky, Heart of Earth," referring to the deity of the ax scepter they hold in their right hands. He linked sky and earth by means of lightning and meteors.

slit drum *Q'ojom*, made from the hollowed trunk of a *sanik che'* or "ant tree" *(Platymiscium dimorphandrum)*, a lowland species whose wood is also used for marimba keys. Slits carved in an H-shape create two tongues of wood that produce distinct tones, with a third tone produced by striking the wood on the outer side of either of the parallel slits.

Sparkling Pumice *Tintot wi Poqlaj*, one of the places where branches of the Rabinal nation suffered losses at the hands of Cawek of the Forest People. Pumice contains small topazes that sparkle in sunlight. Location unknown.

Spilt Water *Pan Amak'a'*, a former Rabinal town occupied by Quiché vassals who were persuaded to leave their original homes by Cawek of the Forest People. Its ruins are located two kilometers southeast of the center of the present Quiché town of Zacualpa.

Standing Jaguar *B'alamwak*, one of the places where branches of the Rabinal nation suffered losses at the hands of Cawek of the Forest People. It is a mountaintop seven kilometers southwest of the center of the present town of Cubulco, marking the southwest corner of its territory. Three kilometers to the south are the ruins of the town of Workers.

striped quail beans *Tzuleyuji*, named for their resemblance of their coloration to that of a species of quail. The term is borrowed from Pipil.

Tepecanic *Tepekanik*, one of the four parts of the fortress of Lord Five Thunder (see Red Mountain). The name is of Pipil origin, from *tepecumit*, "jar mountain."

Thunderclap *Pan Tzajaxaq*, a place visited by Cawek of the Forest People when he was resetting boundaries. Today there is a village named Xajaxac about halfway between the Quiché town center of Chichicastenango and the Cakchiquel town center of Sololá, a short distance beyond the southern limit of Quiché territory.

toponowos An alternative term, borrowed from Pipil, for the slit drum otherwise known as *q'ojom*. The Nahuatl term is *teponaztli*.

Under Ripe Yellow Corn See Below the Cave.

Uxab *Uxab'*, a nation that joined the Pokomam in making war on the Cawuks and Rabinals. They were probably the speakers of Pipil who once lived among the Pokomam.

Walkers *Chakachib'*, a name for the people ruled by Lord Five Thunder and for a place inhabited by their ancestors. The place, whose name also takes the form *Chakachil*, may have been on the ridge top known today as *Kachil* or Plano Grande, twenty-five kilometers northeast of Rabinal.

Water Jar Point *Tzam K'amb'a,* first of the places visited by Cawek of the Forest People on his circuit of the valley ruled from Red Mountain. It is a hilltop two kilometers east of the present town center of Rabinal and three kilometers southeast of Red Mountain.

Whisker Place See Old Camp.

white-winged dove beans *Xtapakal,* named for the resemblance of their coloration to that of the white-winged dove *(Zenaida asiatica).* The term is borrowed from Pipil.

Workers *Samanib',* a name for the people ruled by Lord Five Thunder and for a place inhabited by their ancestors. The place, whose name also takes the form *Tzamanil,* is the ruins known today as Los Cimientos Patzaj, located on a ridge above the hamlet of Tres Cruces, nine kilometers southwest of the present town center of Cubulco. It is the site where the lords of the Rabinal nation established their first seat of government.

Worn-out Trumpet Point *Tzam K'isin Tun,* a place visited by Cawek of the Forest People when he measured the perimeter of the valley ruled from Red Mountain. It is located six kilometers west of the center of the present town of Rabinal, on a ridge that separates its lands from those of Cubulco.

Bibliography

KEY TO LEXICAL CITATIONS

(AB) Barrera Vásquez 1980
(AG) García Hernández et al. 1980
(AT) Ajpacaja Tum et al. 1996
(DB) Basseta 1921
(EH) Haaserijn V. 1979
(FT) Tirado 1787
(FV) Varea 1929

(FX) Ximénez 1985
(LC) Campbell 1985
(MX) Maynard and Xec 1954
(PG) Guzmán 1984
(RS) Siméon 1977
(OS) Stoll 1888
(TC) Coto 1983

Academia de las Lenguas Mayas de Guatemala. 1988. *Lenguas mayas de Guatemala: documento de referencia para la pronunciación de los nuevos alfabetos oficiales.* Guatemala: Instituto Indigenista Nacional.

Acuña, René. 1975. *Introducción al estudio del Rabinal Achi.* Centro de Estudios Mayas, cuaderno 12. México: Instituto de Investigaciones Filológicas, Universidad Nacional Autónoma de México.

Ajpacaja Tum, Pedro Florentino, Manuel Isidro Chox Tum, Francisco Lucas Tepaz Raxuleu, and Diego Adrián Guarchaj Ajtzalam. 1996. *Diccionario K'iche'.* La Antigua Guatemala: Proyecto Lingüístico Francisco Marroquín.

Akkeren, Ruud van. 1988. "Interpretación etnológica del drama 'Rabinal Achi' de Guatemala." *Folklore Americano* 46:99-127.

——. 1999. "Sacrifice at the Maize Tree: *Rab'inal Achi* in its Historical and Symbolic Context." *Ancient Mesoamerica* 10:281-95.

Alcorn, Janis B. 1984. *Huastec Mayan Ethnobotany.* Austin: University of Texas Press.

Álvarez, Silvia. 1991. "Descripción del baile del Rabinal Achí." *Cuadernos de Investigación* 90(1):110-15. Dirección General de Investigación. Guatemala: Universidad de San Carlos. Reprinted as "Danza del Rabinal Achí" in *Rabinal Achí* (1996:45-51).

Anawalt, Patricia Rieff. 1993. "Rabbits, *Pulque,* and Drunkenness: A Study of Ambivalence in Aztec Society." In *Current Topics in Aztec Studies: Essays in Honor of Dr. H.B. Nicholson,* pp. 17-38. San Diego Museum Papers 30. San Diego: San Diego Museum of Man.

Anleu Díaz, Enrique. 1991. "Análisis musicológico del Rabinal Achí." *Cuadernos de Investigación* 90(1):117-26. Dirección General de Investigación. Guatemala:

Universidad de San Carlos. Reprinted as "Música del Rabinal Achí" in *Rabinal Achí* (1996:53-61).

Arnauld, Marie-Carlotte. 1993. "Los territorios políticos de las cuencas de Salamá, Rabinal y Cubulco en el Postclásico." In *Representaciones del espacio político en las tierras altas de Guatemala,* edited by Alain Breton, pp. 43-109. Cuadernos de Estudios Guatemaltecos 2. Guatemala: Centro de Estudios Mexicanos y Centroamericanos.

Baile de la conquista, el. 1981. Texto del Municipio de Cantel. Guatemala: Asociación Tikal and Piedra Santa.

Barrera Vásquez, Alfredo. 1980. *Diccionario maya cordemex, maya-español, español-maya.* Mérida: Ediciones Cordemex.

Basseta, Domingo de. 1921. "Vocabulario en lengua quiché." Paleography by William Gates of a manuscript (?1698) in the Bibliothèque Nationale, Paris. In the J. P. Harrington collection, National Anthropological Archives, Smithsonian Institution, Washington, D.C.

Baudez, Claude-François. 1992. "The Maya Snake Dance." *Res* 21:37-52.

———. 1994. *Maya Sculpture at Copán: The Iconography.* Norman: University of Oklahoma Press.

Bernard, Russel, and Jesús Salinas Pedraza. 1989. *Native Ethnography: A Mexican Indian Describes His Culture.* Newbury Park, Calif.: Sage Publications.

Bertrand, Michel. 1987. *Terre et société coloniale: Les communautés Maya-Quiché de la région de Rabinal du XVIe au XIXe siècle.* Etudes Mesoamericaines 14. México: Centre d'Etudes Mexicaines et Centramericaines.

Bierhorst, John. 1985. *Cantares Mexicanos: Songs of the Aztecs.* Stanford: Stanford University Press.

Bode, Barbara. 1961. "The Dance of the Conquest in Guatemala." Middle American Research Institute pub. 27:204-97. New Orleans: Tulane University.

Boone, Elizabeth Hill. 2000. *Stories in Red and Black: Pictorial Histories of the Aztecs and Mixtecs.* Austin: University of Texas Press.

Brasseur de Bourbourg, Charles Étienne. 1858. *Histoire des nations civilisées du Mexique et de l'Amerique-Centrale,* vol. 2. Paris: Arthus Bertrand.

———. 1861. *Popol Vuh: Le livre sacré et les mythes de l'antiquité américaine.* Collection de documents dans les langues indigenes de l'Amérique ancienne, vol. 1. Paris: Arthus Bertrand.

———. 1862a. *Grammaire de la langue quichée.* Collection de documents dans les langues indigenes de l'Amérique ancienne, vol. 2, pt. 1. Paris: Arthus Bertrand.

———. 1862b. *Rabinal-Achi ou le drame-ballet du tun.* Collection de documents dans les langues indigenes de l'Amérique ancienne, vol. 2, pt. 2. Paris: Arthus Bertrand.

Breton, Alain. 1994. *Rabinal Achi: Un drame dynastique maya du quinzième siècle.* Édition établie d'après le *Manuscrit Pérez.* Nanterre: Société des américanistes & Société d'ethnologie.

———. 1999. *Rabinal Achi: Un drama dinástico maya del siglo XV*. Translated from French by Jorge Mario Martínez. México y Guatemala: Centro Francés de Estudios Mexicanos y Centroamericanos.

Bricker, Victoria Reifler. 1981. *The Indian Christ, the Indian King: The Historical Substrate of Maya Myth and Ritual*. Austin: University of Texas Press.

Brinton, Daniel G. 1885. *The Annals of the Cakchiquels*. Philadelphia: Library of Aboriginal American Literature.

Browne, Walden. 2000. *Sahagún and the Transition to Modernity*. Norman: University of Oklahoma Press.

Burkhart, Louise. 1996. *Holy Wednesday: A Nahua Drama from Early Colonial Mexico*. Philadelphia: University of Pennsylvania Press.

Byland, Bruce E., and John M. D. Pohl. 1994. *In the Realm of 8 Deer: The Archaeology of the Mixtec Codices*. Norman: University of Oklahoma Press.

Calendario de los Indios de Guatemala (1722). Facsimile dated 1877, Berendt Collection, MS 58, University Museum library, University of Pennsylvania, Philadelphia.

Campbell, Lyle. 1977. *Quichean Linguistic Prehistory*. University of California Publications in Linguistics 81. Berkeley: University of California Press.

———. 1985. *The Pipil Language of El Salvador*. Mouton Grammar Library 1. Berlin: Mouton.

Camposeco M., José Balvino. 1992. *Te' son, chinab' o k'ojom: la marimba de Guatemala*. Colección Tierra Adentro 13. Guatemala: Subcentro Regional de Artesanías y Artes Populares.

———. 1994. *An Ch'ech, sajchi' o ki': el maguey y sus usos en Guatemala*. Rancho Palos Verdes, Calif.: Ediciones Yax Te'.

Cardoza y Aragón, Luis. 1972. *Rabinal-Achi (El Varón de Rabinal): Ballet-drama de los indios quichés de Guatemala*. México: Porrua. (Except for the credits on the title page and pagination, this is the same as Raynaud 1953.)

Carmack, Robert M. 1973. *Quichean Civilization: The Ethnohistoric, Ethnographic, and Archaeological Sources*. Berkeley: University of California Press.

———. 1981. *The Quiché Mayas of Utatlán: The Evolution of a Highland Guatemala Kingdom*. Norman: University of Oklahoma Press.

Carmack, Robert M., and James L. Mondloch. 1983. *El título de Totonicapán: texto, traducción y comentario*. Centro de Estudios Mayas, Fuentes para el Estudio de la Cultura Maya 3. México: Universidad Nacional Autónoma de México.

———. 1989. *El título de Yax y otros documentos quichés de Totonicapán, Guatemala*. México: Universidad Nacional Autónoma de México.

Chinchilla Aguilar, Ernesto. 1963. *La danza del sacrificio y otros estudios*. Guatemala: José de Pineda Ibarra.

Chonay, Dionisio José, and Delia Goetz. 1953. *Title of the Lords of Totonicapán*. Norman: University of Oklahoma Press. Bound in the same volume with Recinos and Goetz 1953.

Chun, Marcelino. 1870. *Historia Berdadera de la Conquista de Mexico*. Manuscript copy, made in Cobán, Guatemala, of a manuscript dated 1783. In the Dieseldorff Collection, Latin American Library, Tulane University, New Orleans.

Coe, Michael D. 1978. *Lords of the Underworld: Masterpieces of Classic Maya Ceramics*. Princeton: Princeton Unversity Press.

Coe, Michael D., and Justin Kerr. 1997. *The Art of the Maya Scribe*. London: Thames and Hudson.

Coe, Sophie D., and Michael D. Coe. 1996. *The True History of Chocolate*. New York: Thames and Hudson.

Coto, Thomás de. 1983. *Vocabulario de la lengua cakchiquel*. Edited by René Acuña. México: Universidad Nacional Autónoma de México.

Crónica de Oxkutzcab. n.d. Manuscript in the Tozzer Library, Harvard University, Cambridge, Mass.

Domínguez, Alfredo Méndez. 1984. "La estructura del verso en el Rabinal Achí. *América Indígena* 44:683-701.

Durán, Fray Diego de. 1971. *Book of the Gods and Rites and the Ancient Calendar*. Translated by Fernando Horcasitas and Doris Heyden. Norman: University of Oklahoma Press.

———. 1994. *The History of the Indies of New Spain*. Translated and introduced by Doris Heyden. Norman: University of Oklahoma Press.

Edmonson, Munro S. 1988. *The Book of the Year: Middle American Calendrical Systems*. Salt Lake City: University of Utah Press.

———. 1997. *Quiché Dramas and Divinatory Calendars*. Middle American Research Institute pub. 66. New Orleans: Tulane University.

England, Nora C. 1996. "The Role of Language Standardization in Revitalization." In *Maya Cultural Activism in Guatemala*, edited by Edward F. Fischer and R. McKenna Brown, pp.178-94. Austin: University of Texas Press.

Equipo de Antropología Forense de Guatemala. 1997. *Las masacres en Rabinal: Estudio histórico-antropológico de las masacres de Plan de Sánchez, Chichupac y Río Negro*. Revised edition. Guatemala: Serviprensa.

Fash, William L. 1991. *Scribes, Warriors, and Kings: The City of Copán and the Ancient Maya*. London: Thames and Hudson.

Fox, John W. 1978. *Quiche Conquest: Centralism and Regionalism in Highland Guatemalan State Development*. Albuquerque: University of New Mexico Press.

———. 1987. *Maya Postclassic State Formation: Segmentary Lineage Migration in Advancing Frontiers*. Cambridge: Cambridge University Press.

Freidel, David, Linda Schele, and Joy Parker. 1993. *Maya Cosmos: Three Thousand Years on the Shaman's Path*. New York: William Morrow.

Furst, Jill Leslie. 1978. *Codex Vindobonensis Mexicanus I: A Commentary*. Publications of the Institute for Mesoamerican Studies 4. Albany: State University of New York at Albany.

Furst, Peter T. 1976. *Hallucinogens and Culture*. San Francisco: Chandler & Sharp.

Gall, Francis. 1976. *Diccionario geográfico de Guatemala.* 4 vols., second edition. Guatemala: Instituto Geográfico Nacional.

García Hernández, Abraham, Santiago Yac Sam, and David Henne Pontious. 1980. *Diccionario quiché-español.* Guatemala: Instituto Lingüístico de Verano.

Garibay K., Angel María. 1968. *Poesía Náhuatl.* Vol. 3. México: Universidad Nacional Autónoma de México.

Graham, Ian. 1992. *Corpus of Maya Hieroglyphic Inscriptions,* vol. 4, pt. 2, *Uxmal.* Cambridge: Peabody Museum of Archaeology and Ethnology.

———. 1996. *Corpus of Maya Hieroglyphic Inscriptions,* vol. 7, pt. 1, *Seibal.* Cambridge: Peabody Museum of Archaeology and Ethnology.

Graham, Ian, and Eric Von Euw. 1975. *Corpus of Maya Hieroglyphic Inscriptions,* vol. 2, pt. 1, *Naranjo.* Cambridge: Peabody Museum of Archaeology and Ethnology.

Grube, Nikolai. 1992. "Classic Maya Dance: Evidence from Hieroglyphs and Iconography." *Ancient Mesoamerica* 3:201-218.

Grube, Nikolai, and Simon Martin. 1998. "Deciphering Maya Politics." In *Notebook of the XXIInd Maya Hieroglyphic Forum at Texas,* part II. Austin: University of Texas Department of Art and Art History.

Guerchoux, Anita Padial, and Manuel Vázquez-Bigi. 1991. *Quiché Vinak.* México: Fondo de Cultura Económica.

Guzmán, Pantaleón de. 1984. *Compendio de nombres en lengva cakchiqvel.* Edited by René Acuña. México: Universidad Nacional Autónoma de México.

Haeserijn V., Esteban. 1979. *Diccionario k'ekchi' español.* Guatemala: Piedra Santa.

Harrison, Peter D. 1999. *The Lords of Tikal: Rulers of an Ancient Maya City.* New York: Thames and Hudson.

Hassig, Ross. 1988. *Aztec Warfare: Imperial Expansion and Political Control.* Norman: University of Oklahoma Press.

Horcasitas, Fernando. 1974. *El teatro náhuatl: épocas novohispana y moderna.* Instituto de Investigaciones Históricas, Serie de Cultura Náhuatl 17. México: Universidad Nacional Autónoma de México.

Horspool, Glen Arvel. 1982. *The Music of the Quiché Maya of Momostenango in its Cultural Setting.* Ph.D. dissertation, University of California at Los Angeles. Ann Arbor: University Microfilms.

Houston, Stephen D. 1993. *Hieroglyphs and History at Dos Pilas: Dynastic Politics of the Classic Maya.* Austin: University of Texas Press.

Houston, Stephen D., and David Stuart. 1998. "The Ancient Maya Self: Personhood and Portraiture in the Classic Period." *Res* 33:73-101.

Houston, Stephen D., David Stuart, and Karl A. Taube. 1989. "Folk Classification of Classic Maya Pottery." *American Anthropologist* 91:720-26.

Howell, Steve N. G., and Sophie Webb. 1995. *A Guide to the Birds of Mexico and Northern Central America.* Oxford: Oxford University Press.

Hunt, Eva. 1977. *The Transformation of the Hummingbird: Cultural Roots of a Zinacantecan Mythical Poem.* Ithaca: Cornell University Press.

Ichon, Alain. 1982. "Identification de quelques sites protohistoriques dans la region de Rabinal et de Cubulco." *Cahiers de la R.C.P. 500* 4:54-77. Paris: Institut d'Ethnologie, Centre National de la Recherche Scientifique.

Irving, Thomas Ballantine. 1985. "Warrior of Rabinal: The Ballet of the Sacred Drum." In *The Maya's Own Words* 3:79-96. Culver City, Calif.: Labyrinthos.

Jáuregui, Jesús, and Carlo Bonfiglioli. 1996. "Un relato popular de la conquista de México: el coloquio de Santa Ana Tepetitlán, Zapopan." In *Las danzas de conquista I: México contemporáneo,* edited by Jesús Jáuregui and Carlo Bonfiglioli, pp. 399-437. México: Consejo Nacional para la Cultura y las Artes and Fondo de Cultura Económica.

Köhler, Ulrich. 1989. "Comets and Falling Stars in the Perception of Mesoamerican Indians." In *World Archaeoastronomy,* edited by A. F. Aveni, pp. 289-99. Cambridge: Cambridge University Press.

Kurath, Gertrude, and Samuel Martí. 1964. *Dances of Anáhuac: The Choreography and Music of Precortesian Dances.* Viking Fund Publications in Anthropology 38. New York: Wenner-Gren Foundation.

Laski, Vera. 1958. *Seeking Life.* Memoirs of the American Folklore Society 50. Philadelphia: American Folklore Society.

Leinaweaver, Richard E. 1968. "Rabinal Achí: Commentary and English Translation." *Latin American Theatre Review* 1/2:3-58.

León-Portilla, Miguel. 1963. *Aztec Thought and Culture: A Study of the Ancient Nahuatl Mind.* Norman: University of Oklahoma Press.

———. 1969. *Pre-Columbian Literatures of Mexico.* Translated by Grace Lobanov and Miguel León-Portilla. Norman: University of Oklahoma Press.

Lothrop, Samuel K. 1927. "A Note on Indian Ceremonies in Guatemala." *Indian Notes* 4:68-81.

Lovell, A. C. B. 1954. *Meteor Astronomy.* Oxford: Clarendon Press.

Luján Muñoz, Luis. 1987. *Máscaras y morerías de Guatemala / Masks and Morerías of Guatemala.* Guatemala: Museo del Popol Vuh.

Luján Muñoz, Luis, and Ricardo Toledo Palomo. 1986. *Jícaras y guacales en la cultura Mesoamericana.* Colección Tierra Adentro 5. Guatemala: Subcentro Regional de Artesanías y Artes Populares.

Mace, Carroll Edward. 1967. "Nueva y más reciente información sobre los bailes-drama de Rabinal y del descubrimiento del Rabinal-Achi." *Antropología e Historia de Guatemala* 19(2):20-37.

———. 1970. *Two Spanish-Quiché Dance-Dramas of Rabinal.* Tulane Stusies in Romance Languages and Literature 3. New Orleans: Tulane University.

———. 1973. "Charles Etienne Brasseur de Bourbourg, 1814-1874." In *Guide to Ethnohistorical Sources,* part 2, edited by Howard F. Cline and John B. Glass, pp. 298-318. Handbook of Middle American Indians 13. Austin: University of Texas Press.

———. 1981a. "Algunos apuntes sobre los bailes de Guatemala y de Rabinal." *Mesoamérica* 2:83-136.

———. 1981b. "*Los Negritos* (The Little Black Messengers): A Maya Christmas Comedy." *Xavier Review* 1(1-2):34-52.

———. 1985. "The *Costeño* of Rabinal: Description and Text of a Guatemalan *Baile.*" In *Estudios del reino de Guatemala,* edited by Duncan Kinkead, pp. 149-94. Publicaciones de la Escuela de Estudios Hispano-Americanos de Sevilla 309. Sevilla.

MacLeod, Barbara, and Dorie Reents-Budet. 1994. "The Art of Calligraphy: Image and Meaning." In *Painting the Maya Universe: Royal Ceramics of the Classic Period,* by Dorie Reents-Budet, pp. 106-163. Durham: Duke University Press.

Magno Boyé, Víctor C. 1971. "Análisis preliminar de los elementos dramático-rituales del Rabinal Achí." *Anales de Arqueología y Etnología* 24-25:181-95. Mendoza, Argentina: Universidad Nacional de Cuyo.

Martí, Samuel. 1968. *Instrumentos musicales precortesianos.* Second edition. México: Instituto Nacional de Antropología.

Martin, Simon. 1997. "The Painted King List: A Commentary on Codex-style Dynastic Vases." In *The Maya Vase Book: A Corpus of Rollout Photographs of Maya Vases,* vol. 5, edited by Barbara Kerr and Justin Kerr. New York: Kerr Associates.

Martin, Simon, and Nicolai Grube. 2000. *Chronicle of the Maya Kings and Queens: Deciphering the Dynasties of the Ancient Maya.* New York: Thames and Hudson.

Mathews, Peter. 1992. "A Concordance of the Published Names and Inscriptions of the Rulers of Palenque." In *Notebook for the XVIth Maya Hieroglyphic Workshop at Texas,* edited by Linda Schele, pp. 97-116. Austin: Department of Art and Art History, University of Texas.

Maynard, Gail, and Patricio Xec. 1954. "Diccionario preliminar del idioma quiché." Mimeograph. Quetzaltenango, Guatemala.

McAnany, Patricia A. 1995. *Living with the Ancestors: Kinship and Kingship in Ancient Maya Society.* Austin: University of Texas Press.

McArthur, Harry S. 1966. "Orígenes y motivos del baile del Tz'unum." *Folklore de Guatemala* 2:139-52.

———. 1977. "Releasing the Dead: Ritual and Motivation in Aguacatec Dances." *Cognitive Studies in Mesoamérica,* edited by Helen L. Neuenswander and Dean E. Arnold, pp. 1-34. SIL Museum of Anthropology Pub. 3. Dallas: SIL.

McBryde, Felix Webster. 1947. *Cultural and Historical Geography of Southwest Guatemala.* Institute of Social Anthropology pub. 4. Washington, D.C.: Smithsonian Institution.

Miles, S. W. 1957. "The Sixteenth-Century Pokom-Maya: A Documentary Analysis of Social Structure and Archaeological Setting." *Transactions of the American Philosophical Society* 47 (4):735-781.

Miller, Mary Ellen. 1986. *The Murals of Bonampak.* Princeton: Princeton University Press.

———. 1999. *Maya Art and Architecture.* New York: Thames and Hudson.

Molina, Alonso de. 1970. *Vocabulario en lengua castellana y mexicana y mexicana y castellana.* Estudio preliminar de Miguel León-Portilla. México: Porrua.

Mondloch, James L. 1978. *Basic Quiché Grammar.* Institute for Mesoamerican Studies pub. 2. Albany: State University of New York at Albany.

Monterde, Francisco. 1955. *Rabinal Achí: teatro indígena prehispanico.* México: Biblioteca del Estudiante Universitario.

Morales Hidalgo, Italo A. 1978a. "Las jícaras de San Bernardino." *La Tradición Popular* 18:3-6.

———. 1978b. "Breve estudio sobre el baile del tun en San Bernardino Suchitepéquez desde sus orígines hasta nuestros días." *Anales de la Sociedad de Geografía e Historia de Guatemala* 51:51-66.

———. 1981. "Las jícaras de Rabinal, Baja Verapaz, Guatemala: elaboración y uso." *La Tradición Popular* 33:1-16.

———. 1988a. "El Baile del Tun en el departamento de Suchitepéquez." *Anales de la Academia de Geografía e Historia de Guatemala* 62:131-46.

———. 1988b. *La persistencia de la tradición carolingia en Guatemala y Centroamérica.* Guatemala: Instituto Indigenista Nacional.

Morley, Sylvanus Griswold, and George W. Brainerd. 1956. *The Ancient Maya.* Third edition. Stanford: Stanford University Press.

Nagy, Gregory. 1996. *Poetry as Performance: Homer and Beyond.* Cambridge: Cambridge University Press.

Navarrete, Carlos. 1971. "Prohibición de la Danza de Tigre en Tamulte, Tabasco en 1631." *Tlalocan* 6:374-76.

Ortolani, Benito. 1995. *The Japanese Theatre: From Shamanism to Contemporary Pluralism.* Revised edition. Princeton: Princeton University Press.

Paret-Limardo, Lise. 1963. *La danza del venado en Guatemala.* Guatemala: José de Pineda Ibarra.

Rabinal Achí o danza del tun. 1991. *Cuadernos de Investigación* 90(1). Dirección General de Investigación. Guatemala: Universidad de San Carlos.

Rabinal Achí o danza del tun. 1996. Colección Tierra Adentro 20. Guatemala: Subcentro Regional de Artesanías y Artes Populares.

"Rabinal achi vepu xahoh tun." Holograph copy (with revisions) of the Quiché text in Brasseur (1862b:24-26, 30-118) by Manuel Pérez, 1913. Photocopy in the Latin American Library, Tulane University; facsimiles in *Rabinal Achí* (1991:1-67) and Breton (1994:85-150).

Raynaud, Georges. 1953. *Rabinal-Achi (El Varón de Rabinal): Ballet-drama de los indios quichés de Guatemala.* Translated into Spanish by Luis Cardoza y Aragón. Biblioteca de Cultura Popular 43. Guatemala: Ministerio de Educación Pública.

Raynaud, Georges, and Luis Cardoza y Aragón. 1929-30. "Rabinal-Achi: El Varón de Rabinal." *Anales de la Sociedad de Geografía e Historia de Guatemala* 6, 1:45-51, 2:197-201, 3:347-70, 4:381-391.

Recinos, Adrián. 1957. *Crónicas indígenas de Guatemala.* Guatemala: Editorial Universitaria.

Recinos, Adrián, and Delia Goetz. 1953. *The Annals of the Cakchiquels.* Norman: University of Oklahoma Press.

Recinos, Adrián, Delia Goetz, and Sylvanus Griswold Morley. 1950. *Popol Vuh: The Sacred book of the Quiché Maya of Guatemala.* Norman: University of Oklahoma Press.

Reents-Budet, Dorie. 1991. "The 'Holmul Dancer' Theme in Maya Art." In *Sixth Palenque Round Table,* edited by Merle Greene Robertson, pp. 217-22. Norman: University of Oklahoma Press.

——— 1994. *Painting the Maya Universe: Royal Ceramics of the Classic Period.* Durham: Duke University Press.

Reents-Budet, Dorie, Ronald L. Bishop, and Barbara MacLeod. 1994. "Painting Styles, Workshop Locations and Pottery Production." In *Painting the Maya Universe: Royal Ceramics of the Classic Period,* by Dorie Reents-Budet, pp. 164-233. Durham: Duke University Press.

Reina, Ruben, and Robert M. Hill, II. 1978. *The Traditional Pottery of Guatemala.* Austin: University of Texas Press.

Repetto Tió, Beatriz. 1985. *Desarrolo militar entre los mayas.* Mérida: Maldonado.

Robertson, Merle Greene. 1983. *The Sculpture of Palenque.* Vol. 1, *The Temple of the Inscriptions.* Princeton: Princeton University Press.

———. 1991. *The Sculpture of Palenque.* Vol. 4, *The Cross Group, the North Group, the Olvidado Group, and Other Pieces.* Princeton: Princeton University Press.

Robicsek, Francis, and Donald Hales. 1984. "Maya Heart Sacrifice: Cultural Perspective and Surgical Technique." In *Ritual Human Sacrifice in Mesoamerica,* edited by Elizabeth H. Boone, pp. 49-87. Washington, D.C.: Dumbarton Oaks.

Rodríguez Rouanet, Francisco. 1962. "Notas sobre una representación actual del Rabinal Achí o Baile del Tun." *Guatemala Indígena* 2(1):45-56.

———. 1986. *Rabinal.* Guatemala: Subcentro Regional de Artesanías y Artes Populares.

Roys, Ralph L. 1967. *The Book of Chilam Balam of Chumayel.* Norman: University of Oklahoma Press.

———. 1976. *The Ethno-Botany of the Maya.* Reprint edition supplemented by Sheila Cosminsky. Philadelphia: Institute for the Study of Human Issues.

Rubio, Miguel Ángel. 1996. "Las gestas de caballería: Los doce Pares de Francia." In *Las danzas de conquista I: México contemporáneo,* edited by Jesús Jáuregui and Carlo Bonfiglioli, pp. 145-64. México: Consejo Nacional para la Cultura y las Artes and Fondo de Cultura Económica.

Sacor, Hugo Fidel. 1991. "Rabinal Achí o Danza del Tun." *Cuadernos de Investigación* 90(1):69-107. Dirección General de Investigación. Guatemala: Universidad de San Carlos. Translation reprinted in *Rabinal Achí* (1996:5-44).

Sacor Quiché, Hugo Fidel, and Silvia Álvarez Aguilar. 1986. "Proyecto de investigación estudio etnohistórico, etnográfico y lingüístico del Rabinal Achí: Propuestas de Revitalización." *Tradiciones de Guatemala* 26:121-30.

Sáenz de Santa María, Carmelo. 1977. "Fray Francisco Ximénez, O.P. Su vida y su obra." In *Historia de la provincia de San Vicente de Chiapa y Guatemala de la orden de predicadores,* libros I y II, by Francisco Ximénez, pp.vii-lxi. Biblioteca "Goathemala" 28. Guatemala: Sociedad de Geografía e Historia de Guatemala.

Sahagún, Fray Bernardino de. 1951. *Florentine Codex: General History of the Things of New Spain, Book 2: The Ceremonies.* Translated by Arthur J. O. Anderson and Charles E. Dibble. Monographs of the School of American Research 14(3). Santa Fe: School of American Research.

——. 1954. *Florentine Codex: General History of the Things of New Spain, Book 8: Kings and Lords.* Translated by Arthur J. O. Anderson and Charles E. Dibble. Monographs of the School of American Research 14(9). Santa Fe: School of American Research.

——. 1961. *Florentine Codex: General History of the Things of New Spain, Book 10: The People.* Translated by Arthur J. O. Anderson and Charles E. Dibble. Monographs of the School of American Research 14(11). Santa Fe: School of American Research.

Sam Colop, Luis Enrique. 1993. "Xajoj Tun vs. Quiché Vinak." *Encuentro* May-August, pp. 25-35. Guatemala: Instituto Guatemalteco de Cultura Hispánica.

——. 1994. *Maya Poetics.* Ph.D. dissertation in the Poetics Program, State University of New York at Buffalo. Ann Arbor: University Microfilms.

——. 1998. "Man of Rabinal." Ucha'xik, *Prensa Libre,* May 20. Guatemala.

——. 1999. *Popol Wuj: Versión Poética K'iche'.* Guatemala: Cholsamaj.

Savarese, Nicola. 1991. "Nostalgia or the Passion for a Return." In *A Dictionary of Theatre Anthropology: The Secret Art of the Performer,* edited by Eugenio Barba and Nicola Savarese, pp. 165-70. Translated by Richard Fowler. London: Routledge.

Schele, Linda. 1984. "Human Sacrifice among the Classic Maya." In *Ritual Human Sacrifice in Mesoamerica,* edited by Elizabeth H. Boone, pp. 7-48. Washington: Dumbarton Oaks.

——. 1992. *Workbook for the XVIth Maya Hieroglyphic Work shop at Texas.* Austin: University of Texas Department of Art and Art History.

Schele, Linda, and David Freidel. 1990. *A Forest of Kings: The Untold Story of the Ancient Maya.* New York: William Morrow.

Schele, Linda, and Nikolai Grube. 1997. *Notebook for the XXIst Maya Hieroglyphic Forum at Texas.* Austin: University of Texas Department of Art and Art History.

Schele, Linda, and Peter Mathews. 1998. *The Code of Kings: The Language of Seven Sacred Maya Temples and Tombs.* New York: Scribner.

Schele, Linda, and Mary Ellen Miller. 1986. *The Blood of Kings: Dynasty and Ritual in Maya Art.* Fort Worth: Kimbell Art Museum.

Sharer, Robert J. 1994. *The Ancient Maya.* Fifth edition. Stanford: Stanford University Press.

Shaw, Mary. 1971. *According to Our Ancestors: Folk Texts from Guatemala and Honduras.* Norman: Summer Institute of Linguistics.

Shaw, Mary, and Helen Neuenswander. 1966. "Achí." In *Lenguas de Guatemala,* translated by Julio Vielman, pp. 27-71. Semenario de Integración Social Guatemalteca pub. 20. Guatemala: José de Pineda Ibarra.

Siméon, Rémi. 1977. *Diccionario de la lengua nahuatl o mexicana.* México: Siglo Veintiuno.

Smith, A. Ledyard. 1955. *Archaeological Reconnaissance in Central Guatemala.* Carnegie Institution of Washington pub. 608.

Sondheim, Stephen. 1997. "The Art of the Musical." Interview by James Lipton. *The Paris Review* 142:258-78.

Soto, Leandro. 1998. *"Man of Rabinal* on Stage: Cultural Translation as Metaphor." Program notes for *Man of Rabinal: The Mayan Dance of the Trumpets of Sacrifice.* Buffalo: State University of New York at Buffalo.

Stevenson, Robert. 1968. *Music in Aztec and Inca Territory.* Berkeley: University of California Press.

Stöckli, Matthias. 1997. *"Chirimía* und Trommel im *Baile de la conquista* von Rabinal, Baja Verapaz, Guatemala." *Société suisse des Américanistes / Schwiezerische Amerikanisten-Gesellschaft* Bulletin 61:35-38.

Stoll, Otto. 1888. *Die Sprache der Pokonchí-Indianer.* Die Maya-Sprachen der Pokom-Gruppe, vol. 1. Vienna: Alfred Hölder.

——. 1958. *Etnografía de Guatemala.* Translated by Antonio Goubaud Carrera. Publicaciones del Seminario de Integración Social Guatemalteca 8. Guatemala: Ministerio de Educación Pública.

Stuart, David. 1999. "'The Fire Enters His House': Architecture and Ritual in Classic Maya Texts." In *Function and Meaning in Classic Maya Architecture,* edited by Stephen D. Houston, pp. 373-425. Washington, D.C.: Dumbarton Oaks.

Stuart, David, and Stephen Houston. 1994. *Classic Maya Place Names.* Studies in Pre-Columbian Art and Archaeology 33. Washington, D.C.: Dumbarton Oaks.

Tarn, Nathaniel. 1971. "Rabinal-Achi: Part IV." *Alcheringa* o.s. 2:74-93.

Tate, Carolyn E. 1992. *Yaxchilan: The Design of a Maya Ceremonial City.* Austin: University of Texas Press.

Taube, Karl Andreas. 1992. *The Major Gods of Ancient Yucatán.* Studies in Pre-Columbian Art and Archaeology 32. Washington, D.C.: Dumbarton Oaks.

Tedlock, Barbara. 1981. "Quiché Maya Dream Interpretation." *Ethos* 9:313-30.

——. 1983. "A Phenomenological Approach to Religious Change in Highland Guatemala." In *Heritage of Conquest: Thirty Years Later,* edited by Carl Kendall and John Hawkins, pp. 235-46. Albuquerque: University of New Mexico Press.

——. 1986. "On a Mountain Road in the Dark: Encounters with the Quiche Maya Culture Hero." In *Symbol and Meaning Beyond the Closed Community: Essays in*

Mesoamerican Ideas, edited by Gary H. Gossen, pp. 125-38. Studies on Culture and Society 1. Albany, N.Y.: Institute for Mesoamerican Studies, State University of New York at Albany.

———. 1992. *Time and the Highland Maya*. Revised edition. Albuquerque: University of New Mexico Press.

———. 1999. "Continuities and Renewals in Mayan Literacy and Calendrics." In *Theorizing the Americanist Tradition,* edited by Lisa Philips Valentine and Regna Darnell, pp. 195-208. Toronto: University of Toronto Press.

Tedlock, Barbara, and Dennis Tedlock. 1985. "Text and Textile: Language and Technology in the Arts of the Quiché Maya." *Journal of Anthropological Research* 41: 121-46.

Tedlock, Dennis. 1983a. "Las formas del verso quiché." In *Nuevas perspectivas sobre el Popol Vuh,* edited by Robert Carmack and Francisco Morales Santos, pp. 123-32. Guatemala: Piedra Santa.

———. 1983b. *The Spoken Word and the Work of Interpretation*. Philadelphia: University of Pennsylvania Press.

———. 1985. *Popol Vuh: The Mayan Book of the Dawn of Life*. First edition. New York: Simon & Schuster.

———. 1987. "Hearing a Voice in an Ancient Text: Quiché Maya Poetics in Performance." In *Native American Discourse: Poetics and Rhetoric*, edited by Joel Sherzer and Anthony C. Woodbury, pp. 140-75. Cambridge: Cambridge University Press.

———. 1990. "Drums, Egrets, and the Mother of the Gods: Remarks on the Tablet of the Cross at Palenque." *U Mut Maya* 3:13-14.

———. 1996. *Popol Vuh: The Mayan Book of the Dawn of Life*. Revised and expanded edition. New York: Simon & Schuster.

———. 1997. *Breath on the Mirror: Mythic Voices and Visions of the Living Maya*. Second edition. Albuquerque: University of New Mexico Press.

———. 1998. "Toward a Poetics of Polyphony and Translatability." In *Close Listening: Poetry and the Performed Word,* edited by Charles Bernstein, pp. 178-99. New York: Oxford University Press.

———. 1999. "Dialogues Between Worlds: Mesoamerica After and Before the European Invasion." In *Theorizing the Americanist Tradition,* edited by Lisa Philips Valentine and Regna Darnell, pp. 163-80. Toronto: University of Toronto Press.

Teletor, Celso Narciso. 1955. *Apuntes para una monografía de Rabinal (B.V.) y algo de nuestro folklore*. Guatemala: Ministerio de Educación Pública.

Thompson, J. Eric S. 1960. *Maya Hieroglyphic Writing*. Norman: University of Oklahoma Press.

———. 1970. *Maya History and Religion*. Norman: University of Oklahoma Press.

Tirado, Fermín Joseph. 1787. "Vocabulario de lengua Kiche." Manuscript in the Tozzer Library, Harvard University, Cambridge.

Toledo Palomo, Ricardo. 1965. "Los bailes del tum en los siglos XVI y XVII." *Folklore de Guatemala* 1:61-67.

Townsend, Paul G., Te'c Cham, and Po'x Ich'. 1980. *Ritual Rhetoric from Cotzal.* Guatemala: Instituto Lingüístico de Verano.

Townsend, Richard F. 1992. *The Aztecs.* New York: Thames and Hudson.

Tozzer, Afred M. 1941. *Landa's relación de las cosas de Yucatán.* Papers of the Peabody Museum of American Archaeology and Ethnology 18. Cambridge, Mass.

Underiner, Tamara. 1997. "Cultures Enacted / Cultures in Action: (Intercultural) Theatre in Mayan Mexico." Ph.D. dissertation in drama. Seattle: University of Washington.

Varea, Francisco de. 1929. "Calepino en lengua cakchiquel." Paleography by William Gates of a manuscript (1699) in the American Philosophical Society library, Philadelphia, Pennsylvania. In the Gates collection, Brigham Young University library, Provo, Utah.

Villacorta C., Antonio. 1942. "Rabinal Achí." *Anales de la Sociedad de Geografía e Historia* 17:552-71.

Von Euw, Eric. 1977. *Corpus of Maya Hieroglyphic Inscriptions*, vol. 4, pt. 1, *Itzimte, Pixoy, Tzum.* Cambridge: Peabody Museum of Archaeology and Ethnology.

Waley, Arthur. 1976. *The No Plays of Japan.* Rutland, Vt.: Charles E. Tuttle.

Weeks, John M. 1977. "Evidence for Metalworking on the Periphery of Utatlan." In *Archaeology and Ethnohistory of the Central Quiche*, edited by Dwight T. Wallace and Robert M. Carmack, pp. 55-67. Institute for Mesoamerican Studies pub. 1. Albany: State University of New York at Albany.

Weisshaar, Emmerich, and Rainer Hostnig. 1995a. *Ojer tzij: cuentos y leyendas del pueblo quiché.* Version in Quiché. Guatemala: Foto Publicaiones.

——. 1995b. *Ojer tzij: cuentos y leyendas del pueblo quiché.* Version in Spanish. Guatemala: Foto Publicaiones.

Wolff, Eleanor. 1977. *Rabinal: An Ancient Play of the Quiche Indians of Guatemala.* Lexington, Ky: King Library Press.

Ximénez, Francisco. 1977. *Historia de la provincia de San Vicente de Chiapa y Guatemala de la orden de predicadores.* Libros I y II. Biblioteca "Goathemala" 28. Guatemala: Sociedad de Geografía e Historia de Guatemala.

——. 1985. *Primera parte del tesoro de las lenguas cakchiquel, quiché y zutuhil, en que las dichas lenguas se traducen a la nuestra, española.* Edited by Carmelo Sáenz de Santa María. Academia de Geografía e Historia de Guatemala, special pub. 30. Guatemala: Tipografía Nacional.

Yurchenco, Henrietta. 1958. "Taping History in Guatemala." *American Record Guide* 25:228-229, 282-84.

——. 1978. *Music of the Maya-Quiches of Guatemala: The Rabinal Achi and Baile de las Canastas.* Folkways FE 4226. New York: Folkways Records.

——. 1990. "El Rabinal Achí, un drama del siglo XII de los mayas-quichés de Guatemala." *Anales de la Academia de Geografía e Historia de Guatemala* 64: 169-82.